Human Fertilisation and Embryology:
The New Law

Human Fertilisation and Embryology:
The New Law

Dewinder Birk

Family Law

Published by Family Law
A publishing imprint of Jordan Publishing Limited
21 St Thomas Street, Bristol BS1 6JS

Whilst the publishers and the author have taken every care in preparing the material included in this work, any statements made as to the legal or other implications of particular transactions are made in good faith purely for general guidance and cannot be regarded as a substitute for professional advice. Consequently, no liability can be accepted for loss or expense incurred as a result of relying in particular circumstances on statements made in this work.

British Library Cataloguing-in-Publication Data

A catalogue record for this book is available from the British Library.

ISBN 978 1 84661 138 4

Typeset by Letterpart Ltd, Reigate, Surrey

Printed in Great Britain by CPI Antony Rowe, Chippenham, Wiltshire

DEDICATION

To

The gorgeous trio,

Olivia, Tara and Amir

ACKNOWLEDGEMENTS

It has been a surprise to me as to how much fun it has been to write this book and I have Greg Woodgate at Jordans to thank for approaching me to do it in the first place. I had anticipated the long hours after work that it would entail but not the real fascination of being able to actually work though new legislation. Thanks also to Claire Banyard and Kate Hather at Jordans for all their hard work.

I am grateful to the barristers and the clerks at St Mary's Chambers in Nottingham, a friendly and calm place of work, due in no small measure to our Head of Chambers, Nigel Page. In particular, I would like to thank Tim Clark, Claire Jakens, Rachel Rowley, Sarah Knight, Maria Mulrennan and Jason and Ila Reece for sharing the general fun and frustrations of the Bar over the years.

I would also like to take this opportunity to thank all the wonderful mums whom I have come to know since having my lovely daughter, Olivia, for their sheer generosity and friendship at a time when life has become even more hectic! So thank you in particular to Gail Courtney, Nuala Ryan, Abi Pratt, Anya Zarb, Carola Hogrefe, Sally Wan, Louise Humphrey and Martina Connelly.

Many thanks for the love and support of my large extended family on all sides. Love to my lovely Mum and Dad and of course to my fabulously beautiful and funny sister, Sukhi.

Most special of all, my love to my wonderful husband, Geoff Solomons, whose kindness and patience has never wavered over the years. Long may it continue!

Dewinder Birk
March 2009

PREFACE

The Human Fertilisation and Embryology Act 1990 has stood as the gateway, representing society's need and desire to regulate the fast moving area of assisted reproductive technology. It was an ambitious and controversial piece of legislation which ensured that the UK effectively embraced the new technology and since its commencement it has endeavoured to keep up with the expansion and advances of clinical science and research.

There is now a new Act, the Human Fertilisation and Embryology Act 2008, which works in conjunction with the previous Act. Therefore, it is necessary to understand the workings of both pieces of key legislation to obtain an appreciation of the current boundaries that will exist in regulation.

The aim of this book is to provide that overview to all of those who work, study or have an interest in this exciting area of medical and healthcare law.

Dewinder Birk
March 2009

CONTENTS

Chapter 6
Licences for Treatment

Chapter 7
Licences for Non-medical Fertility Services

Chapter 8
Licences for Storage

Chapter 12
Donors and Information

TABLE OF CASES

References are to paragraph numbers.

TABLE OF STATUTES

References are to paragraph numbers.

TABLE OF STATUTORY INSTRUMENTS

References are to paragraph numbers.

TABLE OF ABBREVIATIONS

DNA	Deoxyribose Nucleic Acid
HFEA and The Authority	Human Fertilisation and Embryology Authority
IVF	*In Vitro* fertilisation
PGD	Pre-Implantation Diagnosis
SI	Statutory Instrument
The 1990 Act	The Human Fertilisation and Embryology Act 1990
The 2008 Act	The Human Fertilisation and Embryology Act 2008
The Code	The Code of Practice
The UK	The United Kingdom

Chapter 1

BACKGROUND

INTRODUCTION

1.1   The new Human Fertilisation and Embryology Act 2008 represents the most radical overhaul and transformation of the United Kingdom's embryology laws since the passing of the original 1990 Human Fertilisation and Embryology Act.

1.2   The new Act, which originated in the House of Lords, represents the culmination of many years of pressure from the government and other quarters, such as the scientific community, for change in this area. The government has striven to ensure that the legislative framework keeps up with the increasingly fast pace of technological, social and medical changes, whilst other interested parties[1] have also found the 1990 Act to be in need of revision.

1.3   The passage of the review of the new embryology laws has been long and challenging. The proposals and counter-proposals that have been put forward have been seen and considered to be controversial and thereby leading to intense debate and discussion. The formulation of the new laws saw once again the re-opening of the debates that have raged since the beginning of the technological and scientific revolution in the 1970s and bring into that debate the moral, philosophical and social arguments which have always shaped and coloured this particular area of medical and scientific endeavour.

1.4   The 1990 Act set out the boundaries of what was determined to be the appropriate level and type of assisted reproductive technology and embryo research that should be permitted in the UK. The two areas of treatment and research are entwined since research on human embryos and gametes has been the groundwork that has subsequently led to procedures becoming available for infertility treatments and, it is hoped, to treat other medical conditions. The 1990 Act reflected what was the general consensus about how science and medicine should intervene in the lives of humans and the concepts of family, research and the rights of an individual.

1.5   What has changed since its enactment has been a society where IVF has become more commonplace and is available in certain circumstances on the

---

[1]   The House of Commons Science and Technology Committee in June 2004 received written evidence from bodies as diverse as the Progress Educational Trust, the Christian Medical Fellowship and the British Infertility Counselling Association.

NHS, and a society where there is more familiarity with technological advances in human embryology and the consequences of these advances.

1.6   The news, on an almost daily basis, focuses on the latest development of embryo research and assisted reproductive treatment. Headlines and articles referring to such terms as animal cloning, human reproductive cloning, therapeutic cloning, 'designer babies', sperm donation, the right to family life and the right to reproduce, multiple births, egg-freezing and human genetics are now prevalent.

1.7   In the light of the dramatically different world that has transpired some 20 years after the passing of the 1990 Act, something new and in keeping with what has changed was required.

THE BACKGROUND TO THE 1990 ACT

The Warnock Committee

1.8   The 1990 Act was borne out of the recommendations of the report published in 1984 from the Warnock Committee,[2] chaired by the now Dame Mary Warnock. This was an inquiry set up specifically to provide the government with recommendations following the dramatic developments in the area of human reproduction using scientific technology, as dramatised by the birth of Louise Brown in 1978 as the first child conceived through *in vitro* fertilisation.

1.9   The concerns raised were seated in the growing unease in allowing the new technologies and medical advances to continue in an unchecked and uncontrolled fashion. The consultations and discussions which resulted showed that there was a diverse range of views. There were those who wished to ban outright any embryo research in principle and those who wished to have no or very limited treatment available for infertility, whilst others were much keener on the continuation of the progress that had been made and wished for a legal framework to allow this to flourish, and others preferred that the scientific and medical communities would self-regulate and should be allowed as much freedom as possible to continue with their work. The apprehension as to the future was sufficiently strong to produce recommendations by the Warnock Committee which clearly sought regulation in some form in this area. It also brought concerns and recommendations in relation to the position and status of surrogacy arrangements, which it was feared would start to rise in number.

1.10   The arguments on all sides of the debate continued long after the publication of the Warnock Report and the government was under pressure to bring forth a piece of legislation which would have a realistic prospect of

---

[2]   *Report of the Committee of Inquiry into Fertilisation and Embryology*, (Cmnd 9314), republished as *A Question of Life* (Oxford, Basil Blackwell, 1985) with a Foreword from Dame Warnock.

control and monitoring in this ever-growing contentious arena. By the end of 1987 the government finally responded by publishing a White Paper outlining and setting out the proposed legislation.[3]

THE 1990 ACT

1.11 The 1990 Act was drawn up on the basis that certain activities involving human embryos outside of the body, or the use of stored or donated gametes, demanded some level of regulation and there needed to be the establishment of clear legal boundaries and limits. The 1990 Act represented the first attempt by the UK to set out a comprehensive regulatory framework for the creation, retention and use of embryos outside of the human body and for the storage and use of gametes to create embryos.

1.12 The Act created a statutory body, the HFEA, which was tasked with imposing regulations for activities which involved dealing with human embryos and gametes. The Act itself prohibited certain activities, such as the placing of non-human embryos or gametes into a woman's body, but other activities were to be capable of being licensed by the HFEA. Licences could be granted for the purpose of fertility treatments, for storage of embryos and gametes and for research using gametes and embryos. The 1990 Act imposed mandatory conditions upon the different types of licence and also allowed for other conditions to be imposed upon licences which were to be granted by the HFEA.

KEY LEGAL DEVELOPMENTS

1.13 It has become necessary to amend the 1990 Act in a piecemeal fashion, as and when situations arose which could not be dealt with by or within the parameters of the 1990 Act. This has been achieved by way of using both primary and secondary legislation.

1.14 There was a relatively speedy amendment by regulation after the 1990 Act came into force. This was to extend the maximum storage period for gametes in respect of people whose fertility since providing the gametes has or is likely to become, in the written opinion of a registered medical practitioner, significantly impaired.[4]

1.15 Another good example of amendment by regulation was the amendments which were made to the 1990 Act by regulations in 2007 for allowing licences to be made available in respect of non-medical fertility

---

[3]   *Human Fertilisation and Embryology: A Framework for Legislation* cm 259 (1987) London.
[4]   The Human Fertilisation and Embryology (Statutory Storage Period) Regulations 1991, SI 1991/1540.

services.[5] A non-medical fertility service is defined as any service which in the course of a business is provided for the purpose of assisting women to carry children, but which is not a medical, surgical or obstetric service. This, therefore, includes the internet-based businesses that arrange for donated sperm to be delivered to women at home for the purposes of self-insemination. Although the number of such businesses was believed to be very small, there was still concern about allowing these services to operate without any regulation or control.

1.16 Leading the way for embryonic stem cell research, which was beginning to herald potential for developing treatments for various common diseases eg diabetes and heart disease, was the extension in the purposes for which embryo research could be licensed. These now include, in addition to the original purposes, the aims of, 'increasing knowledge about the development of embryos', 'increasing knowledge about serious disease' and 'enabling any such knowledge to be applied in developing treatments for serious disease'.[6]

1.17 Statutes have also been used when necessary. For example, when the spectre of cloning humans loomed large as a real possibility over the technological sphere, any attempt to create a child through any process other than fertilisation using sperm and egg was outlawed.[7]

A SUMMARY OF THE IMPETUS TO REFORM

1.18 Over the years the government has endeavoured, as can be seen from above, to keep up with and try to tackle the changes as and when they have arisen. The model of regulation created by the 1990 Act has been faced with the challenges of trying to keep up with the fast pace of change, not only on the technological and scientific front but also in respect of society's expectations and demands.

LEGISLATION WHICH IS 'FIT FOR PURPOSE'

1.19 However, over recent years the government has seen the need for a complete update of the original Act in order to ensure that the regulation is, to use the phrase currently in vogue, 'fit for purpose', and to help maintain what it regards as the UK's position as a world leader in reproductive technologies and embryo research.

---

[5] The Human Fertilisation and Embryology (Quality and Safety) Regulations 2007, SI 2007/1522, Reg 11.
[6] The 1990 Act, Sch 2, para 3A(2), as amended.
[7] The Human Reproductive Cloning Act 2001.

1.20 At the introduction of the new 2008 Act in the Lords, the Parliamentary Under-Secretary of State for the Department of Health, Lord Darzi of Denham stated that:

'We recognised that the 1990 Act had worked well, but like any cutting-edge legislation, needed to be reviewed from time to time. Our aim in undertaking the review was to ensure that the law remained effective and fit for purpose in the 21st century. In particular, we thought our view was timely given the pace of scientific developments and public attitudes associated with them.'[8]

1.21 As explained in the government's public consultation document[9] it was deemed timely and desirable to specifically take account of the development of new procedures and technologies, international developments in the standards that clinics have to meet, the possible changes in public perception and attitudes on complex ethical issues and the need to ensure the continued effectiveness of regulation.

1.22 The government's subsequent White Paper further expanded on its aims for the revised legislation as follows:

• to ensure that legitimate applications of human reproductive technologies continue to flourish;

• to promote public confidence in the development of human reproductive technologies; and

• to secure that regulation accords with better regulation principles and to encourage best regulatory practices.[10]

1.23 As for the legal regulator and licensor, the HFEA had been monitored by the Department of Health through reviews over time, though these tended to centre on the financial costs and implications of the HFEA. The HFEA had been specifically part of the Department of Health's arms length bodies undertaken in 2004 and it was as a result of this that the proposal arose that the HFEA should be merged and replaced. This proposal needed further discussion and consultation as to its far-reaching consequences.

IMPACT OF EUROPEAN LEGISLATION

1.24 The need for further detailed discussions about the future of the HFEA in the light of possible merger proposals was necessary because of the need to

---

[8] HL Hansard 2007-8 vol 696, col 663, 19.11.07.
[9] *Review of the Human Fertilisation and Embryology Act – A Public Consultation.* Department of Health (August 2005) Ref 269640.
[10] *Review of the Human Fertilisation and Embryology Act: Proposals for revised legislation (including establishment of the regulatory Authority for tissue and Embryos)* Cm. 6989, December 2006.

implement effectively European directives into UK legislation. There have been a number of relevant European directives which have had to be observed by the UK and reference has been made to these in the 1990 Act by amendment.[11]

1.25   Under the Human Fertilisation and Embryology (Quality and Safety) Regulations 2007[12] the HFEA is the 'competent authority' in the UK responsible for overseeing the requirements of a number of EU Directives[13] concerned with setting the standards of quality and safety for the donation, procurement, testing, processing, preserving, storing and distribution of human tissues and cells with regards to human gametes and embryos. It is also, under the same Regulations, the 'competent authority' with regard to dealing and communicating with the EEA as to serious adverse incidents.[14]

HUMAN RIGHTS ACT 1998

1.26   The intention of the Human Rights Act 1998[15] was to bring into further effect the rights bestowed on individuals by the Convention for the Protection of Human Rights and Fundamental Freedoms[16] so that those rights could be pursued in the domestic UK courts rather than proceeding in the Strasbourg court.[17]

1.27   This piece of legislation has had an impact on all legislation in the UK in that all primary and secondary legislation must be interpreted by the courts (in so far as it is possible to do so) in a way which is compatible with the Human Rights Convention. If this cannot be done, the courts at the level of the High Court, Court of Appeal and House of Lords must make a 'declaration of incompatibility'[18] and it then remains a matter for Parliament to remedy that incompatibility.

1.28   Of particular relevance in this area are:

- Article 8 which provides that, *'Everyone has the right to respect for his private and family life, his home and his correspondence'.*

- Article 12 which provides that, *'Men and women of marriageable age have the right to marry and to found a family, according to the national laws governing the exercise of this right'.*

---

[11]   The 1990 Act, s 1A.
[12]   SI 2007/1522.
[13]   EU Directives 2004/23/EC, 2006/17/EC, 2006/86/EC and 2004/23/EC.
[14]   The Human Fertilisation and Embryology (Quality and Safety) Regulations 2007, Reg 10.
[15]   The Human Rights Act 1998.
[16]   Set out in Sch 1 of the Human Rights Act 1998.
[17]   Although it does not preclude any individual taking their case to Strasbourg.
[18]   The Human Rights Act 1998, s 4.

- Article 14 which provides that, '*The enjoyment of the rights and freedoms set forth in this Convention shall be secured without discrimination on any ground such as sex, race, colour, language, religion, political or other opinion, national or social origin, association with a national minority, property, birth or other status*'.

1.29 The UK has had to continually consider and ensure that the provisions of the 1990 Act remain 'Human Rights compatible'. The case of *Blood* highlighted that Articles 12 and 8 would have been of relevance if they had been pursued in that case.[19]

1.30 Of further relevance is that public authorities have to act in a way that is compatible with a Convention right.[20] Since health authorities are involved in providing infertility treatment in certain circumstances, the Code of Practice and the way that treatment is provided, which all stems from the legislation, also has to be 'Human Rights compatible'.

THE LEGAL CHALLENGES

1.31 Where there is legislation which directly impinges upon an individual's rights in an area of personal medical care, as is the case where infertile individuals seek fertility treatment, or to widen the scope of what embryo research is possible, there are always going to be legal challenges through the courts to the legislation and the regulator which formulates the relevant decisions and policies.

1.32 The most significant challenges through the legal system have been as follows:

- Challenges to the use of reproductive technology in order to create 'saviour siblings' ie tissue typing in conjunction with pre-genetic diagnosis, where human matter is required for the treatment of a child already in existence.[21]

- Whether sperm could be used when it was taken without written consent.[22]

- Whether embryos could be used where consent to treatment from one of the gamete donors is withdrawn.[23]

---

[19] *R v Human Fertilisation and Embryology Authority Ex p Blood* [1999] 2 WLR 807.
[20] The Human Rights Act 1998, s 6.
[21] *Quintavalle (on behalf of comment on reproductive Ethics) v HFEA* [2005] UKHL 28.
[22] *R v Human Fertilisation and Embryology authority, ex parte Blood* [1996] 3 WLR 1176, [1997] 2 WLR 806 (CA).
[23] *Evans v Amicus Healthcare Ltd and others* [2004] EWCA (civ) 727; *Evans v UK* [2007] 2 FCR 5.

- What are the rights of a child born of donated gametes to have details of the identity of the donor?[24]

- Whether embryos created by cell nuclear replacement are caught by the terms of the 1990 Act.[25]

- What is the legal position where an error occurs due to an egg being inseminated by the incorrect sperm?[26]

1.33 From a legal viewpoint, the government felt that the Department of Health's interpretation of the 1990 Act had been generally upheld in the courts, but it still felt that one of the factors for review was the need to reduce any legal uncertainty and the scope for legal challenge.

THE PARLIAMENTARY PASSAGE

1.34 The government began the process of review in January 2004. The House of Commons Science and Technology Committee produced a report and its recommendations on human reproductive technologies and the law, which was published in March 2005.[27] There was a public consultation in late 2005, where the Committee's recommendations were subjected to further consultation from a wide range of stakeholders, including licence holders, patient's representatives, professional bodies and individuals.

1.35 The Government's White Paper, published in December 2006,[28] contained 25 substantial proposals for changes to the existing legislation.

1.36 The Parliamentary passage was a long and full one. A draft bill entitled the, '*Human Tissue and Embryo (Draft) Bill*'[29] was published in May 2007 for scrutiny by a Joint Committee of both Houses and it considered a wide range of evidence from various stakeholders. The Committee Report was published on 1 August 2007[30] and the government responded on 8 October 2007.[31] The policy proposals were substantially updated from the White Paper following the

---

[24] *R (on the application of Rose and another) v Secretary of State for Health and another* [2002] 3 FCR 731.
[25] *R (on the application of Quintavalle) (on behalf of Prolife Alliance) v Secretary of State for Health* [2003] 1 FCR 577.
[26] *Leeds Teaching Hospital NHS trust v A & another* [2003] 1 FCR 599.
[27] HC 7-1 *Human Reproductive Technologies and the Law*, House of Commons Science and Technology Committee.
[28] *Review of the Human Fertilisation and Embryology Act: Proposals for revised legislation (including establishment of the regulatory Authority for Tissue and Embryos)* Cm. 6989 (December 2006).
[29] Cm. 7087.
[30] HL, Paper 169-1 HC Report 1: Human Tissue and Embryos (Draft) Bill: Joint Committee on the Human Tissue and Embryos (Draft) Bill session 2006–7.
[31] The Government's Response to the Report from the Joint Committee on the Human Tissue and Embryos (Draft) Bill (November 2007).

pre-legislative scrutiny. The new amended Bill, now entitled the Human Fertilisation and Embryology Bill was introduced on 8 November 2007. The Select Committee reported upon it and it was debated in the House of Commons from 19 May 2008 to 12 June 2008.

1.37 It was envisaged that the report and the third reading stage in the Commons would be completed by 14 July 2008; however changes to the parliamentary timetable meant that the Bill's progress was delayed. It was re-opened for final amendment in the Commons on 6 and 22 October 2008. The Commons passed the Act with an overwhelming majority of 355 votes to 129. It returned to the Lords on 23 October 2008 for ratification of its final version and Royal Assent was granted on 13 November 2008.

1.38 In outline, the new Act does not seek to repeal the entirety of the 1990 Act, but instead it is a comprehensive amending statute which imposes considerable changes to the operation of the 1990 Act and the regulation imposed in the area of assisted reproductive technology and embryo research. It amends the Surrogacy Arrangements Act 1985, as did the original 1990 Act. It also introduces new provisions which add onto the existing framework of regulation.

Chapter 2

THE NEW ACT

OVERVIEW

2.1   As the new law operates in the context of the old law and serves to make substantial amendments to it, it is necessary to consider the text of the 1990 Act as it now stands in the light of the amendments to it contained in the 2008 Act. There is an illustrative text of the 1990 Act which contains the amendments imposed by the 2008 Act as Appendix 2 to this book to assist with understanding the new statutory position.

2.2   The 1990 Act also made amendments to the Abortion Act 1967 at s 37, which are beyond the scope of this work.

2.3   The 2008 Act is divided into three separate parts:

(i)   Part 1 (including Schs 1 to 5) makes a wide range of amendments to the 1990 Act to take into account the state of scientific development to date, to reflect the societal changes as ascertained in the consultation process and to improve the HFEA's ability to regulate in line with the principles of better regulation.

(ii)   Part 2 replaces the existing provision under the 1990 Act to determine legal parenthood for future cases involving assisted reproduction. The Act introduces a new concept of parenthood for a mother's female partner in certain circumstances, making equivalent provision to that for opposite sex couples. It also makes provision in relation to surrogacy and parenthood to put same-sex couples and unmarried opposite sex couples in the same position as married couples.

(iii)   Part 3 contains amendments to the Surrogacy Arrangements Act 1985, miscellaneous provisions and general provisions about order and regulation-making powers and power to make consequential and transitional provisions and commencement.

2.4   There are substantial schedules to the Act. Schedule 1 deals with the details concerning the membership of the HFEA, Schs 2 and 3A deal with licences and Sch 3 deals with consent. There are new provisions dealing with counselling set out in Sch 3ZA,[1] Sch 3B deals with inspection, entry search and

---

[1]   As inserted by Sch 4 of the 2008 Act.

seizure[2] and Schs 4 and 7 deal with minor and consequential amendments. Schedule 6 deals with all the amendments relating to new parenthood provisions involving assisted reproduction. This includes separate parts which deal specifically with Scottish legislation and Northern Ireland legislation, which are beyond the scope of this book. Schedule 8 deals with the legislative repeals and revocations.

THE STATUTORY AIMS

2.5   These can be summarised as follows:

- to set detailed parameters for use, storage and research involving gametes and embryos;

- to establish a regulatory body which through the tools of licensing would regulate embryo and gamete use, research and storage;

- to provide definitions for all relevant terms to clarify the law;

- to provide a statute which meets current needs and hopefully is sufficiently elastic to manage future developments in the area of assisted reproductive technology; and

- to amend the Surrogacy Arrangements Act and other legislation.

THE KEY ELEMENTS OF THE LEGISLATION

2.6   The provisions in the 2008 Act follow and enhance the original framework for regulation. The scope of the regulation is set out by express prohibitions, permissions and associated definitions. The combination of this determines the activities which are banned and which activities may be permitted provided certain conditions are met under the provision of a licence issued by the HFEA.

ACTIVITIES INVOLVING EMBRYOS AND GAMETES

2.7   The new legislation has produced amendments with regards to maintaining and extending regulation to the creation and use of all embryos outside of the human body.

2.8   The 2008 Act ensures that all human embryos outside of the human body are subject to its regulation, regardless of the process used in their creation. This was to ensure that the alarm that has always been felt with the

---

[2]   As inserted by Sch 3B of the 2008 Act.

possibility of human cloning being outside of the scope of regulation would not again be raised if a new and different technique of creating an human embryo *in vitro*, other than cloning as it is currently understood and prohibited,[3] was used.

2.9 The original 1990 Act dealt almost exclusively with human embryos, save for prohibiting the combining of human and animal gametes. The 2008 Act clarifies the regulation of human admixed embryos. The new Act allows the creation of human embryos that have been physically mixed with one or more animal cells for research purposes under regulation. However, true human-animal hybrids, made by the fusion of sperm and eggs, remain outlawed. In all cases it will be illegal to allow embryos to grow for more than 14 days or to be implanted into a womb.

2.10 The new provisions increase the scope of legitimate embryo research activities, allowing for hybrid embryos to be allowed to be created for research into serious diseases. The 2008 Act has enforced a ban on the selecting of the sex of offspring for non-medical reasons.

NEW SCIENTIFIC ADVANCES

2.11 Over the years, the ability to use human embryos and gametes, with some input from animal gametes, has been seen as a means of further scientific knowledge and possibility, progressing with the search for treatment for human diseases and conditions.

2.12 The Government staged a climbdown from its original position in 2006 which was to ban all human-animal hybrids. The Public Health Minister at the time, Caroline Flint, stated that the change was because '*We saw this was an area where these could be used for scientific benefit*'.[4]

SEX SELECTION

2.13 There have also been a number of significant developments in the ability of clinicians to screen and select gametes and embryos from those harvested and new techniques have increased the scope for potential parents to make choices about certain characteristics of their potential offspring.

2.14 Some of the developments arise from the possibility of preimplanation genetic diagnosis (PGD) which involves the creation of several embryos and selection of those to be placed in a woman based on the results of a biopsy using one or more cells from the embryos. Preimplantation generic screening (PGS) refers to selecting embryos free from chronomosomal abnormities. There

---

[3]   The Human Reproductive Cloning Act 2001.
[4]   BBC News Health Minister bows to hybrid pressure 25.5.07.

is also the technique of 'sperm sorting' which divides a semen sample into sperm carrying female or male chromosomes to be used for artificial insemination or the creation of an embryo *in vitro.* All of these developments have been met with the public response that scientists are creating 'designer babies' and 'saviour siblings' and have been the subject of contentious debates as to the desirability or otherwise of such developments.

2.15 The line drawn by the new Act is to allow screening provisions for embryos to find a suitable tissue match for an offspring with a serious medical disease. There is a ban on being able to deliberately screen in a disorder or disease e g two deaf parents wishing to have a deaf child. There is also a ban on allowing sex selection of offspring for non-medical reasons.

STORAGE

2.16 A further change has been made in that the statutory storage period is to be extended for embryos from five to ten years. This brings into line the discrepancy that had existed between the storage periods for embryos and gametes, where the storage period had been ten years.

A REGULATORY BODY

2.17 The concept from the start of the legislation under the 1990 Act has been for there to be an independent body which is to act as the legal regulator of those establishments and centres which offered and provided assisted reproductive treatment and those who wish to use human embryos in medical and scientific research.

2.18 The creation of a statutory regulatory body[5] formed a major plank of the scheme of regulation recommended by the Warnock Committee. The HFEA came into operation in 1991 and has continued to operate without interruption since then.

2.19 The HFEA has been the subject of governmental review but the concept and the operation of the HFEA has continued over the years with no real attempts to eradicate or fundamentally change its role and remit.

2.20 However, in an attempt to minimise the bureaucratic overheads and costs of providing a public service[6] the government's proposal in the White Paper was to merge the existing regulatory body in the area of assisted human reproduction technology, the HFEA, with other bodies and provide a new replacement body called the Regulatory Authority for Tissue and Embryos

---

[5]   The predecessor of the HFEA was a voluntary organisation known as the Voluntary Licensing Authority and subsequently the Interim Licensing Authority.

[6]   The *Report on Reconfiguring the Department of Health's Arm's Length Bodies* (July 2004).

(RATE). It would replace two existing bodies, the Human Tissue Authority (HTA) and the Medicines and Healthcare Products Regulatory Agency (MHRA). The proposal was that RATE would then be the regulatory body responsible for the regulation and inspection of all functions relating to human material, namely cells, tissues, organs, gametes, embryos, blood and blood products.

2.21 The government announced its decision to create RATE in July 2004. However, as will be evident from the continued references to the HFEA, this proposal did not survive the final Bill.

2.22 The Joint Committee's recommendations on the draft Human Tissue and Embryo Bill were that the evidence they had received was overwhelming and convincing with regard to retaining the three bodies separately. It concluded that the regulatory oversight provided by the HFEA and the HTA was better than the oversight to be given by RATE.

2.23 The government's response was that this recommendation would be accepted and therefore the proposals for RATE would be dropped. However, it would still bring in certain provisions for the HFEA that would have applied to RATE. These include provisions to allow members of the HFEA to delegate functions to HFEA staff and, with the necessary safeguards, for power to delegate or contract out functions outside the Authority.[7]

2.24 The 2008 Act has brought further clarification of the role and functions of the HFEA. It also provides the HFEA with the scope to streamline their licensing process by allowing the HFEA to delegate its licensing decisions to members of its staff.

DONORS AND INFORMATION

2.25 The 1990 Act and the amendments through the 2008 Act provide, in addition to any general requirements under common law, for specific and extensive requirements for individual consent to a range of activities. Schedule 3 of the Act contains the details of these consent requirements which have been greatly enlarged and detailed. The HFEA's Code of Practice provides further guidance on the issue of consent and it also provides appropriate standards forms for licensed centres to record consents.

2.26 Effective consent ensures that the reproductive decisions that are being made which involve medical interventions are fully understood and informed. Written consent does provide a measure of evidence that there has been some contemplation and reflection on the issues and it also helps to ensure that a

---

[7] The Government's response to the Report from the Joint Committee on the Human Tissue and Embryos (Draft) Bill (November 2007).

person's gametes or embryos cannot be used in ways that they did not intend by providing an enduring record and statement of their wishes.

2.27 A review[8] and subsequently a government consultation[9] had been carried out regarding the various issues associated with people who are unable to provide the necessary consent due to incapacity and this resulted in changes.

2.28 The provisions include the term that donors would be informed if their child is seeking identifying information about them. Also donor-conceived children would be allowed to find out if they have sisters or brothers also conceived through donation, when they reach the age of 18.

2.29 There are also more detailed provisions in the key areas of consent and counselling and the provision of information. There is a one-year cooling off period if consent to embryo storage by one of the couple involved is withdrawn.

There are also changes on the restrictions on the disclosure of treatment dates collected by the HFEA, in order to enable follow-up studies of infertility treatments.

PARENTHOOD

2.30 There are also changes to provide parenthood provisions for civil partners and other same sex couples.

2.31 There is recognition of same sex couples as the legal parents of children conceived through the use of donated sperm, eggs or embryos. Thus enabling, for example, the civil partner of a woman who carried a child following *in vitro* fertilisation to be recognised as the child's legal parent and so providing the child with two legal parents.

2.32 There has been the retention of a duty for those providing fertility treatments to take account of 'the welfare of the child', although the new provisions now refer to the need to take into account 'the need for supportive parenting' rather than 'the need for a father', as was previously the case.

2.33 The 2008 Act also brings forth provisions relating to the circumstances of the people who are to be treated in law as the parents of a child and the recognition of same-sex couples on a par with other legislation, such as in

---

[8] 'Review of the common law provisions relating to the removal of gametes and of the consent provisions in the Human Fertilisation and Embryology Act 1990' (July 1998) and 'Consent and the law. Review of the current position in the Human Fertilisation and Embryology Act 1990 to UK Health Ministers' (September 1997).

[9] 'Human Bodies, Human Choices' *The Law on Human Organs and Tissues in England and Wales*, Department of Health (July 2002).

adoption[10] and in relation to civil partnerships[11] whereby a new legal relationship was created by people of the same sex registering as the civil partner of each other.

THE EUROPEAN DIRECTIVES

2.34 Three relevant Directives from the European Parliament have had an impact on this legislation and are set out in s 1A of the 1990 Act. The details of the requirements for compliance are set out in Chapter Five.[12]

2.35 The First Directive centres on the establishment of standards of quality and safety for the donation, procurement, testing, processing, preservation, storage and distribution of human tissue and cells.[13] The Second Directive is concerned with the technical requirement for the donation, procurement and testing of human tissues and cells.[14] The Third Directive governs traceability requirements, notification of serious adverse reactions and events and certain technical requirements for the coding, processing preservation, shortage and destruction of human tissues and cells.[15]

THE HUMAN RIGHTS ACT 1998

2.36 It is believed by the government and legislators that the 1990 Act and 2008 Act are all 'Human Rights compliant' and the declarations to this effect are carried in all the documentation produced by the Department of Health. However, as it is unlikely that no challenges pursuant to the Human Rights Act will arise, it remains to be seen whether the new legislation and newly improved original legislation has been sufficiently proofed against these future challenges.

REGULATIONS

2.37 To support the 2008 Act in the changes that it will bring into force there are to be a number of new regulations. At the present time the draft regulations are at the consultation stage.[16]

---

[10] The Adoption and Children Act 2002, s 144(4)(b) defines a couple for the purpose of adoption as two people, whether of different sexes or the same sex living together as partners in an enduring family relationship.

[11] The Civil Partnership Act 2004.

[12] The 1990 Act, Sch 3A.

[13] Directive 2004/23/EC of the European Parliament and of the Council of 31 March 2004.

[14] Commission Directive 2006/17/EC of 8 February 2006 implementing Directive 2004/23/EU of the European Parliament and of the Council.

[15] Commission Directive 2006/86/EC of 24 October 2006 implementing Directive 2004/23/EU of the European Parliament and of the Council.

[16] Consultation on Regulations to the Human Fertilisation and Embryology Act 2008, DoH January 2009.

TIMESCALES

2.38   Upon Assent, ss 61–64 and 67–69 of the 2008 Act came into force.[17] Part 2 of the 2008 Act which details the new definitions of parenthood comes into force on 6 April 2009. This early implementation was in order to bring that part of the legislation in line with the existing equality legislation as soon as possible. The amendments to the 1990 Act come into force in October 2009, whilst the provisions relating to parental orders will take effect in April 2010.

TERRITORIAL JURISDICTION

2.39   Part 2 of the 2008 Act and the free standing provisions in Part 3 extend to England and Wales, Scotland and Northern Ireland. The other provision of the Act amends existing legislation and has the same extent as the provision being amended. This results in the provisions under Part 1 extending to England and Wales, Scotland and Northern Ireland.[18]

2.40   The subject matter of the 1990 Act and the subject matter of the Surrogacy Arrangements Act 1985 are reserved matters as regards Scotland and Northern Ireland. Part 2 of the 2008 Act deals with a subject (the legal parenthood children resulting from assisted reproduction) that is already dealt with by ss 27–30 of the 1990 Act. Part 2 therefore also relates to a reserved matter.

2.41   The 2008 Act does not confer any functions on the National Assembly for Wales, and in general it applies to Wales in the same way as it applies to England.

2.42   In Scotland, because the Sewel Convention provides that Westminster will not normally legislate with regard to the devolved matter in Scotland without the consent of the Scottish Parliament, where there are amendments relating to such matters which trigger the Convention, the consent of the Scottish Parliament will need to be sought.

2.43   The Act does not contain provisions that would invoke a legislative consent motion and so consequential amendments for Northern Ireland have been included.

---

[17]   The 2008 Act, s 68(1).
[18]   The 2008 Act, s 67(1) and (2). There are specific provisions in relation to the Bailiwick of Guernsey under the 2008 Act, s 67(4)–(6).

Chapter 3

ACTIVITIES GOVERNED BY THE ACT

INTRODUCTION

3.1   This Chapter deals with the definitions of the key phraseology in embryo research and assisted reproductive technology which have been subject to substantial amendment. The changes have been made in line with one of the key objectives of reform which was to provide a legislative and regulatory system in the UK which would be up-to-date and not lag behind innovation and advances. The regulatory framework established has been one which is prohibitive in terms of certain activities but permits other activities under the governance and control of a licensing system. Clear statutory prohibitions require sanctions to ensure that they are adhered to. Legal enforcement where offences are committed is examined in this Chapter.

3.2   In order to achieve the objective of reducing the likelihood of the Act becoming outdated, or even obsolete, in the light of medical, scientific or legal developments, the mechanism of secondary regulation in the form of regulations is a tool which is regularly used and is now enhanced under the new legislation. An understanding of the scope of the areas subject to change by regulation, how regulations operate and how they fit into the regulatory framework is therefore critical in the implementation of the legislation. This will be considered later in this Chapter and a brief summary given of those regulations which are likely to be imminent in 2009.

DEFINITIONS

3.3   In order to deal with the key elements of change it was clearly necessary to redefine the definitions given in the 1990 Act to the critical components of ART and research, namely the eggs, sperm and embryos.

3.4   The new Act also introduces a new term, 'human admixed embryo' in an endeavour to cover every possible permutation of mixing human and animal genetic material. It also seeks to anticipate and encompass possible future changes by providing the widest possible definition of the principal terms used in human embryology.

3.5   There are also fresh powers provided to the Secretary of State, whereby if it appears necessary or desirable in light of scientific or medical development, there may be further regulations made to provide expansion of the terms to be included within the definitions of 'embryos, eggs, sperm or gametes'. This links in with the perceived need to be able to encompass future developments to ensure that the necessary definitions are kept up-to-date. This ability to regulate and add further detail to the definitions of these key terms does not extend, however, to human admixed embryos, or permit anything which contains nuclear or mitochondria DNA that is not human, in these key definitions. It was clearly accepted that after the considerable debate and controversy that has always surrounded this particular issue, a regulatory power was not an appropriate means to make any changes to the extensively debated definitions provided in the 2008 Act.

The prohibition of activities

3.6   There is a division in the legislation between those activities involving the use of human material which are expressly prohibited in all circumstances and those activities which are prohibited until, and unless, specifically licensed by the HFEA. This allows for treatment and research to be conducted in the permitted areas but also allows the demarcation line to be drawn statutorily at the place which Parliament perceives to be acceptable to the general public and interested sectors generally and which reflects current societal approval.

3.7   The definitions provided below of embryos and gametes are for use in relation to the legislation in general and are specifically stated not to be applied under the new s 4A amendment, which sets out the prohibitions of dealing with genetic material which is not of human origin and provides its own definitions.

The meaning of 'embryo'

3.8   The 1990 Act referred to an 'embryo' as being a live human embryo where fertilisation was complete. The definition also applies to an egg which was in the process of fertilisation.[1] The Act governed only those embryos which were created outside of the human body.[2]

3.9   The 2008 Act wished to make it clear that it applies to the creation of an embryo regardless of the process by which it was created. The technological advances developed since the start of the whole of this scientific and medical endeavour has meant that fertilisation is not the only means by which an embryo can be created.

3.10   So an embryo is defined under the new s 1(1) in much broader terms. An embryo is a live human embryo and this includes an egg which is undergoing fertilisation or '*any other process capable of resulting in an embryo.*'[3] The definition proceeds then to expressly exclude certain types of embryos which have been created by combining together human and animal gametes or human

---

[1]   The 1990 Act, s 1(a) and (b).
[2]   The 1990 Act, s 1(2).
[3]   The 1990 Act, s 1(1), as amended.

embryos which have been altered using animal DNA or animal cells, now referred to as 'human admixed embryos', which are defined later on in the amended 1990 Act under the new s 4A(5). There was a further enlarged definition of 'nuclear DNA' to include both the nucleus and pronucleus of an embryo, so that means it is the genetic material of each gamete in the form of the haploid sets of chromosomes and the genetic material DNA.[4]

3.11   The law is clear in that the statutory regulatory powers apply only to the creation, keeping and using of embryos which are created, kept and used outside of the human body and so that provision from the 1990 Act is retained.[5] It is now the case that the 1990 Act will govern the creation of embryos which are created outside of the human body even if the fertilisation or any other process of creation was not completed outside of the body.[6]

The meaning of 'gametes'

3.12   As with the embryos, the Parliamentary intention was to encompass as wide a definition of gametes as possible. The 1990 Act was amended so that the term 'gametes' expressly includes not only mature eggs and sperm but also immature gametogenic cells such as primary oocytes and spermatocytes.[7]

3.13   The definition of eggs is live human eggs at any stage of maturity, save those eggs which are in the process of fertilisation or undergoing any other process which could result in the production of an embryo, in which case they would fall under the definition of an embryo as set out under s 1(1)(b) as amended.

3.14   The definition of sperm under s 1(4)(b) is live human sperm at any stage of maturity.[8] The previous amendment of the Act continues to remain in place, namely, with the reference to sperm being treated as partner-donated sperm where the donor of the sperm and the recipient of the sperm declare that they have an intimate physical relationship with each other.[9]

Future amendments of the definitions

3.15   In keeping with the need to ensure that the 1990 Act keeps up-to-date with medical and scientific progress, a regulation-making power has been expressly provided for the Secretary of State to expand the definitions in s 1 of the 1990 Act (as amended) of the meaning of 'embryos', 'eggs', 'sperm' or 'gametes', where it becomes necessary or desirable to do so in the light of scientific and medical developments.[10]

---

[4]   The 1990 Act, s 2(1), as amended.
[5]   The 1990 Act, s 1(2).
[6]   The 1990 Act, s 1(2)(a), as amended.
[7]   The 1990 Act, s 1(4)(a) and (b), as amended.
[8]   The 1990 Act, s 1(4)(b), as amended.
[9]   The 1990 Act, s 1(5).
[10]   The 1990 Act, s 1(6), as amended.

3.16 There is a restriction on this power in that it may not provide for anything that contains any nuclear or mitochondrial DNA that is not human, to be treated as an embryo, eggs, sperm or gametes.[11]

Meaning of 'human admixed embryos'

3.17 'Human admixed embryos'[12] is a new term created for inclusion in the legislation and any reference to it indicates that there has been an amendment by the 2008 Act to the 1990 Act.

3.18 Human admixed embryos become highly relevant when dealing with the prohibitions imposed by the new Act. It is essentially a hybrid creation made by mixing human and animal gametes, be they cells or embryos. An animal, for this section, is defined as being anything other than a man.[13]

3.19 It is set out that when defining and referring to human admixed gametes, the eggs and sperm can be at any stage of maturity,[14] and that 'embryo' means an egg that is in the process of fertilisation or undergoing some other process capable of resulting in an embryo.[15]

3.20 The 2008 Act sets out a lengthy, although not necessarily exhaustive definition of a human admixed embryo in the amendment at s 4A(6). The definition includes the following:

(i)   a cytoplasmic hybrid (Cybrids) which are embryos created by techniques used in cloning, using human eggs and animal eggs. The embryos would be mostly human except for the presence of animal mitochondria;[16]

(ii)   a human-animal hybrid embryo created using a human egg and the sperm of an animal or an animal egg and a human sperm or by combining a pro-nucleus of an animal with a human pro-nucleus;[17]

(iii) a human transgenic embryo which is an embryo created by the introduction of animal DNA into one or more cells of the embryo;[18]

(iv)   a human-animal chimera, which are human embryos altered by the addition of one or more cells from an animal;[19]

---

[11]   The 1990 Act, s 1(7), as amended.
[12]   The original term formulated, which can be seen in the earlier consultation documents, was 'inter-species' embryos.
[13]   The 1990 Act, s 4A(7), as amended.
[14]   The 1990 Act, s 4A(9), as amended.
[15]   The 1990 Act, s 4A(8), as amended.
[16]   The 1990 Act, s 4A(6)(a), as amended.
[17]   The 1990 Act, s 4A(6)(b), as amended.
[18]   The 1990 Act, s 4A(6)(c), as amended.
[19]   The 1990 Act, s 4A(6)(d), as amended.

(v)   any embryo which does not fall within any of the categories above but which does contain both human nuclear or mitochondrial DNA and nuclear or mitochondrial DNA of an animal, but where the animal DNA is not predominant.[20]

Future amendments of the definitions

3.21   As with s 1 of the 1990 Act and the definitions included therein, there is a corresponding power to make regulations to specify any further combinations which are to be referred to as a human admixed embryo[21] and to amend, but not repeal, the definitions set out above. There is also a regulation making power to amend such definitions of the terms 'embryo', 'eggs' or gametes' for the purposes of s 4A (which deals with prohibitions), in order to specify things which would otherwise not fall within the definitions.[22]

3.22   The power to amend in respect of the definitions of the human admixed embryos, gametes and eggs has to appear to the Secretary of State to be necessary or desirable in light of scientific or medical developments.

PROHIBITIONS

3.23   There are very important amendments to the 1990 Act as a result of the considerable parliamentary debate on what should or should not be prohibited. The new provisions introduce the concept of dealing only with 'permitted' embryos and 'permitted' eggs and 'permitted' sperm. The references to woman and man under the section dealing with prohibitions of embryos and gametes include respectively a girl and a boy.[23]

Prohibitions in connection with embryos

3.24   Section 3 deals with the prohibitions imposed in connection with embryos. The 1990 Act forbids anyone from creating, keeping or using, an embryo unless they are licensed to do so.[24] No one is permitted to keep or process, without storage, an embryo for human application save in pursuance of a third party agreement.[25] Furthermore, no one is permitted to procure or distribute an embryo intended for human application except in pursuance of a licence or a third party agreement.[26]

---

[20]   The 1990 Act, s 4A(6)(e), as amended.
[21]   The 1990 Act, s 4A(11)(a), as amended.
[22]   The 1990 Act, s 4A(10)(b), as amended.
[23]   The 1990 Act, s 3ZA(6), as amended.
[24]   The 1990 Act, s 3(1), (1A)(a) and (b)(i).
[25]   The 1990 Act, s 3(1A)(b)(ii).
[26]   The 1990 Act, s 3(1B).

3.25   Human application is defined as being used in a human recipient[27] and third party agreements are agreements between licence holders and another person made in compliance with any licence conditions imposed for the purpose of securing compliance with the requirements of the First Directive.[28] Under the third party agreement the other person performs certain duties on behalf of the licence holder, ie the third party could procure, test, process gametes or embryos or supply any goods or services, including distribution services which may affect the quality or safety of gametes or embryos. Third party agreements are further elaborated upon below.

3.26   The amendments under the 2008 Act are set out under s 3(2)(a) and they prohibit the placing in any woman of any embryo other than a 'permitted embryo' which is subsequently defined in s 3ZA. This provides the definition of a permitted embryo as an embryo which has been formed by the fertilisation of a permitted egg by a permitted sperm, whose nuclear or mitochondrial DNA has not been altered and has not had cells added, other than by the division of the embryo's own cells.[29]

3.27   This ensures that embryos created by the use of artificial gametes or genetically modified gametes cannot be placed into a woman. Similarly, genetically modified embryos or embryos created by cloning cannot be placed into a woman. This prevents reproductive cloning and supersedes the Human Reproductive Cloning Act 2001.

3.28   The licence which can be granted is restricted by statute and a licence cannot authorise the following:

- the keeping or using of an embryo after the appearance of the primitive streak.[30] This is a streak which is deemed to have appeared in the embryo not later than the end of the period of 14 days, beginning with the day on which the process of creating the embryo began, not counting any time during which the embryo is stored;[31] or

- keeping or using an embryo in any circumstances in which regulations prohibit its keeping or use;[32] or

- placing an embryo in any animal.[33]

---

[27]   The 1990 Act, s 2(1).
[28]   The 1990 Act, s 2A.
[29]   The 1990 Act, s 3ZA(4).
[30]   The primitive streak has been used as the pragmatic marker, the point at which human life begins to take on moral significance and importance and was adopted by the Warnock Committee when such measure was needed.
[31]   The 1990 Act, s 3(3)(a) and (4).
[32]   The 1990 Act, s 3(3)(c).
[33]   The 1990 Act, s 3(3)(b).

3.29 This ensures that a human embryo which has been created and is over 14 days old, disregarding any time during which it has been frozen, cannot be used or retained. The statute provides that no human embryo may be placed in any animal.

3.30 The relevant regulations were in respect of reproductive cloning but these are now superfluous due to the amendments.

Prohibitions in connection with gametes

3.31 The amendment in s 3(2)(b) provides that no one shall place any gametes into a women other than permitted eggs or permitted sperm and this must only be done in pursuance of a licence.[34]

3.32 The definition of a permitted egg is an egg produced or extracted from the ovaries of a woman and permitted sperm is defined as sperm produced or extracted from the testes of a man.[35] The important aspect of the permitted egg and sperm must be that the egg and sperm must not have been the subject of any alterations of their nuclear or mitochondrial DNA.[36]

3.33 This amendment, therefore, ensures that artificially created gametes or genetically modified gametes cannot be placed into a woman.

3.34 A licence must be obtained in order to store gametes as they may not be stored otherwise.[37] Further, it is not permitted, in the course of providing treatment services for any woman, to use any sperm (other than partner-donated sperm which has been neither processed nor stored), or the woman's eggs after processing or storage, or the eggs of any other woman, except where licensed to do so.

3.35 There can be no procurement, testing, processing or distribution of any gametes intended for human application except in pursuance of a licence or a third party agreement.[38]

3.36 Regulations may be used to specify circumstances where sperm and eggs can be placed into a woman but a licence must nevertheless be obtained and such regulations may accordingly modify the licensing system.[39]

Mitochondrial donation

3.37 There is another regulation-making power which allows the meaning of permitted eggs and permitted embryos to be expanded in order to include eggs

---

[34] The 1990 Act, s 4(3).
[35] The 1990 Act, s 3ZA(2), (3), as amended.
[36] The 1990 Act, s 3ZA (2)(b) and (3)(b), as amended.
[37] The 1990 Act, s 4.
[38] The 1990 Act, s 4(1A).
[39] The 1990 Act, s 4(3) and (4).

or embryos that have been treated in such a way as specified in the regulation to prevent the transmission of serious mitochondrial disease.[40]

3.38 On fertilisation, the mitochondria from the woman's eggs will become the mitochondria for every cell of the embryo created. In circumstances where the woman's mitochondria is susceptible to a genetic medical condition, then this condition will be inherited though her eggs. It was anticipated that in the future, where such circumstances apply, it may be possible to use the woman's eggs, her partner's sperm and healthy donated mitochondria to create healthy embryos. This regulation-making power will enable such embryos and eggs to be implanted in a woman if that technology became available. This, therefore, serves as a good example of the anticipatory nature of the legislation, the drive to remain as up-to-date as possible and the practical use of regulations in such situations.

3.39 The provisions of the 1990 Act make the assumption that only one woman's eggs have been used to produce a child. New provisions now deal with the situation where a permitted egg or permitted embryos were created from material provided by two women. A new provision is inserted into the 1990 Act under s 35A. This provides that where a permitted egg or permitted embryo was created from material provided by two women, regulations may provide for certain provisions to have effect.[41] These are in relation to the type of information provided to those receiving treatment, which involves receiving donor gametes or embryos from persons, the register of information and consent in relation to the use of storage of gametes or embryos and parental orders.[42]

Prohibition in connection with germ cells

3.40 There is a prohibition whereby a person is not permitted to use female germs cells (at any stage of maturity, which includes eggs) taken or derived from an embryo or a foetus or to use embryos created by using such cells, for the purpose of providing any woman with fertility services.[43] Fertility services are defined as medical, surgical or obstetric services provided for the purpose of assisting women to carry children.[44]

Prohibitions in connection with genetic material not of human origin

3.41 There is a new s 4A which provides that certain types of embryo which contain both human and animal DNA, are subject to regulation under the 1990 Act. It expressly prohibits the placing into a woman of a human admixed embryo, which has been defined above in its many permutations. It also

---

[40] The 1990 Act, s 3ZA(5), as amended.
[41] The 1990 Act, s 35A(1), as amended.
[42] The 1990 Act, s 35A(2), as amended.
[43] The 1990 Act, s 3A, as amended.
[44] The 1990 Act, s 3A(2), as amended.

prohibits the placing into a woman of any other embryo which is not a human embryo or any gametes other than human gametes.[45] There is an express prohibition on placing a human admixed embryo in an animal,[46] which was not expressly forbidden in this way in the original legislation.

3.42 It is necessary to have a licence in order to mix human gametes with animal gametes or to create, keep or use a human admixed embryo.[47] In any event, a licence cannot authorise the keeping or use of human admixed embryos after the appearance of the primitive streak or the end of the period of 14 days beginning with the day on which the process of creating the human admixed embryo began, not counting the time during which the human admixed embryo is stored, whichever occurs first.[48] This is consistent with the time limits for keeping human embryos *in vitro* for research purposes.

3.43 An animal is defined for these purposes as an animal other than man.[49] An embryo for the purposes of this section means a live embryo, including an egg that is in the process of fertilisation or is undergoing any process capable of resulting in an embryo.[50]

Third party agreements

3.44 As the clinics practising assisted reproduction technology and embryo research have increased in number and grown in size over the years, ancillary and supportive businesses dealing with human embryos and gametes have become established. To control, manage and regulate this area of relevant growth has led to the inclusion in the 1990 Act of references to a 'third party', ie a person with whom a person who is a licence holder has a third party agreement.[51]

3.45 The 1990 Act references to 'third party agreements' refer to a written agreement between a person who holds a licence and another person. The other person procures, tests or processes gametes or embryos or both on behalf of the holder of the licence, or supplies or distributes to the holder of the licence any goods or services which may affect the quality or safety of gametes or embryos.[52]

3.46 The agreements are made in accordance with any licence conditions imposed by the Authority for the purposes of securing compliance with the requirements of Article 24 of the EU directive,[53] which focuses on the relationship between tissue establishments and third parties.

---

[45]   The 1990 Act, s 4A(1), as amended.
[46]   The 1990 Act, s 4A(4), as amended.
[47]   The 1990 Act, s 4A(2), as amended.
[48]   The 1990 Act, s 4A(3), as amended.
[49]   The 1990 Act, s 4A(7), as amended.
[50]   The 1990 Act, s 4A(8), as amended.
[51]   The 1990 Act, s 2A(2).
[52]   The 1990 Act, s 2A (1).
[53]   The First EU Directive.

3.47 When the 1990 Act refers to persons to whom a third party agreement applies, the relevant parties are the third party, any person designated in the third party agreement as a person to whom the agreement applied and also any person acting under the direction of a third party or of any person so designated.[54]

3.48 The 1990 Act also makes references to 'third party premises'; which means any premises, other than the premises to which the relevant licence relates, on which a third party procures, processes or distributes gametes or embryos on behalf of any person in connection with activities carried out by that person under a licence.[55] It also refers to any premises from which a third party provides any goods or services which may affect the quality and safety of gametes or embryos, and to any person in connection with activities which are carried out by that person under a licence.[56]

Offences under the Act

3.49 There are a number of categories of offences arising from a breach of certain provisions of the Act and in this Chapter the focus will be on those offences arising from the activities concerning embryos and gametes. The aim is to make clear that deviations from those activities which are expressly prohibited and those which can only be carried out with the relevant licence or third party agreement or directions, will be treated seriously.

Statutory defence

3.50 There is a general defence which can be relied upon by a person charged with an offence under the Act, if applicable.

3.51 Under s 41(11), where a person is charged with an offence under the Act, the person charged must show that he was, at the material time, the person to whom a licence or third party agreement applied or to whom directions were given, and that he took all reasonable steps and exercised all due diligence to avoid committing the offence.

The offences

3.52 It is an offence for a person to carry out the following activities:[57]

- to place into a woman an embryo or any gametes save for those permitted embryos, permitted eggs or permitted sperm;[58]

---

[54]　The 1990 Act, s 2A(3).
[55]　The 1990 Act, s 2A(2)(a).
[56]　The 1990 Act, s 2A (2)(b).
[57]　The 1990 Act, s 41(1), as amended.
[58]　Para 3(2) of the 2008 Act.

- to breach the prohibition in connection with germ cells set out in s 3A of the 1990 Act;[59]

- to place into a woman a human admixed embryo, any other embryo which is not a human embryo or any gametes which are not human gametes;[60]

- to mix human gametes with animal gametes, to create, keep or use a human admixed embryo without a licence;[61]

- to keep or use an embryo after the appearance of the primitive streak;[62]

- to place an embryo into an animal;[63]

- to keep or use an embryo which is prohibited by regulations.[64]

3.53 The penalty upon conviction is imprisonment for a term not exceeding ten years or a fine or both.[65]

3.54 There is an offence for a person to do the following in connection with licences and third party agreements:

- to create, use, keep, process, procure, distribute or store gametes and embryos without a licence;[66]

- to contravene any directions given pursuant to s 24(5D) of the 1990 Act as amended, which deals with directions on the keeping of anything or information held in pursuance of a licence to be transferred;[67]

- to provide any information for the purposes of granting a licence which is false or misleading in a material way and he/she knows that the information provided is false or misleading or provides such information recklessly.[68]

3.55 The penalties for conviction are less for this category of offences than those relating to the breach of the strict prohibitions dealt with above. On conviction the penalty for these offences is a custodial sentence of not more

---

[59] Para 3A of the 2008 Act.
[60] The 1990 Act, s 4A(1).
[61] The 1990 Act, s 4A(2).
[62] The 1990 Act, s 3(3)(a).
[63] The 1990 Act, s 3(3)(b).
[64] The 1990 Act, s 3(3)(c).
[65] The 1990 Act, s 41(1).
[66] The 1990 Act, s 41(2), (a)–(c), as amended.
[67] The 1990 Act, s 41(2)(d), as amended.
[68] The 1990 Act, s 41(3).

than two years and/or a fine.[69] On summary conviction, the penalty is imprisonment not exceeding a period of six months and/or a fine not exceeding the statutory maximum.[70]

3.56 There is a defence provided where a person is charged with an offence of doing anything which under ss 3(1), 3(1A), 4(1), 4(1A) or 4A(2), should not be done.[71]

3.57 The defendant has to prove that he was acting under the direction of another and that he believed on reasonable grounds that the other person was at the material time the person responsible under a licence designated by virtue of s 17(2)(b) of this Act as the person to whom the licence applied or person to whom direction had been given under s 24(5A) to (5D) and also that the person charged was authorised by the virtue of the licences, third party agreements or directions to do the thing in question.[72]

3.58 A person who discloses information in breach of s 33A of the Act, as amended, is guilty of an offence. The offence is potentially very wide-reaching and would be committed by those who are in some way involved or connected with the regulation of assisted reproductive technology revealing information on the register of information under s 31(2) as amended.

3.59 The category referred to are those who act in the capacity of a member or employee of the Authority, any person exercising the new functions under the contracting-out and agency arrangements on behalf of the Authority, anyone engaged by the Authority to provide it with services or any of their employees or subcontractors, a person to whom a licence or a third party agreement applies or a person to whom directions have been given.[73]

3.60 The information that is protected from disclosure includes those who are involved in treatment services and the identity of those from whom gametes or embryos have been taken and kept or used.[74] No offence is committed under s 33A of the 1990 Act as amended if any of the lengthy provisos set out in s 33A(2) apply. Otherwise, the statutory defence under s 41(11) above is available in this situation.

3.61 An offence is committed where a person to whom a licence applies or who is the licence holder, gives or receives any money or other benefit which is not authorised by the directions, in respect of any supply of gametes, embryos or human admixed embryos.[75] A person guilty of this offence is liable on

---

[69]   The 1990 Act, s 41(4)(a).
[70]   The 1990 Act, s 41(4)(b).
[71]   These are activities which can only be done under the auspices of a licence or a third party agreement.
[72]   The 1990 Act, s 41(10) and 4(11), as amended.
[73]   The 1990 Act, s 33A(1), as amended.
[74]   The 1990 Act, s 31(2), as amended.
[75]   The 1990 Act, s 41(8).

summary conviction to imprisonment for a term not exceeding six months or a fine not exceeding level five on the standard scale, or both. Again the general defence set out above pursuant to s 41(11) is available.

Regulations relating to offences

3.62 Chapter Four provides more detail about investigating and pursuing the commission of a suspected offence and therefore it suffices to state here that there are powers and procedures set out within the legislation for doing this.

3.63 Provision is made for regulations to provide for details regarding the keeping and examination of gametes or embryos in connection with the investigation of, or proceedings for an offence (wherever it is believed to have been committed), or for the storage of gametes where they are to be used for such purposes, other than treatment services, as may be specified in regulations.[76] There is nothing that makes it unlawful to keep or examine, including for the purposes of performing any tests, any gametes or embryos in pursuant of such regulations.[77]

Consent to prosecution

3.64 In England and Wales, no prosecution proceedings can be instituted without the consent of the Director of Public Prosecutions or alternatively by the Director himself. In Northern Ireland prosecutions cannot be instituted save by or with the consent of the Director of Public Prosecution for Northern Ireland.[78]

THE POWER TO MAKE REGULATIONS

3.65 The use of regulations was to enable the 1990 Act to retain some flexibility, and indeed for the Act to have survived in its basic form for so long reflects in some part the flexibility that the power of making regulations has afforded. There has already been reference in this Chapter above to the changes which can be made by regulations only. However, some parts of the legislation are regarded as providing protection which is so fundamental to the integrity of the legislation that it can only be changed after due parliamentary scrutiny and discussion.

3.66 The regulatory power to amend is given broadly in respect of the key definitions in the legislation ie gametes and embryos. As definitions have just been considered and one of the reasons for amendments was to allow for wider definitions to be inserted into the legislation, it is to be anticipated that these new amended definitions will have some endurance. It is certainly not expected

---

[76] The 1990 Act, s 43(1).
[77] The 1990 Act, s 43(2) and (3).
[78] The 1990 Act, s 42.

that there will be any new regulations in this area of definitions under ss 1 and 4A of the 1990 Act, as amended, in the near future.

3.67   Regulations and power to make consequential provisions are set out in s 45 and the new s 45A respectively. Any power that the Secretary of State or the Authority has to make regulations includes the power to make appropriate transitional, incidental or supplemental provision.[79]

3.68   The Acts employ the two forms of parliamentary scrutiny of secondary legislation, namely the 'negative' and 'affirmative' resolutions of Parliament. Under the 'negative' resolution there is the laying of the statutory instrument before Parliament and the contents will take effect unless there is a prayer of annulment, and then there is the 'affirmative' requirement for a favourable vote to be passed.

3.69   Therefore a copy of the draft regulations are lodged in the office of the clerk to each House of Parliament and the regulations will come into force 40 days after lodging if they have not been made subject to a resolution for annulment passed in either House.

3.70   In contrast, the 'affirmative' resolution involves finding a time slot and space for each House of Parliament to give affirmative approval to the draft statutory instrument. The latter method is clearly more difficult due to competition from other pressing business which also requires parliamentary time and consideration.

3.71   The Act specifies those sections of the legislation which may be changed by affirmative resolution only and that if the regulations are not made in accordance with that procedure where it has been designated, they should be liable to be annulled.[80]

Affirmative resolutions

3.72   The activities which require the affirmative resolution procedure are set out in s 45(4A) and are summarised in the table below:

Provisions	Sections
Redefining the definitions of 'embryos', 'eggs', 'sperm' or 'gametes' for the purposes of s 1 subject to the condition in s 1(7)	The 1990 Act, s 1(6) as amended

---

[79]   The 1990 Act, s 3A, as amended.
[80]   The 1990 Act, s 45(5).

Stating further circumstances in which a licence cannot authorise the keeping or using of an embryo	The 1990 Act, s 3(3)(c)
Allowing eggs or embryos to be termed as 'permitted eggs' or 'permitted embryos' even though the egg or embryos have been treated by a process to prevent the transmission of serious mitochondrial disease	The 1990 Act, s 3ZA(5), as amended
Stating further circumstances in which a licence cannot authorise the storage or use of gametes	The 1990 Act, s 4(2)
Stating further circumstances in which a licence is required to place sperm or eggs into a woman	The 1990 Act, s 4(3)
Redefining the definition of a 'human admixed embryo'	The 1990 Act, s 4A(5)(e), as amended
Amending only (not to repeal) the current statutory definitions of 'human admixed embryo' and to redefine 'embryo', 'eggs' or 'gametes' for the purposes of s 4A	The 1990 Act, s 4A(5)(10), as amended
Requiring or authorising of directions to be given in relation to particular matters which are specified in the regulations and relate to activities involving genetic material of animal origin	The 1990 Act, s 24(4B), as amended
Specifying the information that is to be given about a donor when there is a request for information as to genetic parentage	The 1990 Act, s 31ZA(2)(a), as amended
Providing further exceptions as to where a person may make disclosure of information from the register under s 33A(B), and subject to s 33B(2)	The 1990 Act, s 33B, as amended

Formulating provisions for the disclosure of information from the register for the purposes of medical or other research	The 1990 Act, s 33C, as amended
Formulating provisions for the application of other parts of the Act to have effect where there has been mitochondrial donation	The 1990 Act, s 35A, as amended
Specifying the way in which gametes or embryos can be kept, stored and examined in connection with offences	The 1990 Act, s 43
Specifying other practices which may be licensed for treatment	The 1990 Act, Sch 2, para 1(1)(g), as amended
Amending the circumstances for embryo testing	The 1990 Act, Sch 2, para 1ZC(3), as amended
Specifying further purposes for which a licence for research may be applied for	The 1990 Act, Sch 2, para 3A(1)(c), as amended

Negative resolutions

3.73 Other matters which can be dealt with by regulations are to be dealt with by the 'negative' resolution procedure. For example s 8C(1)(c) permits regulations to set out the functions which cannot be contracted out by the HFEA.[81]

Power to make consequential regulations

3.74 There is a new s 45A inserted into the 1990 Act enabling consequential changes to other legislation to be made as a result of amending any of the current definitions of 'embryo' and 'gametes' under s 1 and human admixed embryo under ss 4A(5)(e) and 4A(10).[82]

3.75 This includes modifying Acts of Parliament, Acts of the Scottish Parliament, Measures or Acts of the Welsh Assembly and Northern Ireland legislation and any secondary legislation made under them (in consultation with the devolved administration where appropriate). The power under s 45A is exercisable by order made by regulation under the affirmative procedure.[83]

---

[81] The 1990 Act, s 45B(3).
[82] The 1990 Act, s 45A(1) and (2).
[83] The 1990 Act, s 45B(4).

New regulations

3.76 The Department of Health has launched a public consultation on the draft regulations to implement the Act. The proposals are in four broad categories, as follows:

(i)   'Storage period for embryos and gametes' – this concerns circumstances in which embryos and gametes might be frozen for longer than previously has been permitted and the issue is whether the same criteria should apply to embryos as to gametes, whether the extended freezing should be permitted in cases of premature infertility eg in children and in cases involving embryo or gamete donation or surrogacy and whether the extended period should be a set time period rather than an age limit;

(ii) 'procedure for revocation, variation or refusal of licences' – this concerns the consideration of licence applications by the HFEA and whether there should be a lay majority on the relevant HFEA committee and whether the relevant HFEA procedures should be detailed in regulations;

(iii) 'appeals' – this concerns reconsideration of licence applications by the HFEA when its decisions are on appeal. The issues centre on whether current and former HFEA members should be prohibited from sitting on appeals committees, and whether the individual heading the appeals committee should be legally qualified;

(iv) 'disclosure of information for research purposes' – this concerns the disclosure of identifiable information held on the HFEA register. It includes circumstances where it is not practicable to obtain consent from the relevant patients. There are issues regarding which of the organisations are best placed to consider applications for information and whether the information that can be disclosed should exclude details of embryo or gamete donation and what conditions should apply to such disclosure of information.

3.77 The specific details of the draft regulations will be considered when the relevant subject matter arises, with the proviso that since the regulations are only available at the draft stage, it is all potentially subject to change.

Chapter 4

THE HUMAN FERTILISATION AND EMBRYOLOGY AUTHORITY

INTRODUCTION

4.1   The Human Fertilisation and Embryology Authority (HFEA) is a non-departmental independent governmental agency which has been operational as a statutory corporation since August 1991. It is central to the regulatory framework of licensing the practice of certain treatments and research involving embryos and gametes, and the storage of gametes and embryos.

4.2   The HFEA has had a succession of Chairmen since its inception in 1989. Its first Chairman was Sir Colin Campbell, followed by Ms Ruth Deech (now Baroness), Ms Suzi Leather (now Dame), Ms Shirley Harrison and its present incumbent is Professor Lisa Jardine CBE. Some Chairmen have been more high profile than others but all of them have led the HFEA in differing styles.

4.3   The first part of this Chapter examines in detail the variety of duties and functions that the HFEA has imposed upon it and how these are performed in practice. The key duty of the HFEA which is to licence those activities which are licensable under the legislation is excluded from this Chapter. Linked to this is the duty to conduct inspections. Both these duties are more properly examined in Chapter 5 where the practical details of the licensing system can be set out in full. However, there is a duty imposed on the HFEA to formulate a Code of Practice[1] which is a key component of the licensing process, and will be examined later in this Chapter.

4.4   The second part of this Chapter looks at the internal organisation of the HFEA and how structurally it sets out to fulfil its various tasks. An important element of this is the membership of the HFEA. This is a relatively small group, which means that invariably the individual personalities and backgrounds of the members must have an impact and influence on the way that the organisation operates.

---

[1]   A Code of Practice is used in other jurisdictions as an effective operating tool of the legislation eg The Mental Capacity Act Code of Practice 2007 and the Human Tissue Act Code of Practice 2006.

THE ROLE OF THE HFEA

4.5　　The HFEA's principal role has been to license and monitor clinics and establishments which carry out certain assisted reproduction procedures for the purpose of treatment and also embryo research. The licensing process is examined in greater detail in Chapter 5. The HFEA operates by formulating and applying a Code of Practice which guides the conduct of these licensed practitioners. However, it also has numerous other important functions.

4.6　　It does not exist in isolation and it has tangent relationships with other bodies operating in similar and closely connected fields, such as the Human Genetics Commission.[2] It also has a public dimension in that it acts as a source of information and advice to the general public about assisted reproduction. For many years it has operated a website[3] which allows it to communicate with the public and where it also provides its agenda, notes of meetings, reports, consultations and further information regarding its work.

4.7　　Some of the changes made by the new amendments are with the intention of enabling the HFEA to function with fewer restrictions than it has done in the past and also to bring it in line with the operational principles by which other organisations and government bodies function.

THE HFEA'S FUNCTIONS AND DUTIES

4.8　　The status and capacity of the HFEA is that it is not to be regarded as a servant or agent of the Crown and likewise does not enjoy any status, privilege or immunity of the Crown.[4] It is stated that 'The Authority shall have the power to do anything which is calculated to facilitate the discharge of its functions, or is incidental or conducive to their discharge, except the power to borrow money'.[5] Its independence is further reinforced by the provision that, subject to the Act, the Authority may regulate its own proceedings and make such arrangements as it thinks appropriate for the discharge of its functions.[6]

4.9　　The HFEA's general functions are to be found in s 8 of the 1990 Act but further additional functions that the HFEA must carry out are scattered throughout the statute. There are some important amendments imposed by the 2008 Act which have now enlarged the scope of the HFEA's duties. The HFEA is still left with the general provision that it may perform such other functions as regulations may specify. This allows an enlargement of its duties through secondary rather than primary legislation.[7]

---

[2]　　The UK's advisory body on new developments in human genetics.
[3]　　http://www.hfea.gov.uk.
[4]　　The 1990 Act, Sch 1, para 1.
[5]　　The 1990 Act, Sch 1, para 2.
[6]　　The 1990 Act, Sch 1, para 9(1).
[7]　　The 1990 Act, s 8(1)(d).

4.10   Each of these duties has been identified and this Chapter will consider what each duty entails and how the HFEA purports to carry out and fulfil its duties. What will be striking is the extent to which the duties extend beyond merely licensing the licensable activities.

The duty to review

4.11   The Authority has to keep under review information about embryos and any subsequent development of embryos and also about the provision of treatment of services and prohibited activities governed by the Act, which by their nature concern embryos and gametes.[8] This, therefore, covers the broad and comprehensive landscape in which the HFEA regulates and the HFEA is in the prime position, with all its others functions, to be the keenest observer and reviewer of the regulated reproductive techniques.

4.12   It has to also advise the Secretary of State on such matters, when asked to do so. This ensures that for the government there is a body whose function it is to keep abreast of all the developments in this field and to whom it can turn for advice, whenever that advice is required at governmental level.

4.13   As a reviewer, the HFEA maintains its independence from the government structure itself. This is evidenced by the committee consultations which took place over the new Act, and the HFEA was able to put forward its own recommendations on the necessary changes to the law and to present its own consultation paper for the consideration of Parliament.[9]

The duty to provide guidance and advice

4.14   The Authority has to publicise its own services and those services provided by others pursuant to their licences.[10] This is provided in the information which can be obtained directly from the HFEA by way of its publication of the treatment and research that are being carried out by all of the licensed clinics and research establishments.

4.15   It also has a duty towards others to give advice and information. This embraces those who are subject to licences, ie the clinics and research establishment, those patients who are receiving treatments and also those donors who are providing gametes or embryos for use for the purposes of the activities governed by the Act or may wish to do so in the future.[11]

4.16   This is primarily provided for by the availability of publications specifically on donors and the success rates of clinics practising IVF.[12] The

---

[8]   The 1990 Act, s 8(1)(a).
[9]   Appendix 7 of the written evidence presented to the House of Commons Science and Technology Committee was a Memorandum from the HFEA.
[10]   The 1990 Act, s 8(1)(b).
[11]   The 1990 Act, s 8(1)(c).
[12]   *The HFEA Guide to Infertility and Directory of Clinics 2007/8*, HFEA.

clinics and research establishments are provided with guidance and information by way of the Code of Practice and also the physical inspections which are carried out on behalf of the HFEA.

4.17   There is an amendment which now gives the Authority the power to charge for some or all of the provision of advice.[13] The Authority has the discretion to fix different fees for different circumstances.[14] This would affect the provision of documentation or specific advice given upon demand but since it only relates to advice and not documentation, it is unlikely that the general public would be charged for publications which offer just information. The intention is that the charge for advice would recover all or part of the costs of providing such advice.

The duty to provide statements and principles

4.18   There are new additional functions requiring the Authority to maintain a statement of its general principles which it considers should be followed in the carrying out of activities governed by the Act and its functions in relation to such activities.[15] This statement should clarify how it perceives its role in relation to each of its various activities and functions.

4.19   When considering the work of the HFEA, the Authority has always defined its general role by reference to its statutory remit. This new requirement is likely to produce a more detailed breakdown of its role in respect of particular and specific activities and functions. In the draft 8th Edition of the Code of Practice, the initial attempt of the HFEA to fulfil this duty can be seen. It states that its principles are to:[16]

- treat people with sensitivity, respect and confidentiality;

- observe the highest standards of integrity and professionalism in putting into effect the governing law;

- consult widely on issues;

- keep abreast of scientific and clinical advances; and

- exercise its functions consistently, proportionally, openly and fairly.

4.20   The way in which the Authority is to carry out its functions is now defined as being, 'effectively, efficiently and economically'[17] and to have regard to the principles of best regulatory practice. The amendments set out expressly that these include the need for transparency, accountability, proportionality,

---

[13]   The 1990 Act, s 8(2), as amended.
[14]   The 1990 Act, s 35B(6), as amended.
[15]   The 1990 Act, s 8(1)(ca), as amended.
[16]   The draft 8th Edition of the Code of Practice, Part 2, para 4.
[17]   The 1990 Act, s 8ZA (1), as amended.

consistency and targeting only those cases in which action is needed. These are all the key principles that other similar quasi-governmental bodies currently have to adhere.

4.21 There is also a new amendment which requires the HFEA to promote compliance with the requirements imposed by or under the Act and the Code of Practice.[18] This expressly defines what as a public regulator the HFEA's role has always been.

The duty to provide directions

4.22 From time to time the Authority can also give directions for specific purposes which are set out in the statute and these are reproduced in the table below. The direction made is then capable of being varied or revoked.[19]

4.23 The person to whom any requirement is made within the direction is then required to comply with that direction.[20] Anything that is done by a person in pursuance of a direction is deemed as being carried out in pursuance of a licence.[21] A failure to comply with directions may lead to a revocation of a licence irrespective of the seriousness of the breach.[22]

4.24 Where directions are made to any particular person, the directions shall be given by serving notice of the direction upon that individual person.[23] Otherwise, directions in pursuant of any licence, which includes a licence which has ceased to have effect, are served on the person who is or was the person responsible, or the person who is or was the holder of the licence, if that is different.[24]

4.25 However, if the directions are general in nature or if the Authority decides that it is not practicable to give notice to the person responsible or the holder of the licence, then it has the discretion to just publish the direction in such a way as the Authority believes is likely to bring the direction to the attention of the person to whom it is applicable.[25]

4.26 There are numerous matters which the Authority has the power to make directions in respect of, and these are summarised in the table below:

---

[18] The 1990 Act, s 8(1)(cb), as amended.
[19] The 1990 Act, s 23(1).
[20] The 1990 Act, s 23(2).
[21] The 1990 Act, s 23(2).
[22] The 1990 Act, s 18(2)(c).
[23] The 1990 Act, s 23(4).
[24] The 1990 Act, s 23(5)(a), as amended.
[25] The 1990 Act, s 23(5)(b).

Provisions	Sections
To implement the draft Code of Practice	The 1990 Act, s 26(5)
To set out what information is required to be recorded and given to the Authority in relation to treatment licences for fertility or non-fertility services	The 1990 Act, s 13(2)
Specify the circumstances and conditions in which gametes or embryos that are not intended for human application may be kept by and on behalf of a person to whom a licence applies, during their passage to and from any premises	The 1990 Act, s 24(3)
Specify the conditions and circumstances in which such gametes or embryos intended for human application may be kept during their carriage between various relevant premises	The 1990 Act, s 24(3A)
The circumstances and conditions to the keeping by or on behalf of a person, to whom a licence applies, of human admixed embryos in the course of their carriage to and from any premises	The 1990 Act, s 24(3B), as amended
The circumstances and conditions for embryos, gametes or admixed human embryos to be imported into or exported from the United Kingdom and to ensure that standards of quality and safety equivalent to those laid down in the Act are met and also have regard to the issue of traceability	The 1990 Act, s 24(4) and (4A), as amended
Where required by Regulations in relation to activities involving genetic material of animal origin	The 1990 Act, s 24(4B)

Provisions	Sections
Directions on such matters as it sees fit concerning the issue of consent	The 1990 Act, Sch 3, para 2(3))
Provision for dealing with the consequences where a licence ceases to have effect or is revoked	The 1990 Act, s 5A to 5E, as amended
On the unique coding assigned to donations of gametes and embryos pursuant to a licence	The 1990 Act, s 24(12)
The information required and measures to be taken where there has been an adverse occurrence, incident or misidentification or mix up involving gametes and embryos intended for human application	The 1990 Act, s 24(13)
Specifying any other animal (rather than a hamster) for the test at Sch 2, para 1(1)(f) or 3(2). However, directions cannot be given until the Secretary of State lays a report before Parliament.	The 1990 Act, s 24(11), as amended
What information must be recorded pursuant to a research licence	The 1990 Act, s 15(2)
What information is to be provided to a person who holds another licence but to whom gametes, embryos or human admixed embryos are supplied	The 1990 Act, s 12(f)

In practice

4.27 The HFEA has been very active in issuing directions on various issues over the years. Some directions have been pedestrian and routine eg bringing into force the latest Code of Practice.[26] Some are clearly more complicated and set out policy and practice.[27] All the directions that have been issued are available on the HFEA website.

---

[26] Direction D2007/5 brings into force the 7th Edition of the Code of Practice.
[27] Direction D2008/5 brought about the multiple births minimisation strategy (30.9.08) which dealt with reducing the clinics' annual multiple birth rates. Each clinic must have its strategy in place by January 2009.

4.28   The use of directions by the HFEA is an effective tool of communication and control. In addition, the Chairman issues letters from time to time and there are press statements setting out the progress or views of the HFEA on particular matters, especially those which have reached the media. Again, these are available on the HFEA website.

The duty to produce an annual report

4.29   The production of an annual report is a statutory requirement and it is prepared for each period of 12 months from the commencement of the HFEA.[28] The contents of the report are stipulated to be the activities of the Authority and also the activities that it proposes to undertake in the forthcoming 12 months.[29] This report is then presented to the Secretary of State who lays it before each House of Parliament.[30] The reports are then available to the public.

4.30   To date, there have been 18 such Annual reports published.[31] The contents and comprehensiveness of the reports has increased over the years in line with the government's endeavours for openness and transparency in the operation of its governmental bodies.

4.31   The annual reports provide a very useful source of information for those involved in this area of healthcare, directly from the regulator. Although there have been changes to the format over the years, the following items can usually be found in these annual reports:

(i)   an account of the role, principles and statutory remit of the HFEA and the Act;

(ii)   the details about the members and the structure of the executive;

(iii)   the remuneration of the members and the executive staff;

(iv)   a list of those establishments which have been granted a licence;

(v)   the highlighting of particular issues concerning the Code of Practice;

(vi)   information on new developments and research;

(vii)   the financial report of the HFEA; and

(viii) the issues that the HFEA is preparing to deal with in the forthcoming year.

---

28   The 1990 Act, s 7(1).
29   The 1990 Act, s 7(2).
30   The 1990 Act, s 7(3).
31   The latest is the HFEA *Annual Report and Accounts 2007/08*.

The duty to produce the Code of Practice

4.32 An important statutory duty of the HFEA is the requirement to maintain and publish a Code of Practice.[32] From the outset, it was always felt that there was a need for assistance for practitioners, in an area of such legal and practical complexity, with the interpretation of the legal provisions in order to ensure that as far as possible regulation was adhered to.

4.33 The Authority also has the ability and opportunity to revise the whole or any part of the Code from time to time.[33] To date there have now been seven editions of the Code.

4.34 The Authority must send in a draft of the proposed revised code to the Secretary of State for approval. Before preparing any draft, the Authority is to consult any such person as the Secretary of State may require it to consult and such other person as the Authority itself considers appropriate.[34] If the draft Code is approved by the Secretary of State it is laid before Parliament and if the Secretary of State does not approve the draft he must give his/her reasons for this conclusion to the Authority.[35] The approved draft Code then comes into force in accordance with the directions.[36]

The contents of the Code

4.35 The purpose of a Code is to give practitioners guidance about the conduct of licensable activities and on the discharge of the functions of the person responsible under the licence and to those others to whom the licence applies.[37] The Code may also give guidance about the use of any technique involving the placing of sperm and eggs in a woman.[38]

4.36 Specifically, the Code must provide guidance to clinics about the account to be taken of the welfare of children who may be born as a result of treatment services and of other children who may be affected by such births. This includes the provision of specific guidance on the resulting child's need for what is now termed as 'supportive parenting', with the 2008 Act replacing the reference to a child's need for a father.[39]

4.37 There is also inserted into the1990 Act a new section[40] which requires the HFEA to provide guidance in the Code about the giving of a suitable opportunity to receive proper counselling and the provision of such relevant information as is proper, as required by the licence condition for clinics under

[32] The 1990 Act, s 25(1) and (5).
[33] The 1990 Act, s 25(4).
[34] The 1990 Act, s 26(3).
[35] The 1990 Act, s 26(4).
[36] The 1990 Act, s 26(5).
[37] The 1990 Act, s 25(1).
[38] The 1990 Act, s 25(3).
[39] The 1990 Act, s 25(2), as amended.
[40] The 1990 Act, s 25(2A), as amended.

the new ss 13(6) and (6A) of the 1990 Act. These new provisions refer to the circumstances where treatment services are being provided to heterosexual couples who are not married and to same-sex couples.

4.38   The format of the Codes has been to set out the legislative provisions in full which require guidance and then for the HFEA to provide its guidance. Each successive Code has to take into account new relevant legislation and is supplemented by further guidance periodically over its duration. This makes for a very full and comprehensive document which it is vital that all licensed clinics and research centres and those involved with related and relevant activities are fully aware of.

Breaches of the Code

4.39   A failure on the part of any person to observe any provisions of the Code shall not of itself make that person liable to any proceedings[41] since the legal force of the Code is ultimately that of guidance and good practice.

4.40   However, the statute imposes upon the Authority the obligation that where it has to consider whether there has been a failure to comply with conditions of the licence, particularly where the conditions require something to be done that is 'proper' or 'suitable', it shall take into account any relevant provisions of the Code.[42] Further, when the HFEA considers whether or not to vary or revoke a licence, it can take into consideration whether there has been any observance of or failure to observe the Code.[43]

4.41   The range of breaches under the Code can clearly stretch from the relatively minor to the catastrophic. The more serious incidences can be dealt with under the criminal enforcement provisions. For the more minor offences, the practice of HFEA has been to flag up the breaches, which often come to light during the inspections (these are set out in the inspection reports) and to then allow for rectification and compliance to take place.

The new Code of Practice

4.42   The current edition of the HFEA Code of Practice[44] was published in July 2007 and so is not the most up-to-date guidance to current practice. In light of the legislative changes, the HFEA is to produce a new Code. This is also to be used as an opportunity for the HFEA to change the format and style of the Code, which has been very similar during its past reincarnations.

4.43   The HFEA has been using the views of the authorised licensed centres panel, which consists of the representatives of the licensed centres, to amend the current Code. The draft 8th Code of Practice has been subject to public

---

[41]   The 1990 Act, s 25(6).
[42]   The 1990 Act, s 25(6)(a), as amended.
[43]   The 1990 Act, s 25(6)(b), as amended.
[44]   7th Code of Practice.

consultation,[45] which sought feedback specifically on the structure and style of the Code and on any benefits or costs for licensed centres resulting from the changes.

4.44 The HFEA proposes that the new Code will not make any additional requirements other than those demanded by the new legislation and will attempt to simplify previous requirements in line with the 'better regulation' principles. Also, considering the legal burden that is upon licensed centres to meet their legal duties and obligations and the need that they and other users have to be able to identify and obtain the information necessary quickly, the HFEA will have to also consider the accessibility and ease with which this information can be provided and updated.

4.45 The draft Code has been re-designed into two parts in order to assist with the new challenges and it will have a section on the HFEA standards which contains specifications that centres are required to show that they can meet, including those required for compliance with the old and new legislation and another section on providing guidance on how these specifications should be met.

4.46 After the end of the consultation period, the HFEA will be able to amend the draft Code accordingly. The 8th Edition of the Code is due for publication prior to July 2009, by which time it will be distributed to the licensed clinic in order to allow practitioners plenty of time to prepare for the changes proposed in the new Act. The new Code will take effect on 1 October 2009. At this stage it is clearly not known what the final Code will look like or to what extent it will differ from the draft Code, so references in this book can only be to the draft Code.

The duty to keep registers

4.47 The HFEA has express duties to keep three forms of different registers. The first is a Register of Information which has been the subject of significant amendments under the new Act. There is a Register of voluntary contact which provides an example of where the HFEA has for some time effectively delegated this function to another organisation on its behalf. There is also a record of licences that have been granted, suspended or revoked.

Under the Freedom of Information Act 2000, there is a public right of access to information that is held by all levels of government and other public bodies, which includes the HFEA. Therefore, potentially any recorded information, in whatever form, is liable to be disclosed under a request pursuant to this statute. The HFEA is obliged to consider the request and will consider the views of those who are opposed to the disclosure but it may still decide to disclose the information requested. The information that can be requested excludes that information which is bound by confidentiality provisions.

---

[45] The consultation period ended on 18 February 2009.

A register of information

4.48   The 1990 Act requires the HFEA to keep a register of information that it obtains from the clinics which relates to the provision of treatment services, the keeping or use of any gametes or embryos taken from a woman or the procurement or distribution of sperm for certain purposes.[46]

4.49   It also requires the HFEA to keep a register of information obtained by it about people born as a result of treatment services.[47] The HFEA has to retain the register of information so that it may provide, if requested, information for people conceived as a result of donated gametes since the 1990 Act came into effect. The information collected on the register contains identifiable information and so is the subject of restrictions.

4.50   The scope and details of the register pertain to the issue of donation of gametes and embryos and so are discussed at greater length in Chapter Twelve below. The access and disclosure of the information contained on the register of information has also been the subject of review and amendment under the 2008 Act and the new provisions are also discussed in Chapter Twelve.

A voluntary contact register

4.51   The Authority also has the power to set up a voluntary contact register, which is a register of persons who have expressed their wish to receive information about any person to whom they are genetically related as a consequence of the provision to any person of treatment services in the UK before 1 August 1991.[48] The Authority has the power to make arrangement with any person who maintains a voluntary contact register to make arrangements for the information contained in the register to be supplied to the authority.[49]

4.52   A voluntary contact register, UK DonorLink,[50] has been run as a national pilot project since 2004 by the voluntary organisation called 'After Adoption Yorkshire'.

4.53   The details of the operation of setting up and maintaining such a register are left very much in the discretion of the HFEA.[51] It has the power to determine the criteria of those who will be included on the register and the details that will be included.[52]

---

[46]   The 1990 Act, s 31(2), as amended.
[47]   The 1990 Act, s 31(4), as amended.
[48]   The 1990 Act, s 31ZF(1), as amended.
[49]   The 1990 Act, s 31ZE(3), as amended.
[50]   http://www.ukdonorlink.org.uk
[51]   The 1990 Act, s 31ZF(2)(a) and (b), as amended.
[52]   The 1990 Act, s 31ZF(2)(c), as amended.

4.54 It has the ability to charge a fee to people who wish their particulars to be entered onto the register and it has the ability to fix different fees for different circumstances.[53] It is intended that the fee charged will recover all or part of the costs of running the register.

4.55 It can arrange for samples of the DNA of such people to be analysed at their request.[54] If there appears to the HFEA to be genetic matches on the register, it can make arrangements for the disclosure of the information on the register between the genetically related persons[55] but the Authority can impose such conditions as it thinks fit to prevent a person disclosing information to a person to whom that person is genetically related if that information would identify any third person who is genetically related to both parties.[56]

4.56 The HFEA has in fact taken advantage of the provisions to give financial assistance to another person to set up and keep a voluntary contact register.[57]

4.57 The HFEA provides the financial assistance for the organisation to do so, in whatever form it chooses, in particular, grants, loans guarantee or incurring expenditure itself for the person maintaining the register.[58] This financial assistance may be given on whatever the HFEA deems to be the appropriate terms and conditions.[59]

A register of licences

4.58 There is an obligation for the HFEA to keep a register which sets out the granting, subsequent suspension or revocation of every licence for treatment or storage which authorises activities in relation to gametes or embryos intended for use for human application and every licence for non-fertility services.[60] The details that have to be included pursuant to this duty are:

- the activities authorised;

- the address of the premises to which the license relates;

- the name of the person responsible and the name of the holder of the licence if that is different; and

- any variations that are made.[61]

---

[53] The 1990 Act, s 31ZF(2)(d) and s 35B(6), as amended.
[54] The 1990 Act, s 31ZF(2)(e), as amended.
[55] The 1990 Act, s 31ZF(2)(f), as amended.
[56] The 1990 Act, s 31ZF(2)(g), as amended.
[57] The 1990 Act, s 31F(1), as amended.
[58] The 1990 Act, s 31ZF(2), as amended.
[59] The 1990 Act, s 31ZG(3), as amended.
[60] The 1990 Act, s 31A(1).
[61] The 1990 Act, s 31A(2).

4.59   The HFEA does have the power, if it considers it appropriate, to make the information on the register available to the public.[62] This builds on the general duty that the HFEA has in relation to providing guidance and advice to the general pubic under s 8(1)(b) of the 1990 Act.

The duty to investigate

4.60   There have been several cases over the years where data or genetic material has been tampered with or negligently dealt with by licensed clinics or establishments.[63] The 1990 Act has been amended over the years in order to make tighter provisions for this and the 2008 Act makes further amendments.

4.61   The HFEA has a clear duty to investigate serious adverse incidents and in order to be an effective regulator the HFEA has to have some powers to inspect, enter, search and seize material or information which would be evidence of a breach of the licence conditions, the Code of practice or the law.

Serious adverse events

4.62   There is imposed upon the HFEA under s 15A(1) of the 1990 Act a duty to investigate serious adverse events and reactions, and then to take the appropriate control measures.

4.63   A serious adverse event refers to any type of gamete or embryo misidentification or mix-up or any untoward occurrence which may be associated with the procurement, testing, process, storage or distribution of gametes or embryos intended for human application. Such an event in relation to a donor of gametes or a person who receives treatment or non-medical fertility services might lead to the transmission of a communicable disease, death or life-threatening disabling or incapacitating condition, or might result in prolonged hospitalisation or illness.[64]

4.64   A serious adverse reaction means an unintended response, linking a communicable disease in a donor of gametes intended for human application or a person who receives treatment or non-medical fertility services, which may be associated with the procurement or human application of gametes or embryos and which is fatal, life-threatening, causes disability, incapacity or which results in prolonged hospitalisation or illness.[65]

4.65   When investigating any such event or reaction, the Authority shall, where it is appropriate, arrange for any premises to which a licence relates and any relevant third party premises to be inspected on its behalf and for a report on the inspection to be made to the Authority.[66]

---

[62]   The 1990 Act, s 31A(3).
[63]   *Leeds Teaching Hospital NHS Trust v A & Another* [2003] 1 FCR 599.
[64]   The 1990 Act, s 2.
[65]   The 1990 Act, s 2.
[66]   The 1990 Act, s 15A(2)(a) and (b).

4.66 If there is a request from a competent authority in an EEA state other than the UK or in Gibraltar to carry out an inspection in relation to a serious adverse event or reaction, then the Authority has to arrange for the inspection to be conducted, a report made of the inspection and for appropriate control measures to be taken.[67]

4.67 In order to deal effectively with serious adverse events and reactions, a duty is imposed upon the HFEA to communicate to competent authorities of other EEA States (other then the UK or Gibraltar) and the European Commission, such information in relation to the serious adverse events and reactions as is necessary for the purpose of enabling appropriate action to be taken. Where necessary, this includes the withdrawal of gametes and embryos which were intended for human application but are known or suspected to be unsuitable for such purpose.[68]

Entry, inspection, search and seizure

4.68 The powers to enter, inspect, search and seize items are to enable the Authority to perform its functions, to enforce the statute and to provide it with the ability to produce and preserve evidence as is necessary. The 2008 Act introduces a new Sch 3B into the 1990 Act[69] which replaces ss 39 and 40 of the 1990 Act and clarifies the powers of the Authority and the courts to enter, inspect, and search premises and to seize items found on premises. It is made plain that it is not unlawful for a member or employee of the Authority to be in possession of any embryo, human admixed embryo or gamete in pursuance of the course of their employment in pursuance of that person's functions.[70]

4.69 The Act also deals with the obtaining and execution of warrants where an offence is suspected.[71] It also provides that a failure to comply with certain requirements under Sch 3B or obstructing the exercise of any right pursuant to it, constitutes an offence.[72]

4.70 It is recognised to be of equal importance that, due to the nature of the powers that can be exercised, a person has to produce evidence of their right and entitlement to exercise such powers, if so required.[73]

4.71 In addition to the statutory powers that are available for entry and inspection, the HFEA when granting a licence must impose as a general condition that any member or employee of the HFEA (providing documentary

---

[67] The 1990 Act, s 15A(3).
[68] The 1990 Act, s 8A.
[69] The 2008 Act, Sch 5.
[70] The 1990 Act, s 38A(2), as amended.
[71] The 1990 Act, Sch 3B paras (5) and (6), as amended.
[72] The 1990 Act, Sch 3B(10)(b), as amended.
[73] The 1990 Act, Sch 3B para (9)(1), as amended.

identification as such if requested), shall at all reasonable times be permitted to enter the licensed premises and inspect them and any equipment or records and observe any activity.[74]

4.72   In this Chapter the powers to inspect in the course of pursuing a criminal offence, breach or some other serious incident are considered rather than the duty to inspect which falls as part of the consideration of a licence application.

The power to enter and inspect premises

4.73   There is a general power for a duly authorised person at a reasonable time to enter and inspect any premises to which a licence relates to any relevant third party premises. This is exercisable in relation to licences and third party agreements.[75]

Entry and search in connection with suspected offences

4.74   There are a number of offences which can be committed under the Act, set out in s 41, and these have been examined in detail in Chapter 3. In order to bring successful prosecutions, there is a need to obtain and secure evidence which could often be found on the licensed premises, in the form of documentary or physical evidence. The HFEA is involved in the entering, searching and seizure of such evidence pursuant to a warrant. The HFEA has the power to authorise other persons on its behalf to be the 'duly authorised person' under the warrant.[76]

Obtaining a warrant

4.75   If there are reasonable grounds for believing that an offence under the Act has been or is being committed on any premises, and provided any of the specified conditions apply, it is possible to apply for a warrant to authorise a duly authorised person, together with any police constables, to enter the premises and, if necessary, for that entry to be by force, and then to search them.[77]

4.76   The four possible applicable conditions are:

- that entry to the premises has been or is likely to be refused and notice of the intention to apply for a warrant has been given to the occupier; or[78]

- that an application for admission to the premises or the giving of notice of the intention to apply for a warrant would defeat the object of entry;[79] or

---

[74]   The 1990 Act, s 12(b).
[75]   The 1990 Act, Sch 3B, para 3, as amended.
[76]   The 1990 Act, Sch 3B para 11(a), as amended.
[77]   The 1990 Act, Sch 3B para 5(11), as amended.
[78]   The 1990 Act, Sch 3B, para 5(1)(a), as amended.
[79]   The 1990 Act, Sch 3B, para 5(1)(d), as amended.

- that the premises are unoccupied;[80] or

- that the occupier is temporarily absent.[81]

4.77 The application for a warrant is to be made to a justice of the peace,[82] ie the magistrates' court or, in the case of Scotland, to the Sheriff of the court.[83] The procedure is by way of laying sworn information or in the case of Northern Ireland, on a complaint on oath[84] or in Scotland by evidence on oath before the court.[85] The duration of the warrant will be until the end of 31 days starting with the date of issue.[86]

Execution of a warrant

4.78 Unless the procedure set out in Sch 3B para 6, as amended, is strictly followed, the entry and search pursuant to a warrant will be unlawful. There is a relevant document which is referred to in the execution procedure which is termed the 'appropriate statement'. This is a written statement containing such information relating to the power of the person executing the warrant and the rights and obligations of the person to whom the statement is given as may be prescribed by the Secretary of State in regulations.[87]

4.79 The first requirement to ensure correct compliance entails a test of reasonableness and the second and third requirements deal with the formalities concerning the occupier.

4.80 The execution of the warrant must be at a reasonable time unless the person who is charged with executing the warrant thinks that the purpose of the search may be frustrated on an entry at a reasonable time. The wording of this subsection allows for the person who is to execute the warrant to have the belief that there would be frustration of the warrant if it was not executed at the time when the person applying thought was appropriate. Provided that he is able to demonstrate that consideration had been given to the issue of the timing of the execution and he is able to justify and give reasons for the timing chosen, then there is no further objective test to satisfy.[88]

4.81 If the occupier of the premises to which the warrant relates to is present when the person executing the warrant seeks to enter the premises, the person executing shall produce the warrant to the occupier and also provide the occupier with a copy of that warrant and an appropriate statement. If the occupier is not present at that time but some other person is present who

---

[80]   The 1990 Act, Sch 3B, para 5(1)(b), as amended.
[81]   The 1990 Act, Sch 3B, para 5(1)(c), as amended.
[82]   The 1990 Act, Sch 3B, para 5(1), as amended.
[83]   The 1990 Act, Sch 3B, para 5(4)(a), as amended.
[84]   The 1990 Act, Sch 3B, para 5(1), as amended.
[85]   The 1990 Act, Sch 3B, para 5(4)(b), as amended.
[86]   The 1990 Act, Sch 3B, para 5(3), as amended.
[87]   The 1990 Act, Sch 3B, para 6(5), as amended.
[88]   The 1990 Act, Sch 3B, para 6(2), as amended.

appears to the person executing the warrant to be in charge of the premises, then the person executing the warrant shall produce the warrant to that other person and give him a copy of the warrant and an appropriate statement and also leave a copy of the warrant in a prominent place on the premises. If, however, the premises to which the warrant relates are unoccupied, the person executing the warrant shall leave a copy of the warrant in a prominent place on the premises.[89]

The power to search

4.82 As with the powers to enter and inspect premises, the power to search permits the accompaniment of such other persons and equipment as the person exercising the power reasonably considers necessary.[90]

4.83 Also the power to search includes in particular the power to inspect any equipment found on the premises and to inspect and take copies of any records found on the premises and where the premise is one to which a licence relates or premises which are relevant third part premises there is the power to observe the carrying on of the licensed activity on the premises.[91]

4.84 It also includes the general power to require any person to afford such facilities and assistance in respect of matters under that person's control as are necessary to enable the power of entry and inspection to be exercised.[92]

4.85 After the inspection and search, there is a requirement for the duly authorised person to prepare a written report on the inspection and search as soon as it is reasonably practicable. A copy of that report is to be provided to the 'appropriate person' upon request. An 'appropriate person' is the person responsible in relation to premises to which a licence relates or in relation to any other premises, the occupier.[93]

Inspections of statutory records

4.86 Upon the request of a duly authorised person, a person can be required to produce for inspection any records which a person is required to keep by virtue of the Act.[94] If the records are kept in some electronic form then that person can be required to produce records for inspection in a visible and legible form or in a form from which they can be readily produced into a visible and legible form.[95] Further, a duly authorised person may inspect and take copies of any records produced for inspection pursuant to this requirement.[96]

---

89   The 1990 Act, Sch 3B, para 6(3) and (4), as amended.
90   The 1990 Act, Sch 3B, para 8(1), as amended.
91   The 1990 Act, Sch 3B, para 8(2), as amended.
92   The 1990 Act, Sch 3B, para 8(3), as amended.
93   The 1990 Act, Sch 3B, para 9(2) and (3), as amended.
94   The 1990 Act, Sch 3B, para 1(1), as amended.
95   The 1990 Act, Sch 3B, para 1(2), as amended.
96   The 1990 Act, Sch 3B, para 1(3), as amended.

The power to seize

4.87 There is a wide-ranging power to seize, upon inspection or search, in order to assist the authority in its licensing and enforcement role.

4.88 A person who is duly authorised to enter and inspect premises under the powers of the Act[97] may in addition seize anything on the premises which that person has reasonable grounds to believe may be required for either of two purposes. The first one is in relation to the granting, revocation, variation or suspension of a licence and the second is to enable appropriate control measures to be taken in the event of a serious adverse event or reaction.[98]

4.89 On an authorised search of premises pursuant to a warrant the duly authorised person may seize anything on the premises which he has reasonable grounds to believe may be required for the purpose of being used in evidence in any proceedings for an offence under the Act.[99]

4.90 In both instances, that of inspection and search, it is possible for such steps to be taken as appear to be necessary for preserving that thing or preventing interference with it. There is then a supplementary power to retain anything seized in exercise of the power, for as long as it may be required for the purposes for which it was seized. When anything is seized, there must be a statement left on the premises giving the particulars of who has seized it and what was seized.[100]

The power of enforcement

4.91 In order to ensure compliance and co-operation with the carrying out of these powers, there are further powers to pursue a criminal offence in the event of an obstruction.

4.92 It is an offence for any person who fails, without a reasonable excuse, to comply with the statutory requirement to produce any records for inspection which are required to be kept under the Act,[101] or to afford such facilities and assistance which are within that person's control, whilst the powers to enter, inspect and search are being exercised, or who intentionally obstructs the exercise of any right under Sch 3B.[102] If found guilty of such an offence he is liable to a summary conviction to a fine not exceeding level 5 on the standard scale.[103]

---

[97]   As set out in the 1990 Act, Sch 3B, para 3, as amended.
[98]   The 1990 Act, Sch 3B, para 7(1), as amended.
[99]   The 1990 Act, Sch 3B, para 7(2), as amended.
[100] The 1990 Act, Sch 3B, para 7(3)–(5), as amended.
[101] The 1990 Act, Sch 3B, para 10(a), as amended.
[102] The 1990 Act, Sch 3B, para 10(b), as amended.
[103] The 1990 Act, Sch 3B, para 10, as amended.

THE STRUCTURE OF THE HFEA

4.93 The HFEA consists of a small body of members, headed by a Chairman. The members sit on the various internal committees which have specific areas and functions to perform and the HFEA makes its decisions as a whole body. The HFEA is assisted in its tasks by an administrative staff headed by the CEO. Section 5 and Sch 1 of the 1990 Act define the role, appointments and tenure of the Chairman and also the members of the HFEA. There are specific changes made in respect of those who can now be appointed and disqualified from serving on the HFEA as members.

4.94 The statute sets out to a large extent how the HFEA is to function in order to fulfil its duties and there are now additional arrangements that the HFEA can engage in. The minutiae of the internal workings of the HFEA cannot be examined in this book, but the overall composition of the organisation can be seen.

Membership composition

4.95 The Authority has to have a Chairman and a deputy chairman[104] and there is no limit on the number of members who can be appointed to the HFEA.[105] It remains the function of the Secretary of State to appoint the members, including the Chairman and deputy chairman. There is a strict mandate that prevents the HFEA becoming an all-male or all-female body,[106] as the issues under consideration have always been regarded as requiring a mixed gender input.

4.96 The membership is obliged to continue, as it has since it was originally formed, to be drawn from each of the following three groups but not exclusively:

(i)   any current or former medical practitioner registered under the Medical Act 1983;

(ii)   any person who is or has been concerned with keeping or using embryos or gametes outside of the human body;

(iii)   any person who is involved in funding or commissioning any research into keeping or using embryos and gametes.

4.97 There must be at least one member from categories (i) and (ii) and at least one-third but less than a half of the membership must be from the above categories.[107] This, therefore, leaves open a diverse cross-section of society who then have to make up the remaining membership.

---

[104]   The 1990 Act, s 5(2)(a).
[105]   The 1990 Act, s 5(2)(b).
[106]   The 1990 Act, Sch 1, para 4(2).
[107]   The 1990 Act, Sch 1, para 4(4).

4.98   In contrast the Chairman and deputy chairman must not be drawn from the above categories.[108] This prevents these two appointments coming from a medical or scientific background. The previous chairmen have been from an academic background, although not exclusively.[109]

4.99   The membership total has tended to be in the region of just over 20 members. It continues to be diverse in terms of the individuals' backgrounds and interests as it has always been.[110] The members are from wide-ranging fields, including academia, medicine, science, religion and charity.[111]

4.100   The vacancies for membership are advertised in the media and the selection process is in accordance with the Nolan principles in that the members are selected on their individual merit as to personal expertise and knowledge rather than as representative for a particular group or viewpoint.

Tenure of membership

4.101   Members are able to continue their tenure for three years[112] and will still be able to reapply for re-appointment at the end of that period. They can reapply in the same or in a different category.[113] The practice has been that many of the members of the HFEA in the past have continued to be members beyond their initial appointment. As with other committees, the issue of achieving a balance between continuity and freshness is important and relevant. Members are able to resign from their post at any time.[114]

Disqualification from membership

4.102   There are provisions for the disqualification from appointment or removal from appointment of members. The Secretary of State has previously had the power during the tenure of a member of the HFEA who has become bankrupt or has made arrangements with his creditors, to remove them from their position in the HFEA.[115] Now there are further detailed conditions for disqualification from appointment based on bankruptcy and criminal convictions, and the grounds for removal have been extended in their application.

---

[108]   The 1990 Act, Sch 1, para 4(3).
[109]   Suzi Leather was from a social policy background, whilst Shirley Harrison was from the HFEA organisation itself and had a short tenure awaiting the appointment of Lisa Jardine. The remainder of the chairmen have been from highly academic backgrounds.
[110]   The list of the current membership is set out in the Annual Reports and is on the HFEA website.
[111]   The current list is in the HFEA's Annual Report 2007/8.
[112]   The 1990 Act, Sch 1, para 5(2).
[113]   The 1990 Act, Sch 1, para 5(4).
[114]   The 1990 Act, Sch 1, para 5(3).
[115]   Under the previous Sch 1, para 5(5).

Disqualification for appointment

4.103   A person seeking to be appointed as a Chairman, deputy chairman or any other member of the HFEA is disqualified from appointment if that person is the subject of bankruptcy restrictions orders or an interim order.[116] This disqualification ceases when the person obtains a discharge or where arrangements with the creditors were made, at the end of a period of five years beginning with the date on which the terms of the deed of composition or arrangement or trusts deed are fulfilled or if the debts are paid in full, if an earlier date.[117]

4.104   There is a further disqualification from appointment to the HFEA for a person who has been convicted in the five years of an offence for which he received a sentence of imprisonment for a period of not less than three months (whether suspended or not) without the option of a fine.[118]

Removal from appointment

4.105   The above grounds for disqualification for appointment to the HFEA as a Chairman, deputy chairman or member are also grounds for removal.[119] The Secretary of State may also remove the Chairman, deputy chairman or member if he is satisfied that the person is unable or unfit to discharge their respective functions.[120] This provision had previously only applied to members of the HFEA. A further ground for removal is if the Secretary of State is satisfied that a member of the Authority has been absent from meetings of the Authority for six consecutive months or longer without the permission of the Authority. This last ground is applicable only to the members.[121]

The committees

4.106   The HFEA has always been at liberty to discharge its many functions by the use of committees or by its members or employees. The internal operation of the HFEA under the 1990 Act was originally set out in s 9 entitled 'Licence committees and other committees'. Section 9, along with s 10 has now been deleted and replaced by a new s 9A. The power to delegate and establish committees is maintained but there are more specific provisions in relation to delegation.

4.107   The HFEA has functioned by establishing a comprehensive structure of committees, sub-committees and working parties which has formed the backbone of its decision making, consultation and information gathering. In addition to the various committees the HFEA also has standing advisory

---

116   The 1990 Act, Sch 1, para 4A(1)(a) and (b), as amended.
117   The 1990 Act, Sch 1, para 4A(2) and (3), as amended.
118   The 1990 Act, Sch 1, para 4A(1)(c) and (5), as amended.
119   The 1990 Act, Sch 1, para 5(4A), as amended.
120   The 1990 Act, Sch 1, para 5(5)(c), as amended.
121   The 1990 Act, Sch 1, para 5(5)(a), as amended.

groups on the issues of ethics and science.[122] There is also a Horizon Scanning Panel which is an international panel of experts who provide early indicators of new developments in the relevant research and treatment.

4.108   The two most important committees are those which the 1990 Act had specifically mentioned and made stipulations about, ie the licensing committee and the appeals committee. Both of these are examined below.

The licensing committee

4.109   Under the 1990 Act there was a specific requirement to maintain a committee or committees which would be known as the 'licence committee', and were charged with the granting, variation, suspension and revocation of the licences. The composition of the licence committee was made up of only members of the Authority.[123] The Human Fertilisation and Embryology (Licence Committee and Appeals) Regulations prescribed the procedures of the HFEA licence committees and also the appeal procedure.[124]

4.110   There is now no longer a specific requirement for a licensing committee to be set up under the amended Act. Instead the amendment merely stipulates that:

> 'The Authority may on application grant a licence to any person if the requirements of subsection (2) below are met.'[125]

4.111   Under the new s 9A(1) the HFEA may delegate its functions to a committee or to a member of the Authority or to the Authority's staff. The Authority may establish committees or sub-committees to advise or to exercise a function delegated to it by the Authority.[126] The new provisions will therefore enable the HFEA to delegate any functions to its staff or to a committee, save those functions which can only be exercised by its members.[127] With regards to licensing, the composition of such a committee and sub-committees can now specifically include persons who are not members of the Authority, which reverses the previous position.[128]

4.112   It was highly unlikely that, even without the express demand to set up a licence committee, the HFEA would contemplate not doing so and formulate and pursue a very different structure for determining and dealing with licensing applications. The HFEA has stated that it intends to establish a Licence Panel

---

[122]   Ethics and Law Advisory Group and Scientific and Clinical Advisory Group.
[123]   Section 9(5) of the 1990 Act, now deleted.
[124]   SI 1991/1889.
[125]   The 1990 Act, s 16(1), as amended.
[126]   The 1990 Act, s 9A(2), as amended.
[127]   The 1990 Act, s 9A(5), as amended.
[128]   The 1990 Act, s 9A(4), as amended.

composed of members of staff with relevant expertise for more routine matters and then issues for revocation, variation or refusal of a licence would be referred onto a Licence Committee.

4.113   The procedure to be operated by the Licence Committee is subject to regulations under s 19(6) of the amended legislation. The draft regulations have been laid open for consultation along with the new regulations to be made on the appeals procedure, replacing the previous regulations.

4.114   Of significance to the operation of the HFEA is that the new draft regulations make provision for there to be either three or five members, including the Chair or deputy chair, sitting on the committee and also specify that there is to be a lay majority on the licensing committee.[129] Further, that the committee shall sit with a legal advisor and it may sit with a clinical, scientific or specialist adviser where the Chair considers it desirable to do so.[130] A member cannot sit on the committee to hear the licensing matter if there is an actual or potential conflict of interest.[131] Further details of the new licensing procedure proposed are more appropriately considered in Chapter 5.

The appeals committee

4.115   The only committee which must be maintained by the HFEA is an appeals committee in respect of the licensing process, the details of which are set out in the new amendment in s 20A of the 1990 Act. There was previously no specific requirement to have an appeals committee, merely an opportunity to appeal the decisions of the licensing committee which was made to the Authority and a requirement that the quorum for a sitting of the Authority to hear an appeal was five.[132]

4.116   The amendments by the 2008 Act stipulate that there may be one or more appeals committees.[133] Save for that stipulation, the statute leaves provision for membership and proceedings to be made by regulations, noting that such regulations may provide in particular for the membership of an appeal committee to be made up wholly or partly of authority members and that a person may be appointed to advise the appeals committee.[134]

4.117   Of relevance here, is that the draft regulations have proposed that there should be seven members on the committee including the Chair and deputy chair although the quorum for a decision must be three and always an uneven

---

[129]   Part 2, para 3(2)(i) and (ii) of the draft Human Fertilisation and Embryology (Procedure for Revocation, Variation or Refusal of Licences) Regulations 2009.

[130]   Part 2, para 3(2)(iv) and (b) of the draft Human Fertilisation and Embryology (Procedure for Revocation, Variation or Refusal of Licences) Regulations 2009.

[131]   Part 2 ,para 3(3) of the draft Human Fertilisation and Embryology (Procedure for Revocation, Variation or Refusal of Licences) Regulations 2009.

[132]   Section 20 of the 1990 Act, now repealed.

[133]   The 1990 Act, s 20A(1) and (2), as amended.

[134]   The 1990 Act, s 20A(3) and 7(4), as amended.

number.[135] It is proposed that the majority of the committee members must not have a professional interest.[136] It is also proposed that current or previous HFEA members cannot sit on an Appeals committee and further that the Chair and deputy chair of an appeals committee are to be legally qualified.[137]

4.118 Under the draft proposals there is also a list of reasons that permit the Authority to remove any member from the committee who in the opinion of the Authority has:

- ceased to be an appropriate person eg by reason of misconduct or criminal conviction;

- seriously and persistently failed to meet the standard of performance level or attendance required of a member in the ordinary course of duties;

- been unable to perform duties because of ill-health;

- improperly disclosed confidential information obtained in the course of that person's membership for the Committee;

- brought the Authority into disrepute;

- acted in such a way that they should no longer continue in the public interest to be a member of the Committee;

- fallen within any of the categories of being a current or former member or employee of the Authority, has fulfilled any of the delegated functions for the Authority, or is a license holder or a person responsible under a licence.

4.119 Although it is stressed again that these and the other draft regulations may not be finalised in their draft form, it does show the intention to raise the standards and the quality of decision making from the committees and also the input that there should be from non-members of the Authority on these committees.

4.120 The practical procedure of the appeals process is very relevant to the licensing regulation and so will be considered in more detail under Chapter 5.

---

[135] Part 2, para 4(i) and 7(i) and (ii) of the draft Human Fertilisation and Embryology (Appeals) Regulations 2009.

[136] Part 2, para 4(5) of the draft Human Fertilisation and Embryology (Appeals) Regulations 2009.

[137] Part 2, para 3(a) and (b) and (4) of the draft Human Fertilisation and Embryology (Appeals) Regulations 2009.

Agency arrangements

4.121 The 2008 Act provides a new section which gives the HFEA the power to make arrangements with a government department, a public authority or the holder of a public office or their staff members for the carrying out any of the functions of the Authority, or to provide administrative, professional or technical services to the Authority.[138] This is to introduce flexibility and expediency where there previously has been none, eg the HFEA could arrange for another public body to conduct its inspections of premises on its behalf rather than recruiting its own body of inspectors.

4.122 The HFEA, however, will still retain the responsibility for carrying out the function.[139] Making subordinate legislation in this way is not permissible.[140]

The power to contract out functions

4.123 There is a similar new power to contract out certain functions of the HFEA to a non-public organisation and its employees,[141] which is to be referred to as 'the authorised person'.

4.124 However there still remains a tight control over the arrangements and functions being contracted out by the HFEA. There are restrictions as to those functions which may not be contracted out, as set out below:[142]

- duties in relation to the granting, revocation or variation of licences;

- the right of entry and power to search and seize;

- the power to make subordinate legislation;

- any function which by any enactment may be exercised only by the Authority's members;

- any function excluded by an order of the Secretary of State.

The liability of the HFEA

4.125 Any person, committee or subcommittee discharging the functions of the HFEA shall do so in accordance with general directions of the Authority.[143]

---

[138] The 1990 Act, s 8B(1), as amended.
[139] The 1990 Act, s 8B(2).
[140] The 1990 Act, s 8B(3).
[141] The 1990 Act, s 8C(3).
[142] The 1990 Act, s 8C(1) and (2).
[143] The 1990 Act, s 9A(4), as amended.

4.126 Even if a function is being carried out by another on its behalf, the Authority can revoke that arrangement at any time and it still does not prevent the Authority from exercising any function to which the arrangements relate.[144]

4.127 Subject to certain provision, the HFEA retains liability for the performance or non-performance of its duties. The Authority is treated as having done or omitted to do anything that has been done or been omitted by the authorised person or its employees in the exercise of, or in connection with, the exercise of any function to which arrangements under this section relate. However, this is inapplicable in the following circumstances:

- for the purposes of that part of the contact between the authorised person and the Authority as relates to the exercise of the function, or

- for the purposes of any criminal proceeding brought in respect of anything done or omitted to be done by the authorised person or its employee.

4.128 The protection which is afforded to members and employees of the Authority of making it lawful for them to keep embryos, human admixes embryos or gametes in pursuance of that person's functions as provided by the new s 38A(2) is extended to the authorised person or the authorised person's employee in the course of the said person exercising the functions of the Authority.[145]

The disclosure of information

4.129 In order for the public or non-public organisation to perform the function assigned to it under an agency arrangement or contract, there will usually be a need to access information which is held by the HFEA and is confidential to the HFEA.

4.130 There are now new provisions which allow for the disclosure of information to those involved for the purposes of exerting any functions of the Authority. These provisions allow the public organisation or non-public organisation and any member of staff or employee or any person exerting functions of the Authority or engaged by the Authority to provide it with a service, to receive and disclose information without there being a breach of confidentiality.[146] The test for such disclosure is whether it is necessary or expedient for the purposes of exercising a relevant function.[147] An example of this could be in respect of disclosing information contained on the HFEA register.

---

[144] The 1990 Act, s 8B(4), as amended.
[145] The 1990 Act, s 8C(7), as amended.
[146] The 1990 Act, s 8D, as amended.
[147] The 1990 Act, s 8D(2), as amended.

4.131 Such provisions were clearly necessary in order for the new powers of agents and contractors to operate effectively.

Interaction with public authorities

4.132 There is a new express power to assist other public authorities if the Authority thinks it is appropriate.[148] The HFEA may provide assistance to any other public authority in the UK for the purpose of aiding that authority in exercising its functions.

4.133 It is able to provide this service on whatever terms it sees fit. It is entitled to charge a fee for this service,[149] which intended to recover the costs of providing that service.

4.134 At this stage it is difficult to see what the HFEA could do for other organisations, but it appears to be a reciprocal power to that contained in para 8B whereby it can enter into arrangements with public authorities for formal assistance in carrying out the functions of the HFEA.

The accounts

4.135 The HFEA is funded partially by the government[150] and partially by the fees it is able to charge the licensed clinics for being able to conduct their licensed activities. The HFEA does not have the power to borrow money[151] and therefore has to endeavour to meet its expenditure, although this is not always successful. It can exercise some control by increasing the fees charged to clinics for their licensed activities and trying to perform its functions as efficiently as possible. The regulator's activities and administration are ultimately governed by the financial constraints of public funding and the need for ratification and approval of its expenditure by the Secretary of State and the Treasury.

4.136 The Authority is charged with keeping proper accounts and records and prepares an annual statement of accounts.[152] The format of the statement of accounts has to comply with any directions given by the Secretary of State with the approval of the Treasury.[153] A statement of accounts is published in its Annual report which is available to the public.

4.137 Within five months of the end of the accounting year[154] the HFEA has to send a copy of the statement of account to the Secretary of State and to the

---

[148] The 1990 Act, s 8E(1), as amended.
[149] The 1990 Act, s 8E(2), as amended.
[150] The 1990 Act, Sch 1, para 3.
[151] The 1990 Act, Sch 1, para (2).
[152] The 1990 Act, s 6(1).
[153] The 1990 Act, s 6(2).
[154] Under the 1990 Act, s 6(6) this is determined as from the date of the establishment of the HFEA to the following 31 March or any later period of 12 months ending with 31 March.

Comptroller and Auditor General, who will then examine and certify and prepare a report, which with a copy of the statement will be laid before each House of Parliament.[155]

The fees

4.138 The area of fees which may be charged is clarified by the new provisions. The circumstances in which the HFEA may charge a fee are specified and centre on the licensing process and the register of information:[156]

(i)   a licence application;

(ii)   the granting or renewal of a licence;

(iii) an application for the revocation or variation of a licence;

(iv)   when the Authority exercises any of its functions whether under the current statute or any other enactment in relation to a licence, licensed premises or previously licensed premises, premises which are or have been relevant third party premises or premises which will be licensed premises or relevant third party premises;

(v)   giving notice where there is a request for information as to genetic parentage under s 31ZA(1) and a request for information as to an intended spouse under s 31ZB(1);

(vi)   the provision of information as to genetic parentage, intended spouses and donor-conceived genetic siblings under s 31ZA, 31ZB and 31ZE respectively.

4.139 The fees that can be charged in relation to the licences (see points (i)–(iv) above) are to be determined by the HFEA under a scheme determined by the Authority, subject to the approval of the Secretary of State and the Treasury.[157] In determining its fees the HFEA may have regard to the costs incurred in exercising its functions under the 1990 Act.[158]

4.140 With regard to charging fees to meet the costs of meeting various statutory requests for information from donor-conceived people, see points (v)–(vi) above. In these cases, the amount of the fee that can be charged can only reflect the costs of dealing with applications under the provision concerned[159] and so is to merely recoup the costs.

---

[155] The 1990 Act, s 6(3) and (4).
[156] The 1990 Act, s 35B (1) and (4).
[157] The 1990 Act, s 35B(2).
[158] The 1990 Act, s 35B(3).
[159] The 1990 Act, s 35B(5).

4.141   In all these circumstances there is discretion for the Authority to fix and charge different fees for different circumstances.[160]

Remuneration

4.142   There is provision within the statute that the Authority may pay remuneration to the Chairman along with a pension, allowances, fees, expenses or gratuities and historically it has always been low.[161] Other members of the Authority may receive all of the above, save for remuneration. This is all within the determination of the Secretary of State with the approval of the Treasury.[162]

4.143   There is also provision for the Authority to pay to members of any committee or sub-committee such fees and allowances as the Secretary of State may, with the consent of the Treasury, determine.

4.144   The Annual Report of the HFEA has set out the details of the amounts paid to the HFEA members. It is also possible and permissible, where the Secretary of State feels that there are special circumstances upon the expiry of the member's tenure, to pay compensation.[163]

The HFEA staff

4.145   The Authority continues to have its own premises in central London and it is able to employ and recruit its own staff on such terms and conditions as it sees fit but with the approval of the Secretary of State and the consent of the Treasury.[164]

4.146   There is a specific requirement that if any employee's functions include the inspection of premises, that person has to be of such a character and qualified by way of training and experience as to be a suitable person to perform that function.[165] The role of inspector is critical in the performance of the Authority as a regulator and licensor since the inspectors prepare the reports on the licensed premises and determine whether prohibited or unlicensed activities are being carried out, whether licences should be granted or continued and the extent of any breaches of the Act or Code.

4.147   Again there are provisions for the payments, pensions, allowances or gratuities and compensation for loss of employment by the Authority of its

---

[160]   The 1990 Act, s 35B(6).

[161]   The most current figures available in the Annual Report 2007/8 at p 54 show that Shirley Harrison was paid between £15,000 to £20,000 for the period 1.4.07 to 31.10.07 plus reimbursements of costs.

[162]   The 1990 Act, Sch 1, para 7(1).

[163]   The 1990 Act, Sch 1, para 7(2).

[164]   The 1990 Act, Sch 1, para 8(1).

[165]   The 1990 Act, Sch 1, para 8(2).

employees with the approval of the Secretary of State.[166] There is also provision if an employee of the HFEA subsequently becomes a member, namely that for the purposes of being a participant in a pension scheme applicable to his previous employment the Secretary of State may determine that his service as a member counts as service as an employee. There have in the past been occasions when employees have become members, namely Shirley Harrison and the CEO, have stepped up when there was a temporary gap in the Chairman's position.

---

[166] The 1990 Act, Sch 1, para 8(3).

Chapter 5

THE LICENSING STRUCTURE

INTRODUCTION

5.1   Arguably the most important function of the HFEA is as a licensing and monitoring body. Only the HFEA may authorise the practice of certain activities involving embryos, gametes and assisted reproduction services, and research involving embryos and gametes. It does this by issuing specific licences to provide the licence holder with the legal right to conduct those specified activities. The legislation deals with four different types of licences and these are each studied in the individual Chapters which follow.

5.2   This Chapter outlines in detail the licensing structure of the HFEA dealing with a licence from making an application to the appeal stage, encompassing the integral inspection process. There has been revision and clarification of the licensing structure by the 2008 Act. The granting of licences is dealt with under s 16, revocations under s 18, with variations of licences under the new s 18A. Suspension of licences is dealt with under the new s 19C. There are powers to reconsider licensing decisions pursuant to the new ss 20 and 20B and to appeal licensing decisions made by the Authority under ss 21 and 20A.

5.3   This Chapter sets out the general conditions that apply to all types of licences and highlights the future changes to the procedure that are imminent, from regulations, the Code of Practice, and directions.

LICENSED ACTIVITIES

5.4   The types of licences that are permitted and the authorised activities are contained in paras 11 and 12, and Sch 2 of the 1990 Act as amended. There are four different types of licences that can be granted. The HFEA can license activities in the course of providing treatment services.[1] These have been defined as medical, surgical or obstetric services provided to the public or a section of the public for the purpose of assisting women to carry children.[2] The 1990 Act has previously been amended to authorise activities in the course of providing non-medical fertility services.[3] This encompasses as any services that

---

[1]   The 1990 Act, s 13 and Sch 1, para 1, as amended.
[2]   The 1990 Act, s 2.
[3]   The 1990 Act, s 13A and Sch 1, para 1A, as amended.

are provided in the course of a business for the purpose of assisting women to carry children, but which are not medical, surgical or obstetric services.[4] There is provision to grant a licence to authorise the storage of gametes which is amended to include embryos or human admixed embryos.[5] Finally, the HFEA can issue licences to authorise activities for the purposes of statutory permitted research.[6] The HFEA's liability to maintain a register of licences has been discussed in Chapter 4.

GENERAL CONDITIONS OF LICENCES

5.5   The general conditions which are applicable to every licence granted under the Act by the HFEA are set out in s 12 of the 1990 Act. It is expressly stated that the mandatory conditions of s 12 are not capable of being varied under the power to vary a licence.[7]

5.6   The activities that are authorised by licences can only be carried on at the premises which have been authorised or, if applicable, third party premises, and under the supervision of the person responsible. These are all details which are clearly set out in the licence.[8] The person responsible is defined as being the individual under whose supervision the activities authorised by a licences are to be carried on.[9]

5.7   It is also a condition that the terms of Sch 3 of the Act which govern the consent to the use or storage of gametes, embryos or human admixed embryos have to be complied with, save for when gametes are used to provide basic partner treatment services.[10] Basic partner treatment services are defined as treatment services for a man and woman together, without using gametes of any other person or embryos created outside of the woman's body.[11]

5.8   This position rectifies the previous position which was that the 1990 Act had been amended so that s 12 exempted non-medical fertility services from the ambit of Sch 3 of the 1990 Act in respect of requiring consent for the use and storage of gametes and embryos. Now the deletion of this exemption under s 12 means that where a person's gametes are to be used for non-medical fertility services, effective consent is required.[12]

---

[4]   The 1990 Act, s 11(1)(aa).
[5]   The 1990 Act, s 14 and Sch 1, para 2, as amended.
[6]   The 1990 Act, s 15 and Sch 1, para 3, as amended.
[7]   The 1990 Act, s 18A(6), as amended.
[8]   The 1990 Act, s 12(1)(a).
[9]   The 1990 Act, s 17(1).
[10] The 1990 Act, s 12(c).
[11] The 1990 Act, s 2.
[12] The 1990 Act, Sch 3(5) is also correspondingly amended so that consent is now required for non-medical fertility services.

5.9   It is also a condition that no money or other benefits shall be given in respect of any supply of gametes or embryos unless authorised by directions.[13] This has now been amended to include not just embryos or gametes but also human admixed embryos. Further, if another person is supplied with gametes or embryos to which another licence applies, that person shall also be provided with such information as the Authority may specify. Again this reference to gametes or embryos now includes human admixed embryos.[14] This all ensures that any research licence granted in connection with a human admixed embryo will be subject to the same relevant licence conditions as for embryos or gametes.

RECORDS AND INFORMATION

5.10   Any member or employee of the Authority shall, upon identification as being such a person, at all reasonable times be permitted to enter those premises and inspect them, any equipment or records, or be able to observe any activity which is being carried out.[15] There is a condition that proper records shall be maintained in such form as may be directed by the Authority.[16] Further, the Authority has a wide range of powers by way of directions, to seek information, copies or extracts from records in such form and at such intervals that it specifies.[17]

5.11   There are further conditions which apply to treatment, non-medical fertility services and storage licences in relation to the provision of information. The licence holder has to record and provide the Authority, when requested, the necessary information needed to allow the traceability of gametes and embryos and also any information in relation to the quality or safety of gametes or embryos.[18]

5.12   The statutory definition of 'traceability'[19] refers to a wide-ranging amount of information which starts with the procurement of embryos and gametes, up to their final destination. The donor and the recipient of any particular gametes or embryos must be capable of identification. The ability to trace also includes the identification and location of gametes and embryos during any step from procurement to use for human application or disposal and also the identity of any person who has carried out any activity in relation to the particular embryos or gametes. It must then be possible to identify and locate all the relevant data relating to products and materials which came into contact with any particular embryos or gametes and which can affect their quality or safety.

---

[13]   The 1990 Act, s 12(e).
[14]   The 1990 Act, s 12(f).
[15]   The 1990 Act, s 12(b).
[16]   The 1990 Act, s 12(d).
[17]   The 1990 Act, s 12(g).
[18]   The 1990 Act, s 12(2) and (3).
[19]   The 1990 Act, s 2.

COMPLIANCE WITH EU DIRECTIVES

5.13 Further details as to the traceability and coding in relation to gametes and embryos intended for human application are set out in Sch 3A of the 1990 Act. This sets out the requirement to adopt systems to secure the traceability and coding of information in compliance with the European Directives.[20]

5.14 There is also the requirement to have systems in place to report, investigate, register and transmit information about serious adverse events and reactions and for recalling from distribution any product which may be related to a serious adverse event or reaction.[21]

5.15 Each licence which permits storage of embryos and gametes must adhere to conditions in relation to the termination of storage activities authorised by the licence and also in relation to third party agreements.[22]

5.16 Where a licence permits the procurement of gametes and/or embryos, the requirements as to the staff, standard operating procedures and appropriate facilities and equipment as set out in the second EU Directive must be complied with.[23] Further requirements as to safety, verification, registration, identification, packaging where there is donation, procurement and reception of gametes and embryos at licensed premises or third party premises are also imposed as a condition of a licence.[24]

5.17 There are also requirements under the second EU Directive in relation to the selection criteria and the laboratory tests which are required for donors of reproductive cells and must form part of the conditions of a licence.[25]

5.18 The apparently onerous record keeping by the licence holder is considered necessary to ensure the safety and ability to deal with any problems or difficulties which may arise at any stage. Without this information it would be even more difficult to follow the process of what happened or is likely to have occurred.

5.19 In addition to these general conditions, there are further express and specific conditions regarding information which must be collected and retained for each of the different types of licence. These are examined in subsequent Chapters.

---

[20]   The 1990 Act, Sch 2, para 1 and 2.
[21]   The 1990 Act, Sch 2, para 3.
[22]   The 1990 Act, Sch 2, para 4.
[23]   The 1990 Act, Sch 2, para 5.
[24]   The 1990 Act, Sch 2, paras 9 and 10
[25]   The 1990 Act, Sch 2, para 6.

THE NEW LICENSING PROCEDURE

5.20   The 2008 Act removes any explicit reference to licence committees (as has already been referred to earlier in Chapter 4) and delegation by the HFEA to its committees or members of staff on licensing matters is now permitted. The intention of the HFEA is to establish a licence panel composed of members of staff with the relevant expertise. The role of the licence panel will be to consider routine initial and renewal applications for treatment, non-medical fertility services and storage licences. The panel will also consider routine applications for renewal of research licences. Where an application was not considered to be routine, however, the panel would refer the matter for consideration to a licence committee. The licence committee would be composed of HFEA members and would also be referred cases from the panel where the latter felt than it was minded to refuse an application or where concerns lead it to recommend that a licence be varied, suspended or revoked.

5.21   Under the new framework, the HFEA will issue directions which will set out the information to be provided and the requirements to be followed when asking for a licence application. The procedure to be followed by the licence panel when considering these applications will be detailed by the Authority by way of standing orders and internal protocols.

5.22   The details of the new procedure for the licence panel have not yet been published but the regulations needed for the licence committee to deal with revocations, variations or refusal of a licence have been published in draft form.[26] Some aspects of the draft regulations in relation to the HFEA structure have already been detailed in Chapter 4. The draft regulations greatly clarify the workings of the licence committee.

The licence committee

5.23   The draft Regulations set out that the licence committee will comprise of three or five members, including the Chair or deputy chair, and will sit with a lay majority. A layman is defined as a person who is not a registered medical practitioner, concerned with keeping or using gametes or embryos outside of the body or directly concerned with commissioning or funding any research involving such keeping or use or who actively participated in any decision to do so. The Committee shall sit with a legal advisor and it may sit with clinical, scientific or special advisors.[27]

5.24   The Authority has the burden of establishing that a licence should be revoked or suspended or varied whilst the person concerned shall bear the burden of establishing that a licence should not be refused.[28]

---

[26]   The draft Human Fertilisation and Embryology (Procedure for Revocation, Variation or Refusal of Licences) Regulations 2009.

[27]   Draft Regulations, Part 2, para 3(2)(a) and (b).

[28]   Draft Regulations, Part 2, para 11(a) and (b).

5.25 The decision of the Committee shall be provided not later than seven days after the date on which it made its decision.[29]

5.26 The draft Regulations then set out the format of the application, in terms of the evidence and documentation, that it is possible to make oral representations at a hearing, the procedure to be followed by the licence committee at the hearing and provisions as to legal representation and evidence.

Application for a licence

5.27 The 1990 Act stipulated that an application for a licence must be in a prescribed form with an initial fee. It may then be granted to anyone provided the conditions are met and any additional fees are paid.[30] The amended s 16 provides that upon an application being made and the requirements of the statute being satisfied, a licence can be granted by the HFEA.[31]

5.28 It is possible for there to be directions stipulating the form and content of applications to be made under the Act and the information to be supplied with such an application.[32]

5.29 There is commission of an offence if a person provides any information for the purposes of granting a licence which is false or misleading in a material detail and the person knows that information to be false or misleading in a material detail or he provided the information recklessly.[33]

Fees

5.30 The fees to be charged under the licensing procedure will be set in accordance with a scheme made by the HFEA under new provisions. As in all monetary matters associated with the HFEA, the scheme has to meet the approval of the Secretary of State and the Treasury.[34]

5.31 The Authority can charge a fee on an application for a licence, a grant or revocation of a licence or in connection with the exercise by the Authority of any other functions conferred on by this or other legislation in relation to a licence or the premises of third party premises to which a licence may apply to or is applicable.[35] The amount to be charged will take into account the costs that will be incurred by exercising its function.[36]

---

[29]   Draft Regulations, Part 2, para 17(1).
[30]   The 1990 Act 1990, s 16(1), now repealed.
[31]   The 1990 Act, s 16(1), as amended.
[32]   The 1990 Act, s 19B(1)(a).
[33]   The 1990 Act, s 41(3).
[34]   The 1990 Act, s 35B(2), as amended.
[35]   The 1990 Act, s 35B(1), as amended.
[36]   The 1990 Act, s 35B(3), as amended.

The duty to inspect

5.32 In order to grant a licence for a licensed activity the Authority needs to be satisfied that the premises where the licensed activity is to take place are appropriate and meet the required standards. So the Authority has a specific power to inspect premises when an application for authorisation for a person to pursue a licensed activity to be carried out is made or where authorisation is sought for licensed activities to be carried out on premises not yet authorised.

5.33 Such inspections can be carried out where the application may have been enquired about or formally made to the Authority. The premises to be inspected will be those where the activity is to be carried out and any relevant third party premises.[37]

5.34 In order to carry out its functions properly in relation to licences and third party agreements, the Authority has the right to appoint a duly authorised person to enter and inspect any premises to which a licence relates to or the relevant third party premises, at any reasonable time.[38]

5.35 The Authority then also has a duty to inspect licensed premises as part of its ongoing obligations. There is a mandatory duty where the Authority has granted a licence for the premises to which the licence relates to be subject to an inspection by a duly authorised person not exceeding a period of two years. There is discretion not to carry out an inspection where the premises in question have been inspected either because there has been an application for authorisation as set out above or where the general power to inspect has been exercised within the previous two years.[39]

5.36 There is a power to take on the inspections, such other persons and equipment as the person exercising the power reasonably considers necessary.[40]

5.37 The power to inspect includes in particular the power to inspect any equipment found on the premises and to inspect and take copies of any records found on the premises and where the premises are such to which a licence relates or premises which are relevant third part premises in relation to a licence, there is the power to observe the carrying on of the licensed activity on the premises.[41]

5.38 It also includes the general power to require any person to afford such facilities and assistance with respect to matters under that person's controls as are necessary to enable the power of entry and inspection to be exercised.[42]

---

[37] The 1990 Act, Sch 3B, 2(1)–(3), as amended.
[38] The 1990 Act, Sch 3B, 3(1) and (2), as amended.
[39] The 1990 Act, Sch 3B, 4(1) and (2), as amended.
[40] The 1990 Act, Sch 3B, para 8(1).
[41] The 1990 Act, Sch 3B, para 8(2).
[42] The 1990 Act, Sch 3B, para 8(3).

5.39   After the inspection and as soon as it is reasonably practicable, the duly authorised person shall prepare a written report on the inspection and if so requested provide a copy of that report. The request has to be made by the appropriate person, who is defined as the person responsible in relation to premises to which a licence relates or, in relation to any other premises, the occupier.[43]

In practice

5.40   The HFEA has refined and changed its process of inspections over the years. Initially it would inspect all premises annually in relation to all aspects and areas dealt with by the Act. This would tend to produce a general overview. As time has passed, there has been a significant increase in the number of clinics and research establishments and a more efficient procedure was needed. In order to become more focused the procedure was changed in 1997 to consist of a general inspection of licensed premises every three years with the intervening years to be covered by more 'focused' inspections.

5.41   The HFEA states its regulatory priorities to be to ensure patient safety and to promote the highest standards of clinical care and effectiveness. The role of the inspection is to assess the quality and effectiveness of the clinics as to their management, the services they provide to patients and donors, the quality of their premises and equipment, the information that is provided to the patients and the HFEA, that the clinical and laboratory processes are in place and the competence of the staff.

5.42   A full inspection team would consist of four members, ordinarily being a scientist, a clinician, a layperson and a member of the HFEA executive staff. The team could include a HFEA member who could play either an active or more of a figurehead role. The agenda, timing and the number of inspectors for the focused inspections would be set by the licence panel or licence committee.

5.43   The inspection reports on the clinics and research establishments and the licence committee meetings notes are now available on the HFEA website.

Granting a licence

5.44   With the inspection report in hand, the HFEA will need to consider the application in relation to the requirements of the legislation and the Code of Practice. The expectation of the HFEA in respect of the licensed establishments and centres is emphasised in the draft 8th Code of Practice which sets out a list of the general regulatory principles which should be adhered to as their conduct and responsibilities.[44]

---

[43]   The 1990 Act, Sch 3B, para 9(2) and (3).
[44]   Draft 8th Code of Practice, Part 2, para 3.

5.45 The HFEA must consider that there are appropriate standards of quality and safety in place. These obligations flow not only from the legislation but also from the Human Fertilisation and Embryology (Quality and Safety) Regulations 2007.[45] It is not being contemplated that the content of these Regulations will be updated. However, consequential amendments will be made to them to take account of the updates in the definition on which they were based, as introduced by the 2008 Act.

5.46 The HFEA has also to consider the suitability of the applicant to hold a licence. Where a licence is being sought for treatment, non-medical fertility services or storage of gametes or embryos intended for human application, the individual must possess a formal qualification in the field of medical or biological sciences up to university level, or some other recognisable qualification, or be otherwise suitably qualified on the basis of academic qualification in the field of nursing and have had at least two years of practical experience which is directly relevant to the activity to be authorised by the licences.[46]

5.47 Where the licence is for the storage of gametes, embryos or human admixed embryos not intended for human application or a research licence, the Authority has to satisfy itself that the qualifications and experience of the individual are such as are required for the supervision of the activities.[47]

5.48 The Authority also has to be satisfied that the individual will discharge the duties of a 'person responsible' pursuant to s 17 of the 1990 Act, as detailed below, and that the premises for which the licence is to be granted and any relevant third party premises are suitable for the activities and that all the other requirements of the Act in relation to granting a licence are satisfied.[48]

5.49 If the Authority decides that the information provided is insufficient to enable a determination of the application, it is not obliged to consider the application until the applicant has provided such further information as may be required.[49]

5.50 A licence cannot be granted unless a copy of the conditions to be imposed by the licence has been shown to and acknowledged in writing by the applicant and, where different, the person under whose supervision the activities are to be carried out.[50]

5.51 The Authority is able to grant a licence but also to make it subject to specific conditions.

---

[45] SI 2007/1522.
[46] The 1990 Act, s 16(2)(c).
[47] The 1990 Act, s 16 (2)(ca).
[48] The 1990 Act, s 16(2)(cb)–(e).
[49] The 1990 Act, s 16(4).
[50] The 1990 Act, s 16(5).

Notice of decision

5.52   Where a decision to grant a licence is made the Authority shall give notice of that decision to the applicant and the person who is to be the person responsible.[51] Where there is a decision not to grant a licence, the decision is provided to the applicant with a statement of the reason for the refusal.[52] An appeal against such a refusal is possible pursuant to s 20(1) and will be explored below.

The 'person responsible'

5.53   The licence is granted to a named person who is the 'person responsible' and it is under that person's supervision that the activities authorised by the licence are carried on. It is that person's duty to secure that the licensed activities are conducted properly by specifically ensuring the following:[53]

- that the other persons to whom the licence applied are of such character and qualified by training and experience so as to be suitable persons to participate in the authorised activities; and

- that proper equipment is used; and

- that proper arrangements are made for the keeping of gametes and embryos and human admixed embryos and for the disposal of the gametes and embryos and human admixed embryos that have been allowed to perish; and

- that suitable practices are used in the course of activities; and

- that the conditions of the license are complied with.

5.54   The term 'nominal licensee' which has been used previously is now omitted since it no longer reflects adequately the responsibilities of a licence holder.

5.55   The 1990 Act provides that the person to whom the licences applies is the person responsible, any person who is designated in the licences, or who is so identified by the aforementioned giving written notice to the Authority, and any person acting under the direction of the person responsible or the person so designated.[54]

---

[51]   The 1990 Act, s 19A(1), as amended.
[52]   The 1990 Act, s 19A(5) and (6), as amended.
[53]   The 1990 Act, s 17(1)(a)–(e).
[54]   The 1990 Act, s 17(2)(a)–(c).

Duration of licences

5.56 All the licences are granted for a specified period and the appropriate length of time for the licence is considered in relation to the circumstances of each individual clinic. A research licence cannot exceed three years[55] whilst all other licences cannot exceed five years in duration.[56] The research licence is shorter due to the nature of the type of licence, which is considered on a project-by-project basis, where other licences are necessary to allow the treatment and storage centres to continue without unnecessary bureaucracy.

5.57 If there is a renewal application of a licence which is still under consideration by the HFEA, then a short term licence may be granted in those circumstances where the clinic's licence is about to expire and the renewal is pending.

5.58 In practice, with regards to treatment licences, if a short-term licence is issued the clinic will be advised to finish off treatment and ensure that arrangements have been made for patients to be transferred to another clinic. If the treatment is due to end after the expiry of the short-term licence then depending upon the terms of the licence, which may mean that treatment cannot be continued at that clinic, the clinic should have contingency plans to ensure that the gametes or embryos, along with supporting documents can be transferred to another clinic. The HFEA will issue a special direction to enable the new clinic to finish off the current treatments.

Revocation of a licence

5.59 The previous s 18 of the 1990 Act is revoked and is substituted by a new s 18 which formulates clearer grounds for the revocation of a licence that has been granted. The 1990 Act gave the power of revocation to the licence committee and the new amendment now gives the power to the Authority. The power to revoke a licence can be exercised on an application by the person responsible or the licence holder (if that is a different person) or of the Authority's own volition.[57]

5.60 The Authority is in a position to revoke a licence of its own volition if any of the following grounds set out in s 18(2) arise:

- the Authority is satisfied that the person responsible has:
  (i) failed to discharge or is unable due to incapacity to discharge his duties as a person responsible under s 17;[58] or
  (ii) failed to comply with directions given in connection with any licence;[59] or

---

55   The 1990 Act, Sch 2, para 3(10).
56   The 1990 Act, Sch 2, para 1(5), (1A)(3) and 2(3).
57   The 1990 Act, s 18(1) and (2), as amended.
58   The 1990 Act, s 18(2)(b), as amended.
59   The 1990 Act, s 18(2)(c), as amended.

(iii) died;[60] or

(iv) has been convicted of an offence under the Act;[61]

- any information given for the purposes of the application was in any material respect false or misleading;[62] or

- the premises specified in the licence or third party premises in relation to a licence are not suitable for the licensed activity;[63] or

- the licence holder is not a suitable person to hold the licence;[64] or

- there have been other material changes of circumstances since the licence was granted.[65]

Notice of decision

5.61 Where there is a decision to revoke a licence, the Authority has to give notice of that decision to the person responsible and the holder of the licence, if that is a different person.[66] A statement of the reasons why there is revocation shall be given where the Authority proceeded to revoke of its own volition, rather than the application being made by the person responsible or the holder of the licence.[67] Where there is a decision not to revoke the licence, notice of this decision shall be given to the applicant.[68] There is the option of an appeal against this type of decision[69] and this will be discussed below.

5.62 The position of the patients of a clinic, when there has been a revocation of a licence, has to be considered by the HFEA. The clinics have to have contingency plans so that, where patients have not yet started their treatment, arrangements should have been made with other clinics for the transfer of those patients to the other clinic. If a patient is in the middle of a treatment, the HFEA has to advise on the best and most suitable options to safeguard the patient's interest. There is the possible option that, if there is no immediate risk to patients, some treatment could continue for a limited time.

Variation of a licence

5.63 During the duration of a licence, there are often circumstances which arise which mean that there need to be changes made to the licence terms and

---

[60] The 1990 Act, s 18(2)(h), as amended.
[61] The 1990 Act, s 18(2)(h), as amended.
[62] The 1990 Act, s 18(2)(a), as amended.
[63] The 1990 Act, s 18(2)(d) and (e), as amended.
[64] The 1990 Act, s 18(2)(g), as amended.
[65] The 1990 Act, s 18(2)(i), as amended.
[66] The 1990 Act, s 19A(2), as amended.
[67] The 1990 Act, s 19A(6), as amended.
[68] The 1990 Act, s 19A(5), as amended.
[69] The 1990 Act, s 20(1), as amended.

conditions. A common reason would be where there needs to be a substitution of the named person responsible with another person who wishes to take over this role.

5.64 It is expressly provided that the power to vary does not include being able to vary the mandatory conditions which are imposed by ss 12–15 of the Act on every licence.[70]

5.65 An application to vary may be made by the person responsible, or the holder of the licence if that is a different person. The Authority would then have to consider the merits of the variation that was being applied for. If the Authority of its own volition decides to vary the licence, it has the options of removing, varying or adding a condition to the licence.[71]

The person responsible

5.66 Under the 1990 Act[72] is was possible for the licence committee to vary the licence to designate another individual in place of the person responsible, on the application of the licence holder and the consent of the other individual intending to take over. This was on the basis that the other individual had the 'character, qualifications and experience' required for the supervision of the activities authorised by the licence and that the individuals would discharge the duty under s 17.

5.67 The new s 18A continues to allow this variation to substitute the person responsible but alters the wording slightly to the Authority having to be, 'satisfied that the other person is a suitable person to supervise the licensed activity'.[73] It is hard to see the difference in practical terms that this new formulation makes to the basis upon which the Authority will decide whether it is appropriate or not to vary the licence.

5.68 Any changes to a person responsible, which is not uncommon in clinics, need not necessarily affect the continuity of the work and treatments being carried out at the clinic.

Notice of decision

5.69 A decision to vary under this provision shall be given by notice to the holder of the licence and the person responsible, if a different person.[74] If there is a decision not to vary, the Authority gives notice of this decision to the applicant, with a statement of reasons for this decision.[75]

---

[70] The 1990 Act, s 18A(6), as amended.
[71] The 1990 Act, s 18A(5), as amended.
[72] The 1990 Act, s 18(5), now repealed.
[73] The 1990 Act, s 18A(1)(b), as amended.
[74] The 1990 Act, s 19A(3), as amended.
[75] The 1990 Act, s 19A(3) and (6), as amended.

Other variations

5.70 As with revocation, a variation may be applied for by the person responsible or the holder of the licence, if different, or by the Authority on the basis that any of the grounds for revocation are applicable. These are discussed above under revocations.

Notice of decision

5.71 If the decision to vary has been made under the other grounds for variation, the Authority shall give notice to the person responsible and to the holder of the licence, if that is a different person.[76] A statement of the reasons for refusal is not strictly required.[77]

Refusal to vary

5.72 The decision to refuse an application to vary is appeallable by way of a reconsideration pursuant to s 20(1) and this avenue will be discussed below.

Suspension of a licence

5.73 A new s 19C substitutes s 22 of the 1990 Act. Where the Authority has reasonable grounds to suspect that that there are grounds for revoking a licence (as set out in s 18(2) above) and is of the opinion that the licence should immediately be suspended, it can do this by the service of a suspension notice which does not exceed three months in the first instance.[78] The Authority has the power to continue this initial suspension by giving further notice.[79] The notice of suspension is served on the person responsible, or where the person responsible has died or appears to be unable because of incapacity to discharge the duty under s 17, then the holder of the licence or alternatively one of the persons to whom the licence applies.[80] This highlights the reason why there may be suspension in the first place, ie the death or incapacity of the person responsible.

5.74 The licence will have no effect whilst there is a suspension notice in force, save that an application can be made under specific sections of the Act in order to allow an application to try and designate another individual as the person responsible, to revoke the licence or to vary the licence in some other way.[81]

5.75 It is also open for the decision to suspend to be appealed against in the same way as other licensing decisions can be appealed against pursuant to the new s 20A. Such appeals are dealt with below.

---

[76]   The 1990 Act, s 19A(4), as amended.
[77]   The 1990 Act, s 19A(7), as amended.
[78]   The 1990 Act, s 19C(1), as amended.
[79]   The 1990 Act, s 19C(2), as amended.
[80]   The 1990 Act, s 19C(3), as amended.
[81]   The 1990 Act, s 19C(5), as amended, refers to ss 18(1) or s 18A(1) or (2).

Reconsideration of licensing decisions

5.76 If an application for the grant, revocation or variation of a licence is refused, the applicant has the option of requiring the Authority to reconsider its decision.[82] If the Authority decides to suspend a licence or to continue its suspension, the Authority can also be requested to reconsider that decision.[83]

Procedure for reconsideration

5.77 Where the application to reconsider is against the decision to vary or revoke a licence, any person to whom the notice of decision was required to be given, other than the person who applied for the variation or revocation, may make the application to reconsider.[84] The timescale for making the application to reconsider is within 28 days of the notice of the decision concerned having been given.[85]

5.78 If the reconsideration is in respect of a suspension or continued suspension of a licence, the time period is within 14 days of the date of decision being given.[86] The decision to suspend the licence or continue the suspension shall not be stayed pending an application for reconsideration.[87]

5.79 The reconsideration will be by way of a fresh decision.[88] However, there can be no further reconsideration of the decision.[89]

5.80 The Act then refers to the regulations being made to set out in detail the procedure that is to be followed.[90] It sets out that such regulations may consider the following issues:

- the rights of the appellant or his representative to appear before and be heard by the appeals committee;

- entitling a representative of the HFEA decision-making person to be heard by the appeals committee;

- allowing the appeals committee to receive and consider any written representation from the appellant and the decision-maker;

- preventing the decision-maker of the decision that is being reconsidered from sitting as a member of the appeals committee dealing with the matter;

---

[82] The 1990 Act, s 20(1), as amended.
[83] The 1990 Act, s 20(4), as amended.
[84] The 1990 Act, s 20(2), as amended.
[85] The 1990 Act, s 20(3), as amended.
[86] The 1990 Act, s 20(5), as amended.
[87] The 1990 Act, s 20(6), as amended.
[88] The 1990 Act, s 20B(1), as amended.
[89] The 1990 Act, s 20(7), as amended.
[90] The 1990 Act, s 20B(2), as amended.

- the giving and admissibility of evidence and the production of documents;

- requiring the applicant and any other prescribed person to be given notice of the decision on reconsideration and a statement of the reasons of the appeal committee's decision;[91]

- the considerations regarding the making of different provisions about the procedure, depending upon whether the decision under reconsideration is one for refusal to grant, revoke or vary a decision or it is a decision in respect of suspension.[92]

5.81 The draft Regulations have been published for consultation and reference is made to them below, in order to provide some concept of the new appeals system which might be formulated.

Appeals

5.82 The new provisions under s 20A provide that the HFEA must maintain one or more appeals committees.[93] The constitution of the appeals committee and the appeal procedure require regulations to be made by the Secretary of State.[94] It is stipulated that the regulations may also provide for advisors to be appointed to the appeals committee so that the committee can receive scientific, legal and other advice.[95] It also stipulates that the regulations may provide for the membership of an appeals committee to be made wholly or partly from persons who are not members of the Authority.[96]

5.83 The new s 21 provides that a further appeal may be made to the High Court (or in the case of Scotland, to the Court of Session) by a person aggrieved by the appeals committee's decision, but only on a point of law.

New Regulations

5.84 Pursuant to the new amendments, the power to make regulations under s 20A(3) and 20B(2) has already been the subject of draft Regulations. Some aspects of the draft appeals Regulations have already been detailed in Chapter 4 in relation to the HFEA. The anticipation is that the new appeals process will be underway by October 2009 and that in the summer of 2009 the current Regulations, the HFE (Licence Committee and Appeals) Regulations 1991[97] will be replaced by the new Regulations.[98]

---

[91] The 1990 Act, s 20B(3) (a)–(g), as amended.
[92] The 1990 Act, s 20B(4), as amended.
[93] The 1990 Act, s 20A(1), as amended.
[94] The 1990 Act, s 20A(3), as amended.
[95] The 1990 Act, s 20A(4)(b), as amended.
[96] The 1990 Act, s 20A(4)(a), as amended.
[97] SI 1991/1889.
[98] The draft Human Fertilisation and Embryology (Appeals) Regulations 2009.

5.85 In summary, Part 3 of the draft Regulations deals with the appointment of advisors to the committee as it deems appropriate from time to time. The function of the expert is to advise the committee on any areas within the expert's expertise and to intervene to advise the appeals committee on an issue where it appears that without an intervention there is the possibility of an error being made. The advisors, although permitted to be present in meetings, hearings and private deliberations of the committee, cannot participate in the decision-making or vote. Where the advice of the advisor is not accepted by the committee, reasons shall be given and recorded by the Chair for declining the advice that was tendered.[99]

5.86 There is provision for a reconsideration to be made on paper, or for a hearing to be convened with oral evidence and documentation to be presented. Representation at the hearing would also be permitted. The draft Regulations set out the procedure for the hearing in detail.[100]

5.87 There is provision that the written notice of the committee's decision and a statement setting out the reasons for the committee's decision shall be provided to the parties no later than seven days after the date of the committee making its decision.[101]

---

[99]   Draft Regulations, Part 3, paras 10, 11 and 14.
[100]   Draft Regulations, Part 4, paras 16 to 28.
[101]   Draft Regulations, Part 4, para 29.

Chapter 6

LICENCES FOR TREATMENT

INTRODUCTION

6.1   There has been an enormous growth since the inception of the 1990 Act in the number of people who have sought the various forms of fertility treatments which are now available. Most of this treatment for assisted conception is supplied by private clinics, although some of these treatments, such as IVF, have become available on the NHS, albeit a much more limited scale. The technological advances have meant that more choice and possibilities have become available and the demands, desires and expectations of those seeking particular treatment have risen. For example there are individuals who wish to have a sibling who could be a tissue match for a child already in existence who has a medical need or who wish to 'balance' their family by choosing the sex of their next child. This has meant that the regulatory lines have had to be reconsidered.

6.2   In order to practise and offer these services, a clinic has to be in possession of a treatment licence. This Chapter will concentrate on the permitted activities that can be pursued under a treatment licence and the conditions that have to be or can be attached to such licences. The provisions for treatment licences have been extensively amended under the 2008 Act and are contained primarily in s 13 and Sch 2 of the 1990 Act as amended.

ACTIVITIES PERMITTED PURSUANT TO A TREATMENT LICENCE

6.3   The activities permitted under a licence for providing treatment services are set out in Sch 2, ss 1–1ZC.

6.4   A licence for providing treatment services may provide for the creation of embryos *in vitro*, procuring, keeping, testing, processing or destroying embryos, or procuring, testing and processing and distributing or using gametes and other practices designed to secure that embryos are in a suitable condition to be placed in a woman.[1]

---

[1]   The 1990 Act, Sch 2, para 1(1)(a)(b), (c) and (d), as amended.

6.5   A treatment licence can allow the placing of the newly defined permitted embryos in a woman.[2] The meaning of a 'permitted embryo'[3] being if it has been created by the fertilisation of an egg which has been produced or extracted from the ovaries of a woman, with sperm which has been produced or extracted from the testes of a man, and where the nuclear or mitochondrial DNA of any cell of the embryo has not been altered nor added to other than by the division of the embryo's own cells.[4] Further, there can be no alteration of the nuclear or mitochondrial DNA of a cell whilst it forms part of an embryo, unless it remains something that will be defined as an permitted embryo under the definition in s 3ZA(5) of the amended Act, which deals with preventing the transmission of serious mitochondrial disease.[5] This is a matter for future regulations.

6.6   There is an amendment which now permits using embryos for the purposes of training embryo biopsy, embryo storage or other embryological techniques.[6] This is on condition that the Authority is satisfied that it is necessary to use the embryos for that purpose.[7]

6.7   There remains the practice of the 'hamster test' which allows for the mixing of sperm with the egg of a hamster or other animal as specified in the direction, for the purpose of testing the fertility or normality of the sperm, but only where anything which forms is destroyed when the test is complete and in any event not later than the two cell stage.[8] The test allows a decision to be made based on the percentage of eggs which have been penetrated by the sperm as to the motility and normality of the sperm. As a significant number of patients who seek IVF suffer male infertility difficulties, this is still considered to be a valuable test.

6.8   It is also still possible for other practices, as may be specified by regulations, to be authorised under a treatment license. This allows for the possibility of there being further suitable and appropriate tests. However, there is a prohibition upon such regulations being able to provide for practices which would involve the mixing of human gametes with animal gametes, the creation of a human admixed embryo or the keeping or using of a human admixed embryo.[9]

6.9   There is the proviso that the Authority has to consider that an activity is necessary or desirable for the purposes of providing treatment services before it can be authorised.[10]

---

[2]   The 1990 Act, Sch 2, para 1(1)(e), as amended.
[3]   The 1990 Act, Sch 2, para 1(6), as amended.
[4]   The 1990 Act, s 3ZA(2)–(4), as amended.
[5]   The 1990 Act, Sch 2, para 1(4), as amended.
[6]   The 1990 Act, Sch 2, para 1(1)(ca), as amended.
[7]   The 1990 Act, Sch 1, para 1(4A), as amended.
[8]   The 1990 Act, Sch 2, para 1(1)(f), as amended.
[9]   The 1990 Act, Sch 2, para 1(1)(g), as amended.
[10]   The 1990 Act, Sch 2, para 1(3), as amended.

6.10 A treatment licence can be granted for the period set out in the licence but it cannot exceed five years.[11]

RESTRICTIONS ON THE USE OF GAMETES AND EMBRYOS

6.11 There are new amendments which deal with which gametes and embryos are to be preferred for use in providing treatment services.

6.12 Certain statutory provisions apply when considering and determining any of the following circumstances set out below:[12]

- in respect of persons who are to provide gametes for use where consent is required for the use in question under Sch 3, Part 5;

- in respect of a woman from whom an embryo is to be taken for use where her consent is required for use under Sch 3, Part 7;

- in respect of which of the two or more embryos are to be placed into a woman.

6.13 The conditions are that if the person or the embryos are known to have a gene, chromosome or mitochondrion abnormality which involves a significant risk that a person with that abnormality will have or develop a serious physical or mental disability, serious illness or some other serious medical condition, then they are not to be preferred to those that are not known to have such an abnormality.[13]

6.14 Further conditions are where embryos which are known to be of a particular sex and to carry a particular risk compared with embryos of that sex in general and where any resulting child will have or develop a gender-related serious physical or mental disability or serious illness or any other gender-related serious medical condition, then likewise they must not be preferred to those that are not known to carry such a risk.[14] The definition of gender-related is if the physical or mental disability, illness or other medical condition affects only one sex or it affects one sex significantly more than the other sex.[15]

6.15 Further, it is not possible to keep or use in the provision of treatment services any embryo which has been appropriated for training in embryological techniques.[16]

---

[11] The 1990 Act, Sch 2, para 1(5), as amended.
[12] The 1990 Act, s 13(8), as amended.
[13] The 1990 Act, s 13(9), as amended.
[14] The 1990 Act, s 13(10), as amended.
[15] The 1990 Act, s 13(11), as amended.
[16] The 1990 Act, s 13(12), as amended.

RESTRICTIONS ON THE TYPE OF TREATMENT

6.16 The type of treatments that are and should be made available has been part of the controversial discussions and consultations that have taken place about the amendments that should be imposed. The Act now makes specific references to the type of treatments that can be licensed and the restrictions that are placed upon them.

Embryo testing

6.17 Under the 1990 Act the HFEA has had a relatively wide discretion to license the use of techniques such as Preimplantation Genetic Diagnosis. Following public consultation in 1999 the HFEA's policy has been to licence uses of Preimplantation Genetic Diagnosis to screen for serious diseases only. These have generally been diseases which are characterised by early onset and for which effective treatments are not available.

6.18 The new amendments set out circumstances in which embryos can be tested in pursuance of a treatment licence. These amendments in Sch 2, para 1ZA permit the testing of an embryo for specific purposes only. The testing can be for one or more of the reasons but it cannot be authorised for any other reason.

6.19 The five specific purposes for embryo testing are as follows:

Genetic abnormality

6.20

(1) To establish whether an embryo has a gene, chromosome or mitochondrial abnormality that may affect its capacity to result in a live birth.[17]

(2) Where there is a risk of such genetic abnormality, to establish whether it has that abnormality.[18]

6.21 Purpose (1) could authorise testing to establish whether an embryo contained an abnormal number of chromosomes likely to result in miscarriage, referred to as pre-implantation genetic screening. Whereas purpose (2) could be used to determine the presence of absence of a genetic disorder referred to as preimplantation genetic diagnosis.

6.22 If the purpose set out in (2) above is to be pursued, there is a further condition, namely the Authority must show that it is satisfied that in relation to the abnormality for which there is a particular risk and also any other abnormality for which the embryo will be tested, that there is a significant risk

---

[17] The 1990 Act, Sch 2, para 1ZA (1)(a), as amended.
[18] The 1990 Act, Sch 2, para 1ZA(1)(b), as amended.

that a person with the abnormality will have or develop a serious physical or mental disability, a serious illness or any other serious medical condition.[19]

Gender-related

6.23

(3) To establish the sex of an embryo where there is a particular risk that the resulting child will have or develop a gender-related serious physical or mental disability, serious illness or any other gender-related serious medical condition.[20]

6.24 Therefore sex selection is permissible for conditions such as Duchenne Muscular Dystrophy and also where there is a strong family history of breast cancer where the mother has been affected and is probably a carrier of the faulty gene, in order to avoid passing this cancer onto a daughter.

6.25 To establish whether the physical or mental disability, illness or other medical condition is gender-related, the HFEA must be satisfied that it affects only one sex or that it affects one sex significantly more than the other.[21]

Tissue-typing

6.26

(4) To establish whether the embryo would result in a child whose tissue was compatible with that of an existing child (the sibling).[22]

6.27 This provides for the situation where a child of the person whose gametes are used to bring about the creation of the embryos suffers from a serious medical condition which could use certain human material being available for its treatment. The material that can be used is the umbilical cord blood stem cells, bone marrow or other tissue but does not include any whole organ.[23]

Identification

6.28

(5) Where there is uncertainty as to whether the embryo is one of those whose creation was brought about by using the gamete of particular persons, to try and identify whether it is.

---

[19] The 1990 Act, Sch 2, para 1ZA (2), as amended.
[20] The 1990 Act, Sch 2, para 1ZA (1)(c), as amended.
[21] The 1990 Act, Sch 2, para 1ZA (3), as amended.
[22] The 1990 Act, Sch 2, para 1ZA (1)(d), as amended.
[23] The 1990 Act, Sch 2, para 1ZA (1)(d) and (4), as amended.

Sex selection

6.29 The HFEA has not allowed sex selection techniques to be used, save for medical reasons. The Act maintains this position in Sch 2, para 1ZB(1) which provides a clear prohibition of any practice which is designed to secure that any resulting child born of assisted reproductive treatment will be one sex rather than the other, eg sperm sorting.[24]

6.30 However, para 1ZB does not prevent any embryo testing practices that may be permitted under the preceding para 1ZA. So the subsequent amendments[25] reiterate that the embryo testing which is permitted under Sch 2 continues and is not prevented by this ban on sex selection testing, especially where the practice is to try and establish the sex of a resulting child, is deemed necessary and has been authorised in relation to the development or presence of a gender-related disability, condition or illness.

Future amendments

6.31 There is a specific power provided for regulations to be made to make any amendments to the provisions of embryo testing as set out in Sch 2, para 1ZA.[26] If any such amendments necessitate having consequential amendments to the sex selection provisions under Sch 2, para IZB (2)–(4), then that can be done.[27]

6.32 Although amendments in this section expressly contain the power to add to as well as repeal,[28] the regulations are restricted in that they cannot authorise the testing of embryos for the purpose of establishing their sex or any other practices designed to secure the sex of a child to be one rather than the other as prohibited in para 1ZB(1), except on the grounds relating to the health of any resulting child.[29]

Conditions imposed on treatment licences

6.33 The general conditions that are imposed on treatment licences under s 12 have already been referred to in Chapter 5. There are specific conditions which treatment licences have to adhere to concerning the treatments that are provided and the persons to whom they are providing such services.

The welfare of the child

6.34 A condition of all treatment licences is the consideration that must be given to the welfare of any child born of assisted reproduction technology. The

24   The 1990 Act, Sch 2, para 1ZB (1), as amended.
25   The 1990 Act, Sch 2, para 1ZB (2 to (4), as amended.
26   The 1990 Act, Sch 2, para 1ZC (1), as amended.
27   The 1990 Act, Sch 2, para 1ZC (2), as amended.
28   The 1990 Act, Sch 2, para 1ZC (4), as amended.
29   The 1990 Act, Sch 2, para 1ZC (3), as amended.

deliberations of the Warnock Committee and the ensuing parliamentary debates revealed that it was important for there to be some recognition in the provision of these new treatments of the importance of the family structure.

6.35 This resulted in s 13(5) of the 1990 Act which requires that 'A woman shall not be provided with treatment services unless account has been taken of the welfare of any child who may be born as result of the treatment (including the need of that child for a father), and of any other child who may be affected by the birth'.

6.36 This was a wide-ranging requirement leaving the clinic to consider a theoretical and complex matter before providing treatment. The HFEA was expressly required to provide guidance on this issue. The Code of Practice in its current form provides to the licence holders the guidance[30] that:

> 'Where the child will have no legal father the treatment centre should assess the prospective mother's ability to meet the child's/childrens' needs and the ability of other persons within the family or social circle willing to share responsibility for those needs.'

6.37 The subsequent debate has centred upon the availability of treatment for same sex female couples or single females who wish to have treatment with this restrictive condition in place.

6.38 There is still an express requirement that no woman shall be provided with treatment services unless account has been taken of the welfare of any child which may be born as a result and also to take account of any other child who may be affected by the birth. This clearly refers to any existing children of the persons undertaking the treatment and those of any surrogate mother.

6.39 However, the new Act under s 13(5) removes the phrase 'need for a father' when considering the welfare of the resulting child and substitutes instead the phrase 'supportive parenting'.

6.40 There is still a corresponding requirement for the HFEA to provide guidance on the new s 13(5). The draft 8th Code of Practice provides guidance in the following terms.[31]

> 'Supportive parenting is a sustained commitment to the health, well-being and development of the child. In considering whether this commitment exists, the centre may take into account the wider family and social network within which the child will be raised. All prospective parents are presumed to be supportive parents, in the absence of any reasonable cause for concern that either the child to be born, or any other child, may be at risk of significant harm or neglect.'

---

[30] HFEA Code of Practice, 7th edition, G.3.3.3.
[31] Draft 8th Code of Practice, Part 8, para 9.

There is therefore an examination of a much wider family and social network than just having a male partner present and the presumption of supportive parenting being available makes the need for exclusion from treatment to be on clear and strong evidential grounds, as the requirements are to show significant harm or neglect rather than anything more general.

Counselling

6.41 Counselling for infertile couples was considered by the Warnock report to be relevant because it ensured that they understood the implications of what they were embarking upon, what their rights and duties were and where they could anticipate difficulties to arise in their individual cases. These were also the considerations behind ensuring that appropriate information was provided before consent was given. The type of information to be provided by the licensed centres was to include a range of issues, including medical and legal matters, as well as the centre's policy in selecting patients and information about costs. The elements of counselling and provision of information formed part of the 1990 Act. Guidance on both counselling and the provision of appropriate information is provided through the HFEA's Code of Practice. The draft 8th Code of Practice specifically refers to providing the opportunity for counselling before treatment and, at every stage of the treatment process, for it to be carried out by a qualified counsellor and for it to be provided on an individual or couple basis.[32]

6.42 The existing statutory provisions of counselling were amended as it was felt that it was not sufficiently clear or strong that the opportunity for counselling must be given before treatment is provided and also because of the difficulties that there had been in instances where one party or the other had withdrawn consent.[33]

6.43 It is a condition of a treatment licence that a woman shall not be provided with any treatment services as specified under the amended Sch 3ZA part 1 unless she and any partner of that woman (male or female) who are being treated together have been given a suitable opportunity to receive counselling before treatment is provided and given such relevant information as is proper.[34]

6.44 The treatments were those that involved the use of the gametes of any person from whom consent was required for that use, the use of any embryos created *in vitro* or treatment which involved the use of an embryo taken from a woman where her consent was needed.[35]

---

[32] Draft 8th Code of Practice, Part 3, paras 2–12.
[33] *Evan v Amicus Healthcare & Others* [2003] EWHC 2161.
[34] The 1990 Act, s 13(6), as amended.
[35] The 1990 Act, Sch 3zA, Part 1.

Record keeping requirements

6.45 There are further requirements regarding information which must be recorded, which the HFEA can specify in directions.

6.46 The information that needs to be recorded is detailed in s 13(2) and the records must be maintained and no information can be removed from the records maintained in pursuance of the licence, before the expiry period given in directions dealing with such records.[36]

6.47 The information to be recorded is detailed in broad terms in s 13(2) and is not exhaustive as the regulations can specify other matters such as:[37]

- the persons for whom the services are provided;

- the services which are provided for them;

- the person whose gametes are kept or used for the purposes of the services provided or whose gametes have been used in bringing about the creation of the embryos so kept or used;

- any child appearing to the person responsible to have been born as a result of the treatment provided;

- any mixing of the gametes and taking of an embryo from a woman or other acquisition of an embryo;[38]

- any consents that are required under Sch 3.[39]

---

[36] The 1990 Act, s 13(4), as amended. Where the 'person responsible' does not know if any child was born following treatment, other than basic partner treatment, then the period of retaining information is not less than 50 years from the date when the information was first recorded under s 24(1) of the 1990 Act.

[37] The 1990 Act, s 13(2)(f), as amended.

[38] The 1990 Act, s 13(2)(a)–(e), as amended.

[39] The 1990 Act, s 13(3), as amended.

Chapter 7

LICENCES FOR NON-MEDICAL FERTILITY SERVICES

INTRODUCTION

7.1 'Non-medical fertility services' means any services which are provided, in the course of business, for the purpose of assisting women to carry children, but are not medical, surgical or obstetric services.[1]

7.2 Such activities come within the ambit of the legislation and are licensed activities. The main relevant provisions are contained in s 13A and now Sch 2 of the Act.

A LICENCE FOR NON-MEDICAL FERTILITY SERVICES

Activities

7.3 There is a licence permitted for processing sperm and distributing sperm in the course of providing non-medical fertility services.[2] The HFEA may attach such conditions related to the licensed activities and the performance of such activities in the licence subject to the provision of the Act.[3]

7.4 However, there is now a specific amendment which provides that a licence cannot authorise the procurement or distribution of sperm to which there has been applied any process designed to secure that any resulting child will be of one sex rather than the other.[4]

7.5 The duration of the licence shall be as specified in the licence but it cannot exceed five years.[5]

Conditions of a licence

7.6 The general conditions which attach to all licences set out in s 12 have been already set out in Chapter 5, but there are some further specific requirements which attach to the licence.

---

[1]   The 1990 Act, s 2(1).
[2]   The 1990 Act, Sch 2, para IA(1).
[3]   The 1990 Act, Sch 2, para IA(2).
[4]   The 1990 Act, Sch 2, para IA(1A), as amended.
[5]   The 1990 Act, Sch 2, para IA(3).

Record keeping

7.7   Under s 13A it is a specific requirement that s 13(2)–(4) and (7) has to be complied with.[6] The provisions under s 13(2)–(4) relate to the keeping, recording and retaining of information that is sought by the HFEA in relation to services provided and these have been examined under Chapter 6 dealing with treatment licences. The requirement under s 13(7) is to ensure that there are suitable procedures for determining the persons who provide gametes and embryos and also to ensure that consideration is paid to the use of practices which do not require a licence.

7.8   There are further record keeping requirements, in that there must be sufficient information to ensure that there is traceability of gametes and embryos and a record of any information relating to the quality or the safety of the gametes or embryos which can then be provided upon request to the Authority.[7]

7.9   There is also the stipulation that a woman shall not be provided with any non-medical fertility services involving the use of sperm other than partner-donated sperm unless the woman being provided with the services has been given the opportunity to receive proper counselling about the implications of taking the proposed steps and has been provided with relevant information.[8]

7.10   There is a new amendment which now requires that if a person's gametes are to be used for the purposes of non-medical fertility services, there must be effective consent by that person for the gametes to be so used and the gametes must be used in accordance with the terms of the consent given.[9]

---

[6]   The 1990 Act, s 13A(2).
[7]   The 1990 Act, s 12(2) and (3).
[8]   The 1990 Act, s 13A(3).
[9]   The 1990 Act, Sch 3, para 5(1), as amended.

Chapter 8

LICENCES FOR STORAGE

INTRODUCTION

8.1 The meaning of storing gametes, embryos or human admixed embryos is defined in broad terms as preserving such entities, whether by cryopreservation or in any other way.[1]

8.2 As has been mentioned earlier, the provision of treatments pursuant to a treatment licence and research into gametes and embryos will inevitably involve the keeping of embryos or gametes to create an embryo *in vitro*. The 1990 Act permits the storage of gametes or embryos or both under a licence for storage.[2] There is now an amendment to include the storage of human admixed embryos regardless of whether the licence holder is already permitted by licence to store embryos or gametes.[3]

8.3 In this Chapter, the specific conditions that have to be attached to storage licences in addition to the general conditions set out in s 12 will be examined. These conditions are set out in s 14 which has been substantially amended by the 2008 Act. Section 13 of the Act introduces Sch 3 of the Act which deals with the issue of consent to the storage of gametes, embryos or human admixed embryos. An outline of the issue of consent will be provided here but further details of the circumstances and conditions for effective consent will be examined in full in Chapter 10. The period of storage is also the subject–matter of fresh regulations and the draft provisions will be considered.

CONDITIONS FOR STORAGE LICENCES

8.4 A licence for the storage of gametes, embryos or human admixed embryos can be granted subject to the conditions that are contained in it.[4] In addition, as with licences for treatment and research, there are particular conditions which must attach to a licence to store embryos and gametes which are now set in para 14 and also by reference to Sch 3 of the 1990 Act. There is

---

[1]   The 1990 Act, s 2(1).
[2]   The 1990 Act, Sch 2, para 2(10).
[3]   The 1990 Act, Sch 2, para 2(1A) as amended.
[4]   The 1990 Act, Sch 2, para 2(2).

an amendment to ensure that human admixed embryos are to be subject to the same storage conditions as for gametes and embryos.[5]

The storage of gametes

8.5   There are specified circumstances in which gametes from a particular person can be stored:

(i)   they have to be received from that person;[6]

(ii)   the acquired gametes do not have to have that person's consent to storage due to the application of certain statutory provisions set out in Sch 3, paras 9 or 10;[7]

(iii)   they are acquired from a person to whom a licence or third party agreement applies;[8]

(iv)   stored gametes shall not be supplied to a person otherwise than in the course of providing treatment services unless that person is a person to whom a licence applies;[9]

(v)   that no gamete is allowed to be kept in storage for longer than the statutory storage period and, if in storage at the end of that period, they shall be allowed to perish;[10]

(vi)   the statutory storage for gametes is a period as may be specified in the licence but not exceeding ten years;[11]

(vii) the statutory storage period for gametes is subject to changes regarding the length of the period by regulation;[12]

(viii) the licence for storage shall be granted for such period as specified in the licence but not exceeding five years;[13]

(ix)   the Authority may specify in regulations whose consent is required under Sch 3 of the Act, the terms of their consent, the circumstances of the storage and other matters, including the maintenance of records in

---

5   The 1990 Act, s 14(1), as amended.
6   The 1990 Act, s 14(1)(a)(i), as amended.
7   The 1990 Act, s 14(1)(a)(ii), as amended.
8   The 1990 Act, s 14(1)(a)(iii), as amended.
9   The 1990 Act, s 14(1)(b).
10   The 1990 Act, s 14(1)(c).
11   The 1990 Act, s 14(3).
12   The 1990 Act, s 14(5).
13   The 1990 Act, Sch 2, para (2)(3).

pursuance of the licence. Such information is not to be removed from the records before the expiry of the period specified in directions for the records of the class in question.[14]

The storage of embryos

8.6 There are specified circumstances in which embryos from a particular person can be stored:

(i) the embryos taken from a woman have to be received from that woman or acquired from a person to whom a licence or third party agreements applies;[15]

(ii) they are acquired from a person to whom a licence or third party agreement applies;[16]

(iii) that an embryo that has been created *in vitro* but not in pursuance of a licence shall be placed in storage only if acquired from a person to whom a licence or third party agreement applies;[17]

(iv) stored embryos shall not be supplied to a person otherwise than in the course of providing treatment services unless that person is a person to whom a licence applies;[18]

(v) that no embryo is allowed to be kept in storage for longer than the statutory storage period and, if in storage at the end of that period, they shall be allowed to perish;[19]

(vi) the statutory storage for embryos is such period as may be specified in the licence but not exceeding ten years;[20]

(vii) the statutory storage period for embryos is subject to changes regarding the length of the period by regulations;[21]

(viii) the licence for storage shall be granted for such period as specified in the licence but not exceeding five years;[22]

(ix) the Authority may specify in regulations whose consent is required under Sch 3 of the Act the terms of their consent, the circumstances of the storage and other matters, including the maintenance of records in

14 The 1990 Act, s 14(1)(d) and (2).
15 The 1990 Act, s 14(1)(aa), as amended.
16 The 1990 Act, s 14(1)(aa)(iii), as amended.
17 The 1990 Act, s 14(1)(ab), as amended.
18 The 1990 Act, s 14(1)(b).
19 The 1990 Act, s 14(1)(c).
20 The 1990 Act, s 14(4).
21 The 1990 Act, s 14(5).
22 The 1990 Act, Sch 2, para (2)(3).

pursuance of the licence. Such information is not to be removed from the records before the expiry of the period specified in directions for the records of the class in question.[23]

The storage of human admixed embryos

8.7   There are specified circumstances in which human admixed embryos may be stored:

(i)   where a human admixed embryo has been created *in vitro* but not in pursuance of a licence it shall be placed in storage only if acquired from a person to whom a licence under Sch 2 ,para 2 or 3 applied; namely a storage or a research licence;[24]

(ii)   human admixed embryos shall not be supplied to a person unless that person is a person to whom a licence applies;[25]

(iii)   that no human admixed embryo is allowed to be kept in storage for longer than the statutory storage period and, if in storage at the end of that period, they shall be allowed to perish;[26]

(iv)   the statutory storage for human admixed embryos is such period as may be specified in the licence but not exceeding ten years;[27]

(v)   the statutory storage period for human admixed embryos is subject to changes regarding the length of the period by regulations;[28]

(vi)   the Authority may specify in regulations whose consent is required under Sch 3 of the Act, the terms of their consent, the circumstances of the storage and other matters, including the maintenance of records in pursuance of the licence. Such information is not to be removed from the records before the expiry of the period specified in directions for the records of the class in question.[29]

CONSENT

8.8   To avoid repetition, when understanding the concept of consent as it applies in this Act and the procedure for obtaining effective consent, reference must be made to Chapter 10.

---

[23]   The 1990 Act, s 14(1)(d) and (2).
[24]   The 1990 Act, s 14(1)(ac), as amended.
[25]   The 1990 Act, s 14(1)(ba), as amended.
[26]   The 1990 Act, s 14(1)(c), as amended.
[27]   The 1990 Act, s 14(4A), as amended.
[28]   The 1990 Act, s 14(5).
[29]   The 1990 Act, s 14(1)(d) and (2).

8.9　It is abundantly clear from the Act that there must be effective consent by the person whose gametes are to be stored to their storage and that they must be stored in accordance with the terms of the consent given.[30] Where an embryo is taken from a woman, there must be effective consent by her to its storage and it must be stored in accordance with the terms of that consent.[31] The consent to the storage of any gametes, any embryo or any human admixed embryo must specify the maximum period of storage, if less than the statutory storage periods, and state what is to be done with the gametes, embryos or human admixed embryo if the person who gave the consent dies or is unable because of incapacity to vary the terms of the consent or to revoke it. The consent may also specify other conditions subject to which the gametes, embryos or human admixed embryo may remain in storage.[32]

8.10　The HFEA can provide for other matters by way of directions that need to be considered or applied under the consent provisions under Sch 3.[33]

8.11　The terms of consent can be varied from time to time and consent may also be withdrawn by the giving of notice by the person who gave the consent to the person keeping the gametes, human cells, embryos or human admixed embryo to which the consent relates.[34]

8.12　Where there is a notice of withdrawal of consent to storage, the storage of an embryo remains lawful until the end of a 12-month period beginning with the day on which the notice was received.[35] This is in relation to straightforward notice of withdrawal of consent to storage. Where there is consent to use involved, different provisions apply and these are discussed and referred to more sensibly under the chapters dealing with those different types of licences.

8.13　With regards to an embryo which was created *in vitro*, there must be effective consent for storage from each of the relevant persons in relation to the embryo and the embryo must then be stored in accordance with the consent.[36] The consent that is required is from the following:

- each person whose gametes or human cells were used to bring about the creation of the embryo;[37]

---

[30]　The 1990 Act, Sch 3, para 8(1).
[31]　The 1990 Act, Sch 3, para 8(3).
[32]　The 1990 Act, Sch 3, para 2(2), as amended.
[33]　The 1990 Act, Sch 3, para 2(3), as amended.
[34]　The 1990 Act, Sch 3, para 4(1), as amended.
[35]　The 1990 Act, Sch 3, para 4(4), as amended.
[36]　The 1990 Act, Sch 3, para 8(2), as amended.
[37]　The 1990 Act, Sch 3, para 8(2A)(a), as amended.

- each person whose gametes or human cells were used to bring about the creation of any other embryo, *in vitro*, which was then used to bring about the creation of the embryo in question;[38]

- each person whose gametes or human cells were used to bring about the creation of any human admixed embryos, the creation of which was brought about *in vitro*, which was then used to bring about the creation of the embryo in question.[39]

CASES WHERE CONSENT IS NOT REQUIRED

8.14　The new Act brings about some very important changes to the consent provisions in order to widen the use of the facility of storage in more circumstances and also to bring assistance into situations where previously the legal bounds were much tighter and restrictive. There are new provisions which set out in detail those situations where gametes can be lawfully stored but there must now be strict compliance with the rules regarding consent.

8.15　A new amendment to Sch 3 to the 1990 Act will allow the storage of gametes without written consent in two different scenarios; one of a child donor and the other of an incapacitated patient. The consent that would be ordinarily required is circumvented by the use of a medical practitioner being able to certify that the conditions as set out in those paragraphs have been met. Another safeguard imposed is that the gametes retrieved and stored cannot be used for any purpose unless the gamete provider becomes competent and consents to such use. In any event, the person's gametes which are stored under these two exceptions are not to be kept in storage after the person's death.[40]

8.16　The references made in this section to capacity to consent are to be read in accordance with the Mental Capacity Act 2005.[41]

The 'child donor'

8.17　A child who is expected to undergo medical treatment which in the opinion of a registered medical practitioner is likely to cause a significant impairment of the fertility of the child, eg chemotherapy or radiotherapy, could if time allows prior to their treatment try and preserve that fertility by placing their gametes in storage. However in some cases the patient might not have the capacity to give consent to storage. In the case of early childhood cancer, a child may be too young to be considered competent enough to consent to storage of their gametes.

---

[38]　The 1990 Act, Sch 3, para 8(2A)(b), as amended.
[39]　The 1990 Act, Sch 3, para 8(2A)(c), as amended.
[40]　The 1990 Act, Sch 3, para 10(12), as amended.
[41]　The 1990 Act, Sch 3, para 10(11), as amended.

8.18 Provided that certain provisions can be satisfied it is possible to keep the gametes of the 'child donor' without the child's consent. The statutory conditions are as follows:

(i)   before the child attains the age of 18 the gametes have to be lawfully taken or provided by the child donor;[42]

(ii)   before the initial storage of the gametes, a registered practitioner must certify in writing that the child donor is expected to undergo medical treatment and that in his opinion that treatment is likely to cause a significant impairment of the fertility of the child donor and that the storage of the gametes is in the best interest of the child donor;[43]

(iii) at the time of the first initial storage the child donor has not attained the age of 16 years and is not competent enough to deal with the issue of the storage of the gametes[44] or he has reached the age of 16 but lacks the competence to deal with the issue of consent to the storage but does have the capacity to consent to storage;[45]

(iv)   the child donor has not, since becoming competent enough to deal with the issue of consent to the storage of the gametes, given consent to storage of the gametes or given written notice to the person keeping the gametes that he does not wish them to consent to be stored.[46]

8.19 There are some slight differences in relation to the situation as it applies in Scotland. The relevant age is before the child donor attains the age of 16[47] and when the gametes are first stored, that the donor does not have the capacity to consent in accordance with the relevant Scottish statute.[48] Also that with regards to point (iv) above it is 'acquiring such capacity' rather than 'becoming competent to deal with the issue of storage of the gametes'.[49]

The 'incapacitated patient'

8.20 This covers the situation where an adult suffers a serious physical injury where the treatment that is administered could result in that person becoming infertile. However, they were not in a position, due to their injuries, to give consent. Again there are provisions which would be able to protect their fertility by allowing the gathering and storage of their gametes. For example,

---

[42] The 1990 Act, Sch 3, para 9(2), as amended.
[43] The 1990 Act, Sch 3, para 9(3), as amended.
[44] The 1990 Act, Sch 3, para 9(4)(a), as amended.
[45] The 1990 Act, Sch 3, para 9(4)(b), as amended.
[46] The 1990 Act, Sch 3, para 9(5), as amended.
[47] The 1990 Act, Sch 3, para 9(6)(a), as amended.
[48] The Age of Legal Capacity (Scotland) Act 1991, s 2(4).
[49] The 1990 Act, Sch 3, para 9(6)(c), as amended.

this would apply where a severe injury resulted in a coma and this rendered the adult unable to give consent or direct another person to do so on his or her behalf.

8.21 Provided that certain provisions can be satisfied it is possible to keep the gametes of the 'incapacitated patient' without the patient's consent. The statutory conditions are as follows:

(i)   the gametes are lawfully taken from or provided by the patient after the patient is aged over 16; and[50]

(ii)   before the gametes are first stored, a registered medical practitioner certifies in writing that the patient is expected to undergo medical treatment and that he is of the opinion that the treatment is likely to cause a significant impairment of the patient's fertility, that the patient lacks the capacity to consent to storage of the gametes, that the patient is likely to regain that capacity and that the storage of the gametes is in the patient's best interests; and[51]

(iii) at the time of the first storage that the patient lacks capacity to their storage; and

(iv)   that the patient has not, after regaining capacity to give consent, given consent to the storage of the gametes or given written notice to the person keeping the gametes that the patient does not wish for them to continue in storage.

THE STORAGE PERIODS

8.22 The 1990 Act set maximum storage periods, reflecting the idea that long term or indefinite storage of gametes and embryos were neither necessary nor desirable.

8.23 Gametes can be stored for ten years.[52] This period can be extended as set out in the Human Fertilisation and Embryology (Statutory Storage) Regulations 1991.[53] There can only be an extension if the gametes are intended to be used by the person who provided them and that person has or is likely to have significantly impaired fertility. The maximum storage under the Regulations is until the person who provided the gamete attains the age of 55 years.

---

[50]   The 1990 Act, Sch 3, para 10(2), as amended.
[51]   The 1990 Act, Sch 3, para 10(3), as amended.
[52]   The 1990 Act, s 14(3).
[53]   SI 1991/1540.

8.24 Embryos were originally only able to be stored for five years and this has now been changed to ten years by the new amendment.[54] It was possible, under the terms of the Human Fertilisation and Embryology (Statutory Storage Periods for Embryos) Regulations 1996,[55] for the frozen embryos to be kept for a further five years after the expiry of the initial five years if one of the gametes providers, or the woman to be treated with the embryo was or was likely to become prematurely and completely infertile. The storage period could be extended if the woman being treated was a surrogate mother. There was an upper limit of the extension until the person reached the age of 55 years. It was also possible to extend the period to ten years, or when the person who intended to use the embryo reached 55 years of age, whichever was the shorter period, if the person had, or was likely to develop, significantly impaired fertility. There could also be an extension to the age of 55 if one of the persons was a carrier of a genetic condition which caused a risk of a serious medical condition.

8.25 Now, with the amendment, it is possible to keep the embryos, admixed human embryos and gametes for ten years from the outset. After the expiry of the maximum statutory period of storage allowed for the gametes or the embryos, the gametes or the embryos must then be allowed to perish.[56] The Act provided that storage periods were capable of being changed to a shorter or longer period by Parliamentary regulations.[57]

THE NEW REGULATIONS

8.26 Although the 2008 Act does not repeal the storage regulations, there are already draft Regulations to reflect the changes to the statutory storage period for embryos and also in respect of defining circumstances in which storage periods for gametes and embryos can be extended beyond ten years. These new Regulations are intended to replace the current two sets of Regulations referred to above.[58] These new Regulations only require the negative procedure and so are not required to be debated in Parliament.

8.27 Frozen gametes and embryos are usually used within a few years of them being stored and frozen but it is envisaged that there are circumstances when it can be necessary to store them for longer. The situations that have been envisaged are where the cancer patient is very young and it may be a long time before his stored gametes are used to start a family. Also where a couple are seeking a surrogate, it provides more time for them to set up a surrogacy arrangement.

---

[54] The 1990 Act, s 14(4).
[55] SI 1996/373.
[56] The 1990 Act, s 14(1)(c).
[57] The 1990 Act, s 14(5)(a) and (b).
[58] Para 10 of the draft Regulations would revoke the current Regulations save for the purposes of the draft Regulations 7 and 9, which means that these Regulations will continue to have effect for any gametes or embryos which are remaining in storage under the existing Regulations.

8.28　Other considerations have included the reflection that the cut-off age of 55 imposes an age limit on treatment which is not specified anywhere else in the legislation and there was also a consideration of the propriety of this under the Human Rights Act 1998. There is also the consideration that there should be a broadening of the circumstances in which a person can extend storage and for that to extend to situations for persons other than the gamete providers.

The aims of the new Regulations

8.29　The aims of the Regulations are therefore to have the same infertility criteria and overall time limits applicable to the extension for both gametes and embryos, to allow the extension of time where someone has or will become significantly and prematurely infertile, including cases where the person to be treated is not the gametes provider, for extensions in cases of using donated gametes or embryos and to remove the age limit for the storage of gametes and embryos and replace it with an overall time limit of 55 years, irrespective of the age of the person who put them into storage.

Storage periods for embryos

8.30　The new Regulations make provision for the statutory storage period for an embryo to be 55 years if the following conditions are met:[59]

- each of the persons whose gametes were used to create the embryo have consented to the embryo being stored for longer than ten years in writing; and

- during any time within the ten years' storage period a medical practitioner has given a written opinion that one of the gamete providers or the person to be treated has or is likely to develop significant and premature infertility.

8.31　The 'person to be treated' would be a named recipient of a donated embryo and this will be either:[60]

(i)　the woman who it is intended will be treated using the embryo in question; or

(ii)　the woman to whom the embryo has been allocated by a clinic, eg a woman intending to use a donated embryo with a surrogate mother; or

(iii)　the man to whom the embryo has been allocated by a clinic, eg a known donor could donate an embryo to the man to be used in treatment with his female partner or using a surrogate.

---

[59]　Draft Human Fertilisation and Embryology (Statutory Storage Period for Embryos and Gametes) Regulations 2009, Reg 3.

[60]　Draft Human Fertilisation and Embryology (Statutory Storage Period for Embryos and Gametes) Regulations 2009, Reg 2(a).

Storage periods for gametes

8.32 The same provisions that apply under the Regulations to the embryos permitting their extension would also apply to gametes.[61]

Embryo testing

8.33 An embryo can be stored for up to 55 years if the following requirements are met:

- each person who provided gametes to create the embryo consents in writing for the embryo to be stored for longer than ten years; and

- at any time within the ten-year period the embryo has been tested by a licence holder for the specified purposes set out in the 1990 Act as follows:
  (ii) to establish if the embryo carried a particular risk of having a genetic abnormality which gives rise to a significant risk of a serious medical condition, has that abnormality or other genetic abnormality;
  (ii) to establish the sex of the embryo if there is a particular risk of the embryo having a gender-related serious medical condition; or
  (iii) to establish the tissue type of the embryo where there is an older sibling that could be treated using such tissue.

Transitional provisions

8.34 These are set out in paras 6–9 of the draft Regulations. It is expected that the date for the new Regulations will be October 2009. If the persons whose gametes were used to create an embryo have it in storage at the date that the Regulations come into force then the storage period can be extended to 55 years if there is consent in writing before the original storage period of five years expires and if the applicable conditions set out in regulations[62] are met at any point before the ten years has expired. If these conditions are not met it will be a storage period of ten years.[63]

8.35 This would allow those whose embryos are currently stored for five years under the 1990 Act to benefit from the new extended initial storage period under the 2008 Act.

8.36 The same provisions described above for embryos would also apply to any gametes in storage on the date that the Regulation comes into force.[64]

---

[61] Draft Human Fertilisation and Embryology (Statutory Storage Period for Embryos and Gametes) Regulations 2009, Reg 5.

[62] Draft Human Fertilisation and Embryology (Statutory Storage Period for Embryos and Gametes) Regulations 2009, Regs 3 and 4.

[63] Draft Human Fertilsition and Embryology (Statutory storage period for Embryos and Gametes) Regulations 2009, Reg 6.

[64] Draft Human Fertilsition and Embryology (Statutory storage period for Embryos and Gametes) Regulations 2009, Reg 8.

8.37   If the embryos are already extended under the 1996 Regulations then the storage period for those embryos in storage on the date of the enforcement of the new Regulations will be 55 years if the conditions set out are met any time before the expiry of the extended storage period; or where those conditions are not met, it will be the period extended under the 1996 Regulations.[65]

8.38   The same would apply for gametes which are stored under the extended storage period for gametes under the 1991 Regulations.[66]

---

[65]   Draft Human Fertilisation and Embryology (Statutory Storage Period for Embryos and Gametes) Regulations 2009, Reg 7.

[66]   Draft Human Fertilisation and Embryology (Statutory Storage Period for Embryos and Gametes) Regulations 2009, Reg 9.

Chapter 9

LICENCES FOR RESEARCH

INTRODUCTION

9.1   Each new development and breakthrough in the science behind assisted reproduction treatment is the work of many years of research using human gametes and embryos. A need was felt for this scientific research to continue, in the hope not only of providing further refinements of the techniques that can assist those who are infertile or have difficulties in conceiving, but also to possibly assist in providing greater understanding and possibly treatment of the wider areas of human healthcare, such as Parkinsons' Disease and cancer. Simultaneously there was the need for such research, since it involved human embryos and gametes, to be strictly regulated to ensure the safety and the quality of such human matter and also respect for the human genetic material that was being used.

9.2   The 1990 Act has been revised and amended over the years in an endeavour to keep up with the developments. This Chapter examines where the new boundary lines have been drawn and the provisions that have been made in the legislation to enable it to keep up-to-date and not fall behind the latest advances. The scope of the permitted research purposes has been expanded over time and Sch 3A now represents the definitive list. This supersedes the Human Fertilisation and Embryology (Research Purposes) Regulations 2001[1] which are therefore revoked.[2]

A LICENCE FOR RESEARCH

9.3   The relevant schedules setting out the scope for research in the 1990 Act have been completely revised. There are now new paras 3 and 3A for Sch 2.

9.4   Research may authorise the bringing into creation of embryos *in vitro* and keeping or using embryos for the purposes of a project of research which is specified in the licence which is granted.[3]

9.5   The mixing of sperm with the eggs of a hamster (the 'hamster test') or any other animal specified in directions, for the purpose of developing more

---

[1]   SI 2001/188.
[2]   The 2008 Act, Sch 8, Part 2.
[3]   The 1990 Act, Sch 2, para 3(1), as amended.

effective techniques for determining the fertility or normality of sperm is permitted but the form which has been created has to be destroyed at the end of that piece of research and in any event, must be destroyed before the passing of the 2 cell stage.[4]

9.6   There is a new provision to deal with the newly defined human admixed embryos. A research licence may be issued to create, keep and use human admixed embryos for the purposes of a project of research.[5] However, such a licence does not authorise the 'hamster test'.[6]

9.7   It is possible for regulations to provide the creation *in vitro*, keeping and using things that are defined by those regulations as being human admixed embryos[7] and also to provide for conditions which must specifically be attached to such a licence.[8]

9.8   A licence can specify the manner in which the performance of all of these activities referred to above have to be performed.[9]

9.9   The Authority has to be satisfied that the proposed use of embryos or human admixed embryos is necessary for the purposes of the proposed research before it will grant a licence.

CONDITIONS FOR RESEARCH LICENCES

9.10   There are general conditions which attach to every licence granted,[10] which are set out in and examined as part of the licensing system in Chapter 5.

9.11   There are some express requirements set out in s 15 which apply to all research licences. It is a requirement that no embryo which has been appropriated for the purposes of any project for research shall only be used or kept for that purpose and not any other.[11]

9.12   Records must be maintained under a research licence, which includes such information as the Authority may set out in directions, and no information can be removed from any records before the expiry of the period as may be specified in the directions for the records of the class in question.[12]

---

[4]   The 1990 Act, Sch 2, para 3(2), as amended.
[5]   The 1990 Act, Sch 2, para 3(3), as amended.
[6]   The 1990 Act, Sch 2, para 3(4), as amended.
[7]   The 1990 Act, Sch 2, para 3(5), as amended, refers to the power to regulate under s 4A(5)(e).
[8]   The 1990 Act, Sch 2, para 3(8), as amended.
[9]   The 1990 Act, Sch 2, para 3(9), as amended.
[10]   The 1990 Act, s 12.
[11]   The 1990 Act, s 15(4).
[12]   The 1990 Act, s 15(2) and (3).

9.13 The licence itself can set out such conditions as shall be applicable to that individual licence.[13]

9.14 A licence may be granted for a period as stipulated in the licence but not exceeding three years.[14]

9.15 Furthermore, a licence can only be applicable to one project of research and it has to be under the supervision of one individual as designated under the licence and the activities are only authorised to be carried on in premises which are specified in the licence.[15] In the case of activities of keeping or processing, without storage, or procuring or distributing an embryo intended for human application, the licence can apply to relevant third party premises under a third party agreement but under the supervision of the person designated in the licence.[16]

THE SCOPE FOR RESEARCH

9.16 For a research licence to be granted it must fulfil one of the statutory principal purposes:

(i)   increasing knowledge about serious diseases or other serious conditions;[17]

(ii)   developing treatments for serious diseases or other serious medical conditions;[18]

(iii) increasing knowledge about the causes of any congenital disease or congenital medical condition which does not fall into the category of serious disease or serious medical condition;[19]

(iv)   promoting advances in the treatment of infertility;[20]

(v)   increasing knowledge about the causes of miscarriage;[21]

(vi)   developing more effective techniques of contraception;[22]

(vii) developing methods for detecting the presence of gene, chromosome or mitochondrion abnormalities in embryos before implantation;[23] or

---

[13]   The 1990 Act, Sch 2, para 3(7), as amended.
[14]   The 1990 Act, Sch 2, para 3(7), as amended.
[15]   The 1990 Act, Sch 2, para 4(2).
[16]   The 1990 Act, Sch 2, para 4(1).
[17]   The 1990 Act, Sch 2, para 3A(2)(a), as amended.
[18]   The 1990 Act, Sch 2, para 3A(2)(b), as amended.
[19]   The 1990 Act, Sch 2, para 3A(2)(c), as amended.
[20]   The 1990 Act, Sch 2, para 3A(2)(d), as amended.
[21]   The 1990 Act, Sch 2, para 3A(2)(e), as amended.
[22]   The 1990 Act, Sch 2, para 3A(2)(f), as amended.
[23]   The 1990 Act, Sch 2, para 3A(2)(g), as amended.

(viii) increasing knowledge about the development of embryos.[24]

9.17 In addition to meeting one of the above principal purposes, the Authority must be satisfied that the activity requiring to be authorised is necessary or desirable for specified principal purposes or that it is necessary or desirable for the purposes of providing knowledge that may be capable of being applied to point (i) or (ii) of the specified purposes of increasing knowledge, or that it is necessary or desirable for such other purposes as may be specified for the regulations.[25]

FUTURE DEVELOPMENTS

9.18 The list of principal purposes includes some new amendments set out in points (i) and (ii) above. The ability to undertake research to increase knowledge about other serious medical conditions and treatments for those conditions, coupled with the ability to conduct research which may be capable of application for those purposes, considerably widens the scope of the areas where research licences may now be sought.

9.19 It is also of note that there has been a deletion of a previous restriction on altering the genetic structure of the cells of an embryo and so it is possible for there to be application for a research licence involving the genetic modification of embryos, providing the principal purposes and the other conditions of a research licence can be satisfied.

---

[24]   The 1990 Act, Sch 2, para 3A(2)(h), as amended.
[25]   The 1990 Act, Sch 2, para 3A(1), as amended.

Chapter 10

THE CONSENT PROVISIONS

INTRODUCTION

10.1   Medical law is very familiar with the concept of consent in respect of the medical practices and procedure that are carried out on patients. In relation to the area of human fertilisation and embryology there have been cases and incidents which have involved the issue of whether consent has been given or not to the particular procedures in question. Therefore, the emphasis has been on establishing effective consent, not only in this area but across all other areas of medical and healthcare practice.

10.2   The new amendments have enlarged the scope of those areas where consent is required and this Chapter studies those areas. Consent is a relevant consideration in respect of all of the licences which can be granted, as consent is required from the gametes and embryo providers for the use of those embryos and gametes for the purposes of research. Consent is needed from those participating in assisted reproduction treatment and those wishing to acquire the status of parent under the statutory provisions. Consent is also required from those who wish to fulfil the criteria for storage of their gametes and embryos.

10.3   The legislation deals with constructing what makes consent 'effective consent' and also setting out the situation in which consent is necessary. Hand-in-hand with the issue of consent, there is the issue of counselling.[1] The provision of counselling has been extended and this is discussed later on in this Chapter. New provisions have been made in respect of consent and counselling and these are set out in Schs 3 and 3ZA respectively. The Code of Practice gives guidance on the ways that consent and counselling should be dealt with and proforma consent forms for different situations are provided to the clinics by the Authority.

---

[1]   Counselling is also referred to in the legislation in a different context pursuant to s 31ZA(3), whereby a donor-conceived person at the age of 16 requests information in respect of the donor, such information will only be provided if the applicant has been given a suitable opportunity to receive proper counselling.

CONSENT IN RELATION TO GAMETES, EMBRYOS, HUMAN ADMIXED EMBRYOS AND HUMAN CELLS

10.4 Schedule 3 of the new Act substantially amended the previous Sch 3 of the 1990 Act which governed consent. The amendments take into account that that there is now the possibility of creating further embryos by using embryos and human admixed embryos.[2] It is therefore possible to create a chain of embryos and consent if necessary, for the gametes and human cells to be used to create the original embryo, and then for their consent to be necessary for the subsequent use of that embryo to create other embryos or human admixed embryos.

10.5 Scientific progress also means that embryos can be altered or created using human cells, including human admixed embryos.[3] The definition of human cells excludes human cells which are reproductive cells.[4] Consent is therefore now relevant to the creation, use and storage of gametes, embryos, human admixed embryos and human cells.

10.6 The Authority can issue directions providing for other matters which must be dealt with concerning consent.[5]

Consent to the use of embryos and gametes

10.7 There must be consent to use a person's gametes for the purposes of treatment services or non-medical fertility services.[6]

10.8 To use an embryo there must be consent to one or more of the following purposes:

(i)   providing treatment services to the person giving consent or that person and another specified person together;[7] or

(ii)   donation for the treatment of others, not including the person giving consent;[8] or

(iii)   use for the purpose of any project of research;[9] or

(iv)   use for the purposes of training people in embryo biopsy, embryo storage or other embryological techniques.[10]

---

[2]   The 1990 Act, Sch 3, para 16(2) and (3), as amended.
[3]   The 1990 Act, Sch 3, para 16(4), as amended.
[4]   The 1990 Act, Sch 3, para 16(1), as amended.
[5]   The 1990 Act, Sch 3, para 2(3).
[6]   The 1990 Act, Sch 3, para 5(1), as amended.
[7]   The 1990 Act, Sch 3, para 2(1)(a).
[8]   The 1990 Act, Sch 3, para 2(1)(a).
[9]   The 1990 Act, Sch 3, para 2(1)(c).
[10]   The 1990 Act, Sch 3, para 2(1)(ba), as amended.

10.9 Each relevant person must consent to the use of gametes or human cells to bring about the creation of an embryo *in vitro* for one or more of the purposes listed at points (i)–(iii) above. A relevant person is each of the following:

(i) each person whose gametes or human cells were used to bring about the creation of the embryo (embryo A);

(ii) each person whose gametes or human cells were used to bring about the creation of an embryo *in vitro* which was then used to create embryo A;

(iii) each person whose gametes or human cells were used to bring about the creation of a human admixed embryo *in vitro* which was then used to create embryo A.

10.10 A line of predecessor embryos or human admixed embryos is created.[11] In respect of the provider of the gametes or human cells which go on to create an embryo or human admixed embryo, the terms of the consent may be varied or withdrawn either in general terms and in relation to a particular embryo or embryos or a particular human admixed embryo or embryos.

Consent to the creation, use and storage of human admixed embryos

10.11 The consent to the use of any human admixed embryos in research must clearly specify that it is for use for the purposes of a project of research.[12]

Consent to the storage of gametes

10.12 A person's gametes must not be kept in storage unless there is an effective consent by that person to their storage and they are stored in accordance with that consent.[13] The consent must specify the maximum period of storage (subject to the statutory maximum) and state what is to be done with the gametes or embryos if the person who gave the consent dies or is unable because of incapacity to vary the terms of the consent or to revoke it, and it may also specify conditions subject to which the gametes may remain in storage.[14]

10.13 The Authority may specify in directions the information which must be included in the records maintained in pursuance of the licences about the person whose consent is required under Sch 3, including the terms of their consent and the circumstances of the storage and any other matters. This

---

[11] The 1990 Act, Sch 3, para 2(4), as amended.
[12] The 1990 Act, Sch 3, para 2(1A), as amended.
[13] The 1990 Act, Sch 3, para 8(1), as amended.
[14] The 1990 Act, Sch 3, para 8(2), as amended.

information cannot be removed from the records before the expiry of any period that may be specified in the directions for records of the category in question (para 14 (1)(d) and (2)).

10.14   The amendments set out that the gametes of a person shall be placed in storage only if received from that person and acquired in circumstances where by virtue of Sch 3, para 9 or 10 that person's consent to storage is not required or if it is acquired from a person to whom a licence or third party agreement applies.

Cases where consent is not required for storage

10.15   This deals with two very different situations, the 'child donor' and also the incapable patient and these have been already dealt with in Chapter 8.

Consent to storage of embryos

10.16   Effective consent is necessary for the storage of embryos.[15]

10.17   The consent provisions are subject to the provisions of Sch 3, para 4A(4) which allows the lawful continuation of storage of an embryo for up to 12 months despite the withdrawal of consent by one of the gamete-providers.

10.18   The amendments provide that an embryo taken from a woman shall be placed in storage only if it is received from that woman or acquired from a person to whom a licence or a third party agreement applies.

10.19   There is the ability for an embryo which has been created *in vitro* but not in pursuance of a storage licence to be placed into storage only if acquired from that person to whom a licence or third party agreement applied. With regards to admixed human embryos brought about *in vitro* but not in pursuance of a licence they shall be placed into storage only if acquired from a person to whom a licence under paras 2 or 3 of Sch 2 applies, namely a treatment licence or a licence for non-medical fertility services.

THE FORMALITIES OF OBTAINING CONSENT

Giving consent

10.20   The procedure for giving consent aims to provide effective consent which is clear and unambiguous. The definition of 'effective consent' means consent that has been given in accordance with Sch 3 and not been withdrawn.[16]

---

[15]   The 1990 Act, Sch 3, para 8(1), as amended.
[16]   The 1990 Act, Sch 3, para 1(3), as amended.

10.21 It is therefore insisted upon that consent is given in writing and signed by the person giving it.[17]

10.22 Where a person is unable to sign a consent, or to give any subsequent notice of withdrawal or variation of consent because of illness, injury or physical disability, it will be taken to have been duly signed if it is signed at the direction of that incapacitated person in the presence of the incapacitated person and in the presence of at least one witness who attests the signature.[18]

Counselling

10.23 The new Sch 3ZA sets out the statutory requirements of counselling and the circumstances in which counselling must be offered before consent is given. The amendments inserted into the 1990 Act at s 13(6)–(6E) serve to extend the circumstances in which services will not be provided unless there has been a suitable opportunity to receive proper counselling.

10.24 Under the new s 13(6) it is a requirement of all treatment licences that a woman may not be provided with any treatment service which involves donated gametes or embryos or the use of an embryo which has been created *in vitro*, unless prior to treatment she and any partner (male or female) with whom she is being treated have been provided with the relevant information and have been offered counselling about the implications of the treatment that she is seeking. The same provisions apply where two people consent to the parenthood of any child that may be born as a result of the treatment.[19] This is in respect of any intended second parent as provided for by the agreed fatherhood and female parenthood provisions under the amended Act.[20]

10.25 Where the situation is that treatment services that are going to be provided involve the use of donated gametes or embryos taken from a woman who is not receiving those services, then the information that is to be provided to parties under ss 13(6) and 13(6A) must also include such information as is proper about the importance of giving information to the resulting child at an early age about how the child was conceived using donor gametes and to consider suitable methods of informing the child about their conception.[21]

10.26 The circumstances under Part 1 of Sch 3ZA where counselling must be offered are where the treatment services involve the use of donated gametes or embryos taken from a woman who is not receiving the services and the use of embryos which were created *in vitro*. In such circumstances, counselling must be offered in compliance with the new conditions imposed by s 13(6) as described above. The events where there must be the offer of counselling are where there

---

[17] The 1990 Act, Sch 3, para 1(1), as amended.
[18] The 1990 Act, Sch 3, para 1(2), as amended.
[19] The 1990 Act, s 13(6A), as amended.
[20] The 1990 Act, s 13(6B), as amended.
[21] The 1990 Act, s 13(6C), as amended.

is giving of the notice of consent in relation to parties involved in invoking the new fatherhood and female parenthood provisions.

VARIATION AND WITHDRAWAL OF CONSENT

10.27 Having originally given consent to the use or storage of gametes, embryos or human admixed embryos, there are significant repercussions if the consent is thereafter withdrawn or varied. However, there must be provision for the consent to be varied from time to time as the circumstances of the person who gave consent change and there must be the option of withdrawing consent. The statutory provisions are in place to ensure that the withdrawal and variation is communicated to the relevant persons and to set out the consequences of such a variation or withdrawal of consent.

Procedure for withdrawal or variation of consent

10.28 It is required that a withdrawal or variation of the consent to the storage and/or use of gametes or embryos or human admixed embryos is to be provided in writing and signed by the person withdrawing the consent.[22] As with the giving of consent, if the person is incapacitated though illness, injury or physical disability and is so unable to sign then the signature is valid to a withdrawal or variation if it is signed at the direction of the incapacitated person, in the presence of at least one other witness.[23] The notice of withdrawal or variation must be given to the person responsible at the establishment where the gametes or embryos are held.

Withdrawal of consent for use of embryos in treatment

10.29 New provisions were introduced for dealing with the situation which arose in the long running case of *Evans*,[24] where there were frozen embryos in storage created by a couple. After the couple separated, the male partner then withdrew his consent to allow the embryos to be used by the female partner by herself for fertility treatment. This required the embryos in storage to be destroyed. The case was perceived to be particularly difficult and poignant due to the female partner's inability to conceive naturally due to her illness. The aim is to introduce a 'cooling period' which would allow for time for the discussions and a possible resolution to be reached by the persons involved concerning the future of the embryos.

10.30 The new provisions apply where the permitted embryo created *in vitro* is in storage and it was created from the use of providing treatment services, but before it is used in providing treatment services one of the persons whose gametes were used to bring about its creation gives notice to the person keeping

---

[22]   The 1990 Act, Sch 3, para 1(1), as amended.
[23]   The 1990 Act, Sch 3, para 1(2), as amended.
[24]   *Evans v Amicus Healthcare & Others* [2003] EWHC 2161.

the embryo withdrawing consent to the storage of the embryo.[25] The person withdrawing their consent could be one of the partners of the couple who were seeking treatment services or, where donated gametes were used, the gamete donor.

10.31 In such circumstances, the person who is responsible for keeping the embryo must as soon as possible take all reasonable steps to give notice to each of the interested persons involved in relation to the embryo of the withdrawal of consent notice.[26] The interested person would be the person who was to use the embryo in their treatment services.[27]

10.32 There is then a period of 12 months beginning with the day of the receipt of the withdrawal of consent notice when the embryo will not be destroyed. Storage remains lawful during that 12-month period or until the last notice is received from each of the persons notified of the withdrawal, setting out each of their consents to the destruction of the embryo.[28]

10.33 Therefore, this opportunity of time may be used to reach a resolution between the interested parties. Alternatively if the interested persons do not agree to the embryos being removed from storage or there is no response to the notification of withdrawal then the embryo will remain in storage for 12 months, at the end of which it will be allowed to perish.

Withdrawal of consent to parenthood

10.34 There are also new provisions which state that where a partner withdraws consent to agreed fatherhood or agreed female parenthood, that responsibility falls on the person responsible for the clinic to notify the other partner who was to be provided with treatment and this will then halt the placing of an embryo or sperm and eggs in the woman, or being artificially inseminated, until the woman has been so informed.[29]

10.35 Where a woman being provided with treatment withdraws her consent for the other partner to be the parent of any resulting child, the person responsible at the clinic has the duty to inform the other partner of the withdrawal of consent.[30]

Withdrawal of variation of consent to gametes and human cells

10.36 As has been seen earlier, where providers of the gametes or human cells go on to create an embryo or human admixed embryo, the terms of the consent

---

[25] The 1990 Act, Sch 3, para 4A(1), as amended.
[26] The 1990 Act, Sch 3, para 4A(2), as amended.
[27] The 1990 Act, Sch 3, para 4A(3), as amended.
[28] The 1990 Act, Sch 3, para 4A(4), as amended.
[29] The 1990 Act, s 13(6D), as amended.
[30] The 1990 Act, s 13(6E), as amended.

may be varied or withdrawn either in general terms and in relation to a particular embryo or embryos or a particular human admixed embryo or embryos.[31]

Variations and withdrawals not permitted

10.37   Consent may be withdrawn or varied by the giving of due notice to the person who is keeping the gametes, human cells, embryos or human admixed embryos. However, there are circumstances where this ability to vary or revoke consent ceases.

10.38   The circumstances are as follows:

(i)   the embryo has already been used in providing treatment services;[32]

(ii)   the embryo has been used in training persons in embryo biopsy, embryo storage or other embryological techniques;[33]

(iii)   the embryo has been used for the purposes of any research project;[34]

(iv)   where there was consent for an embryo to be used in the creation of an embryo or a human admixed embryo which has been used for the purposes set out in points (i)–(iii) above, there can be no variation or withdrawal of the use of the original embryo;[35]

(v)   the use of a human admixed embryo once it has been used in point (iii) above.[36]

---

[31]   The 1990 Act, Sch 3, para 2(5), as amended.
[32]   The 1990 Act, Sch 3, para 4(2)(a), as amended.
[33]   The 1990 Act, Sch 3, para 4(2)(aa), as amended.
[34]   The 1990 Act, Sch 3, para 4(2)(b), as amended.
[35]   The 1990 Act, Sch 3, para 4(3), as amended.
[36]   The 1990 Act, Sch 3, para 4, as amended.

Chapter 11

PARENTHOOD IN CASES INVOLVING ASSISTED REPRODUCTION

INTRODUCTION

11.1 The review of the 1990 Act has allowed not only the opportunity for taking into account new forms of technology which were either omitted or not considered at the time of passing that piece of legislation but it has also allowed the reconsideration of the whole area of parenthood in the context of where assisted reproduction technology has been used, including that of surrogacy.

11.2 This Chapter will examine the conferment of parenthood upon those involved in assisted reproduction and also the status of the resulting child. Part 2 of the 2008 Act sets out the changes and provisions as to the status of those involved in assisted reproduction treatment. The 2008 Act introduces the concepts of 'fatherhood' and 'female parenthood' and explains their meaning and effect. The law on parenthood is updated and further elaborated upon in ss 33–53 of the 2008 Act. Sch 6 deals at length with the impact that the new provisions have upon the existing legislation and a substantial list of the changes is set out. This Chapter will also deal with the new parental orders which will replace the provisions currently set out in s 30 of the 1990 Act.

IMPLEMENTATION

11.3 The importance of the provisions relating to parenthood can be seen in the fact that they are to be enacted ahead of the rest of the Act on 6 April 2009. When the substantial passages of the 2008 Act which deal with parenthood in relation to those involved in assisted reproduction, namely ss 33–48 come into force, then ss 27–29 of the 1990 Act will be repealed and will cease to have effect.[1] Regulations in respect of the parental orders have not yet been drafted and so the new provisions will take effect in April 2010.

---

[1]   The 2008 Act, s 57(1) and (2).

THE LEGAL STATUS

11.4 There is a vested interest for society in clarifying the circumstances in which status of parenthood is acquired and for the legal status of the child born as a result of assisted reproduction technology to be established and clear. There are varieties of possibilities regarding the legal status that could result from the variety of ways in which such a child could be created and issues such as the impact of donation and consent needed to be clarified.

11.5 The common law position is that the genetic link between parent and child is the determining factor of parenthood,[2] save where there are statutory provisions which intervene and override that position. The issue was initially tackled by the Family Law Reform Act 1987 which provided that the husband of a wife giving birth following artificial insemination should be taken to be the father of the child unless an absence of consent on his part to the insemination could be demonstrated.[3] The 1990 Act repealed that provision[4] and instead replaced it with more detailed provisions in order to deal with other situations and possible scenarios.

11.6 The 1990 Act, as can be seen from the Warnock Report and the parliamentary debates that ensued,[5] was concerned with the notion of marriage being significant and important to society and the need to uphold it as such, and there were also concerns about children being labelled 'illegitimate' or being born 'fatherless'. The societal landscape in which the 2008 Act was passed was after there had been greater acceptance of same-sex couples and unmarried couples and their rights to a family. It had also seen the passing of legislation which was aimed at creating the equality of same-sex couples with heterosexual couples.[6]

DEFINITIONS OF MARRIAGE AND CIVIL PARTNERSHIP

11.7 These are terms which are used throughout Part 2 and clear definitions are provided. A marriage has to be a subsisting one without a judicial separation in force. This would include a legal separation obtained in a country outside of the British islands and recognised in the UK.[7]

11.8 However a marriage would include a void marriage if either or both of the parties reasonably believed at the time that the marriage was valid. There is

---

[2]   *Re B (parentage)* [1996] 2 FLR 15.
[3]   Family Law Reform Act 1987, s 27.
[4]   The 1990 Act, s 49(4).
[5]   See the debates on the concept of the 'welfare of the child'.
[6]   The Civil Partnership Act 2004.
[7]   The 2008 Act, s 49(1)(a) and (2).

a presumption for the purpose of this section that one of the parties did reasonably believe at that time that the marriage was valid, unless the contrary can be shown.[8]

11.9   References to parties to a civil partnership mean one that is subsisting unless there is a separation order in force.[9] A separation order is defined as a separation order or a decree of separation under the respective provisions of the Civil Partnership Act 2004 or a legal separation obtained in a country outside of the UK and recognised in the UK.[10]

11.10   The same presumption and proviso that is raised with a void marriage is also raised with regards to a void civil partnership.[11] This includes the situation where there is reference to a civil partnership in the context of where a person is a second parent at the time of artificial insemination or the placing of the embryo or sperm and egg in their partner by virtue of s 43 but by the time the child is born, the parties have entered into a civil partnership, so the child becomes the legitimate child of the second parent as set out in para 48(6)(b).[12]

THE MEANING OF 'MOTHER'

11.11   It remains the case now, as under the 1990 Act, that the woman who carries a child following assisted reproduction anywhere in the world is the child's mother unless the child is subsequently adopted or parenthood is transferred through a parental order.[13]

11.12   This would appear to cause no difficulty in the ordinary situation where the female is part of a heterosexual couple seeking treatment together and are intending to raise the resulting child together. This means the genetic, gestational and social aspects of mothering are all embodied in one person.

11.13   Adoption will involve the intervention of a court order to this effect and parental orders will be discussed below.

THE MEANING OF 'FATHER'

11.14   Donor insemination is an option under assisted reproduction technology where there are difficulties with male infertility. Without the statutory provisions, the donor of the sperm would be regarded as the genetic and social father of the resulting child.

---

[8]   The 2008 Act, s 49(1)(b).
[9]   The 2008 Act, s 50(1)(a).
[10]   The 2008 Act, s 50(1)(b).
[11]   The 2008 Act, s 50(2).
[12]   The 2008 Act, s 50(2).
[13]   The 2008 Act, s 33.

11.15 The relevant time for the statutory provisions under the 2008 Act governing the status of becoming the 'father' in that situation is when the gametes or the embryo is placed in the woman or at the time that she is artificially inseminated.[14]

11.16 The provisions under s 35 of the 2008 Act provide that where a woman is married at the time of treatment when there was placed in her an embryo or the gametes involving donor sperm, her husband will be treated as the father of the conceived child.[15] The proviso is if it is shown that he did not consent to his wife's treatment. This provision applies whether the wife was in the UK or elsewhere in the world.[16] There is further provision that if a person is treated as the father then no other person may be treated as the father. This reinforces the position of the sperm donor being unable to have the status of father.[17]

11.17 There is statutory provision that s 35 is subject to the common law presumption that a child is the legitimate child of a married couple.[18]

11.18 In practical terms, this means that in the situation where a woman got married between the conception of a donor-conceived child and its birth, the presumption will be that her new husband is the father of the child. This would apply even if the agreed fatherhood conditions, which are explained below, were satisfied in relation to a different man at the time when the gametes or embryos were transferred.

11.19 This presumption does not operate in common law for people who enter into a civil partnership so the provisions which would otherwise apply to determine parenthood would not be affected by the mother entering into a civil partnership after the embryos or gametes have been transferred.

THE 'FATHERHOOD' CONDITIONS

11.20 Where a woman becomes a mother using donor-sperm and is not married and has no female partner but she does have a male partner to whom she is not married, there are now provisions which enable an unmarried man to be the father of a donor-conceived child.

11.21 There are a number of conditions which must be satisfied, including those of 'fatherhood' before he is able to be treated as the legal father:[19]

- the woman must be treated in a UK licensed clinic;

---

14   The 2008 Act, s 34.
15   The 2008 Act, s 35(1).
16   The 2008 Act, s 35(2).
17   The 2008 Act, s 38(1).
18   The 2008 Act ss 38(2) and 32(3).
19   The 2008 Act, s 36.

- the sperm is not that of her unmarried male partner who seeks to become the father;

- the man who seeks to become the father is alive at the time;

- the 'fatherhood' conditions as prescribed by s 37 of the 2008 Act are met.

11.22 The new 'fatherhood' conditions are to ensure that the mother and prospective father are fully aware and give clear evidence of their intention for the unmarried man to become the father. The constraint that the couple have to be a couple treated in a licensed clinic in the UK is to ensure that the parents' intention about fatherhood are carefully and properly documented.

11.23 The 'fatherhood' provisions that have to be satisfied are as follows:

- at the time the embryo or gametes have been placed into the woman or at the time she is artificially inseminated, the couple must each have given notice of consent to him being treated as the father;[20]

- neither of them must have given notice withdrawing that consent;[21]

- the woman must not, since giving the above notice, subsequently give notice of consent to another man or woman being treated as the child's parent;[22]

- the couple must not be within the prohibited degrees of relationship in relation to each other.[23]

NOTICES OF CONSENT

11.24 The notices of consent as set out above must be provided to the 'person responsible' at the clinic,[24] which is the person under whose supervision the licensed activities are being carried out. The consents have to be in writing and signed by the person providing the consent,[25] although there is provision that if any of the parties involved are unable to sign the consent because of illness, injury or physical disability then there will be valid consent as to the signature if it is signed at the direction of the incapacitated party, in their presence and also in the presence of at least one witness who attests the signature.[26]

---

[20] The 2008 Act, s 37(1)(a) and (b).
[21] The 2008 Act, s 37(1)(c).
[22] The 2008 Act, s 37(1)(d).
[23] The 2008 Act, s 37(1)(e).
[24] The 2008 Act, s 37(1).
[25] The 2008 Act, s 37(2).
[26] The 2008 Act, s 37(3).

11.25   Clinics will have been sent prior to the commencement date of these provisions, guidance notes and consent forms for parenthood which have been the subject of the consultation in respect of consent forms.

11.26   If the circumstances are that a woman has given notice of consent to several people being the father of a child, and there are corresponding notices given by the other persons, then the latest set of consents that have been provided to the clinic would apply.

11.27   After the transfer of the gametes or embryo, neither the man nor the woman can withdraw their consent to the man being treated as the child's father unless the woman does not conceive and a new cycle of treatment has to begin. Changes to the conditions which must be included in all treatment licences, will require that, if the man withdraws his consent at an earlier stage, the woman must be told before the treatment proceeds. She therefore will have the opportunity to decide whether she wishes to go ahead in these circumstances. If the woman withdraws her agreement to the man being the father, he must be told as soon as possible but he would not, through these provisions, be able to stop her going ahead if she wishes to do so.

PROHIBITED RELATIONSHIPS

11.28   If the two people involved are within the prohibited degrees of relationship they are unable to give valid notice of consent, as such close relatives will not be jointly treated as the parents of the resulting child. The definition of the prohibited relationships includes parents, grandparents, siblings, uncles and aunts and refers to those relationships if of full or half blood. In the case of those who have been adopted, this would include those relationships as would subsist but for the adoption and includes the relationship of a child with his adoptive or former adoptive parents.[27]

11.29   The Act will maintain the situation that if an unmarried couple carry out self-insemination with donor sperm at home or elsewhere, not as part of licensed treatment, then the male partner would not be the legal parent. He would have to take steps to acquire formal parental responsibility, e g adopting the child. An unmarried man cannot become a parent where donor sperm is provided under a licence under para 1A of Sch 2 of the 1990 Act (non-medical fertility series) unless the donor sperm is also used in treatment services.

POSTHUMOUS USE OF SPERM

11.30   There were amendments to the 1990 Act by the 2003 Act dealing with deceased fathers.[28] The amendments allowed a man to be registered as the

---

[27]   The 2008 Act, s 58(2).
[28]   The Human Fertilisation and Embryology (Deceased Fathers) Act 2003.

father of a child conceived after his death using his sperm or using an embryo created with his sperm before his death.

11.31 Section 39 replaces the provisions inserted in the 1990 Act. Where the woman has a child as a result of there being placed in her an embryo, or sperm and eggs, or by artificial insemination she conceives a child created with the man's sperm and where the creation of that embryo was brought about by using the sperm of a man after his death or by using his sperm before his death but the embryo was placed in the woman after his death, then the man who provided the sperm is to be treated as the child's father for the purposes of birth registration only if various conditions are met.[29] These provisions apply whether the embryo or gametes were transferred to the women in the UK or elsewhere.[30]

11.32 The conditions are as follows:

- the man must have consented in writing to the use of the sperm or embryo after his death and to being treated for any resulting child as the child's father for the purposes of birth registration;[31]

- the man did not withdraw this specific consent;[32]

- the woman must elect in writing that he should be treated in this way within 42 days[33] of the child's birth;[34]

- no one else is to be treated as the father by virtue of the provisions in ss 35, 36 or 38(2) or (3) (marriage, fatherhood provisions or the common law presumption);[35]

- no one else is to be treated as a parent of the child by virtue of ss 42 or 43 (a woman in a civil partnership or agreed female parenthood);[36]

- no one else is to be treated as a parent of the child by virtue of adoption.[37]

---

[29] The 2008 Act, s 39(1)(a) and (b) and (3).
[30] The 2008 Act, s 39(2).
[31] The 2008 Act, s 39(1)(c)(i) and (ii).
[32] The 2008 Act, s 39(1)(c).
[33] The 2008 Act, s 39(4) states that it is 21 days in Scotland.
[34] The 2008 Act, s 39(1)(d).
[35] The 2008 Act, s 39(1)(e)(i).
[36] The 2008 Act, s 39(1)(e)(ii).
[37] The 2008 Act, s 39(1)(e)(ii).

USE OF DONATED SPERM WHERE THE COUPLE ARE MARRIED

11.33   Where donated sperm has been used in the creation of the embryo and the husband of the woman in whom the embryo was transferred dies before the placing of the embryo into the woman then there are similar provisions to ensure that the husband can be treated as the father of the resulting child.[38] These provisions apply whether the embryo or gametes were transferred to the women in the UK or elsewhere.[39]

11.34   Again various conditions have to be satisfied and these are as follows:

- the woman was married when the embryo which used donor sperm was created;[40]

- the husband died before the placing of the embryo in the woman;[41]

- the husband consented in writing to the placing of the embryo in his wife and to being treated for any resulting child as the child's father for the purposes of birth registration;[42]

- the man did not withdraw this specific consent;[43]

- the woman must elect in writing that he should be treated in this way within 42 days[44] of the child's birth;[45]

- no one else is to be treated as the father by virtue of the provisions in ss 35, 36 or 38(2) or (3) (marriage, fatherhood provisions or the common law presumption);[46]

- no one else is to be treated as a parent of the child by virtue of ss 42 or 43 (a woman in a civil partnership to agreed female parenthood);[47]

- no one else is to be treated as a parent of the child by virtue of adoption.[48]

---

[38]   The 2008 Act, s 40(1).
[39]   The 2008 Act, s 40(3).
[40]   The 2008 Act, s 40(1)(b).
[41]   The 2008 Act, s 40(1)(d).
[42]   The 2008 Act, s 40(1)(e).
[43]   The 2008 Act, s 40(1)(e).
[44]   The 2008 Act, s 40(5) states that it is 21 days in Scotland.
[45]   The 2008 Act, s 40(1)(f).
[46]   The 2008 Act, s 40(1)(g)(i).
[47]   The 2008 Act, s 40(1)(g)(ii).
[48]   The 2008 Act, s 40(1)(g)(ii).

USE OF DONATED SPERM WHERE COUPLE ARE NOT MARRIED

11.35 If the woman and man were not married nor in a civil partnership at the time of the embryo creation, and donated sperm was used to create the embryo, then all of the above conditions which apply for a married couple also apply in order to ensure that the man is to be treated as the child's father.[49] In addition, the fatherhood conditions set out in s 37 must have been met immediately before the man's death and the embryo must have been created in the course of licensed treatment services in the UK.[50]

PERSONS NOT TO BE TREATED AS THE FATHER

11.36 These are clarifying sections which denote who is not the father of the child. A man who donates sperm and has consented for it to be used for the treatment or the non-medical fertility services of another is not to be treated as the father.[51] Neither is a man who has not consented to his sperm being used after his death.[52] This applies whether the woman is in the UK or elsewhere at the time of the placing into her of the embryo or the sperm and eggs or at the time of her artificial insemination.[53]

THE FEMALE PARENTHOOD CONDITIONS

11.37 New provisions are brought into the legislation providing for female civil partners to be brought into line with those provisions which apply to married couples. Where a female civil partner gives birth to a child conceived as a result of donor insemination, anywhere in the world, she is the mother of the child[54] and her civil partner will automatically be the other parent, unless she did not consent to the mother's treatment.[55]

11.38 Where the relationship is not that of a civil partnership and one of the women has a child as a result of donor insemination then provided certain conditions are met, the other woman will be treated as a legal parent of the resulting child.[56]

11.39 The necessary conditions to be met are the embryo or the sperm and eggs were placed in the woman, or she was inseminated in a UK licensed clinic and at that time the agreed female parenthood conditions were met in respect

---

[49]   The 2008 Act, s 40(2), (3),(4) and (5).
[50]   The 2008 Act, s 40(2)(f).
[51]   The 2008 Act, s 41(1).
[52]   The 2008 Act, s 41(2).
[53]   The 2008 Act, s 40(3).
[54]   The 2008 Act, s 33(1).
[55]   The 2008 Act, s 42(1) and (2).
[56]   The 2008 Act, s 43.

of the other woman in relation to the treatment that is being provided to the woman who will bear the child, and that the woman seeking to be the other parent is still alive.

11.40   The agreed female parenthood conditions that have to be fulfilled are as follows:

- at the time the embryo or gametes have been placed into the woman or at the time she is artificially inseminated, the couple must each have given notice of consent to her being treated as the parent;[57]

- neither of them must have given notice withdrawing that consent;[58]

- the woman must not have since giving the notice as above then subsequently given notice of consent to another woman being treated as the child's parent;[59]

- the woman must not have since giving the notice as above then subsequently given notice of consent to another man being treated as the child's father under s 37(1)(b);[60]

- the couple must not be within the prohibited degrees of relationship in relation to each other;[61]

- the couple must have in place, at the time of transfer of the sperm or embryo which results in conception, current notices of consent to the other woman being treated as a parent and then she will be a legal parent. This reflects the provisions for an unmarried heterosexual couple who have a child.

Notices of consent

11.41   The same situation exists with the consent provisions as with those which apply to those who seek fatherhood. The notices of consent as set out above must be provided to the 'person responsible' at the clinic,[62] which is the person under whose supervision the licensed activities are being carried out. The consents have to be in writing and signed by the person providing the consent,[63] although there is provision that if any of the parties involved are unable to sign the consent because of illness, injury or physical disability then

---

[57]   The 2008 Act, s 44(1)(a) and (b).
[58]   The 2008 Act, s 44(1)(c).
[59]   The 2008 Act, s 44(1)(d)(i).
[60]   The 2008 Act, s 44(1)(d)(ii).
[61]   The 2008 Act, s 44(1)(e).
[62]   The 2008 Act, s 44(1).
[63]   The 2008 Act, s 44(2).

there will be valid consent as to the signature if it is signed at the direction of the incapacitated party, in their presence and also in the presence of at least one witness who attests the signature.[64]

11.42　If the circumstances are that a woman has given notice of consent to several people being the parent or father of the child, and there are corresponding notices given by the other persons, then the latest set of consents that have been provided to the clinic would apply.

11.43　After the transfer of the gametes or embryo neither party can withdraw their consent to the woman being treated as the child's parent unless the woman does not conceive and a new cycle of treatment has to begin. Changes to the conditions which must be included in all treatment licences, will require that, if the woman withdraws her consent at an earlier stage, then the woman seeking to have the placement of the embryo must be told before the treatment proceeds. She therefore will have the opportunity to decide whether she wishes to go ahead in these circumstances. If the woman withdraws her agreement to the other woman being the parent, she must be told as soon as possible but she would not be able to stop her going ahead with the transfer if she wishes to do so.

Prohibited relationships

11.44　If the two women involved are within the prohibited degrees of relationship then they are unable to give valid notice of consent as such close relatives will not be jointly treated as the parents of the resulting child. The definition of the prohibited relationships include parents, grandparents, siblings, uncles and aunts and refers to those relationships if of full or half blood. In the case of those who have been adopted this would include those relationships as would subsist but for the adoption and include the relationship of a child with his adoptive or former adoptive parents.[65]

The effect of female parenthood

11.45　Where a woman is to be treated as a parent of the child by being in a civil relationship with the mother or fulfilling the criteria to be a parent under the female parenthood provisions, then no man is to be treated as the father of the child.[66] However, the provisions in ss 42 and 43 will not affect who is to be considered the parent of child in cases of the common law presumption that a child is the legitimate child of a married couple[67] or if the child has been adopted.[68]

---

[64]　The 2008 Act, s 44(3).
[65]　The 2008 Act, s 58(2).
[66]　The 2008 Act, s 45(1).
[67]　The 2008 Act, s 45(2) and (3).
[68]　The 2008 Act, s 45(4).

THE DEATH OF A SAME SEX PARTNER

11.46   There are new provisions about the registration of a deceased same sex partner as a child's parent in the register of births in certain circumstances. The provision for civil partners is comparable to that under s 40 for married couples using donor sperm whilst the provision for other same sex couples is comparable to that for unmarried couples using donor sperm.

Embryo transfer after the death of a civil partner

11.47   Where a child is created from an embryo that was placed in a woman, which had been created at the time when the woman was a party to a civil partnership and her partner dies before the placement of that embryo, then provided certain requirements have been met the deceased partner may be treated as the parent of the child.[69]

11.48   The requirements are as follows:

- the woman was in a civil partnership when the embryo was created;[70]

- the other party died before the placing of the embryo in the woman;[71]

- the other party consented in writing to the placing of the embryo in the woman and to being treated for any resulting child as the child's parent for the purposes of birth registration;[72]

- the man did not withdraw this specific consent;[73]

- the woman must elect in writing that her partner should be treated in this way within 42 days[74] of the child's birth;[75]

- no one else is to be treated as the father by virtue of the provisions in ss 35, 36 or 38(2) or (3) (marriage, fatherhood provisions or the common law presumption);[76]

- no else is to be treated as a parent of the child by virtue of ss 42 or 43 (a woman in a civil partnership to agreed female parenthood);[77]

---

[69]   The 2008 Act, s 46(1).
[70]   The 2008 Act, s 46(1)(b).
[71]   The 2008 Act, s 46(1)(c).
[72]   The 2008 Act, s 46(1)(d)(i) and (ii).
[73]   The 2008 Act, s 40(1)(d).
[74]   The 2008 Act, s 46(4) states that it is 21 days in Scotland.
[75]   The 2008 Act, s 4691)(e).
[76]   The 2008 Act, s 46(1)(f)(i).
[77]   The 2008 Act, s 46(1)(f)(ii).

- no else is to be treated as a parent of the child by virtue of adoption.[78]

Embryo transfer after the death of intended female parent

11.49 If the same sex female couple were not in a civil partnership at the time of the embryo creation and nor was the woman who carried the child in a marriage, then it is provided that certain conditions are met for the woman's female partner (not a civil partner) who then dies before the transfer of the embryo to be registered as the legal parent of the child.[79]

11.50 The criterion that has to be met is that the female partner consented in writing (and this was not withdrawn) to the placing of the embryo in the woman after her own death and to herself becoming the parent of any resulting child. The partner has to have died before the placing of the embryo into the woman and the female parenthood conditions set out in s 44 must have been met immediately before the female's death and the embryo must have been created in the course of licensed treatment services in the UK.[80] The woman bearing the child has elected not later then a period of 42 days[81] for her partner to have been treated as a parent of the child.[82] Further, that no one else is to be treated as the father by virtue of the provisions in ss 35, 36 or 38(2) or (3), or a parent by virtue of s 42 or 43 or by adoption.[83] These provisions apply whether the woman was anywhere in the world when the embryo was placed in her.[84]

EGG DONATION

11.51 The provisions make it clear that where a woman has not carried a child she will only be treated as a parent if the provisions relating to parenthood or the mother's partner apply, or if she has adopted the child. Therefore being an egg donor will not make a woman the parent of a child carried by another woman, although it is open for parenthood to be conferred by other legal provisions e g if a woman donated an egg to her female partner and then agreed female parenthood conditions were met in relation to the egg donor.

THE EFFECT OF THE PARENTHOOD PROVISIONS

11.52 Where the section's application treats a person as the mother, father or parent of a child then this will apply for all legal purposes and likewise where

---

[78]   The 2008 Act, s 46(1)(f)(ii).
[79]   The 2008 Act, s 46(2) and (4).
[80]   The 2008 Act, s 46(2)(a)–(e).
[81]   The 2008 Act, s 46(5) states that it is 21 days in Scotland.
[82]   The 2008 Act, s 46(2)(f).
[83]   The 2008 Act, s 46(2)(g).
[84]   The 2008 Act, s 46(3).

the provisions provide that a person is not a mother, father or parent then he or she cannot be treated as a parent for any purpose.[85]

11.53 Where the statutory provisions above permit a deceased man or a deceased woman to be treated in law as the father or parent of a child, then this is only applicable for purposes of the registration of the birth and not any other purpose.[86]

11.54 The new parenthood provisions do not affect the succession to any dignity or title of honour in England, Wales and Northern Ireland or any property rights that relate to them.[87] The provisions do not apply to any titles, coat of arms, honour or dignity in Scotland or any property interest.[88]

THE REGISTER OF BIRTHS

11.55 The relevant register of births which is referred to for the deceased father or parent who is to be permitted entry of their particulars, provided they could satisfy the necessary conditions, depends upon where the child is born. In England and Wales it would be the register of live-birth or still-births kept under the Births and Deaths Registration Act 1953.[89]

LATE ELECTION BY MOTHER WITH CONSENT OF REGISTRAR GENERAL

11.56 There is provision for the allowing for an extension of the period during which a woman may elect for her deceased partner to be treated as her child's parent for the purposes of birth registration with the consent of the relevant Registrar General (depending upon whether the matter is dealt with in English and Wales, Scotland or Northern Ireland).[90] The Registrar General has to be satisfied that there is a compelling reason for him to consent to the making of a late election.[91]

---

[85]   The 2008 Act, s 48(1) and (2).
[86]   The 2008 Act, s 48(3) and (4).
[87]   The 2008 Act, s 48(7).
[88]   The 2008 Act, s 48(8).
[89]   The 2008 Act, s 51. In Scotland it would be the register of births or still-births under the Registration of Births, Deaths and Marriages (Scotland) Act 1965 and in Northern Ireland it would be the register of live births or still-births kept under the Births and Deaths Registration (Northern Ireland) Order 1976 (SI 1976/1041 (N.I.14).
[90]   The 2008 Act, s 52(1) and (3).
[91]   The 2008 Act, s 52(2).

STATUTORY AMENDMENTS RELATING TO PARENTHOOD

11.57   Section 53 of the 2008 Act and Sch 6 of the 2008 Act set out that for interpretation of other enactments, deeds or other instruments or documents whenever passed or made, references to a child's father will in relevant cases be read as references to a woman who is one of the child's parents by virtue of the provisions for parent in Part 2 of the 2008 Act.

11.58   An enactment is such as in contained in or is an instrument in an Act of Parliament, an Act of the Scottish Parliament, a Measure or Act of the National Assembly for Wales or Northern Ireland legislation.[92]

11.59   Section 56 sets out that Sch 6 contains an extensive list of legislation that is expressly amended to take account of the possibility that a child may have two female parents. Parts 2 and 3 of the Sch deal with specific legislation relating to Scotland and Northern Ireland respectively. Part 1 deals with a whole raft of general legislation which is amended when the new Act comes into force.

AMENDMENTS TO GENERAL LEGISLATION

11.60   The precise amendments are set out in full in Sch 6 and therefore only the effects of the various amendments to each piece of legislation are highlighted here.

Amendments in Part 1

11.61

(i)   Population (Statistics) Act 1938 – enables the insertion of second female parent and the date of the formation of any civil partnership.

(ii)   Births and Deaths Registration Act 1953 – enables the details to be inserted of the woman who is parent of the child by virtue of ss 42 or 43 of the 2008 Act to be treated as the father, where the woman is a civil partner of the mother to be treated as the second female parent and of both fathers and women who are treated as parents by virtue of s 46 of the 2008 Act. It also allows for re-registration where the parents are not married so that a woman can be inserted as a parent of child by virtue of ss 42 or 46(1) or (2) of the 2008 Act. Also a woman who is parent of child by virtue of ss 42 or 43 of the 2008 Act is to be treated in the same way as a father of a child. It also allows for the amendments of the Legitimacy Act 1976 as set out below to be reflected so that there can be re-registration of the births of legimated persons to show that such a

---

[92]   The 2008 Act, s 58(1).

legitimated person is the child of a person who is the parent of the child by virtue of s 43 of the 2008 Act. Finally, there is the provision for corrections of the register where a woman is wrongly registered as a parent of a person by virtue of ss 42, 43 or 46(1) or (2) of the 2008 Act.

(iii) Legitimacy Act 1976 – is amended so that women who enter into a civil partnership and who have had children together previously by assisted conception can legitimise those children as from the date of their civil partnership.

(iv) Registration of Births, Deaths and Marriages (Special Provisions) Act 1957 – amendments allow for correction of the register where the woman is wrongly registered as a parent of a person by virtue of ss 42, 43 or 46(1) or (2) of the 2008 Act. There is also provision for the second female parent by virtue of s 43 of the 2008 Act to be registered or re-registered as the parent of a child following the subsequent formation of a civil partnership between the child's parents.

(v) Family Law Reform Act 1969 – amends the definition of 'excluded' in s 25 so as to include a reference to ss 33 to 47 of the 2008 Act. The relevance of this is where the parentage of any person falls to be determined in civil proceedings under s 20 of the 1969 Act.

(vi) Congenital Disabilities (Civil Liability) Act 1976 – extends the meaning of parent to include a person who would be a parent and the reference of 'father'; to include a woman who is a second female parent under ss 42 or 43 of the 2008 Act.

(vii) Magistrates' Courts Act 1980 – replaces the references to s 30 (parental orders) with the new s 54 of the 2008 Act.

(viii) Supreme Court Act 1981 – assigns s 54 (parental orders) of the 2008 Act as matters to be dealt with by the Family Division of the High Court.

(ix) British Nationality Act 1981 – includes a father to be a person who is treated as 'father' under s 28 of the 1990 Act or ss 35 or 26 of the 2008 Act or second female parent under ss 42 or 43 of the 2008 Act.

(x) Family Law Reform Act 1986 – is amended by reference to the new s 2A of the Legitimacy Act 1976 to extend the definition of a legitimated person.

(xi) Family Law Reform Act 1987 – amends references to married couples to include female civil partners and those who had female parenthood agreement at the time of the mother's treatment and were civil partners either at the time of the child's birth or between treatment and birth. It permits void civil partnerships to be treated as valid civil partnerships where either or both partners believed the civil partnership to be valid.

There are also amendments to the succession of intestacy so that references to 'father' include a second female parent under s 43 of the 2008 Act. There is also a presumption that a person is not survived by an unmarried father.

(xii) Children Act 1989 – is amended to enable a second female parent to have parental responsibility for a child. This is automatic where she and the mother were in a civil partnership at the time of the fertility treatment or where the two were civil partners either at the child's birth or at any time between treatment and the child's birth. It is also possible for the second female parent to acquire parental responsibility by registering as the child's parent in the register of births by means of a parental responsibility agreement or court order. A second female parent also acquires parental responsibility under a residence order if she does not already have it by the court making a parental responsibility order. The duration of orders and agreements is until the child attains the age of 18 unless it is terminated earlier. A second female parent is also included in the definition of father under the financial provision of Sch 1.

(xiii) Human Fertilisation and Embryology Act 1990 – amendments permit the HFEA to comply with a request from the Registrar General to disclose information from the HFEA's register in respect of the parenthood of a child and in respect of proceedings under the Congenital Disabilities (Civil Liability) Act 1976, where there are second female parents under ss 42 or 43 of the 2008 Act.

(xiv) Child Support Act 1991 – amendments are made to include references to the new parental orders and parenthood provisions.

(xv) Family Law Act 1996 – replaces the references to s 30 (parental orders) with the new s 54 of the 2008 Act.

(xvi) Access to Justice Act 1999 – replaces the references to s 30 (parental orders) with the new s 54 of the 2008 Act.

(xvii)Adoption and Children Act 2002 – amends the section on adoption by one person to include a reference to cases where there is no other parent by virtue of ss 34 to 47 of the 2008 Act.

(xviii)Mental Capacity Act 2005 – the amendments mean that the provisions of the Mental Capacity Act 2005 do not enable a decision on the giving of consent to be made on behalf of another person.

Amendments in Part 2

11.62

(i) Children and Young Persons (Scotland) Act 1937 – allows for the second female parent to be deemed to have parental responsibilities for the purpose of offences even if not so registered.

(ii) Registration of Births, Deaths and Marriages (Scotland) Act 1965 – amendments mean that a second female parent pursuant to s 42 of the 2008 Act is obliged to give information relating to a birth. There is also parity created with unmarried fathers and second female parents in respect of other provisions within the 1965 Act.

(iii) Family Law (Scotland) 1985 – extends the definition of a child of the family to include a child where both partners were by virtue of ss 33 and 42 civil partners at the time of treatment.

(iv) Children (Scotland) Act 1995 – inserts provisions in relation to the second female partner in circumstances concerning parental responsibility and definitions of a child of the family.

(v) Criminal Law (Consolidation) (Scotland) Act 1995 – amendments mean that the offence of incest applies as between mothers, fathers and second female partners on one hand and their children on the other, where that legal relationship is created by the 2008 Act.

(vi) Adoption and Children (Scotland) Act 2007 – extends the section on adoption by one person who is the child's natural parent to include a reference to cases where there is no other parent by virtue of ss 28 to 47 of the 2008 Act.

Amendments in Part 3

11.63

(i) Legitimacy Act (Northern Ireland) 1928 – makes provision for legitimisation of a person born to a woman as a result of assisted conception if there was a female parenthood agreement with which she entered into a civil partnership after the birth of the child, provided that the second female is domiciled in Northern Ireland.

(ii) Births and Deaths Registration (Northern Ireland) Order 1976 – extends references to father to include a civil partner of the mother or a second female parenthood agreement and a qualified applicant to include a second female parent with parental responsibility. There is also provision made in respect of registration of births where a parenthood agreement is in place.

(iii)   Family Law Reform (Northern Ireland) Order 1977– is amended so that a person who is a parent by virtue of the 2008 Act provisions is not excluded as a legal parent on the basis of DNA tests.

(iv)   Adoption (Northern Ireland) Order 1987 – amends the section whereby s 28 of the 1990 Act means that there is no parent other than the mother to include those children where there is no other parent by virtue of ss 34 to 47 of the 2008 Act.

(v)   Child Support (Northern Ireland) Order 1991 – amendments are made to include references to the new parental orders and parenthood provisions.

(vi)   Children (Northern Ireland) Order 1995 – replaces the references to s 30 (parental orders) with the new s 54 of the 2008 Act. Provision is made with regard to second female parents and parental responsibility and legitimacy. A second female parent is also included in the definition of father under Sch 1 and in respect of succession in cases of intestacy.

(vii)   Family Homes and Domestic Violence (Northern Ireland) Order 1998 – in respect of recognised family proceedings. The references to s 30 (parental orders) are replaced with the new s 54 of the 2008 Act.

PARENTAL ORDERS

11.64   Parental orders allow court orders to be made in favour of couples where a child has been conceived using the gametes of at least one of the couple, and has been carried by a surrogate mother for the child to be treated in law as the child of the applicants. A parental order is in one sense a 'fast-track' adoption because as from November 2004 it was possible for the legal parenthood to be transferred to the commissioning couple of a child who was born to a surrogate mother under a parental order rather than through a full adoption procedure.[93]

11.65   The 2008 Act repeals s 30 of the 1990 Act which dealt with the parental orders which could be made in favour of gamete donors. The new provisions for parental orders are set out in s 54. The new provisions now extend the categories that are able to apply from just married couples to civil partners, unmarried opposite-sex couples or same-sex couples not in a civil partnership. The new provisions are not expected to be in force until 6 April 2010 and new regulations will need to be drafted to implement the new statutory provisions. There are no draft regulations available at the moment and such regulations will take into account a review by the Ministry of Justice and also the review of surrogacy to be undertaken by the Department of Health later in 2009.

---

[93]   The Parental Orders (Human Fertilisation and Embryology) Regulations 1994 brought into effect s 30 of the 1990 Act.

Procedure to apply for a parental order

11.66   The application is for an order for the applicant to treat the child in law as their child. The child must have been carried by a woman who is not one of the applicants as a result of the placing in her of an embryo or eggs or sperm or by artificial insemination[94] and this can take place anywhere in the world,[95] and the gametes of at least one of the applicants should have been used to bring about the creation of the embryos.[96]

The application

11.67   The application for a parental order in England and Wales is deemed to be 'family proceedings' for the purposes of the Children Act 1989 and jurisdiction is determined under s 92(7)–(10) and Part 1 of Sch 11 to the Children Act 1989.[97]

11.68   In Scotland, the court means the Court of Session or the Sheriff Court in the sheriffdom within which the child is and in Northern Ireland this means the High Court or the county court depending upon the division in which the child is.[98]

11.69   The application has to be made by two people, who must either be married, or civil partners of each other or two persons who are living as partners in an enduring family relationship and who are not within prohibited degrees of relationship in relation to each other.[99]

11.70   Therefore a single person remains unable to apply, but such a person would be able to apply to adopt the child from the surrogate mother pursuant to the Adoption and Children Act 2002.

11.71   The application must be made within six months from the day that the child is born,[100] save where the application is in respect of a child who was born before the coming into force of this s 54 and is made by two people who throughout the period that s 30 (2) of the 1990 Act applied (ie a married heterosexual couple) were not eligible to apply for a parental order. In that case the application for a parental order can be made within the period of six months beginning from the date on which s 54 comes into force.[101]

11.72   In addition to the above, the court can make a parental order if the following conditions are satisfied:

---

[94]   The 2008 Act, s 54(1)(a).
[95]   The 2008 Act, s 54(10).
[96]   The 2008 Act, s 54(1)(b).
[97]   The 2008 Act, s 54(9).
[98]   The 2008 Act, s 54(9)(b) and (c).
[99]   Prohibited family relationships are set out in s 58(2) and described above.
[100]   The 2008 Act, s 54(3).
[101]   The 2008 Act, s 54(11).

(i) the application is made by two people;[102] and

(ii) the child has been carried by a surrogate who has been artificially inseminated or had the placement of an embryo or gametes[103] and this can take place in the UK or anywhere else;[104] and

(iii) the gametes of at least one of the applicants were used in the creation of the embryo;[105] and

(iv) the child's home must be with the applicants;[106] and

(v) at least one of the applicants must be domiciled in the UK, the Channel Islands or the Isle of Man;[107]

(vi) the applicants must both have been aged 18 or over;[108] and

(vii) the court also must be satisfied of the following:
- that the woman who carried the child and any other person who is a parent of the child but is not one of the applicants has freely and with full understanding of what is involved agreed unconditionally to the making of the parental order;
- that the consent of the woman who carried the child is ineffective for these purposes if given by her less than six weeks after the child's birth;
- that the agreement of a person who cannot be found or is incapable of giving agreement is ineffective;
- that no money or other benefit (save for reasonable expenses incurred) shall have been given or received by either of the applicants for or in consideration of making the order, any agreement required for the making of this application, the handing over of the child to the applicants or the making of arrangements with a view to the making of the order, unless authorised by the court.[109]

REGULATIONS

11.73 There is a power given to the Secretary of State to make such regulations to modify the main enactments about adoption to take into

---

[102] The 2008 Act, s 54(1).
[103] The 2008 Act, s 54(1)(a).
[104] The 2008 Act, s 54(10).
[105] The 2008 Act, s 54(1)(b).
[106] The 2008 Act, s 54(4)(a).
[107] The 2008 Act, s 54(4)(b).
[108] The 2008 Act, s 54(5).
[109] The 2008 Act, s 54(8).

account s 54 and to make any enactments as are necessary or desirable to make incidental or supplementary provisions.[110]

---

[110] The 2008 Act, s 55.

Chapter 12

DONORS AND INFORMATION

INTRODUCTION

12.1 Assisted reproduction technology has always relied upon donors to come forward to donate gametes and embryos in order to provide a better chance of conception for those having difficulty to conceive a child. The UK has rejected the payment of these donors but instead has opted for voluntary gamete and embryo donors to whom reasonable expenses and reimbursements may be made by the clinics and centres, as set out in the Code of Practice.[1]

12.2 There has been a tension between those who donate their sperm and eggs and the right that they have expressed to do that anonymously and the rights of the resulting child to know details and/or the identity of the donor, who is a genetic parent to them. The 1990 Act proceeded on the basis that donations could be made anonymously and that the balance should be in favour of providing donations so at least prospective parents who were prepared to use donated gametes had the opportunity of bearing children. There have been judicial challenges to donor anonymity and the law was changed with the introduction of The Human Fertilisation and Embryology (Disclosure of Donor Information) Regulations 2004[2] which removed the right of new donors to remain anonymous once the child has reached the age of 18 years.

12.3 The HFEA is under a statutory duty to keep a register of information that it obtains which relate to the provision of treatment services, the keeping or use of any gametes or an embryo taken from a woman or the procurement or destruction of sperm for certain purposes. The HFEA also have to keep a register of information obtained by it about the resulting children of treatment services. There are provisions to request and release certain information in relation to donor-conceived children.

12.4 This Chapter looks at the extensive changes which have been introduced by the 2008 Act to the issues of the register of information and the disclosure

---

[1] Draft 8th Code of Practice, Part 13 provides for the reimbursement of all reasonable out-of-pocket expenses incurred in the UK in connection with the donation eg travel to the centre and the loss of earnings limited to a maximum amount of £250 per day. Egg donors who become ill as a direct result of the donation may claim reasonable expenses arising from the illness.

[2] SI 2004/1511.

of information in respect of donors and donor-conceived children. The previous s 31 has been replaced by new provisions at s 31–31(ZG) of the 1990 Act.

12.5 There are also other types of disclosure which will be examined at the end of the Chapter.

THE REGISTER OF INFORMATION

12.6 The HFEA has to keep a register of the information which relates to the following matters:[3]

(i) identifying the individual for whom treatment services, other than basic partner treatment services, were provided;

(ii) the procurement or distribution of any sperm, save that which is partner-donated sperm and has not been stored, in the course of providing non-medical fertility services for any identifiable individual;

(iii) the keeping of the gametes of any identifiable individual;

(iv) the keeping of an embryo taken from any identifiable woman;

(v) the use of gametes of any identifiable individual other than for their use for the purpose of basic partner treatment services;

(vi) the use of an embryo taken from any identifiable woman;

(vii) identifying an individual who was or may have been born in consequence of treatment services, other than basic partner treatment services;

(viii) identifying an individual who was or may have been born in consequence of the procurement or distribution of any sperm, other than partner-donor sperm which has not been stored for the use of providing non-medical services.

12.7 The definition of basic partner treatment services refers to treatment services provided to a woman and a man together without using the gametes of any other person or the creation of an embryo *in vitro*.[4]

12.8 The register of information will not contain information which has been provided for the purposes of the voluntary contact register under s 31ZF(1) which is dealt with below.

---

[3] The 1990 Act, s 31(2) and (4).
[4] The 1990 Act, s 2(1).

12.9 The HFEA obtains this information from the licensed clinics and it holds and retains the information that it held immediately before the commencement of the amended s 31.[5]

REQUESTS FOR INFORMATION

12.10 These take different forms and the information that is released is dependent upon the age of the applicant, the request that is being made and whether the regulations allow the release of identifying information or not. The relevant regulations are the 2004 Regulations which will remain in force save for being updated in terms of consequential amendments to take into account the new definitions now provided by the 2008 Act.

Information about genetic parentage

12.11 A donor-conceived person who is aged 16 may request by notice that the Authority state whether or not the information contained in the register would show that he could or might be the resulting child of gamete donation. The information that can be requested at this stage, if the reply to the request is affirmative is:[6]

- give as much information as the Authority requires under regulations; or

- whether there are other persons that could be his/her donor-conceived half siblings through the use of the gametes of the same donor but are not the donor's legal children, and if so how many, the sex of each of them and the year of their birth.

12.12 The request shall only be complied with if the information in the register shows that the applicant is a 'relevant individual', meaning an individual who was born of treatment services or through the use of sperm which was not partner-donated sperm in the course of providing non-medical fertility services and that the applicant has been given a suitable opportunity to receive proper counselling about the implications of the request.[7]

12.13 Whilst the applicant is under 18 years of age, only non-identifying information can be disclosed.[8] Further, the Authority has a discretion not to comply with the request in relation to half-siblings where it takes the view that special circumstances exist which would increase the likelihood that if the information was given it would enable the applicant to identify the donor, in a case where under regulations, the Authority is not required to give that information or that it would identify the genetic half-sibling.[9]

---

[5]   The 1990 Act, s 319(1), as amended.
[6]   The 1990 Act, s 31ZA(2), as amended.
[7]   The 1990 Act, s 31ZA(3), as amended.
[8]   The 1990 Act, s 31ZA(4), as amended.
[9]   The 1990 Act, s 31ZA(6), as amended.

Information related to intended relationships

12.14　Donor-conceived people are able to find out whether they would be related to the person they intend to marry, enter into a civil partnership with or an intimate physical relationship with or with whom they are already having an intimate physical relationship.[10] In respect of those intending to marry or enter into a civil partnership there is no age limit, but in respect of the physical relationship the applicant has to be aged 16 or over.[11]

12.15　The application has to specify the person whom he may be related to.[12] The Authority will respond to the request if the information in the register shows that the applicant is or might be a donor-conceived child and the specified person consents in writing to the request being made, that consent had not been withdrawn and that the applicant and the specified person have each been given a suitable opportunity for proper counselling about the implications of the request.[13]

12.16　The 2004 Regulations specify the information which the HFEA must provide if a request is made by a donor-conceived person. Where information was provided by a donor before 1 April 2005, certain specified non-identifying information must be provided to the donor-conceived person. Where identifying information was provided by a donor after 31 March 2005, certain identifying and non-identifying information must be provided. Those who ask for information from the register must be given an opportunity to receive counselling.

12.17　Donors who made their donation before 31 March 2005 but after the 1990 Act came into force can opt to re-register as identifiable and identifying information could also be released about them if a request was made by a person conceived as a result of their donation.

12.18　The donor-conceived people will be able to request identifying information about their donor from 2023 onwards, in relation to donors who donated identifiably from April 2005. This could happen sooner if someone donated before April 2005 and elected to re-register as identifiable and a person conceived from his or her donation requested identifying information from the HFEA.

12.19　In practice, the HFEA would try and forewarn the donor before identifying information was given to the donor-conceived applicant. However, this would not always be possible if the donor has failed to provide his up-to-date address. There is no corresponding exchange of information; the HFEA may not disclose identifying information about the donor-conceived person to the donor.

---

[10]　The 1990 Act, s 31ZB(2), as amended.
[11]　The 1990 Act, s 31ZB(4) and (5), as amended.
[12]　The 1990 Act, s 31ZB(2), as amended.
[13]　The 1990 Act, s 31ZB(3), as amended.

Power to inform donor of request

12.20 The HFEA is given the power to inform the donor of the fact that a donor-conceived person has requested information about him, but it may not disclose the identity of the applicant or any information relating to the applicant.[14] This provides protection to the applicants who have sought information from the HFEA and allays any fears that they may have about the donor contacting them.

Request by donor of information

12.21 There are new provisions which enable a donor now or in the past to be provided with information on request about the number, sex and year of birth of children born as a result of their donations.[15]

12.22 They may ask the clinic where they donated or the HFEA, if the clinic has closed, or unable to, or fails to, provide the information. The information can be withheld from the donor if the HFEA is aware that circumstances exist which would mean that releasing the information would increase the likelihood that the donor would be able to identify a child born as a result of their donation.

Information about donor-conceived genetic siblings

12.23 There is a new section which enables donor-conceived people to request and obtain identifying information about their genetic half-siblings who were conceived using gametes from the same donor, where neither is the donor's legal offspring.

12.24 The procedure is where the information contained in the register shows that a donor-conceived individual ('A') is the donor-conceived genetic sibling of another donor-conceived individual ('B') and A has provided information to the Authority that permits A's identity to be disclosed to any of his donor-conceived genetic siblings or to such siblings of a specified description which includes B, then the Authority may disclose the information.[16] However certain conditions have to be met before disclosure takes place, which are as follows:[17]

- A and B have each attained the age of 18;[18] and

- B has requested the disclosure to B of information about any donor-conceived genetic sibling of B;[19] and

---

14 The 1990 Act, s 31ZC(1), as amended.
15 The 1990 Act, s 31ZD(1) and (3), as amended.
16 The 1990 Act, s 31ZE (1) and (2), as amended.
17 The 1990 Act, s 31ZE(2), as amended.
18 The 1990 Act, s 31ZE(3)(a), as amended.
19 The 1990 Act, s 31ZE(3)(b), as amended.

- A and B have each had the opportunity to receive proper counselling about the implication of disclosure;[20]

- the Authority will not disclose information which will lead to the identification of a donor by A or B without the donor's consent unless regulations provide that his or her identity could be released to either of the donor-conceived people on request ie he or she is an anonymous donor.[21]

A voluntary contact register

12.25 A power introduced for the HFEA to set up, or keep, a voluntary contact register of people who would like to receive information about any person to whom they are genetically related to, as a consequence of the provision to any person of assisted conception treatment services in the UK involving donors before the HFEA's register began on 1 August 1991. The terms and operation of such a register have been set out in Chapter 4 as part of the HFEA's duties.

Disclosure of information

12.26 It is necessary on occasions to have disclosure of the information contained on the register. A new s 33A replaces the previous provisions in relation to disclosure.

12.27 The section starts on the premise that the information falling within s 31(2) (that is the information contained in the register) is prohibited from being disclosed. There can be no disclosure of that information in a person's capacity as set out below, unless further provisions apply. The list of those who cannot disclose such protected information is:

- a member or employee of the Authority;[22]

- any person who is exercising the functions of the Authority under agency or contractual arrangements, including their staff and employees;[23]

- any person engaged by the Authority to provide services to the Authority or their sub-contractors;[24]

- any licence holder;[25]

---

[20] The 1990 Act, s 31ZE(3)(c), as amended.
[21] The 1990 Act, s 31ZE(4), as amended.
[22] The 1990 Act, s 33A(1)(a), as amended.
[23] The 1990 Act, s 33A(1)(b), as amended.
[24] The 1990 Act, s 33A(1)(c) and (d), as amended.
[25] The 1990 Act, s 33A(1)(e), as amended.

- any person to whom a third party agreement applies;[26]

- any person to whom directions have been given;[27]

12.28 Disclosure can only occur by reference to the categories of persons or in the circumstances specified in the new s 33A(2). There is now disclosure permitted to other persons or bodies discharging a regulatory function and disclosure permitted to authorised people who are performing functions contracted out to them by the HFEA or under third party agreements, or with the consent of those to whom the information relates in certain circumstances. There is the power to make further regulations to make further exceptions to the prohibition.[28]

12.29 In general, when considering whether it is lawful to disclose the relevant information, the Data Protection Act 1998 or any confidentiality rights will still need to be adhered to and respected.

Disclosure for research purposes

12.30 It has been canvassed that the duties collected by the HFEA on its register of patient information could be usefully used for research. One of the areas which is commonly raised is the need for follow up studies on the safety of IVF and views have been expressed that the information could be of great use to researchers who would wish follow up studies on different treatments or to research the effectiveness of particular treatments and techniques. The absolute ban on the disclosure of any information for these purposes, including where the patient has consented to the information being released, has always hindered this.

12.31 The new legislation enables the Secretary of State to make provision, in regulations, requiring or regulating the disclosure of such protected information falling within s 31(2) for medical research purposes where the Secretary of State considers it necessary or expedient or in the interest of improving patient care.[29]

12.32 The authorisation of disclosure of protected information will not be granted where that information is such that an individual may be identified if it would be reasonably practicable to achieve the aim of the research by some other means, having regard to the costs and technology that is available for that.

12.33 The new provisions under s 33C(2) provide what may be contained in such regulations and it will be seen below that all the statutory guidance has been considered within the drawing up of the draft Regulations. Fees may be

[26] The 1990 Act, s 33A(1)(f), as amended.
[27] The 1990 Act, s 33A(1)(g), as amended.
[28] The 1990 Act, s 33B(1), as amended.
[29] The 1990 Act, s 33C(1)(a), as amended.

charged in accordance with regulations made by the Secretary of State for these purposes. The fees will be of a prescribed amount to be paid to the HFEA and it is intended that the fees charged would recover all or part of the costs of providing the information.

NEW REGULATIONS

12.34   There are draft Regulations pursuant to s 33D of the amended 1990 Act which are formulated to govern the procedure for application for the authorisations for the disclosure and use of protected information for medical or other research purposes.

12.35   The draft Regulations are currently under consultation.[30] As before, whilst making the Regulations the Secretary of State must consult such appropriate bodies who appear to represent the interests of those who are likely to be affected by the Regulations.[31] It is hoped that the Regulations will be in place for the commencement of the new Act in October 2008, but this regulation requires affirmative resolution procedure so the Regulations are to be debated in both houses of parliament.

Outline of the draft Regulations

12.36   The principal aim of the Regulations is to allow information that is held on the HFEA register to be made available to researchers in certain limited circumstances. The protected information means information entered on the register between 1 August 1991 and the coming into force of the Regulations which relates to or identifies individuals but it excludes donor information, which can only be released with consent.[32]

12.37   The key proposals are that the HFEA will consider the applications for the information relying on the expertise and resources of the Patient Information Advisory Group which currently approves access to NHS data.

12.38   The process of authorisation set out is for the request to be made in writing by an appropriate person nominated by the research establishment,[33] which is a university or other body or institution that carried our medical or other research in the UK.[34] The request has to set out, *inter alia,* details about the applicant and the research that is being undertaken and what the projected information wants to process, why it is necessary for the purpose of the research project, why such protected information cannot be obtained by other

---

[30]   The draft Human Fertilisation and Embryology (Disclosure of Information for Research Purposes) Regulations 2009.
[31]   The 1990 Act, s 33C(3)(8), as amended.
[32]   Reg 2(1)(a)–(f).
[33]   Reg 4(2).
[34]   Draft Regulations, reg 2(1)(f).

means and a description of the security arrangements in place at the premises where the protected information will be processed.[35]

12.39 The HFEA is able to levy fees for processing the application and where approved for the collating and issuing of the projected information.[36] It is also able to enter into agency arrangements for the provision of its statutory functions or to contract those functions out to a third party.[37]

12.40 There is provision that if approval has been given under s 251 of the National Health Services Act 2006 then that will be considered sufficient approval under these Regulations, unless the HFEA has special reasons for not releasing the protected information.[38]

12.41 The application will be refused if the research does have ethics committee approval, identifying information that is not needed to achieve the aims of the research project, security arrangements that have to be provided for or if it remains practicable to obtain consent from the person to whom the information relates. There are also grounds for revoking the authorisation.[39]

12.42 There will be conditions attached to the use of the protected information, and the HFEA can add additional conditions. Any authorisation given can be suspended if there is a failure to comply with what the conditions disclose or if inaccurate information has been supplied to the HFEA.[40]

12.43 There is a three-year maximum period for a single authorisation and the HFEA has to release the protected information in 90 days from the date of notification of the decision. The information must be destroyed when the authorisation expires the purpose for which it is sought, or is satisfied or the authorisation is revoked.[41]

12.44 The applicant has to submit an annual report to the HFEA to allow for the monitoring of the use of the protected information with the HFEA able to specify what should be contained in such reports. There is a power for the HFEA to inspect the research centres if necessary with the consent of the research centre. The HFEA is to establish an Oversight committee to monitor the operation of the application process and the processing of protected information.[42]

---

[35] Reg 4(3).
[36] Reg 5.
[37] Reg 6.
[38] Reg 7.
[39] Reg 17.
[40] Reg 16.
[41] Reg 18.
[42] Reg 21.

DISCLOSURE IN THE INTERESTS OF JUSTICE

12.45   In court proceedings to determine whether or not a person is the parent of a child by virtue of ss 27 to 29 of the 1990 Act or ss 33 to 47 of 2008 Act, a party may apply for to the court for an order requiring the Authority to disclose whether there is any relevant information contained in the Register of Information under s 31 and if there is to disclose the information that is sought in that court order.[43] However, such a court order could not seek the disclosure of information about the keeping of gametes and the use of gametes taken from any identifiable persons save if the use is for their own basic partner treatment nor the keeping or use of embryos taken from any identifiable woman.[44]

12.46   The court would grant such an order if it is satisfied that it is in the interests of justice to do so, and this involves taking into consideration any representations made by any individuals who could be affected by the disclosure and the welfare of the child, if under the age of 18 and of any other person under that age who may also be affected by the disclosure.[45]

12.47   In civil proceedings, it is open to the court to consider if all or any part of the proceedings shall be conducted in camera.[46] An application for such closed proceedings shall under this provision be heard in camera unless the court directs otherwise.[47]

CONGENITAL DISABILITIES

12.48   There are amendments to the Congenital Disabilities (Civil Liability) Act 1976 that deal with civil actions arising from a child being born disabled which extends the ambit of liability to cover infertility treatments.[48] There are also provisions in 1990 Act to deal with when and how liability falls.[49] There is a new amendment under the 2008 Act so that references to father now will include references to a second female parent.[50]

12.49   Where for the purposes of such proceedings it is necessary to identify a person who would or might be the parent of the child but for the provisions of ss 27 to 29 of the 1990 Act and ss 33 to 47 of the 2008 Act, then the court can be requested to require the Authority to disclose any identifying information in

---

43   The 1990 Act, s 34(1), as amended.
44   The 1990 Act, s 34(1)(b), as amended.
45   The 1990 Act, s 34(2).
46   The 1990 Act, s 34(3).
47   The 1990 Act, s34(4).
48   The 1990 Act, s 44(1A), as amended.
49   The 1990 Act, s 44.
50   The 2008 Act, Sch 6, para 14.

the Register of Information.[51] Corresponding provisions are made for any action or prospective action for damages in such cases in Scotland.[52]

---

[51] The 1990 Act, s 35(1) and (2A), as amended.
[52] The 1990 Act, s 35(2), as amended.

Chapter 13

MISCELLANEOUS PROVISIONS AND AMENDMENTS TO SURROGACY PROVISIONS

13.1 This Chapter will set out the amendments and the position in relation to surrogacy in terms of the link it has with assisted reproduction technology and the means by which it is sought to regulate this area. There is also provision in relation to conscientious objections.

SURROGACY

Background

13.2 A surrogate mother is a woman who carries a child for another with the intention that after the birth of the child the child shall be handed over to another. That person is referred to as the commissioning person or commissioning couple. The surrogate mother may be a stranger or a woman known to the commissioning person or couple eg a friend or relative. There is a distinction to be drawn between a 'full' surrogacy where the commissioning couple's sperm and egg are fertilised *in vitro* and implanted into the surrogate mother, and 'partial' surrogacy where the surrogate mother's egg is inseminated using the commissioning male's sperm.

13.3 Surrogacy is usually entered into for medical reasons concerning the commissioning couple. For example, where the commissioning female has difficulty with or cannot carry a child to term or where the commissioning couple are a male homosexual couple.

13.4 As full surrogacy involves *in vitro* fertilisation it comes within the remit of the HFEA's regulation. On the other hand, 'partial' surrogacy can be carried out by the parties themselves without involving treatment in fertility clinics and is not able to be effectively controlled or regulated. It also does not allow for effective monitoring of the incidences and the outcome of partial surrogacy in contrast with the obtaining and maintaining of information and records that the HFEA is charged with carrying out in respect of other treatments.

13.5 The Warnock Committee's remit included looking at surrogacy as concerns were raised about the ethics of it and controlling it.[1] The resulting legislation reflected the competing aims of trying to discourage the practice of surrogacy but at the same time attempting to provide the children born of such arrangements some protection and also the aim of trying to provide some protection for the surrogate mother.

13.6 Under the Surrogacy Arrangements Act 1985 surrogacy arrangements are not enforceable in law.

13.7 There was also a move to avoid commercialisation of surrogacy, the 1985 Act prohibits organisations or people other than the intended parents or surrogate mothers themselves from undertaking certain activities relating to surrogacy on a commercial basis.

13.8 There is an amendment which allows bodies that operate on a not-for-profit basis to receive payment for providing some surrogacy services. It does so by exempting them from the prohibition in the current law.

13.9 This clause separates out into four categories the activities which are prohibited if done on a commercial basis. Not-for-profit bodies are permitted to receive payments for carrying out the initial negotiations with a view to making of surrogacy arrangements. For example, it may charge for the interested parties to meet each other to discuss the possibility of surrogacy arrangements between them. The second is compiling information about surrogacy. The not-for-profit bodies would be able to charge for establishing and keeping lists of people willing to be surrogate mothers or intended parents wishing to have discussions with a potential surrogate mother.

13.10 It will remain the position that non-for-profit organisations will not be permitted to receive payment for offering to negotiate a surrogacy arrangement or for taking part in negotiations about surrogacy arrangements. However, these activities are not unlawful if there is no charge.

13.11 The Act changes in relation to advertising by non-profit making bodies. The 1985 Act makes it an offence to publish or distribute an advertisement that someone may be willing to enter into surrogacy arrangements, or that anyone is looking for a surrogate mother, or that anyone is willing to facilitate or negotiate such an arrangement. The clause provides that this prohibition does not apply to an advertisement placed by, or on behalf of, a non-profit making body provided that the advertisement only refers to activities which may legally be undertaken on a commercial basis. This would mean that a not-for-profit body could advertise that it held a list of people seeking surrogate mothers and a list of people willing to be involved in surrogacy, and that it could bring them

---

[1]   The conclusions of the Warnock Committee were that it considered surrogacy arrangements nearly always to be unethical but there was a recognition that the practice would nevertheless continue.

together for discussion. It remains illegal for anyone to advertise that they want a surrogate mother or to be a surrogate mother.

CONSCIENTIOUS OBJECTION

13.12 The 1990 Act provides a 'conscientious objection' clause in the event that if someone has a 'conscientious objection' to participating in any activity governed by the statutes eg assisted reproduction treatment or embryo research, then they would not be bound to perform or undertake it.[2] This provision was imposed due to the ethical element that many of the activities governed by the Act could have. It is a similar provision to that contained in s 4 of the Abortion Act 1967. It is not a means by which potential patients who are seeking treatment can be permitted or refused that treatment on personal views or religious convictions, eg under the provisions of s 13(5) of the 1990 Act. The draft 8th Code of Practice refers to the duty imposed on the person responsible to ensure that this provision is not being used to perpetrate unlawful discrimination.[3]

13.13 In legal proceedings, the burden of proof of conscientious objection rests upon the person claiming it.[4] This burden of proof is discharged in any Scottish court proceedings by the person providing a statement on oath to the effect that he has a conscientious objection to participating in a particular activity governed by the Acts.[5]

---

[2]   The 1990 Act, s 38(1).
[3]   Draft 8th Code of Practice, Part 29, para 9.
[4]   The 1990 Act, s 38(2).
[5]   The 1990 Act, s 38(3).

Appendix 1

HUMAN FERTILISATION AND EMBRYOLOGY ACT 2008

ARRANGEMENT OF SECTIONS

PART 1

AMENDMENTS OF THE HUMAN FERTILISATION AND
EMBRYOLOGY ACT 1990

Principal terms used in the 1990 Act

PART 1
AMENDMENTS OF THE HUMAN FERTILISATION AND EMBRYOLOGY ACT 1990

Principal terms used in the 1990 Act

1 Meaning of "embryo" and "gamete"

(1) Section 1 of the 1990 Act (meaning of "embryo", "gamete" and associated expressions) is amended as follows.

(2) For subsection (1) substitute—

(1) In this Act (except in section 4A or in the term "human admixed embryo")—

(a) embryo means a live human embryo and does not include a human admixed embryo (as defined by section 4A(6)), and

(b) references to an embryo include an egg that is in the process of fertilisation or is undergoing any other process capable of resulting in an embryo.

(3) In subsection (2), for paragraph (a) substitute—

(a) references to embryos the creation of which was brought about in vitro (in their application to those where fertilisation or any other process by which an embryo is created is complete) are to those where fertilisation or any other process by which the embryo was created began outside the human body whether or not it was completed there, and.

(4) For subsection (4) substitute—

(4) In this Act (except in section 4A)—

(a) references to eggs are to live human eggs, including cells of the female germ line at any stage of maturity, but (except in subsection (1)(b)) not including eggs that are in the process of fertilisation or are undergoing any other process capable of resulting in an embryo,

(b) references to sperm are to live human sperm, including cells of the male germ line at any stage of maturity, and

(c) references to gametes are to be read accordingly.

(5) After subsection (5) insert—

(6) If it appears to the Secretary of State necessary or desirable to do so in the light of developments in science or medicine, regulations may provide that in this Act (except in section 4A) "embryo", "eggs", "sperm" or "gametes" includes things specified in the regulations which would not otherwise fall within the definition.

(7) Regulations made by virtue of subsection (6) may not provide for anything containing any nuclear or mitochondrial DNA that is not human to be treated as an embryo or as eggs, sperm or gametes.

2 Meaning of "nuclear DNA"

In section 2(1) of the 1990 Act (other terms), after the definition of "non-medical fertility services" insert—

'nuclear DNA', in relation to an embryo, includes DNA in the pronucleus of the embryo.

Activities governed by the 1990 Act

3 Prohibitions in connection with embryos

(1) Section 3 of the 1990 Act (prohibitions in connection with embryos) is amended as follows.

(2) For subsection (2) substitute—

    (2) No person shall place in a woman—

        (a)   an embryo other than a permitted embryo (as defined by section 3ZA), or

        (b)   any gametes other than permitted eggs or permitted sperm (as so defined)."

(3) In subsection (3)—

        (a)   at the end of paragraph (b), insert "or", and

        (b)   omit paragraph (d) and the word "or" immediately before it.

(4) In subsection (4), for "the day when the gametes are mixed" substitute "the day on which the process of creating the embryo began.

(5) After section 3 insert—

3ZA Permitted eggs, permitted sperm and permitted embryos

(1) This section has effect for the interpretation of section 3(2).

(2) A permitted egg is one—

        (a)   which has been produced by or extracted from the ovaries of a woman, and

        (b)   whose nuclear or mitochondrial DNA has not been altered.

(3) Permitted sperm are sperm—

        (a)   which have been produced by or extracted from the testes of a man, and

        (b)   whose nuclear or mitochondrial DNA has not been altered.

(4) An embryo is a permitted embryo if—

        (a)   it has been created by the fertilisation of a permitted egg by permitted sperm,

        (b)   no nuclear or mitochondrial DNA of any cell of the embryo has been altered, and

        (c)   no cell has been added to it other than by division of the embryo's own cells.

(5) Regulations may provide that—

        (a)   an egg can be a permitted egg, or

        (b)   an embryo can be a permitted embryo, even though the egg or embryo has had applied to it in prescribed circumstances a prescribed process designed to prevent the transmission of serious mitochondrial disease.

(6) In this section—

(a) "woman" and "man" include respectively a girl and a boy (from birth), and

(b) "prescribed" means prescribed by regulations.

(6) The Human Reproductive Cloning Act 2001 (c. 23) (which is superseded by the preceding provisions of this section) ceases to have effect.

4 Prohibitions in connection with genetic material not of human origin

(1) In section 4 of the 1990 Act (prohibitions in connection with gametes)—

(a) in subsection (1), omit—
(i)   paragraph (c), and
(ii) the word "or" immediately before it, and

(b) in subsection (5), after "section 3" insert "or 4A".

(2) After section 4 of the 1990 Act insert—

4A Prohibitions in connection with genetic material not of human origin

(1) No person shall place in a woman—

(2) No person shall—

(a) mix human gametes with animal gametes,
(b) bring about the creation of a human admixed embryo, or
(c) keep or use a human admixed embryo, except in pursuance of a licence.

(3) A licence cannot authorise keeping or using a human admixed embryo after the earliest of the following—

(a) the appearance of the primitive streak, or
(b) the end of the period of 14 days beginning with the day on which the process of creating the human admixed embryo began, but not counting any time during which the human admixed embryo is stored.

(4) A licence cannot authorise placing a human admixed embryo in an animal.

(5) A licence cannot authorise keeping or using a human admixed embryo in any circumstances in which regulations prohibit its keeping or use.

(6) For the purposes of this Act a human admixed embryo is—

(a) an embryo created by replacing the nucleus of an animal egg or of an animal cell, or two animal pronuclei, with—
(i)   two human pronuclei,
(ii)   one nucleus of a human gamete or of any other human cell, or
(iii) one human gamete or other human cell,
(b) any other embryo created by using—
(i)   human gametes and animal gametes, or
(ii) one human pronucleus and one animal pronucleus,
(c) a human embryo that has been altered by the introduction of any sequence of nuclear or mitochondrial DNA of an animal into one or more cells of the embryo,
(d) a human embryo that has been altered by the introduction of one or more animal cells, or

(e) any embryo not falling within paragraphs (a) to (d) which contains both nuclear or mitochondrial DNA of a human and nuclear or mitochondrial DNA of an animal ("animal DNA") but in which the animal DNA is not predominant.

(7) In subsection (6)—

(a) references to animal cells are to cells of an animal or of an animal embryo, and

(b) references to human cells are to cells of a human or of a human embryo.

(8) For the purposes of this section an "animal" is an animal other than man.

(9) In this section "embryo" means a live embryo, including an egg that is in the process of fertilisation or is undergoing any other process capable of resulting in an embryo.

(10) In this section—

(a) references to eggs are to live eggs, including cells of the female germ line at any stage of maturity, but (except in subsection (9)) not including eggs that are in the process of fertilisation or are undergoing any other process capable of resulting in an embryo, and

(b) references to gametes are to eggs (as so defined) or to live sperm, including cells of the male germ line at any stage of maturity.

(11) If it appears to the Secretary of State necessary or desirable to do so in the light of developments in science or medicine, regulations may—

(a) amend (but not repeal) paragraphs (a) to (e) of subsection (6);

(b) provide that in this section "embryo", "eggs" or "gametes" includes things specified in the regulations which would not otherwise fall within the definition.

(12) Regulations made by virtue of subsection (11)(a) may make any amendment of subsection (7) that appears to the Secretary of State to be appropriate in consequence of any amendment of subsection (6).

The Human Fertilisation and Embryology Authority

5 Membership of Authority: disqualification and tenure

Schedule 1 contains amendments of Schedule 1 to the 1990 Act (which are about disqualification for appointment to membership of the Authority and the tenure of office of members).

6 Additional general functions of Authority

(1) In section 8 of the 1990 Act (general functions of the Authority), renumber the existing provision as subsection (1) of that section.

(2) In that subsection—

(a) omit the word "and" immediately after paragraph (c), and

(b) after that paragraph insert—

(ca) maintain a statement of the general principles which it considers should be followed—

(i) in the carrying-on of activities governed by this Act, and

(ii) in the carrying-out of its functions in relation to such activities,

(cb) promote, in relation to activities governed by this Act, compliance with—

(i) requirements imposed by or under this Act, and

(ii) the code of practice under section 25 of this Act, and.

(3) After that subsection, insert—

(2) The Authority may, if it thinks fit, charge a fee for any advice provided under subsection (1)(c).

7 Duties in relation to carrying out its functions

After section 8 (general functions of the Authority) insert—

8ZA Duties in relation to carrying out its functions

(1) The Authority must carry out its functions effectively, efficiently and economically.

(2) In carrying out its functions, the Authority must, so far as relevant, have regard to the principles of best regulatory practice (including the principles under which regulatory activities should be transparent, accountable, proportionate, consistent and targeted only at cases in which action is needed).

8 Power to contract out functions etc

After section 8A of the 1990 Act (duty of Authority to communicate with competent authorities of other EEA states) insert—

8B Agency arrangements and provision of services

(1) Arrangements may be made between the Authority and a government department, a public authority or the holder of a public office ("the other authority") for—

(a)   any functions of the Authority to be exercised by, or by members of the staff of, the other authority, or

(b)   the provision by the other authority of administrative, professional or technical services to the Authority.

(2) Arrangements under subsection (1)(a) do not affect responsibility for the carrying-out of the Authority's functions.

(3) Subsection (1)(a) does not apply to any function of making subordinate legislation (within the meaning of the Interpretation Act 1978).

8C Contracting out functions of Authority

(1) This section applies to any function of the Authority other than—

(a)   any function which, by virtue of any enactment, may be exercised only by members of the Authority,

(b)   a function excluded from this section by subsection (2), or

(c)   a function excluded from this section by the Secretary of State by order.

(2) A function is excluded from this section if—

(a) it relates to the grant, revocation or variation of any licence,

(b) it is a power or right of entry, search or seizure into or of any property, or

(c) it is a function of making subordinate legislation (within the meaning of the Interpretation Act 1978).

(3) The Authority may make arrangements with any person ("the authorised person") for the exercise by that person, or by the employees of that person, of any function of the Authority to which this section applies.

(4) Any arrangements made by the Authority under this section—

(a) may be revoked at any time by the Authority, and

(b) do not prevent the Authority from exercising any function to which the arrangements relate.

(5) Subject to subsection (6), anything done or omitted to be done by or in relation to the authorised person (or an employee of the authorised person) in, or in connection with, the exercise or purported exercise of any function to which the arrangements relate is to be treated for all purposes as done or omitted to be done by or in relation to the Authority.

(6) Subsection (5) does not apply—

(a) for the purposes of so much of any contract between the authorised person and the Authority as relates to the exercise of the function, or

(b) for the purposes of any criminal proceedings brought in respect of anything done or omitted to be done by the authorised person (or any employee of the authorised person).

(7) Section 38A(2) of this Act (which relates to the keeping of embryos, human admixed embryos and gametes) applies in relation to the authorised person or any employee of the authorised person, when exercising functions of the Authority, as it applies in relation to any member or employee of the Authority exercising functions as member or employee.

8D Disclosure of information where functions of Authority exercised by others

(1) This section applies to—

(a) the Authority,

(b) any public authority or other person exercising functions of the Authority by virtue of section 8B,

(c) any member of staff of any person falling within paragraph (b),

(d) any person exercising functions of the Authority by virtue of section 8C,

(e) an employee of any person falling within paragraph (d), or

(f) any person engaged by the Authority to provide services to the Authority.

(2) No obligation of confidence is to prevent the disclosure of information by a person to whom this section applies to another such person if the disclosure is necessary or expedient for the purposes of the exercise of any function of the Authority.

9 Power to assist other public authorities

After section 8D (inserted by section 8 above) insert—

8E Power to assist other public authorities

(1) The Authority may if it thinks it appropriate to do so provide assistance to any other public authority in the United Kingdom for the purpose of the exercise by that authority of its functions.

(2) Assistance provided by the Authority under this section may be provided on such terms, including terms as to payment, as it thinks fit.

10 Power to delegate and establish committees

For section 9 (licence committees and other committees) of the 1990 Act substitute—

9A Power to delegate and establish committees

(1) The Authority may delegate a function to a committee, to a member or to staff.

(2) The Authority may establish such committees or sub-committees as it thinks fit (whether to advise the Authority or to exercise a function delegated to it by the Authority).

(3) Subject to any provision made by regulations under section 20A (appeals committees), the members of the committees or subcommittees may include persons who are not members of the Authority.

(4) Subsection (1) has effect subject to any enactment requiring a decision to be taken by members of the Authority or by a committee consisting of members of the Authority.

Scope of licences

11 Activities that may be licensed

(1) In section 11 of the 1990 Act (licences for treatment, storage and research), in subsection (1)(b), for "and embryos" substitute ", embryos or human admixed embryos".

(2) Schedule 2 contains amendments of Schedule 2 to the 1990 Act (which relates to the activities for which licences may be granted under the Act).

(3) The Human Fertilisation and Embryology (Research Purposes) Regulations 2001 (S.I. 2001/188) (which are superseded by the amendments made by Schedule 2) cease to have effect.

Licence conditions

12 General conditions of licences

(1) Section 12 of the 1990 Act (general conditions of licences under that Act) is amended as follows.

(2) In subsection (1)—

    (a)   in paragraph (c)(condition relating to compliance with Schedule 3 to the Act), omit "or non-medical fertility services", and

    (b)   in paragraphs (e) and (f) (which relate to the supply of gametes or embryos), for "or embryos" substitute ", embryos or human admixed embryos".

(3) In subsection (2)—

    (a)   omit the "and" at the end of paragraph (a), and

    (b)   at the end of paragraph (b) insert ", and

    (c)   every licence under paragraph 3 of that Schedule, so far as authorising activities in connection with the derivation from embryos of stem cells that are intended for human application.

13 Consent to use or storage of gametes, embryos, human admixed embryos etc

Schedule 3 contains amendments of Schedule 3 to the 1990 Act (which relates to consent to the use or storage of gametes or embryos).

14 Conditions of licences for treatment

(1) Section 13 of the 1990 Act (conditions of licences for treatment) is amended in accordance with subsections (2) to (4).

(2) In subsection (5)—

    (a)   omit ", other than basic partner treatment services,", and

    (b)   for "a father" substitute "supportive parenting".

(3) For subsection (6) substitute—

(6) A woman shall not be provided with treatment services of a kind specified in Part 1 of Schedule 3ZA unless she and any man or woman who is to be treated together with her have been given a suitable opportunity to receive proper counselling about the implications of her being provided with treatment services of that kind, and have been provided with such relevant information as is proper.

(6A) A woman shall not be provided with treatment services after the happening of any event falling within any paragraph of Part 2 of Schedule 3ZA unless (before or after the event) she and the intended second parent have been given a suitable opportunity to receive proper counselling about the implications of the woman being provided with treatment services after the happening of that event, and have been provided with such relevant information as is proper.

(6B) The reference in subsection (6A) to the intended second parent is a reference to—

    (a)   any man as respects whom the agreed fatherhood conditions in section 37 of the Human Fertilisation and Embryology Act 2008 ("the 2008 Act") are for the time being satisfied in relation to treatment provided to the woman mentioned in subsection (6A), and

    (b)   any woman as respects whom the agreed female parenthood conditions in section 44 of the 2008 Act are for the time being satisfied in relation to treatment provided to the woman mentioned in subsection (6A).

(6C) In the case of treatment services falling within paragraph 1 of Schedule 3ZA (use of gametes of a person not receiving those services) or paragraph 3 of that Schedule (use of embryo taken from a woman not receiving those services), the information provided by virtue of subsection (6) or (6A) must include such information as is proper about—

    (a)   the importance of informing any resulting child at an early age that the child results from the gametes of a person who is not a parent of the child, and

    (b)   suitable methods of informing such a child of that fact.

(6D) Where the person responsible receives from a person ("X") notice under section 37(1)(c) or 44(1)(c) of the 2008 Act of X's withdrawal of consent to X being treated as the parent of any child resulting from the provision of treatment services to a woman ("W"), the person responsible—

    (a)   must notify W in writing of the receipt of the notice from X, and

    (b)   no person to whom the licence applies may place an embryo or sperm and eggs in W, or artificially inseminate W, until W has been so notified.

(6E) Where the person responsible receives from a woman ("W") who has previously given notice under section 37(1)(b) or 44(1)(b) of the 2008 Act that she consents to another person ("X") being treated as a parent of any child resulting from the provision of treatment services to W—

    (a)   notice under section 37(1)(c) or 44(1)(c) of the 2008 Act of the withdrawal of W's consent, or

    (b)   a notice under section 37(1)(b) or 44(1)(b) of the 2008 Act in respect of a person other than X,

the person responsible must take reasonable steps to notify X in writing of the receipt of the notice mentioned in paragraph (a) or (b).

(4) After subsection (7) insert—

(8) Subsections (9) and (10) apply in determining any of the following—

    (a)   the persons who are to provide gametes for use in pursuance of the licence in a case where consent is required under paragraph 5 of Schedule 3 for the use in question;

    (b)   the woman from whom an embryo is to be taken for use in pursuance of the licence, in a case where her consent is required under paragraph 7 of Schedule 3 for the use of the embryo;

    (c)   which of two or more embryos to place in a woman.

(9) Persons or embryos that are known to have a gene, chromosome or mitochondrion abnormality involving a significant risk that a person with the abnormality will have or develop—

    (a)   a serious physical or mental disability,

    (b)   a serious illness, or

    (c)   any other serious medical condition, must not be preferred to those that are not known to have such an abnormality.

(10) Embryos that are known to be of a particular sex and to carry a particular risk, compared with embryos of that sex in general, that any resulting child will have or develop—

    (a)   a gender-related serious physical or mental disability,

(b)   a gender-related serious illness, or

(c)   any other gender-related serious medical condition, must not be preferred to those that are not known to carry such a risk.

(11) For the purposes of subsection (10), a physical or mental disability, illness or other medical condition is gender-related if—

(a)   it affects only one sex, or

(b)   it affects one sex significantly more than the other.

(12) No embryo appropriated for the purpose mentioned in paragraph 1(1)(ca) of Schedule 2 (training in embryological techniques) shall be kept or used for the provision of treatment services.

(13) The person responsible shall comply with any requirement imposed on that person by section 31ZD.

(5) After Schedule 3 to the 1990 Act insert the Schedule set out in Schedule 4 to this Act (circumstances in which offer of counselling required as condition of licence for treatment).

(6) In any licence under paragraph 1 of Schedule 2 to the 1990 Act (licences for treatment) that is in force immediately before the commencement of subsection (2)(b) of this section, the condition required by virtue of section 13(5) of that Act is to have effect as the condition required by that provision as amended by subsection (2)(b) of this section.

15 Conditions of storage licences

(1) Section 14 of the 1990 Act (conditions of storage licences) is amended as follows.

(2) In subsection (1)—

(a)   for "authorising the storage of gametes or embryos" substitute "authorising the storage of gametes, embryos or human admixed embryos",

(b)   for paragraph (a) substitute—

(a)   that gametes of a person shall be placed in storage only if—

(i)   received from that person,

(ii)   acquired in circumstances in which by virtue of paragraph 9 or 10 of Schedule 3 that person's consent to the storage is not required, or

(iii)   acquired from a person to whom a licence or third party agreement applies,

(aa)   that an embryo taken from a woman shall be placed in storage only if—

(i)   received from that woman, or

(ii)   acquired from a person to whom a licence or third party agreement applies,

(ab)   that an embryo the creation of which has been brought about in vitro otherwise than in pursuance of that licence shall be placed in storage only if acquired from a person to whom a licence or third party agreement applies, (ac) that a human admixed embryo the creation of which has been brought about in vitro otherwise than in pursuance of that licence shall be placed in storage only if acquired from a person to whom a licence under paragraph 2 or 3 of Schedule 2 applies,

(c) after paragraph (b) insert—

(ba) that human admixed embryos shall not be supplied to a person unless that person is a person to whom a licence applies,", and

(d) in paragraph (c), for "or embryos" substitute ", embryos or human admixed embryos.

(3) In subsection (4), for "five years" substitute "ten years".

(4) After subsection (4) insert—

(4A) The statutory storage period in respect of human admixed embryos is such period not exceeding ten years as the licence may specify.

(5) In subsection (5)—

(a) for "or (4)" substitute ", (4) or (4A)", and
(b) omit "or, as the case may be, five years".

Grant, revocation and suspension of licences

16 Grant of licence

(1) Section 16 of the 1990 Act (grant of licence) is amended as follows.

(2) For subsection (1) substitute—

(1) The Authority may on application grant a licence to any person if the requirements of subsection (2) below are met.

(3) In subsection (2)—

(a) for "licence committee" substitute "Authority" in each place it occurs,
(b) in paragraph (c), after "application" insert "or a licence under paragraph 3 of that Schedule authorising activities in connection with the derivation from embryos of stem cells that are intended for human application",
(c) in paragraph (ca)—
    (i) for "or embryos" substitute ", embryos or human admixed embryos", and
    (ii) after "that Schedule" insert "authorising activities otherwise than in connection with the derivation from embryos of stem cells that are intended for human application", and
(d) in paragraph (d), after "granted" insert "and any premises which will be relevant third party premises.

(4) In subsection (4) for "licence committee" substitute "Authority".

(5) In subsection (5) for "licence committee" substitute "Authority".

(6) Omit subsections (6) and (7) (which concern the power to charge fees).

17 The person responsible

(1) Section 17 of the 1990 Act (the person responsible) is amended as follows.

(2) In subsection (1)(c)—

 (a) for "and embryos" substitute ", embryos and human admixed embryos", and
 (b) for "or embryos" substitute ", embryos or human admixed embryos".

(3) Omit subsection (3) (which defines "the nominal licensee").

18 Revocation and variation of licence

For section 18 of the 1990 Act (revocation and variation of licence) substitute—

18 Revocation of licence

(1) The Authority may revoke a licence on application by—

 (a) the person responsible, or
 (b) the holder of the licence (if different).

(2) The Authority may revoke a licence otherwise than on application under subsection (1) if—

 (a) it is satisfied that any information given for the purposes of the application for the licence was in any material respect false or misleading,
 (b) it is satisfied that the person responsible has failed to discharge, or is unable because of incapacity to discharge, the duty under section 17,
 (c) it is satisfied that the person responsible has failed to comply with directions given in connection with any licence,
 (d) it ceases to be satisfied that the premises specified in the licence are suitable for the licensed activity,
 (e) it ceases to be satisfied that any premises which are relevant third party premises in relation to a licence are suitable for the activities entrusted to the third party by the person who holds the licence,
 (f) it ceases to be satisfied that the holder of the licence is a suitable person to hold the licence,
 (g) it ceases to be satisfied that the person responsible is a suitable person to supervise the licensed activity,
 (h) the person responsible dies or is convicted of an offence under this Act, or
 (i) it is satisfied that there has been any other material change of circumstances since the licence was granted.

18A Variation of licence

(1) The Authority may on application by the holder of the licence vary the licence so as to substitute another person for the person responsible if—

 (a) the application is made with the consent of that other person, and
 (b) the Authority is satisfied that the other person is a suitable person to supervise the licensed activity.

(2) The Authority may vary a licence on application by—

(a)   the person responsible, or
(b)   the holder of the licence (if different).

(3) The Authority may vary a licence without an application under subsection (2) if it has the power to revoke the licence under section 18(2).

(4) The powers under subsections (2) and (3) do not extend to making the kind of variation mentioned in subsection (1).

(5) The Authority may vary a licence without an application under subsection (2) by—

(a)   removing or varying a condition of the licence, or
(b)   adding a condition to the licence.

(6) The powers conferred by this section do not extend to the conditions required by sections 12 to 15 of this Act.

19 Procedure for refusal, variation or revocation of licence

For section 19 of the 1990 Act (procedure for refusal, variation or revocation of licence) substitute—

19 Procedure in relation to licensing decisions

(1) Before making a decision—

(a)   to refuse an application for the grant, revocation or variation of a licence, or
(b)   to grant an application for a licence subject to a condition imposed under paragraph 1(2), 1A(2), 2(2) or 3(6) of Schedule 2, the Authority shall give the applicant notice of the proposed decision and of the reasons for it.

(2) Before making a decision under section 18(2) or 18A(3) or (5) the Authority shall give notice of the proposed decision and of the reasons for it to—

(a)   the person responsible, and
(b)   the holder of the licence (if different).

(3) Where an application has been made under section 18A(2) to vary a licence, but the Authority considers it appropriate to vary the licence otherwise than in accordance with the application, before so varying the licence the Authority shall give notice of its proposed decision and of the reasons for it to—

(a)   the person responsible, and
(b)   the holder of the licence (if different).

(4) A person to whom notice is given under subsection (1), (2) or (3) has the right to require the Authority to give him an opportunity to make representations of one of the following kinds about the proposed decision, namely—

(a)   oral representations by him, or a person acting on his behalf;
(b)   written representations by him.

(5) The right under subsection (4) is exercisable by giving the Authority notice of the exercise of the right before the end of the period of 28 days beginning with the day on which the notice under subsection (1), (2) or (3) was given.

(6) The Authority may by regulations make such additional provision about procedure in relation to the carrying out of functions under sections 18 and 18A and this section as it thinks fit.

19A Notification of licensing decisions

(1) In the case of a decision to grant a licence, the Authority shall give notice of the decision to—

    (a)   the applicant, and

    (b)   the person who is to be the person responsible.

(2) In the case of a decision to revoke a licence, the Authority shall give notice of the decision to—

    (a)   the person responsible, and

    (b)   the holder of the licence (if different).

(3) In the case of a decision to vary a licence on application under section 18A(1), the Authority shall give notice of the decision to—

    (a)   the holder of the licence, and

    (b)   (if different) the person who is to be the person responsible.

(4) In the case of any other decision to vary a licence, the Authority shall give notice of the decision to—

    (a)   the person responsible, and

    (b)   the holder of the licence (if different).

(5) In the case of a decision to refuse an application for the grant, revocation or variation of a licence, the Authority shall give notice of the decision to the applicant.

(6) Subject to subsection (7), a notice under subsection (2), (4) or (5) shall include a statement of the reasons for the decision.

(7) In the case of a notice under subsection (2) or (4), the notice is not required to include a statement of the reasons for the decision if the decision is made on an application under section 18(1) or 18A(2).

19B Applications under this Act

(1) Directions may make provision about—

    (a)   the form and content of applications under this Act, and

    (b)   the information to be supplied with such an application.

(2) The Secretary of State may by regulations make other provision about applications under this Act.

(3) Such regulations may, in particular, make provision about procedure in relation to the determination of applications under this Act and may, in particular, include—

    (a)   provision for requiring persons to give evidence or to produce documents;

    (b)   provision about the admissibility of evidence.

20 Power to suspend licence

After section 19B (inserted by section 19 above) insert—

19C Power to suspend licence

(1) Where the Authority—

    (a)   has reasonable grounds to suspect that there are grounds for revoking a licence, and

    (b)   is of the opinion that the licence should immediately be suspended,

it may by notice suspend the licence for such period not exceeding three months as may be specified in the notice.

(2) The Authority may continue suspension under subsection (1) by giving a further notice under that subsection.

(3) Notice under subsection (1) shall be given to the person responsible or where the person responsible has died or appears to be unable because of incapacity to discharge the duty under section 17—

    (a)   to the holder of the licence, or

    (b)   to some other person to whom the licence applies.

(4) Subject to subsection (5), a licence shall be of no effect while a notice under subsection (1) is in force.

(5) An application may be made under section 18(1) or section 18A(1) or (2) even though a notice under subsection (1) is in force.

21 Reconsideration and appeals

For sections 20 and 21 of the 1990 Act (appeals to Authority against determinations of licence committees and further appeals) substitute—

20 Right to reconsideration of licensing decisions

(1) If an application for the grant, revocation or variation of a licence is refused, the applicant may require the Authority to reconsider the decision.

(2) Where the Authority decides to vary or revoke a licence, any person to whom notice of the decision was required to be given (other than a person who applied for the variation or revocation) may require the Authority to reconsider the decision.

(3) The right under subsections (1) and (2) is exercisable by giving the Authority notice of exercise of the right before the end of the period of 28 days beginning with the day on which notice of the decision concerned was given under section 19A.

(4) If the Authority decides —

    (a)   to suspend a licence under section 19C(1), or

    (b)   to continue the suspension of a licence under section 19C(2), any person to whom notice of the decision was required to be given may require the Authority to reconsider the decision.

(5) The right under subsection (4) is exercisable by giving the Authority notice of exercise of the right before the end of the period of 14 days beginning with the day on which notice of the decision concerned was given under section 19C.

(6) The giving of any notice to the Authority in accordance with subsection (5) shall not affect the continuation in force of the suspension of the licence in respect of which that notice was given.

(7) Subsections (1), (2) and (4) do not apply to a decision on reconsideration.

20A Appeals committee

(1) The Authority shall maintain one or more committees to carry out its functions in pursuance of notices under section 20.

(2) A committee under subsection (1) is referred to in this Act as an appeals committee.

(3) Regulations shall make provision about the membership and proceedings of appeals committees.

(4) Regulations under subsection (3) may, in particular, provide—

(a)   for the membership of an appeals committee to be made up wholly or partly of persons who are not members of the Authority, and

(b)   for the appointment of any person to advise an appeals committee on prescribed matters.

(5) For the purposes of subsection (4) "prescribed" means prescribed by regulations under subsection (3).

20B Procedure on reconsideration

(1) Reconsideration shall be by way of a fresh decision.

(2) Regulations shall make provision about the procedure in relation to reconsideration.

(3) Regulations under subsection (2) may, in particular, make provision—

(a)   entitling a person by whom reconsideration is required, ("the appellant") to require that the appellant or the appellant's representative be given an opportunity to appear before and be heard by the appeals committee dealing with the matter,

(b)   entitling the person who made the decision which is the subject of reconsideration to appear at any meeting at which such an opportunity is given, and to be heard in person or by a representative,

(c)   requiring the appeals committee dealing with the matter to consider any written representations received from the appellant or the person who made the decision which is the subject of reconsideration,

(d)   preventing any person who made the decision which is the subject of reconsideration from sitting as a member of the appeals committee dealing with the matter,

(e)   requiring persons to give evidence or to produce documents,

(f)   concerning the admissibility of evidence, and

(g)   requiring the appellant and any prescribed person to be given notice of the decision on reconsideration and a statement of reasons for the appeals committee's decision.

(4) Regulations under subsection (2) may, in particular, make different provision about the procedure on reconsideration depending upon whether the reconsideration is in pursuance of a notice under section 20(3) or a notice under section 20(5).

(5) Such regulations may, in particular, make provision—

(a)   in relation to cases where a person requires reconsideration of a decision to suspend a licence and reconsideration of a decision to continue the suspension of that licence, and

(b)   in relation to cases where reconsideration of a decision is required under section 20(2) by only one of two persons by whom it could have been required.

(6) In this section—

(a)   "prescribed" means prescribed by regulations under subsection (2), and

(b)   "reconsideration" means reconsideration in pursuance of a notice under section 20.

21 Appeal on a point of law

A person aggrieved by a decision on reconsideration in pursuance of a notice under section 20 may appeal to the High Court or, in Scotland, the Court of Session on a point of law.

Directions and guidance

22 Directions

(1) Section 24 of the 1990 Act (directions as to particular matters) is amended as follows.

(2) After subsection (3A) insert—

(3B) Directions may authorise, in such circumstances and subject to such conditions as may be specified in the directions, the keeping, by or on behalf of a person to whom a licence applies, of human admixed embryos in the course of their carriage to or from any premises.

(3) In subsection (4) for "or embryos", in both places, substitute ", embryos or human admixed embryos".

(4) After subsection (4A) insert—

(4B) Regulations may make provision requiring or authorising the giving of directions in relation to particular matters which are specified in the regulations and relate to activities falling within section 4A(2) (activities involving genetic material of animal origin).

(5) For subsections (5) to (10) substitute—

(5A) Directions may make provision for the purpose of dealing with a situation arising in consequence of—

(a)   the variation of a licence, or

(b)   a licence ceasing to have effect.

(5B) Directions under subsection (5A)(a) may impose requirements—

(a)　on the holder of the licence,

(b)　on the person who is the person responsible immediately before or immediately after the variation, or

(c)　on any other person, if that person consents.

(5C) Directions under subsection (5A)(b) may impose requirements—

(a)　on the person who holds the licence immediately before the licence ceases to have effect,

(b)　on the person who is the person responsible at that time, or

(c)　on any other person, if that person consents.

(5D) Directions under subsection (5A) may, in particular, require anything kept, or information held, in pursuance of the licence to be transferred in accordance with the directions.

(5E) Where a licence has ceased to have effect by reason of the death or dissolution of its holder, anything subsequently done by a person before directions are given under subsection (5A) shall, if the licence would have been authority for doing it, be treated as authorised by a licence.

(6)　In subsection (11), for "3(5)" substitute "3(2)".

23　Code of practice

(1)　Section 25 of the 1990 Act (code of practice) is amended as follows.

(2)　In subsection (2), for "a father" substitute "supportive parenting".

(3)　After that subsection insert—

(2A)　The code shall also give guidance about—

(a)　the giving of a suitable opportunity to receive proper counselling, and

(b)　the provision of such relevant information as is proper, in accordance with any condition that is by virtue of section 13(6) or (6A) a condition of a licence under paragraph 1 of Schedule 2.

(4)　In subsection (6)(a) and (b), for "a licence committee" substitute "the Authority".

Information

24　Register of information

For section 31 of the 1990 Act (the Authority's register of information) substitute—

31　Register of information

(1) The Authority shall keep a register which is to contain any information which falls within subsection (2) and which—

(a)　immediately before the coming into force of section 24 of the Human Fertilisation and Embryology Act 2008, was contained in the register kept under this section by the Authority, or

(b)　is obtained by the Authority.

(2) Subject to subsection (3), information falls within this subsection if it relates to—

- (a) the provision for any identifiable individual of treatment services other than basic partner treatment services,
- (b) the procurement or distribution of any sperm, other than sperm which is partner-donated sperm and has not been stored, in the course of providing non-medical fertility services for any identifiable individual,
- (c) the keeping of the gametes of any identifiable individual or of an embryo taken from any identifiable woman,
- (d) the use of the gametes of any identifiable individual other than their use for the purpose of basic partner treatment services, or
- (e) the use of an embryo taken from any identifiable woman, or if it shows that any identifiable individual is a relevant individual.

(3) Information does not fall within subsection (2) if it is provided to the Authority for the purposes of any voluntary contact register as defined by section 31ZF(1).

(4) In this section "relevant individual" means an individual who was or may have been born in consequence of—

- (a) treatment services, other than basic partner treatment services, or
- (b) the procurement or distribution of any sperm (other than partner-donated sperm which has not been stored) in the course of providing non-medical fertility services.

31ZA Request for information as to genetic parentage etc

(1) A person who has attained the age of 16 ("the applicant") may by notice to the Authority require the Authority to comply with a request under subsection (2).

(2) The applicant may request the Authority to give the applicant notice stating whether or not the information contained in the register shows that a person ("the donor") other than a parent of the applicant would or might, but for the relevant statutory provisions, be the parent of the applicant, and if it does show that—

- (a) giving the applicant so much of that information as relates to the donor as the Authority is required by regulations to give (but no other information), or
- (b) stating whether or not that information shows that there are other persons of whom the donor is not the parent but would or might, but for the relevant statutory provisions, be the parent and if so—
  - (i) the number of those other persons,
  - (ii) the sex of each of them, and
  - (iii) the year of birth of each of them.

(3) The Authority shall comply with a request under subsection (2) if—

- (a) the information contained in the register shows that the applicant is a relevant individual, and
- (b) the applicant has been given a suitable opportunity to receive proper counselling about the implications of compliance with the request.

(4) Where a request is made under subsection (2)(a) and the applicant has not attained the age of 18 when the applicant gives notice to the Authority under subsection (1), regulations cannot require the Authority to give the applicant any information which identifies the donor.

(5) Regulations cannot require the Authority to give any information as to the identity of a person whose gametes have been used or from whom an embryo has been taken if a person to whom a licence applied was provided with the information at a time when the Authority could not have been required to give information of the kind in question.

(6) The Authority need not comply with a request made under subsection (2)(b) by any applicant if it considers that special circumstances exist which increase the likelihood that compliance with the request would enable the applicant—

    (a)   to identify the donor, in a case where the Authority is not required by regulations under subsection (2)(a) to give the applicant information which identifies the donor, or

    (b)   to identify any person about whom information is given under subsection (2)(b).

(7) In this section—

    "relevant individual" has the same meaning as in section 31;
    "the relevant statutory provisions" means sections 27 to 29 of this Act and sections 33 to 47 of the Human Fertilisation and Embryology Act 2008.

31ZB Request for information as to intended spouse etc

(1) Subject to subsection (4), a person ("the applicant") may by notice to the Authority require the Authority to comply with a request under subsection (2).

(2) The applicant may request the Authority to give the applicant notice stating whether or not information contained in the register shows that, but for the relevant statutory provisions, the applicant would or might be related to a person specified in the request ("the specified person") as—

    (a)   a person whom the applicant proposes to marry,

    (b)   a person with whom the applicant proposes to enter into a civil partnership, or

    (c)   a person with whom the applicant is in an intimate physical relationship or with whom the applicant proposes to enter into an intimate physical relationship.

(3) Subject to subsection (5), the Authority shall comply with a request under subsection (2) if—

    (a)   the information contained in the register shows that the applicant is a relevant individual,

    (b)   the Authority receives notice in writing from the specified person consenting to the request being made and that notice has not been withdrawn, and

    (c)   the applicant and the specified person have each been given a suitable opportunity to receive proper counselling about the implications of compliance with the request.

(4) A request may not be made under subsection (2)(c) by a person who has not attained the age of 16.

(5) Where a request is made under subsection (2)(c) and the specified person has not attained the age of 16 when the applicant gives notice to the Authority under subsection (1), the Authority must not comply with the request.

(6) Where the Authority is required under subsection (3) to comply with a request under subsection (2), the Authority must take all reasonable steps to give the applicant and the specified person notice stating whether or not the information contained in the register shows that, but for the relevant statutory provisions, the applicant and the specified person would or might be related.

(7) In this section—

> "relevant individual" has the same meaning as in section 31;
> "the relevant statutory provisions" has the same meaning as in section 31ZA.

31ZC Power of Authority to inform donor of request for information

(1) Where—

    (a)   the Authority has received from a person ("the applicant")a notice containing a request under subsection (2)(a) of section 31ZA, and

    (b)   compliance by the Authority with its duty under that section has involved or will involve giving the applicant information relating to a person other than the parent of the applicant who would or might, but for the relevant statutory provisions, be a parent of the applicant ("the donor"), the Authority may notify the donor that a request under section 31ZA(2)(a) has been made, but may not disclose the identity of the applicant or any information relating to the applicant.

(2) In this section "the relevant statutory provisions" has the same meaning as in section 31ZA.

31ZD Provision to donor of information about resulting children

(1) This section applies where a person ("the donor") has consented under Schedule 3 (whether before or after the coming into force of this section) to—

    (a)   the use of the donor's gametes, or an embryo the creation of which was brought about using the donor's gametes, for the purposes of treatment services provided under a licence, or

    (b)   the use of the donor's gametes for the purposes of non-medical fertility services provided under a licence.

(2) In subsection (1)—

    (a)   "treatment services" do not include treatment services provided to the donor, or to the donor and another person together, and

    (b)   "non-medical fertility services" do not include any services involving partner-donated sperm.

(3) The donor may by notice request the appropriate person to give the donor notice stating—

(a)   the number of persons of whom the donor is not a parent but would or might, but for the relevant statutory provisions, be a parent by virtue of the use of the gametes or embryos to which the consent relates,

(b)   the sex of each of those persons, and

(c)   the year of birth of each of those persons.

(4) Subject to subsections (5) to (7), the appropriate person shall notify the donor whether the appropriate person holds the information mentioned in subsection (3) and, if the appropriate person does so, shall comply with the request.

(5) The appropriate person need not comply with a request under subsection (3) if the appropriate person considers that special circumstances exist which increase the likelihood that compliance with the request would enable the donor to identify any of the persons falling within paragraphs (a) to (c) of subsection (3).

(6) In the case of a donor who consented as described in subsection (1)(a), the Authority need not comply with a request made to it under subsection (3) where the person who held the licence referred to in subsection (1)(a) continues to hold a licence under paragraph 1 of Schedule 2, unless the donor has previously made a request under subsection (3) to the person responsible and the person responsible—

(a)   has notified the donor that the information concerned is not held, or

(b)   has failed to comply with the request within a reasonable period.

(7) In the case of a donor who consented as described in subsection (1)(b), the Authority need not comply with a request made to it under subsection (3) where the person who held the licence referred to in subsection (1)(b) continues to hold a licence under paragraph 1A of Schedule 2, unless the donor has previously made a request under subsection (3) to the person responsible and the person responsible—

(a)   has notified the donor that the information concerned is not held, or

(b)   has failed to comply with the request within a reasonable period.

(8) In this section "the appropriate person" means—

(a)   in the case of a donor who consented as described in paragraph

(a)   of subsection (1)—

    (i)   where the person who held the licence referred to in that paragraph continues to hold a licence under paragraph 1 of Schedule 2, the person responsible, or

    (ii)   the Authority, and

(b)   in the case of a donor who consented as described in paragraph

(b)   of subsection (1)—

    (i)   where the person who held the licence referred to in that paragraph continues to hold a licence under paragraph 1A of Schedule 2, the person responsible, or

    (ii)   the Authority.

(9) In this section "the relevant statutory provisions" has the same meaning as in section 31ZA.

31ZE Provision of information about donor-conceived genetic siblings

(1) For the purposes of this section two relevant individuals are donor conceived genetic siblings of each other if a person ("the donor") who is not the parent of either of them would or might, but for the relevant statutory provisions, be the parent of both of them.

(2) Where—

    (a)   the information on the register shows that a relevant individual ("A") is the donor-conceived genetic sibling of another relevant individual ("B"),

    (b)   A has provided information to the Authority ("the agreed information") which consists of or includes information which enables A to be identified with the request that it should be disclosed to—

        (i)   any donor-conceived genetic sibling of A, or

        (ii)   such siblings of A of a specified description which includes B, and

    (c)   the conditions in subsection (3) are satisfied, then, subject to subsection (4), the Authority shall disclose the agreed information to B.

(3) The conditions referred to in subsection (2)(c) are—

    (a)   that each of A and B has attained the age of 18,

    (b)   that B has requested the disclosure to B of information about any donor-conceived genetic sibling of B, and

    (c)   that each of A and B has been given a suitable opportunity to receive proper counselling about the implications of disclosure under subsection (2).

(4) The Authority need not disclose any information under subsection (2) if it considers that the disclosure of information will lead to A or B identifying the donor unless—

    (a)   the donor has consented to the donor's identity being disclosed to A or B, or

    (b)   were A or B to make a request under section 31ZA(2)(a), the Authority would be required by regulations under that provision to give A or B information which would identify the donor.

(5) In this section—

    "relevant individual" has the same meaning as in section 31;
    "the relevant statutory provisions" has the same meaning as in section 31ZA.

31ZF Power of Authority to keep voluntary contact register

(1) In this section and section 31ZG, a "voluntary contact register" means a register of persons who have expressed their wish to receive information about any person to whom they are genetically related as a consequence of the provision to any person of treatment services in the United Kingdom before 1 August 1991.

(2) The Authority may—

    (a)   set up a voluntary contact register in such manner as it thinks fit,

    (b)   keep a voluntary contact register in such manner as it thinks fit,

    (c)   determine criteria for eligibility for inclusion on the register and the particulars that may be included,

(d)   charge a fee to persons who wish their particulars to be entered on the register,

(e)   arrange for samples of the DNA of such persons to be analysed at their request,

(f)   make such arrangements as it thinks fit for the disclosure of information on the register between persons who appear to the Authority to be genetically related, and

(g)   impose such conditions as it thinks fit to prevent a person ("A") from disclosing information to a person to whom A is genetically related ("B") where that information would identify any person who is genetically related to both A and B.

(3) The Authority may make arrangements with any person by whom a voluntary contact register is kept before the commencement of this section for the supply by that person to the Authority of the information contained in the register maintained by that person.

31ZG Financial assistance for person setting up or keeping voluntary contact register

(1) The Authority may, instead of keeping a voluntary contact register, give financial assistance to any person who sets up or keeps a voluntary contact register.

(2) Financial assistance under subsection (1) may be given in any form, and in particular, may be given by way of—

(a)   grants,

(b)   loans,

(c)   guarantees, or

(d)   incurring expenditure for the person assisted.

(3) Financial assistance under subsection (1) may be given on such terms and conditions as the Authority considers appropriate.

(4) A person receiving assistance under subsection (1) must comply with the terms and conditions on which it is given, and compliance may be enforced by the Authority.

25 Restrictions on disclosure of information

For section 33 of the 1990 Act (restrictions on disclosure of information) substitute—

33A Disclosure of information

(1) No person shall disclose any information falling within section 31(2) which the person obtained (whether before or after the coming into force of section 24 of the Human Fertilisation and Embryology Act 2008) in the person's capacity as—

(a)   a member or employee of the Authority,

(b)   any person exercising functions of the Authority by virtue of section 8B or 8C of this Act (including a person exercising such functions by virtue of either of those sections as a member of staff or as an employee),

(c)   any person engaged by the Authority to provide services to the Authority,

(d)   any person employed by, or engaged to provide services to, a person mentioned in paragraph (c),

(e)   a person to whom a licence applies,

(f)   a person to whom a third party agreement applies, or

(g)   a person to whom directions have been given.

(2) Subsection (1) does not apply where—

(a)   the disclosure is made to a person as a member or employee of the Authority or as a person exercising functions of the Authority as mentioned in subsection (1)(b),

(b)   the disclosure is made to or by a person falling within subsection (1)(c) for the purpose of the provision of services which that person is engaged to provide to the Authority,

(c)   the disclosure is made by a person mentioned in subsection (1)(d) for the purpose of enabling a person falling within subsection (1)(c) to provide services which that person is engaged to provide to the Authority,

(d)   the disclosure is made to a person to whom a licence applies for the purpose of that person's functions as such,

(e)   the disclosure is made to a person to whom a third party agreement applies for the purpose of that person's functions under that agreement,

(f)   the disclosure is made in pursuance of directions given by virtue of section 24,

(g)   the disclosure is made so that no individual can be identified from the information,

(h)   the disclosure is of information other than identifying donor information and is made with the consent required by section 33B,

(i)   the disclosure—

    (i)   is made by a person who is satisfied that it is necessary to make the disclosure to avert an imminent danger to the health of an individual ("P"),

    (ii)   is of information falling within section 31(2)(a) which could be disclosed by virtue of paragraph (h) with P's consent or could be disclosed to P by virtue of subsection (5), and

    (iii)   is made in circumstances where it is not reasonably practicable to obtain P's consent,

(j)   the disclosure is of information which has been lawfully made available to the public before the disclosure is made,

(k)   the disclosure is made in accordance with sections 31ZA to 31ZE,

(l)   the disclosure is required or authorised to be made—

    (i)   under regulations made under section 33D, or

    (ii)   in relation to any time before the coming into force of the first regulations under that section, under regulations made under section 251 of the National Health Service Act 2006,

(m)   the disclosure is made by a person acting in the capacity mentioned in subsection (1)(a) or (b) for the purpose of carrying out the Authority's duties under section 8A,

(n)   the disclosure is made by a person acting in the capacity mentioned in subsection (1)(a) or (b) in pursuance of an order of a court under section 34 or 35,

(o)   the disclosure is made by a person acting in the capacity mentioned in subsection (1)(a) or (b) to the Registrar General in pursuance of a request under section 32,

(p)   the disclosure is made by a person acting in the capacity mentioned in subsection (1)(a) or (b) to any body or person discharging a regulatory function for the purpose of assisting that body or person to carry out that function,

(q)   the disclosure is made for the purpose of establishing in any proceedings relating to an application for an order under subsection (1) of section 54 of the Human Fertilisation and Embryology Act 2008 whether the condition specified in paragraph (a) or (b) of that subsection is met,

(r)   the disclosure is made under section 3 of the Access to Health Records Act 1990,

(s)   the disclosure is made under Article 5 of the Access to Health Records (Northern Ireland) Order 1993, or

(t)   the disclosure is made necessarily for—

    (i)   the purpose of the investigation of any offence (or suspected offence), or

    (ii)   any purpose preliminary to proceedings, or for the purposes of, or in connection with, any proceedings.

(3) Subsection (1) does not apply to the disclosure of information in so far as—

(a)   the information identifies a person who, but for sections 27 to 29 of this Act or sections 33 to 47 of the Human Fertilisation and Embryology Act 2008, would or might be a parent of a person who instituted proceedings under section 1A of the Congenital Disabilities (Civil Liability) Act 1976, and

(b)   the disclosure is made for the purpose of defending such proceedings, or instituting connected proceedings for compensation against that parent.

(4) Paragraph (t) of subsection (2), so far as relating to disclosure for the purpose of the investigation of an offence or suspected offence, or for any purpose preliminary to, or in connection with proceedings, does not apply—

(a)   to disclosure of identifying donor information, or

(b)   to disclosure, in circumstances in which subsection (1) of section 34 of this Act applies, of information relevant to the determination of the question mentioned in that subsection, made by any person acting in a capacity mentioned in any of paragraphs (c) to (g) of subsection (1).

(5) Subsection (1) does not apply to the disclosure to any individual of information which—

(a)   falls within subsection (2) of section 31 of this Act by virtue of any of paragraphs (a) to (e) of that subsection, and

(b)   relates only to that individual or, in the case of an individual who is treated together with, or gives a notice under section 37 or 44 of the Human Fertilisation and Embryology Act 2008 in respect of, another, only to that individual and that other.

(6) In subsection (2)—

(a)   in paragraph (p) "regulatory function" has the same meaning as in section 32 of the Legislative and Regulatory Reform Act 2006, and

(b)   in paragraph (t) references to "proceedings" include any formal procedure for dealing with a complaint.

(7) In this section "identifying donor information" means information enabling a person to be identified as a person whose gametes were used in accordance with consent given under paragraph 5 of Schedule 3 for the purposes of treatment services or non-medical fertility services in consequence of which an identifiable individual was, or may have been, born.

33B Consent required to authorise certain disclosures

(1) This section has effect for the purposes of section 33A(2)(h).

(2) Subject to subsection (5), the consent required by this section is the consent of each individual who can be identified from the information.

(3) Consent in respect of a person who has not attained the age of 18 years ("C") may be given—

(a)   by C, in a case where C is competent to deal with the issue of consent, or
(b)   by a person having parental responsibility for C, in any other case.

(4) Consent to disclosure given at the request of another shall be disregarded unless, before it is given, the person requesting it takes reasonable steps to explain to the individual from whom it is requested the implications of compliance with the request.

(5) In the case of information which shows that any identifiable individual ("A") was, or may have been, born in consequence of treatment services, the consent required by this section does not include A's consent if the disclosure is necessarily incidental to the disclosure of information falling within section 31(2)(a).

(6) The reference in subsection (3) to parental responsibility is—

(a)   in relation to England and Wales, to be read in accordance with the Children Act 1989;
(b)   in relation to Northern Ireland, to be read in accordance with the Children (Northern Ireland) Order 1995;
(c)   in relation to Scotland, to be read as a reference to parental responsibilities and parental rights within the meaning of the Children (Scotland) Act 1995.

33C Power to provide for additional exceptions from section 33A(1)

(1) Regulations may provide for additional exceptions from section 33A(1).

(2) No exception may be made under this section for—

(a)   disclosure of a kind mentioned in paragraph (a) or (b) of subsection (4) of section 33A, or
(b)   disclosure in circumstances in which section 32 of this Act applies of information having the tendency mentioned in subsection (2) of that section, made by any person acting in a capacity mentioned in any of paragraphs (c) to (g) of subsection (1) of section 33A.

33D Disclosure for the purposes of medical or other research

(1) Regulations may—

(a)　make such provision for and in connection with requiring or regulating the processing of protected information for the purposes of medical research as the Secretary of State considers is necessary or expedient in the public interest or in the interests of improving patient care, and

(b)　make such provision for and in connection with requiring or regulating the processing of protected information for the purposes of any other research as the Secretary of State considers is necessary or expedient in the public interest.

(2) Regulations under subsection (1) may, in particular, make provision—

(a)　for requiring or authorising the disclosure or other processing of protected information to or by persons of any prescribed description subject to compliance with any prescribed conditions (including conditions requiring prescribed undertakings to be obtained from such persons as to the processing of such information),

(b)　for securing that, where prescribed protected information is processed by a person in accordance with the regulations, anything done by that person in so processing the information must be taken to be lawfully done despite any obligation of confidence owed by the person in respect of it,

(c)　for requiring fees of a prescribed amount to be paid to the Authority in prescribed circumstances by persons in relation to the disclosure to those persons of protected information under those regulations,

(d)　for the establishment of one or more bodies to exercise prescribed functions in relation to the processing of protected information under those regulations,

(e)　as to the membership and proceedings of any such body, and

(f)　as to the payment of remuneration and allowances to any member of any such body and the reimbursement of expenses.

(3) Where regulations under subsection (1) require or regulate the processing of protected information for the purposes of medical research, such regulations may enable any approval given under regulations made under section 251 of the National Health Service Act 2006 (control of patient information) to have effect for the purposes of the regulations under subsection (1) in their application to England and Wales.

(4) Subsections (1) to (3) are subject to subsections (5) to (8).

(5) Regulations under subsection (1) may not make any provision requiring or authorising the disclosure or other processing, for any purpose, of protected information, where that information is information from which an individual may be identified, if it would be reasonably practicable to achieve that purpose otherwise than pursuant to such regulations, having regard to the cost of and technology available for achieving that purpose.

(6) Regulations under this section may not make provision for or in connection with the processing of protected information in a manner inconsistent with any provision made by or under the Data Protection Act 1998.

(7) Subsection (6) does not affect the operation of provisions made under subsection (2)(b).

(8) Before making any regulations under this section the Secretary of State shall consult such bodies appearing to the Secretary of State to represent the interests of those likely to be affected by the regulations as the Secretary of State considers appropriate.

(9) In this section—

"prescribed" means prescribed by regulations made by virtue of this section,

"processing", in relation to information, means the use, disclosure, or obtaining of the information or the doing of such other things in relation to it as may be prescribed for the purposes of this definition, and

"protected information" means information falling within section 31(2).

Mitochondrial donation

26 Mitochondrial donation

After section 35 of the 1990 Act insert—

Mitochondrial donation

35A Mitochondrial donation

(1) Regulations may provide for any of the relevant provisions to have effect subject to specified modifications in relation to cases where—

  (a)   an egg which is a permitted egg for the purposes of section 3(2) by virtue of regulations made under section 3ZA(5), or

  (b)   an embryo which is a permitted embryo for those purposes by virtue of such regulations,

has been created from material provided by two women.

(2) In this section "the relevant provisions" means—

  (a)   the following provisions of this Act—
     (i)   section 13(6C) (information whose provision to prospective parents is required by licence condition),
     (ii) section 31 (register of information),
     (iii) sections 31ZA to 31ZE (provision of information), and
     (iv) Schedule 3 (consents to use or storage of gametes, embryos or human admixed embryos etc), and

  (b)   section 54 of the Human Fertilisation and Embryology Act 2008 (parental orders).

Miscellaneous

27 Fees

After section 35A of the 1990 Act (as inserted by section 26 above) insert—

Fees

35B Fees

(1) The Authority may charge a fee in respect of any of the following—

  (a)   an application for a licence,

    (b)   the grant or renewal of a licence,

    (c)   an application for the revocation or variation of a licence, or

    (d)   the exercise by the Authority of any other function conferred on it by or under this Act or by or under any other enactment—

        (i)   in relation to a licence,

        (ii)   in relation to premises which are or have been premises to which a licence relates,

        (iii)   in relation to premises which are or have been relevant third party premises in relation to a licence, or

        (iv)   in relation to premises which, if an application is granted, will be premises to which a licence relates or relevant third party premises.

(2) The amount of any fee charged by virtue of subsection (1) is to be fixed in accordance with a scheme made by the Authority with the approval of the Secretary of State and the Treasury.

(3) In fixing the amount of any fee to be charged by virtue of that subsection, the Authority may have regard to the costs incurred by it—

    (a)   in exercising the functions conferred on it by or under this Act (apart from sections 31ZA to 31ZG and 33D), and

    (b)   in exercising any other function conferred on it by or under any other enactment.

(4) The Authority may also charge such fee as it thinks fit in respect of any

of the following—

    (a)   the giving of notice under section 31ZA(1) or 31ZB(1), or

    (b)   the provision of information under section 31ZA, 31ZB or 31ZE.

(5) In fixing the amount of any fee to be charged by virtue of subsection (4) the Authority may have regard to the costs incurred by it in exercising the function to which the fee relates.

(6) When exercising its power to charge fees under section 8(2), 31ZF(2)(d) or this section, the Authority may fix different fees for different circumstances.

28 Inspection, entry, search and seizure

(1) Before section 39 of the 1990 Act (but after the heading "Enforcement" immediately before that section) insert—

38A Inspection, entry, search and seizure

(1) Schedule 3B (which makes provisions about inspection, entry, search and seizure) has effect.

(2) Nothing in this Act makes it unlawful for a member or employee of the Authority to keep any embryo, human admixed embryo or gametes in pursuance of that person's functions as such.

(2) After Schedule 3A to the 1990 Act insert the Schedule set out in Schedule 5 to this Act (inspection, entry, search and seizure).

(3) Section 39 of the 1990 Act (powers of members and employees of Authority) and section 40 of that Act (power to enter premises) (which are superseded by the amendments made by subsection (2)) cease to have effect.

29 Offences under the 1990 Act

(1) Section 41 of the 1990 Act (offences) is amended as follows.

(2) In subsection (1)(a), for "4(1)(c)" substitute "4A(1) or (2)".

(3) In subsection (2)—

    (a)   after paragraph (a) insert—

        (aa)   contravenes section 3(1B) of this Act,

    (b)   after paragraph (ba) insert—

        (bb)   contravenes section 4(1A) of this Act,", and

    (c)   in paragraph (d), for "section 24(7)(a)" substitute "section 24(5D)".

(4) In subsection (4), omit ", other than an offence to which subsection (4B) applies,".

(5) In subsection (5), for "section 33" substitute "section 33A".

(6) In subsection (7), for "section 10(2)(a)" substitute "section 19B(3)(a) or 20B(3)(e)".

(7) In subsection (8)—

    (a)   for "or the nominal licensee" substitute "or the holder of the licence", and
    (b)   for "or embryos" substitute ", embryos or human admixed embryos".

(8) In subsection (9), omit "(6),".

(9) For subsection (10) substitute—

    (10) It is a defence for a person ("the defendant") charged with an offence of doing anything which, under section 3(1) or (1A), 4(1) or 4A(2), cannot be done except in pursuance of a licence to prove—

        (a)   that the defendant was acting under the direction of another, and
        (b)   that the defendant believed on reasonable grounds—
            (i)   that the other person was at the material time the person responsible under a licence, a person designated by virtue of section 17(2)(b) of this Act as a person to whom a licence applied, or a person to whom directions had been given under section 24(5A) to (5D), and
            (ii)   that the defendant was authorised by virtue of the licence or directions to do the thing in question. (10A) It is a defence for a person ("the defendant") charged with an offence of doing anything which, under section 3(1A) or (1B) or 4(1A), cannot be done except in pursuance of a licence or a third party agreement to prove—

    (a)   that the defendant was acting under the direction of another,
    and

(b) that the defendant believed on reasonable grounds—
   (i) that the other person was at the material time the person responsible under a licence, a person designated by virtue of section 17(2)(b) of this Act as a person to whom a licence applied, a person to whom a third party agreement applied, or a person to whom directions had been given under section 24(5A) to (5D), and
   (ii) that the defendant was authorised by virtue of the licence, third party agreement or directions to do the thing in question.

(10) Omit subsections (2A), (4A), (4B) and (6).

(11) Section 41(2) of the 1990 Act as amended by subsection (3) is to be treated as a relevant enactment for the purposes of section 282 of the Criminal Justice Act 2003 (c. 44) (increase in maximum term that may be imposed on summary conviction of offence triable either way).

30 Regulations under the 1990 Act

(1) Section 45 of the 1990 Act (regulations) is amended as follows.

(2) After subsection (1) insert—

(1A) Subsection (1) does not enable the Secretary of State to make regulations by virtue of section 19(6) (which confers regulation-making powers on the Authority).

(3) In subsection (2), after "regulations" insert "under this Act".

(4) For subsection (3) substitute—

(3) The power to make regulations under this Act may be exercised—

(a) either in relation to all cases to which the power extends, or in relation to those cases subject to specified exceptions, or in relation to any specified cases or classes of case, and
(b) so as to make, as respects the cases in relation to which it is exercised—
   (i) the full provision to which the power extends or any less provision (whether by way of exception or otherwise);
   (ii) the same provision for all cases in relation to which the power is exercised, or different provision as respects the same case or class of case for different purposes;
   (iii) any such provision either unconditionally, or subject to any specified condition.

(3A) Any power of the Secretary of State or the Authority to make regulations under this Act includes power to make such transitional, incidental or supplemental provision as the Secretary of State or the Authority considers appropriate.

(5) For subsection (4) substitute—

(4) The Secretary of State shall not make regulations by virtue of any of the provisions specified in subsection (4A) unless a draft has been laid before and approved by a resolution of each House of Parliament.

(4A) Those provisions are—

section 1(6);
section 3(3)(c);
section 3ZA(5);
section 4(2) or (3);
section 4A(5) or (11);
section 20A(3);
section 20B(2);
section 24(4B);
section 31ZA(2)(a);
section 33C;
section 33D;
section 35A;
section 43;
paragraph 1(1)(g), 1ZC or 3A(1)(c) of Schedule 2.

(6) In subsection (5), after "regulations" insert "made by the Secretary of State".

31 Power to make consequential provision

After section 45 of the 1990 Act (regulations) insert—

45A Power to make consequential provision

(1) The Secretary of State may by order make such provision modifying any provision made by or under any enactment as the Secretary of State considers necessary or expedient in consequence of any provision made by regulations under any of the relevant provisions of this Act.

(2) For the purposes of subsection (1), "the relevant provisions of this Act" are—

    (a)   section 1(6) (power to include things within the meaning of "embryo" and "gametes" etc);

    (b)   section 4A(11) (power to amend definition of "human admixed embryo" and other terms).

(3) Before making an order under this section containing provision which would, if included in an Act of the Scottish Parliament, be within the legislative competence of that Parliament, the Secretary of State must consult the Scottish Ministers.

(4) Before making an order under this section containing provision which would be within the legislative competence of the National Assembly for Wales if it were included in a Measure of the Assembly (or, if the order is made after the Assembly Act provisions come into force, an Act of the Assembly), the Secretary of State must consult the Welsh Ministers.

(5) Before making an order under this section containing provision which would if included in an Act of the Northern Ireland Assembly, be within the legislative competence of that Assembly, the Secretary of State must consult the Department of Health, Social Services and Public Safety.

(6) In this section—

    "enactment" means—

    (a)   an Act of Parliament (other than this Act),

(b)   an Act of the Scottish Parliament,

(c)   a Measure or Act of the National Assembly for Wales, or

(d)   Northern Ireland legislation,

whenever passed or made;

> "modify" includes amend, add to, revoke or repeal;
> "the Assembly Act provisions" has the meaning given by section 103(8) of
> the Government of Wales Act 2006.

32 Orders under the 1990 Act

After section 45A (inserted by section 31 above) insert—

45B Orders

(1) The power to make an order under section 8C(1)(c) or 45A of this Act shall
be exercisable by statutory instrument.

(2) The power to make an order under section 8C(1)(c) or 45A of this Act
includes power to make such transitional, incidental or supplemental provision as
the Secretary of State considers appropriate.

(3) A statutory instrument containing an order made by the Secretary of State by
virtue of section 8C(1)(c) shall be subject to annulment in pursuance of a
resolution of either House of Parliament.

(4) The Secretary of State shall not make an order by virtue of section 45A unless
a draft has been laid before and approved by a resolution of each House of
Parliament.

PART 2
PARENTHOOD IN CASES INVOLVING ASSISTED REPRODUCTION

Meaning of "mother"

33 Meaning of "mother"

(1) The woman who is carrying or has carried a child as a result of the placing
in her of an embryo or of sperm and eggs, and no other woman, is to be treated
as the mother of the child.

(2) Subsection (1) does not apply to any child to the extent that the child is
treated by virtue of adoption as not being the woman's child.

(3) Subsection (1) applies whether the woman was in the United Kingdom or
elsewhere at the time of the placing in her of the embryo or the sperm and eggs.

Application of sections 35 to 47

34 Application of sections 35 to 47

(1) Sections 35 to 47 apply, in the case of a child who is being or has been
carried by a woman (referred to in those sections as "W") as a result of the
placing in her of an embryo or of sperm and eggs or her artificial insemination,
to determine who is to be treated as the other parent of the child.

(2) Subsection (1) has effect subject to the provisions of sections 39, 40 and 46 limiting the purposes for which a person is treated as the child's other parent by virtue of those sections.

Meaning of "father"

35 Woman married at time of treatment

(1) If—

   (a)   at the time of the placing in her of the embryo or of the sperm and eggs or of her artificial insemination, W was a party to a marriage, and
   (b)   the creation of the embryo carried by her was not brought about with the sperm of the other party to the marriage, then, subject to section 38(2) to (4), the other party to the marriage is to be treated as the father of the child unless it is shown that he did not consent to the placing in her of the embryo or the sperm and eggs or to her artificial insemination (as the case may be).

(2) This section applies whether W was in the United Kingdom or elsewhere at the time mentioned in subsection (1)(a).

36 Treatment provided to woman where agreed fatherhood conditions apply

If no man is treated by virtue of section 35 as the father of the child and no woman is treated by virtue of section 42 as a parent of the child but—

   (a)   the embryo or the sperm and eggs were placed in W, or W was artificially inseminated, in the course of treatment services provided in the United Kingdom by a person to whom a licence applies,
   (b)   at the time when the embryo or the sperm and eggs were placed in W, or W was artificially inseminated, the agreed fatherhood conditions (as set out in section 37) were satisfied in relation to a man, in relation to treatment provided to W under the licence,
   (c)   the man remained alive at that time, and
   (d)   the creation of the embryo carried by W was not brought about with the man's sperm,

then, subject to section 38(2) to (4), the man is to be treated as the father of the child.

37 The agreed fatherhood conditions

(1) The agreed fatherhood conditions referred to in section 36(b) are met in relation to a man ("M") in relation to treatment provided to W under a licence if, but only if,—

   (a)   M has given the person responsible a notice stating that he consents to being treated as the father of any child resulting from treatment provided to W under the licence,
   (b)   W has given the person responsible a notice stating that she consents to M being so treated,

    (c)   neither M nor W has, since giving notice under paragraph (a) or (b), given the person responsible notice of the withdrawal of M's or W's consent to M being so treated,

    (d)   W has not, since the giving of the notice under paragraph (b), given the person responsible—

        (i)   a further notice under that paragraph stating that she consents to another man being treated as the father of any resulting child, or

        (ii)   a notice under section 44(1)(b) stating that she consents to a woman being treated as a parent of any resulting child, and

    (e)   W and M are not within prohibited degrees of relationship in relation to each other.

(2) A notice under subsection (1)(a), (b) or (c) must be in writing and must be signed by the person giving it.

(3) A notice under subsection (1)(a), (b) or (c) by a person ("S") who is unable to sign because of illness, injury or physical disability is to be taken to comply with the requirement of subsection (2) as to signature if it is signed at the direction of S, in the presence of S and in the presence of at least one witness who attests the signature.

38 Further provision relating to sections 35 and 36

(1) Where a person is to be treated as the father of the child by virtue of section 35 or 36, no other person is to be treated as the father of the child.

(2) In England and Wales and Northern Ireland, sections 35 and 36 do not affect any presumption, applying by virtue of the rules of common law, that a child is the legitimate child of the parties to a marriage.

(3) In Scotland, sections 35 and 36 do not apply in relation to any child who, by virtue of any enactment or other rule of law, is treated as the child of the parties to a marriage.

(4) Sections 35 and 36 do not apply to any child to the extent that the child is treated by virtue of adoption as not being the man's child.

39 Use of sperm, or transfer of embryo, after death of man providing sperm

(1) If—

    (a)   the child has been carried by W as a result of the placing in her of an embryo or of sperm and eggs or her artificial insemination,

    (b)   the creation of the embryo carried by W was brought about by using the sperm of a man after his death, or the creation of the embryo was brought about using the sperm of a man before his death but the embryo was placed in W after his death,

    (c)   the man consented in writing (and did not withdraw the consent)—

        (i)   to the use of his sperm after his death which brought about the creation of the embryo carried by W or (as the case may be) to the placing in W after his death of the embryo which was brought about using his sperm before his death, and

> (ii)   to being treated for the purpose mentioned in subsection (3) as the father of any resulting child,
>
> (d)   W has elected in writing not later than the end of the period of 42 days from the day on which the child was born for the man to be treated for the purpose mentioned in subsection (3)as the father of the child, and
>
> (e)   no-one else is to be treated—
>
> > (i)   as the father of the child by virtue of section 35 or 36 or by virtue of section 38(2) or (3), or
> >
> > (ii)   as a parent of the child by virtue of section 42 or 43 or by virtue of adoption,

then the man is to be treated for the purpose mentioned in subsection (3) as the father of the child.

(2) Subsection (1) applies whether W was in the United Kingdom or elsewhere at the time of the placing in her of the embryo or of the sperm and eggs or of her artificial insemination.

(3) The purpose referred to in subsection (1) is the purpose of enabling the man's particulars to be entered as the particulars of the child's father in a relevant register of births.

(4) In the application of this section to Scotland, for any reference to a period of 42 days there is substituted a reference to a period of 21 days.

40 Embryo transferred after death of husband etc who did not provide sperm

(1) If—

> (a)   the child has been carried by W as a result of the placing in her of an embryo,
>
> (b)   the embryo was created at a time when W was a party to a marriage,
>
> (c)   the creation of the embryo was not brought about with the sperm of the other party to the marriage,
>
> (d)   the other party to the marriage died before the placing of the embryo in W,
>
> (e)   the other party to the marriage consented in writing (and did not withdraw the consent)—
>
> > (i)   to the placing of the embryo in W after his death, and
> >
> > (ii)   to being treated for the purpose mentioned in subsection (4) as the father of any resulting child,
>
> (f)   W has elected in writing not later than the end of the period of 42 days from the day on which the child was born for the man to be treated for the purpose mentioned in subsection (4) as the father of the child, and
>
> (g)   no-one else is to be treated—
>
> > (i)   as the father of the child by virtue of section 35 or 36 or by virtue of section 38(2) or (3), or
> >
> > (ii)   as a parent of the child by virtue of section 42 or 43 or by virtue of adoption,

then the man is to be treated for the purpose mentioned in subsection (4) as the father of the child.

(2) If—

(a) the child has been carried by W as a result of the placing in her of an embryo,

(b) the embryo was not created at a time when W was a party to a marriage or a civil partnership but was created in the course of treatment services provided to W in the United Kingdom by a person to whom a licence applies,

(c) a man consented in writing (and did not withdraw the consent)—

   (i)   to the placing of the embryo in W after his death, and

   (ii) to being treated for the purpose mentioned in subsection (4) as the father of any resulting child,

(d) the creation of the embryo was not brought about with the sperm of that man,

(e) the man died before the placing of the embryo in W,

(f) immediately before the man's death, the agreed fatherhood conditions set out in section 37 were met in relation to the man in relation to treatment proposed to be provided to W in the United Kingdom by a person to whom a licence applies,

(g) W has elected in writing not later than the end of the period of 42 days from the day on which the child was born for the man to be treated for the purpose mentioned in subsection (4) as the father of the child, and

(h) no-one else is to be treated—

   (i)   as the father of the child by virtue of section 35 or 36 or by virtue of section 38(2) or (3), or

   (ii) as a parent of the child by virtue of section 42 or 43 or by virtue of adoption,

then the man is to be treated for the purpose mentioned in subsection (4) as the father of the child.

(3) Subsections (1) and (2) apply whether W was in the United Kingdom or elsewhere at the time of the placing in her of the embryo.

(4) The purpose referred to in subsections (1) and (2) is the purpose of enabling the man's particulars to be entered as the particulars of the child's father in a relevant register of births.

(5) In the application of this section to Scotland, for any reference to a period of 42 days there is substituted a reference to a period of 21 days.

41 Persons not to be treated as father

(1) Where the sperm of a man who had given such consent as is required by paragraph 5 of Schedule 3 to the 1990 Act (consent to use of gametes for purposes of treatment services or non-medical fertility services) was used for a purpose for which such consent was required, he is not to be treated as the father of the child.

(2) Where the sperm of a man, or an embryo the creation of which was brought about with his sperm, was used after his death, he is not, subject to section 39, to be treated as the father of the child.

(3) Subsection (2) applies whether W was in the United Kingdom or elsewhere at the time of the placing in her of the embryo or of the sperm and eggs or of her artificial insemination.

Cases in which woman to be other parent

42 Woman in civil partnership at time of treatment

(1) If at the time of the placing in her of the embryo or the sperm and eggs or of her artificial insemination, W was a party to a civil partnership, then subject to section 45(2) to (4), the other party to the civil partnership is to be treated as a parent of the child unless it is shown that she did not consent to the placing in W of the embryo or the sperm and eggs or to her artificial insemination (as the case may be).

(2) This section applies whether W was in the United Kingdom or elsewhere at the time mentioned in subsection (1).

43 Treatment provided to woman who agrees that second woman to be parent

If no man is treated by virtue of section 35 as the father of the child and no woman is treated by virtue of section 42 as a parent of the child but—

- (a) the embryo or the sperm and eggs were placed in W, or W was artificially inseminated, in the course of treatment services provided in the United Kingdom by a person to whom a licence applies,
- (b) at the time when the embryo or the sperm and eggs were placed in W, or W was artificially inseminated, the agreed female parenthood conditions (as set out in section 44) were met in relation to another woman, in relation to treatment provided to W under that licence, and
- (c) the other woman remained alive at that time, then, subject to section 45(2) to (4), the other woman is to be treated as a parent of the child.

44 The agreed female parenthood conditions

(1) The agreed female parenthood conditions referred to in section 43(b) are met in relation to another woman ("P") in relation to treatment provided to W under a licence if, but only if,—

- (a) P has given the person responsible a notice stating that P consents to P being treated as a parent of any child resulting from treatment provided to W under the licence,
- (b) W has given the person responsible a notice stating that W agrees to P being so treated,
- (c) neither W nor P has, since giving notice under paragraph (a)or (b), given the person responsible notice of the withdrawal of P's or W's consent to P being so treated,
- (d) W has not, since the giving of the notice under paragraph (b), given the
person responsible—

      (i)   a further notice under that paragraph stating that W consents to a woman other than P being treated as a parent of any resulting child, or

      (ii)   a notice under section 37(1)(b) stating that W consents to a man being treated as the father of any resulting child, and

  (e)   W and P are not within prohibited degrees of relationship in relation to each other.

(2) A notice under subsection (1)(a), (b) or (c) must be in writing and must be signed by the person giving it.

(3) A notice under subsection (1)(a), (b) or (c) by a person ("S") who is unable to sign because of illness, injury or physical disability is to be taken to comply with the requirement of subsection (2) as to signature if it is signed at the direction of S, in the presence of S and in the presence of at least one witness who attests the signature.

45 Further provision relating to sections 42 and 43

(1) Where a woman is treated by virtue of section 42 or 43 as a parent of the child, no man is to be treated as the father of the child.

(2) In England and Wales and Northern Ireland, sections 42 and 43 do not affect any presumption, applying by virtue of the rules of common law, that a child is the legitimate child of the parties to a marriage.

(3) In Scotland, sections 42 and 43 do not apply in relation to any child who, by virtue of any enactment or other rule of law, is treated as the child of the parties to a marriage.

(4) Sections 42 and 43 do not apply to any child to the extent that the child is treated by virtue of adoption as not being the woman's child.

46 Embryo transferred after death of civil partner or intended female parent

(1) If—

  (a)   the child has been carried by W as the result of the placing in her of an embryo,

  (b)   the embryo was created at a time when W was a party to a civil partnership,

  (c)   the other party to the civil partnership died before the placing of the embryo in W,

  (d)   the other party to the civil partnership consented in writing (and did not withdraw the consent)—

      (i)   to the placing of the embryo in W after the death of the other party, and

      (ii)   to being treated for the purpose mentioned in subsection (4) as the parent of any resulting child,

  (e)   W has elected in writing not later than the end of the period of 42 days from the day on which the child was born for the other party to the civil partnership to be treated for the purpose mentioned in subsection (4) as the parent of the child, and

(f)   no one else is to be treated—
    (i)   as the father of the child by virtue of section 35 or 36 or by virtue of section 45(2) or (3), or
    (ii)   as a parent of the child by virtue of section 42 or 43 or by virtue of adoption,

then the other party to the civil partnership is to be treated for the purpose mentioned in subsection (4) as a parent of the child.

(2) If—

(a)   the child has been carried by W as the result of the placing in her of an embryo,

(b)   the embryo was not created at a time when W was a party to a marriage or a civil partnership, but was created in the course of treatment services provided to W in the United Kingdom by a person to whom a licence applies,

(c)   another woman consented in writing (and did not withdraw the consent)—
    (i)   to the placing of the embryo in W after the death of the other woman, and
    (ii)   to being treated for the purpose mentioned in subsection (4) as the parent of any resulting child,

(d)   the other woman died before the placing of the embryo in W,

(e)   immediately before the other woman's death, the agreed female parenthood conditions set out in section 44 were met in relation to the other woman in relation to treatment proposed to be provided to W in the United Kingdom by a person to whom a licence applies,

(f)   W has elected in writing not later than the end of the period of 42 days from the day on which the child was born for the other woman to be treated for the purpose mentioned in subsection (4)as the parent of the child, and

(g)   no one else is to be treated—
    (i)   as the father of the child by virtue of section 35 or 36 or by virtue of section 45(2) or (3), or
    (ii)   as a parent of the child by virtue of section 42 or 43 or by virtue of adoption,

then the other woman is to be treated for the purpose mentioned in subsection (4) as a parent of the child.

(3) Subsections (1) and (2) apply whether W was in the United Kingdom or elsewhere at the time of the placing in her of the embryo.

(4) The purpose referred to in subsections (1) and (2) is the purpose of enabling the deceased woman's particulars to be entered as the particulars of the child's other parent in a relevant register of births.

(5) In the application of subsections (1) and (2) to Scotland, for any reference to a period of 42 days there is substituted a reference to a period of 21 days.

47 Woman not to be other parent merely because of egg donation

A woman is not to be treated as the parent of a child whom she is not carrying and has not carried, except where she is so treated—

(a)   by virtue of section 42 or 43, or

(b)   by virtue of section 46 (for the purpose mentioned in subsection (4) of that section), or

(c)   by virtue of adoption.

Effect of sections 33 to 47

48 Effect of sections 33 to 47

(1) Where by virtue of section 33, 35, 36, 42 or 43 a person is to be treated as the mother, father or parent of a child, that person is to be treated in law as the mother, father or parent (as the case may be) of the child for all purposes.

(2) Where by virtue of section 33, 38, 41, 45 or 47 a person is not to be treated as a parent of the child, that person is to be treated in law as not being a parent of the child for any purpose.

(3) Where section 39(1) or 40(1) or (2) applies, the deceased man—

(a)   is to be treated in law as the father of the child for the purpose mentioned in section 39(3) or 40(4), but

(b)   is to be treated in law as not being the father of the child for any other purpose.

(4) Where section 46(1) or (2) applies, the deceased woman—

(a)   is to be treated in law as a parent of the child for the purpose mentioned in section 46(4), but

(b)   is to be treated in law as not being a parent of the child for any other purpose.

(5) Where any of subsections (1) to (4) has effect, references to any relationship between two people in any enactment, deed or other instrument or document (whenever passed or made) are to be read accordingly.

(6) In relation to England and Wales and Northern Ireland, a child who—

(a)   has a parent by virtue of section 42, or

(b)   has a parent by virtue of section 43 who is at any time during the period beginning with the time mentioned in section 43(b) and ending with the time of the child's birth a party to a civil partnership with the child's mother,

is the legitimate child of the child's parents.

(7) In relation to England and Wales and Northern Ireland, nothing in the provisions of section 33(1) or sections 35 to 47, read with this section—

(a)   affects the succession to any dignity or title of honour or renders any person capable of succeeding to or transmitting a right to succeed to any such dignity or title, or

(b)   affects the devolution of any property limited (expressly or not) to devolve (as nearly as the law permits) along with any dignity or title of honour.

(8) In relation to Scotland—

(a)   those provisions do not apply to any title, coat of arms, honour or dignity transmissible on the death of its holder or affect the succession to any such title, coat of arms or dignity or its devolution, and

(b)   where the terms of any deed provide that any property or interest in property is to devolve along with a title, coat of arms, honour or dignity, nothing in those provisions is to prevent that property or interest from so devolving.

References to parties to marriage or civil partnership

49 Meaning of references to parties to a marriage

(1) The references in sections 35 to 47 to the parties to a marriage at any time there

referred to—

(a)   are to the parties to a marriage subsisting at that time, unless a judicial separation was then in force, but

(b)   include the parties to a void marriage if either or both of them reasonably believed at that time that the marriage was valid; and for the purposes of those sections it is to be presumed, unless the contrary is shown, that one of them reasonably believed at that time that the marriage was valid.

(2) In subsection (1)(a) "judicial separation" includes a legal separation obtained in a country outside the British Islands and recognised in the United Kingdom.

50 Meaning of references to parties to a civil partnership

(1) The references in sections 35 to 47 to the parties to a civil partnership at any

time there referred to—

(a)   are to the parties to a civil partnership subsisting at that time, unless a separation order was then in force, but

(b)   include the parties to a void civil partnership if either or both of them reasonably believed at that time that the civil partnership was valid; and for the purposes of those sections it is to be presumed, unless the contrary is shown, that one of them reasonably believed at that time that the civil partnership was valid.

(2) The reference in section 48(6)(b) to a civil partnership includes a reference to a void civil partnership if either or both of the parties reasonably believed at the time when they registered as civil partners of each other that the civil

partnership was valid; and for this purpose it is to be presumed, unless the contrary is shown, that one of them reasonably believed at that time that the civil partnership was valid.

(3) In subsection (1)(a), "separation order" means—

    (a)   a separation order under section 37(1)(d) or 161(1)(d) of the Civil Partnership Act 2004 (c. 33),

    (b)   a decree of separation under section 120(2) of that Act, or

    (c)   a legal separation obtained in a country outside the United Kingdom and recognised in the United Kingdom.

Further provision about registration by virtue of section 39, 40 or 46

51 Meaning of "relevant register of births"

For the purposes of this Part a "relevant register of births", in relation to a birth, is whichever of the following is relevant—

    (a)   a register of live-births or still-births kept under the Births and Deaths Registration Act 1953 (c. 20),

    (b)   a register of births or still-births kept under the Registration of Births, Deaths and Marriages (Scotland) Act 1965 (c. 49), or

    (c)   a register of live-births or still-births kept under the Births and Deaths Registration (Northern Ireland) Order 1976 (S.I. 1976/1041 (N.I. 14)).

52 Late election by mother with consent of Registrar General

(1) The requirement under section 39(1), 40(1) or (2) or 46(1) or (2) as to the making of an election (which requires an election to be made either on or before the day on which the child was born or within the period of 42 or, as the case may be, 21 days from that day) is nevertheless to be treated as satisfied if the required election is made after the end of that period but with the consent of the Registrar General under subsection (2).

(2) The Registrar General may at any time consent to the making of an election after the end of the period mentioned in subsection (1) if, on an application made to him in accordance with such requirements as he may specify, he is satisfied that there is a compelling reason for giving his consent to the making of such an election.

(3) In this section "the Registrar General" means the Registrar General for England and Wales, the Registrar General of Births, Deaths and Marriages for Scotland or (as the case may be) the Registrar General for Northern Ireland.

Interpretation of references to father etc where woman is other parent

53 Interpretation of references to father etc

(1) Subsections (2) and (3) have effect, subject to subsections (4) and (6), for the interpretation of any enactment, deed or any other instrument or document (whenever passed or made).

(2) Any reference (however expressed) to the father of a child who has a parent by virtue of section 42 or 43 is to be read as a reference to the woman who is a parent of the child by virtue of that section.

(3) Any reference (however expressed) to evidence of paternity is, in relation to a woman who is a parent by virtue of section 42 or 43, to be read as a reference to evidence of parentage.

(4) This section does not affect the interpretation of the enactments specified in subsection (5) (which make express provision for the case where a child has a parent by virtue of section 42 or 43).

(5) Those enactments are—

- (a) the Legitimacy Act (Northern Ireland) 1928 (c. 5 (N.I.)),
- (b) the Schedule to the Population (Statistics Act 1938 (c. 12),
- (c) the Births and Deaths Registration Act 1953 (c. 20),
- (d) the Registration of Births, Deaths and Marriages (Special Provisions) Act 1957 (c. 58),
- (e) Part 2 of the Registration of Births, Deaths and Marriages (Scotland) Act 1965 (c. 49),
- (f) the Congenital Disabilities (Civil Liability) Act 1976 (c. 28),
- (g) the Legitimacy Act 1976 (c. 31),
- (h) the Births and Deaths Registration (Northern Ireland) Order 1976 (S.I. 1976/1041 (N.I. 14)),
- (i) the British Nationality Act 1981 (c. 61),
- (j) the Family Law Reform Act 1987 (c. 42),
- (k) Parts 1 and 2 of the Children Act 1989 (c. 41),
- (l) Part 1 of the Children (Scotland) Act 1995 (c. 36),
- (m) section 1 of the Criminal Law (Consolidation) (Scotland) Act 1995 (c. 39), and
- (n) Parts 2, 3 and 14 of the Children (Northern Ireland) Order 1995 (S.I. 1995/755 (N.I.2)).

(6) This section does not affect the interpretation of references that fall to be read in accordance with section 1(2)(a) or (b) of the Family Law Reform Act 1987 or Article 155(2)(a) or (b) of the Children (Northern Ireland) Order 1995 (references to a person whose father and mother were, or were not, married to each other at the time of the person's birth).

Parental orders

54 Parental orders

(1) On an application made by two people ("the applicants"), the court may make an order providing for a child to be treated in law as the child of the applicants if—

- (a) the child has been carried by a woman who is not one of the applicants, as a result of the placing in her of an embryo or sperm and eggs or her artificial insemination,

(b) the gametes of at least one of the applicants were used to bring about the creation of the embryo, and

(c) the conditions in subsections (2) to (8) are satisfied.

(2) The applicants must be—

(a) husband and wife,

(b) civil partners of each other, or

(c) two persons who are living as partners in an enduring family relationship and are not within prohibited degrees of relationship in relation to each other.

(3) Except in a case falling within subsection (11), the applicants must apply for the order during the period of 6 months beginning with the day on which the child is born.

(4) At the time of the application and the making of the order—

(a) the child's home must be with the applicants, and

(b) either or both of the applicants must be domiciled in the United Kingdom or in the Channel Islands or the Isle of Man.

(5) At the time of the making of the order both the applicants must have attained the age of 18.

(6) The court must be satisfied that both—

(a) the woman who carried the child, and

(b) any other person who is a parent of the child but is not one of the applicants (including any man who is the father by virtue of section 35 or 36 or any woman who is a parent by virtue of section 42 or 43), have freely, and with full understanding of what is involved, agreed unconditionally to the making of the order.

(7) Subsection (6) does not require the agreement of a person who cannot be found or is incapable of giving agreement; and the agreement of the woman who carried the child is ineffective for the purpose of that subsection if given by her less than six weeks after the child's birth.

(8) The court must be satisfied that no money or other benefit (other than for expenses reasonably incurred) has been given or received by either of the applicants for or in consideration of—

(a) the making of the order,

(b) any agreement required by subsection (6),

(c) the handing over of the child to the applicants, or

(d) the making of arrangements with a view to the making of the order, unless authorised by the court.

(9) For the purposes of an application under this section—

(a) in relation to England and Wales, section 92(7) to (10) of, and Part 1 of Schedule 11 to, the Children Act 1989 (c. 41) (jurisdiction of courts) apply for the purposes of this section to determine the meaning of "the court" as they apply for the purposes of that Act and proceedings on the application are to be "family proceedings" for the purposes of that Act,

(b)   in relation to Scotland, "the court" means the Court of Session or the sheriff court of the sheriffdom within which the child is, and

(c)   in relation to Northern Ireland, "the court" means the High Court or any county court within whose division the child is.

(10) Subsection (1)(a) applies whether the woman was in the United Kingdom or elsewhere at the time of the placing in her of the embryo or the sperm and eggs or her artificial insemination.

(11) An application which—

(a)   relates to a child born before the coming into force of this section, and

(b)   is made by two persons who, throughout the period applicable under subsection (2) of section 30 of the 1990 Act, were not eligible to apply for an order under that section in relation to the child as husband and wife,

may be made within the period of six months beginning with the day on which this section comes into force.

55 Parental orders: supplementary provision

(1) The Secretary of State may by regulations provide—

(a)   for any provision of the enactments about adoption to have effect, with such modifications (if any) as may be specified in the regulations, in relation to orders under section 54, and applications for such orders, as it has effect in relation to adoption, and applications for adoption orders, and

(b)   for references in any enactment to adoption, an adopted child or an adoptive relationship to be read (respectively) as references to the effect of an order under section 54, a child to whom such an order applies and a relationship arising by virtue of the enactments about adoption, as applied by the regulations, and for similar expressions in connection with adoption to be read accordingly.

(2) The regulations may include such incidental or supplemental provision as appears to the Secretary of State to be necessary or desirable in consequence of any provision made by virtue of subsection (1)(a) or (b).

(3) In this section "the enactments about adoption" means—

(a)   the Adoption (Scotland) Act 1978 (c. 28),

(b)   the Adoption and Children Act 2002 (c. 38),

(c)   the Adoption and Children (Scotland) Act 2007 (asp 4), and

(d)   the Adoption (Northern Ireland) Order 1987 (S.I. 1987/2203 (N.I. 22)).

Amendments of enactments

56 Amendments relating to parenthood in cases involving assisted reproduction

Schedule 6 contains amendments related to the provisions of this Part.

General

57 Repeals and transitional provision relating to Part 2

(1) Sections 33 to 48 have effect only in relation to children carried by women as a result of the placing in them of embryos or of sperm and eggs, or their artificial insemination (as the case may be), after the commencement of those sections.

(2) Sections 27 to 29 of the 1990 Act (which relate to status) do not have effect in relation to children carried by women as a result of the placing in them of embryos or of sperm and eggs, or their artificial insemination (as the case may be), after the commencement of sections 33 to 48.

(3) Section 30 of the 1990 Act (parental orders in favour of gamete donors) ceases to have effect.

(4) Subsection (3) does not affect the validity of any order made under section 30 of the 1990 Act before the coming into force of that subsection.

58 Interpretation of Part 2

(1) In this Part "enactment" means an enactment contained in, or in an instrument

made under—

  (a)   an Act of Parliament,
  (b)   an Act of the Scottish Parliament,
  (c)   a Measure or Act of the National Assembly for Wales, or
  (d)   Northern Ireland legislation.

(2) For the purposes of this Part, two persons are within prohibited degrees of relationship if one is the other's parent, grandparent, sister, brother, aunt or uncle; and in this subsection references to relationships—

  (a)   are to relationships of the full blood or half blood or, in the case of an adopted person, such of those relationships as would subsist but for adoption, and
  (b)   include the relationship of a child with his adoptive, or former adoptive, parents, but do not include any other adoptive relationships.

(3) Other expressions used in this Part and in the 1990 Act have the same meaning in this Part as in that Act.

PART 3
MISCELLANEOUS AND GENERAL

Miscellaneous

59 Surrogacy arrangements

(1) The Surrogacy Arrangements Act 1985 (c. 49) is amended as follows.

(2) In section 1 (meaning of various terms), after subsection (7) insert—

(7A) "Non-profit making body" means a body of persons whose activities are not carried on for profit.

(3) In section 2 (negotiating surrogacy arrangements on a commercial basis), in subsection (1)—

(a)   in paragraph (a) omit "or take part in", and
(b)   after paragraph (a) insert—

(aa)   take part in any negotiations with a view to the making of a surrogacy arrangement,.

(4) After subsection (2) insert—

(2A) A non-profit making body does not contravene subsection (1) merely because—

(a)   the body does an act falling within subsection (1)(a) or (c) in respect of which any reasonable payment is at any time received by it or another, or
(b)   it does an act falling within subsection (1)(a) or (c) with a view to any reasonable payment being received by it or another in respect of facilitating the making of any surrogacy arrangement.

(2B) A person who knowingly causes a non-profit making body to do an act falling within subsection (1)(a) or (c) does not contravene subsection (1) merely because—

(a)   any reasonable payment is at any time received by the body or another in respect of the body doing the act, or
(b)   the body does the act with a view to any reasonable payment being received by it or another person in respect of the body facilitating the making of any surrogacy arrangement.

(2C) Any reference in subsection (2A) or (2B) to a reasonable payment in respect of the doing of an act by a non-profit making body is a reference to a payment not exceeding the body's costs reasonably attributable to the doing of the act.

(5) After subsection (5) of that section insert—

(5A) A non-profit making body is not guilty of an offence under subsection (5), in respect of the receipt of any payment described in that subsection, merely because a person acting on behalf of the body takes part in facilitating the making of a surrogacy arrangement.

(6) After subsection (8) of that section insert—

(8A) A person is not guilty of an offence under subsection (7) if—

(a)   the body of persons referred to in that subsection is a non-profit making body, and

(b) the only activity of that body which falls within subsection (8) is facilitating the making of surrogacy arrangements in the United Kingdom.

(8B) In subsection (8A)(b) "facilitating the making of surrogacy arrangements" is to be construed in accordance with subsection (8).

(7) In section 3 (advertisements about surrogacy), after subsection (1) insert—

(1A) This section does not apply to any advertisement placed by, or on behalf of, a non-profit making body if the advertisement relates only to the doing by the body of acts that would not contravene section 2(1) even if done on a commercial basis (within the meaning of section 2).

60 Exclusion of embryos from definition of "organism" in Part 6 of the EPA 1990

(1) Section 106 of the Environmental Protection Act 1990 (c. 43) (meaning of "genetically modified organisms" etc) is amended as follows.

(2) In subsection (2), for "or human embryos" substitute ", human embryos or human admixed embryos".

(3) After subsection (3) insert—

(3A) For the purposes of subsection (2) above—

(a) "human embryo" means an embryo within the meaning given in the provisions of the Human Fertilisation and Embryology Act 1990 (apart from section 4A) by virtue of section 1(1) and (6) of that Act, and

(b) "human admixed embryo" has the same meaning as it has in that Act by virtue of section 4A(6) and (11) of that Act.

General

61 Orders and regulations: general provisions

(1) Any power of the Secretary of State to make an order or regulations under this Act is exercisable by statutory instrument.

(2) Any power of the Secretary of State to make an order or regulations under this Act may be exercised—

(a) either in relation to all cases to which the power extends, or in relation to those cases subject to specified exceptions, or in relation to any specified cases or classes of case, and

(b) so as to make, as respects the cases in relation to which it is exercised—

(i) the full provision to which the power extends or any less provision (whether by way of exception or otherwise);

(ii) the same provision for all cases in relation to which the power is exercised, or different provision as respects the same case or class of case for different purposes;

(iii) any such provision either unconditionally, or subject to any specified condition.

(3) Any power of the Secretary of State to make an order or regulations under this Act includes power to make such transitional, saving, incidental or supplemental provision as the Secretary of State considers appropriate.

62 Orders and regulations: parliamentary control

(1) Orders made by the Secretary of State under this Act are subject to annulment in pursuance of a resolution of either House of Parliament.

(2) Subsection (1) does not apply to—

  (a)   an order to which subsection (3) applies, or
  (b)   an order under section 68 (commencement).

(3) No order under section 64 (power to make consequential and transitional provision etc) which includes provision made by virtue of subsection (2) of that section may be made unless a draft of the order has been laid before, and approved by a resolution of, each House of Parliament.

(4) No regulations under section 55 (parental orders: supplementary provision) may be made unless a draft of the regulations has been laid before, and approved by a resolution of, each House of Parliament.

63 Meaning of "the 1990 Act"

In this Act, "the 1990 Act" means the Human Fertilisation and Embryology Act 1990 (c. 37).

64 Power to make consequential and transitional provision etc

(1) The Secretary of State may by order make—

  (a)   any supplementary, incidental or consequential provision, and
  (b)   any transitional or saving provision,

that the Secretary of State considers necessary or expedient for the purposes of, in consequence of, or for giving full effect to, any provision of this Act.

(2) An order under this section may modify—

  (a)   any enactment passed or made before the passing of this Act, and
  (b)   any enactment passed or made before the end of the Session in which this Act is passed.

(3) An order under this section which modifies an enactment in consequence of any provision of Part 2 may modify subsection (5) of section 53 (interpretation of references to father etc).

(4) An order under this section may provide for any provision of this Act which comes into force before any other provision comes into force to have effect, until that other provision has come into force, with specified modifications.

(5) Before making an order under this section containing provision which would, if included in an Act of the Scottish Parliament, be within the legislative competence of that Parliament, the Secretary of State must consult the Scottish Ministers.

(6) Before making an order under this section containing provision which would be within the legislative competence of the National Assembly for Wales if it were included in a Measure of the Assembly (or, if the order is made after the Assembly Act provisions come into force, an Act of the Assembly), the Secretary of State must consult the Welsh Ministers.

(7) Before making an order under this section containing provision which would, if included in an Act of the Northern Ireland Assembly, be within the legislative competence of that Assembly, the Secretary of State must consult the Department of Health, Social Services and Public Safety.

(8) Nothing in this section limits the power under section 61 to include transitional or saving provision in a commencement order under section 68(2).

(9) The modifications that may be made by virtue of subsection (2) are in addition to those that are made by any other provision of this Act.

(10) In this section—

"enactment" means an enactment contained in, or in an instrument made under—

(a)   an Act of Parliament,
(b)   an Act of the Scottish Parliament,
(c)   a Measure of the National Assembly for Wales, or
(d)   Northern Ireland legislation;

"modify" includes amend, add to, revoke or repeal, and references to "modifications" are to be read accordingly;
"the Assembly Act provisions" has the meaning given by section 103(8) of the Government of Wales Act 2006 (c. 32).

65 Minor and consequential amendments

Schedule 7 contains minor and consequential amendments.

66 Repeals and revocations

Schedule 8 contains repeals and revocations.

67 Extent

(1) Subject to the following provisions, this Act extends to England and Wales, Scotland and Northern Ireland.

(2) Any amendment or repeal made by this Act has the same extent as the enactment to which it relates (ignoring extent by virtue of an Order in Council).

(3) Subsection (2) is subject to paragraph 1(2) of Schedule 6.

(4) Her Majesty may by Order in Council provide for any of the provisions of this Act to extend, with or without modifications, to the Bailiwick of Guernsey.

(5) Subsection (4) does not authorise the extension to the Bailiwick of Guernsey of a provision of this Act so far as the provision amends an enactment that does not itself extend there and is not itself capable of being extended there in exercise of a power conferred on Her Majesty in Council.

(6) Subsection (4) does not apply in relation to the extension to the Bailiwick of Guernsey of a provision which extends there by virtue of subsection (2).

(7) Subsection (3) of section 61 applies to the power to make an Order in Council under this section as it applies to any power of the Secretary of State to make an order under this Act, but as if the references in that subsection to the Secretary of State were references to Her Majesty in Council.

68 Commencement

(1) The following provisions of this Act come into force on the day on which this Act is passed—

sections 61 to 64;
section 67, this section and section 69.

(2) The remaining provisions of this Act come into force in accordance with provision made by the Secretary of State by order.

69 Short title

This Act may be cited as the Human Fertilisation and Embryology Act 2008.

Schedule 1

Section 5

Amendments to Schedule 1 to the 1990 Act Relating to Membership of the Authority

1 Schedule 1 to the 1990 Act (supplementary provision about Authority) is amended as follows.

2 After paragraph 4 (appointment of members) insert—

4A

(1) A person ("P") is disqualified for being appointed as chairman, deputy chairman, or as any other member of the Authority if—

    (a)   P is the subject of a bankruptcy restrictions order or interim order,

    (b)   a bankruptcy order has been made against P by a court in Northern Ireland, P's estate has been sequestered by a court in Scotland, or under the law of Northern Ireland or Scotland, P has made a composition or arrangement with, or granted a trust deed for, P's creditors, or

    (c)   in the last five years P has been convicted in the United Kingdom, the Channel Islands or the Isle of Man of an offence and has had a qualifying sentence passed on P.

(2) Where P is disqualified under sub-paragraph (1)(b) because a bankruptcy order has been made against P or P's estate has been sequestered, the disqualification ceases—

    (a)   on P obtaining a discharge, or

    (b)   if the bankruptcy order is annulled or the sequestration of P's estate is recalled or reduced, on the date of that event.

(3) Where P is disqualified under sub-paragraph (1)(b) because of P having made a composition or arrangement with, or granted a trust deed for, P's creditors, the disqualification ceases—

    (a)   at the end of the period of five years beginning with the date on which the terms of the deed of composition or arrangement or trust deed are fulfilled, or

    (b)   if, before then, P pays P's debts in full, on the date on which the payment is completed.

(4) For the purposes of sub-paragraph (1)(c), the date of conviction is to be taken to be the ordinary date on which the period allowed for making an appeal or application expires or, if an appeal or application is made, the date on which the appeal or application is finally disposed of or abandoned or fails by reason of its non prosecution.

(5) In sub-paragraph (1)(c), the reference to a qualifying sentence is to a sentence of imprisonment for a period of not less than three months (whether suspended or not) without the option of a fine.

3 In paragraph 5—

    (a)   after sub-paragraph (4), insert—

    (4A) A person holding office as chairman, deputy chairman or other member of the Authority is to cease to hold that office if the person becomes disqualified for appointment to it.", and

    (b)   in sub-paragraph (5)—

        (i)   omit paragraph (b) and the word "or" immediately after it,

        (ii)   in paragraph (c) for "functions of a member" substitute "person's functions as chairman, deputy chairman or other member", and

        (iii)   in the full-out words, for the words from "declare" to the end substitute "remove the member from office as chairman, deputy chairman or other member".

Schedule 2

Section 11

Activities that may be Licensed under the 1990 Act

Introductory

1 Schedule 2 to the 1990 Act (activities for which licences may be granted) is amended as follows.

Licences for treatment

2

(1) Paragraph 1 (licences for treatment) is amended as follows.

(2) In sub-paragraph (1)—

    (a)   after paragraph (c) insert—

        (ca)   using embryos for the purpose of training persons in embryo biopsy, embryo storage or other embryological techniques,

    (b)   in paragraph (d), omit the words from "or" onwards,

    (c)   in paragraph (e), for "embryo" substitute "permitted embryo", and

    (d)   in paragraph (g), after "practices" insert ", apart from practices falling within section 4A(2),".

(3) For sub-paragraph (4) substitute—

(4) A licence under this paragraph cannot authorise altering the nuclear or mitochondrial DNA of a cell while it forms part of an embryo, except for the purpose of creating something that will by virtue of regulations under section 3ZA(5) be a permitted embryo.

(4) After sub-paragraph (4) insert—

(4A) A licence under this paragraph cannot authorise the use of embryos for the purpose mentioned in sub-paragraph (1)(ca) unless the Authority is satisfied that the proposed use of embryos is necessary for that purpose.

(5) At the end insert—

(6) In this paragraph, references to a permitted embryo are to be read in accordance with section 3ZA.

Embryo testing and sex selection

3 After paragraph 1 insert—

Embryo testing

    1ZA

(1) A licence under paragraph 1 cannot authorise the testing of an embryo, except for one or more of the following purposes—

(a)   establishing whether the embryo has a gene, chromosome or mitochondrion abnormality that may affect its capacity to result in a live birth,

(b)   in a case where there is a particular risk that the embryo may have any gene, chromosome or mitochondrion abnormality, establishing whether it has that abnormality or any other gene, chromosome or mitochondrion abnormality,

(c)   in a case where there is a particular risk that any resulting child will have or develop—

(i)   a gender-related serious physical or mental disability,

(ii)   a gender-related serious illness, or

(iii)   any other gender-related serious medical condition,

establishing the sex of the embryo,

(d)   in a case where a person ("the sibling") who is the child of the persons whose gametes are used to bring about the creation of the embryo (or of either of those persons) suffers from a serious medical condition which could be treated by umbilical cord blood stem cells, bone marrow or other tissue of any resulting child, establishing whether the tissue of any resulting child would be compatible with that of the sibling, and

(e)   in a case where uncertainty has arisen as to whether the embryo is one of those whose creation was brought about by using the gametes of particular persons, establishing whether it is.

(2) A licence under paragraph 1 cannot authorise the testing of embryos for the purpose mentioned in sub-paragraph (1)(b) unless the Authority is satisfied—

(a)   in relation to the abnormality of which there is a particular risk, and

(b)   in relation to any other abnormality for which testing is to be authorised under sub-paragraph (1)(b), that there is a significant risk that a person with the abnormality will have or develop a serious physical or mental disability, a serious illness or any other serious medical condition.

(3) For the purposes of sub-paragraph (1)(c), a physical or mental disability, illness or other medical condition is gender-related if the Authority is satisfied that—

(a)   it affects only one sex, or

(b)   it affects one sex significantly more than the other.

(4) In sub-paragraph (1)(d) the reference to "other tissue" of the resulting child does not include a reference to any whole organ of the child.

Sex selection

1ZB

(1) A licence under paragraph 1 cannot authorise any practice designed to secure that any resulting child will be of one sex rather than the other.

(2) Sub-paragraph (1) does not prevent the authorisation of any testing of embryos that is capable of being authorised under paragraph 1ZA.

(3) Sub-paragraph (1) does not prevent the authorisation of any other practices designed to secure that any resulting child will be of one sex rather than the other in a case where there is a particular risk that a woman will give birth to a child who will have or develop—

(a)   a gender-related serious physical or mental disability,
(b)   a gender-related serious illness, or
(c)   any other gender-related serious medical condition.

(4) For the purposes of sub-paragraph (3), a physical or mental disability, illness or other medical condition is gender-related if the Authority is satisfied that—

(a)   it affects only one sex, or
(b)   it affects one sex significantly more than the other.

Power to amend paragraphs 1ZA and 1ZB

1ZC

(1) Regulations may make any amendment of paragraph 1ZA (embryo testing).

(2) Regulations under this paragraph which amend paragraph 1ZA may make any amendment of sub-paragraphs (2) to (4) of paragraph 1ZB (sex selection) which appears to the Secretary of State to be necessary or expedient in consequence of the amendment of paragraph 1ZA.

(3) Regulations under this paragraph may not enable the authorisation of—

(a)   the testing of embryos for the purpose of establishing their sex, or
(b)   other practices falling within paragraph 1ZB(1), except on grounds relating to the health of any resulting child.

(4) For the purposes of this paragraph, "amend" includes add to and repeal, and references to "amendment" are to be read accordingly.

Licences for non-medical fertility services

4 In paragraph 1A (licences for non-medical fertility services) after subparagraph (1) insert—

(1A) A licence under this paragraph cannot authorise the procurement or distribution of sperm to which there has been applied any process designed to secure that any resulting child will be of one sex rather than the other.

Licences for storage

5 In paragraph 2 (licences for storage)—

(a)   after sub-paragraph (1) insert—

(1A) A licence under this paragraph or paragraph 3 may authorise the storage of human admixed embryos (whether or not the licence also authorises the storage of gametes or embryos or both)., and

(b)   in sub-paragraph (2), after "such storage" insert "as is mentioned in sub-paragraph (1) or (1A)".

Licences for research

6 For paragraph 3 substitute—

Licences for research

3

(1) A licence under this paragraph may authorise any of the

following—

    (a)   bringing about the creation of embryos in vitro, and

    (b)   keeping or using embryos,

for the purposes of a project of research specified in the licence.

(2) A licence under this paragraph may authorise mixing sperm with the egg of a hamster, or other animal specified in directions, for the purpose of developing more effective techniques for determining the fertility or normality of sperm, but only where anything which forms is destroyed when the research is complete and, in any event, no later than the two cell stage.

(3) A licence under this paragraph may authorise any of the following—

    (a)   bringing about the creation of human admixed embryos in vitro, and

    (b)   keeping or using human admixed embryos, for the purposes of a project of research specified in the licence.

(4) A licence under sub-paragraph (3) may not authorise the activity which may be authorised by a licence under sub-paragraph (2).

(5) No licence under this paragraph is to be granted unless the Authority is satisfied that any proposed use of embryos or human admixed embryos is necessary for the purposes of the research.

(6) Subject to the provisions of this Act, a licence under this paragraph may be granted subject to such conditions as may be specified in the licence.

(7) A licence under this paragraph may authorise the performance of any of the activities referred to in sub-paragraph (1), (2) or (3) in such manner as may be so specified.

(8) A licence under this paragraph may be granted for such period not exceeding three years as may be specified in the licence.

(9) This paragraph has effect subject to paragraph 3A.

Purposes for which activities may be licensed under paragraph 3

3A

(1) A licence under paragraph 3 cannot authorise any activity unless the activity appears to the Authority—

    (a)   to be necessary or desirable for any of the purposes specified in sub-paragraph (2) ("the principal purposes"),

    (b)   to be necessary or desirable for the purpose of providing knowledge that, in the view of the Authority, may be capable of being applied for the purposes specified in subparagraph (2)(a) or (b), or

    (c)   to be necessary or desirable for such other purposes as may be specified in regulations.

(2) The principal purposes are—

    (a)   increasing knowledge about serious disease or other serious medical conditions,

    (b)   developing treatments for serious disease or other serious medical conditions,

    (c)   increasing knowledge about the causes of any congenital disease or congenital medical condition that does not fall within paragraph (a),

    (d)   promoting advances in the treatment of infertility,

    (e)   increasing knowledge about the causes of miscarriage,

    (f)   developing more effective techniques of contraception,

    (g)   developing methods for detecting the presence of gene, chromosome or mitochondrion abnormalities in embryos before implantation, or

    (h)   increasing knowledge about the development of embryos.

Schedule 3

Section 13

Consent to use or storage of gametes, embryos or human admixed embryos etc

Introductory

1

Schedule 3 to the 1990 Act (giving of consent to use or storage of gametes or embryos) is amended as follows.

2

In the title to that Schedule, for "OF GAMETES OR EMBRYOS", substitute "OR STORAGE OF GAMETES, EMBRYOS OR HUMAN ADMIXED EMBRYOS ETC".

General requirements as to consent

3

For paragraph 1 substitute—

    1

    (1) A consent under this Schedule, and any notice under paragraph 4 varying or withdrawing a consent under this Schedule, must be in writing and, subject to sub-paragraph (2), must be signed by the person giving it.

    (2) A consent under this Schedule by a person who is unable to sign because of illness, injury or physical disability (a "person unable to sign"), and any notice under paragraph 4 by a person unable to sign varying or withdrawing a consent under this Schedule, is to be taken to comply with the requirement of sub-paragraph (1) as to signature if it is signed at the direction of the person

unable to sign, in the presence of the person unable to sign and in the presence of at least one witness who attests the signature.

(3) In this Schedule "effective consent" means a consent under this Schedule which has not been withdrawn.

Terms of consent

4

(1) Paragraph 2 (terms etc of consent) is amended as follows.

(2) In sub-paragraph (1), for the "or" at the end of paragraph (b) substitute—

(ba) use for the purpose of training persons in embryo biopsy, embryo storage or other embryological techniques, or.

(3) After sub-paragraph (1) insert—

(1A) A consent to the use of any human admixed embryo must specify use for the purposes of any project of research and may specify conditions subject to which the human admixed embryo may be so used.

(4) For sub-paragraph (2) substitute—

(2) A consent to the storage of any gametes, any embryo or any human admixed embryo must—

    (a)   specify the maximum period of storage (if less than the statutory storage period),

    (b)   except in a case falling within paragraph (c), state what is to be done with the gametes, embryo or human admixed embryo if the person who gave the consent dies or is unable, because the person lacks capacity to do so, to vary the terms of the consent or to withdraw it, and

    (c)   where the consent is given by virtue of paragraph 8(2A) or 13(2), state what is to be done with the embryo or human admixed embryo if the person to whom the consent relates dies, and may (in any case) specify conditions subject to which the gametes, embryo or human admixed embryo may remain in storage.

(2A) A consent to the use of a person's human cells to bring about the creation in vitro of an embryo or human admixed embryo is to be taken unless otherwise stated to include consent to the use of the cells after the person's death.

(2B) In relation to Scotland, the reference in sub-paragraph (2)(b) to the person lacking capacity is to be read as a reference to the person—

    (a)   lacking capacity within the meaning of the Age of Legal Capacity (Scotland) Act 1991, or

    (b)   being incapable within the meaning of section 1(6) of the Adults with Incapacity (Scotland) Act 2000.

(5) For sub-paragraph (4) substitute—

(4) A consent under this Schedule may apply—

    (a)   to the use or storage of a particular embryo or human admixed embryo, or

    (b)   in the case of a person providing gametes or human cells, to the use or storage of—

      (i)   any embryo or human admixed embryo whose creation may be brought about using those gametes or those cells, and

      (ii)   any embryo or human admixed embryo whose creation may be brought about using such an embryo or human admixed embryo.

(5) In the case of a consent falling within sub-paragraph (4)(b), the terms of the consent may be varied, or the consent may be withdrawn, in accordance with this Schedule either generally or in relation to—

      (a)   a particular embryo or particular embryos, or

      (b)   a particular human admixed embryo or particular human admixed embryos.

Information to be given to a person giving consent

5

In paragraph 3 (procedure for giving consent), in sub-paragraph (2), after "paragraph 4" insert "and, if relevant, paragraph 4A".

Variation and withdrawal of consent

6

(1) Paragraph 4 (variation and withdrawal of consent) is amended as follows.

(2) In sub-paragraph (1), for "or embryo" substitute ", human cells, embryo or human admixed embryo".

(3) In sub-paragraph (2)—

    (a)   for "The" substitute "Subject to sub-paragraph (3), the", and

    (b)   for the "or" at the end of paragraph (a) substitute—

        (aa)   in training persons in embryo biopsy, embryo storage or other embryological techniques, or.

(4) After sub-paragraph (2) insert—

    (3) Where the terms of any consent to the use of an embryo ("embryo A") include consent to the use of an embryo or human admixed embryo whose creation may be brought about in vitro using embryo A, that consent to the use of that subsequent embryo or human admixed embryo cannot be varied or withdrawn once embryo A has been used for one or more of the purposes mentioned in sub-paragraph (2)(a) or (b).

    (4) Subject to sub-paragraph (5), the terms of any consent to the use of any human admixed embryo cannot be varied, and such consent cannot be withdrawn, once the human admixed embryo has been used for the purposes of any project of research.

    (5) Where the terms of any consent to the use of a human admixed embryo ("human admixed embryo A") include consent to the use of a human admixed embryo or embryo whose creation may be brought about in vitro using human admixed embryo A, that consent to the use of that subsequent human admixed embryo or embryo cannot be varied or withdrawn once human admixed embryo A has been used for the purposes of any project of research.

Withdrawal of consent to storage: notification of interested persons

7

4A

(1) This paragraph applies where—

    (a)   a permitted embryo, the creation of which was brought about in vitro, is in storage,

    (b)   it was created for use in providing treatment services,

    (c)   before it is used in providing treatment services, one of the persons whose gametes were used to bring about its creation ("P") gives the person keeping the embryo notice withdrawing P's consent to the storage of the embryo, and

    (d)   the embryo was not to be used in providing treatment services to P alone.

(2) The person keeping the embryo must as soon as possible take all reasonable steps to notify each interested person in relation to the embryo of P's withdrawal of consent.

(3) For the purposes of sub-paragraph (2), a person is an interested person in relation to an embryo if the embryo was to be used in providing treatment services to that person.

(4) Storage of the embryo remains lawful until

(5) The reference in sub-paragraph (1)(a) to a permitted embryo is to be read in accordance with section 3ZA.

Application of consent provisions to non-medical fertility services

8

In paragraph 5 (use of gametes for treatment of others), in sub-paragraph (1), after "treatment services" insert "or non-medical fertility services".

In vitro fertilisation and subsequent use of embryo

9

(1) Paragraph 6 (in vitro fertilisation and subsequent use of embryo) is amended as follows.

(2) In sub-paragraph (1)—

    (a)   after "person's gametes" insert "or human cells",

    (b)   after "to any embryo" insert a comma,

    (c)   after "those gametes" insert "or human cells,", and

    (d)   for "paragraph 2(1)" substitute "paragraph 2(1)(a), (b) and (c)".

(3) In sub-paragraph (2)—

    (a)   for the words from "each person" to "creation of" substitute "each relevant person in relation to", and

    (b)   for "paragraph 2(1)" substitute "paragraph 2(1)(a), (b), (ba) and (c)".

(4) In sub-paragraph (3), for the words from "person" to "creation of" substitute "relevant person in relation to".

(5) After sub-paragraph (3) insert—

> (3A) If the Authority is satisfied that the parental consent conditions in paragraph 15 are met in relation to the proposed use under a licence of the human cells of a person who has not attained the age of 18 years ("C"), the Authority may in the licence authorise the application of sub-paragraph (3B) in relation to C.
>
> (3B) Where the licence authorises the application of this subparagraph, the effective consent of a person having parental responsibility for C—
>
> > (a)   to the use of C's human cells to bring about the creation of an embryo in vitro for use for the purposes of a project of research, or
> >
> > (b)   to the use for those purposes of an embryo in relation to which C is a relevant person by reason only of the use of C's human cells, is to be treated for the purposes of sub-paragraphs (1) to (3) as the effective consent of C.
>
> (3C) If C attains the age of 18 years or the condition in paragraph 15(3) ceases to be met in relation to C, paragraph 4 has effect in relation to C as if any effective consent previously given under subparagraphs (1) to (3) by a person having parental responsibility for C had been given by C but, subject to that, sub-paragraph (3B) ceases to apply in relation to C. (3D) Sub-paragraphs (1) to (3) have effect subject to paragraphs 16 and 20.
>
> (3E) For the purposes of sub-paragraphs (2), (3) and (3B), each of the following is a relevant person in relation to an embryo the creation of which was brought about in vitro ("embryo A")—
>
> > (a)   each person whose gametes or human cells were used to bring about the creation of embryo A,
> >
> > (b)   each person whose gametes or human cells were used to bring about the creation of any other embryo, the creation of which was brought about in vitro, which was used to bring about the creation of embryo A, and
> >
> > (c)   each person whose gametes or human cells were used to bring about the creation of any human admixed embryo, the creation of which was brought about in vitro, which was used to bring about the creation of embryo A.

Use of embryos obtained by lavage etc

10

(1) Paragraph 7 (embryos obtained by lavage etc) is amended as follows.

(2) In sub-paragraph (3), for "This paragraph does" substitute "Sub-paragraphs (1) and (2) do".

(3) After sub-paragraph (3) insert—

> (4) An embryo taken from a woman must not be used to bring about the creation of any embryo in vitro or any human admixed embryo in vitro.

Consents in relation to storage

11

(1) Paragraph 8 (storage of gametes and embryos) is amended as follows.

(2) In sub-paragraph (2), for the words from "person" to "creation of" substitute "relevant person in relation to".

(3) After sub-paragraph (2) insert—

> (2A) Where a licence authorises the application of paragraph 6(3B) in relation to a person who has not attained the age of 18 years ("C"), the effective consent of a person having parental responsibility for C to the storage of an embryo in relation to which C is a relevant person by reason only of the use of C's human cells is to be treated for the purposes of sub-paragraph (2) as the effective consent of C.

> (2B) If C attains the age of 18 years or the condition in paragraph 15(3) ceases to be met in relation to C, paragraph 4 has effect in relation to C as if any effective consent previously given under subparagraph (2) by a person having parental responsibility for C had been given by C but, subject to that, sub-paragraph (2A) ceases to apply in relation to C.

> (2C) For the purposes of sub-paragraphs (2) and (2A), each of the following is a relevant person in relation to an embryo the creation of which was brought about in vitro ("embryo A")—
>
> > (a) each person whose gametes or human cells were used to bring about the creation of embryo A,
> > (b) each person whose gametes or human cells were used to bring about the creation of any other embryo, the creation of which was brought about in vitro, which was used to bring about the creation of embryo A, and
> > (c) each person whose gametes or human cells were used to bring about the creation of any human admixed embryo, the creation of which was brought about in vitro, which was used to bring about the creation of embryo A.

(4) After sub-paragraph (3) insert—

> (4) Sub-paragraph (1) has effect subject to paragraphs 9 and 10; and sub-paragraph (2) has effect subject to paragraphs 4A(4), 16 and 20.

12

After paragraph 8 insert—

Cases where consent not required for storage

9

> (1) The gametes of a person ("C") may be kept in storage without C's consent if the following conditions are met.

> (2) Condition A is that the gametes are lawfully taken from or provided by C before C attains the age of 18 years.

> (3) Condition B is that, before the gametes are first stored, a registered medical practitioner certifies in writing that C is expected to undergo medical treatment and that in the opinion of the registered medical practitioner—

   (a)   the treatment is likely to cause a significant impairment of C's fertility, and
   (b)   the storage of the gametes is in C's best interests.

(4) Condition C is that, at the time when the gametes are first stored, either—

   (a)   C has not attained the age of 16 years and is not competent to deal with the issue of consent to the storage of the gametes, or
   (b)   C has attained that age but, although not lacking capacity to consent to the storage of the gametes, is not competent to deal with the issue of consent to their storage.

(5) Condition D is that C has not, since becoming competent to deal with the issue of consent to the storage of the gametes—

   (a)   given consent under this Schedule to the storage of the gametes, or
   (b)   given written notice to the person keeping the gametes that C does not wish them to continue to be stored.

(6) In relation to Scotland, sub-paragraphs (1) to (5) are to be read with the following modifications—

   (a)   for sub-paragraph (4), substitute—
          (4) Condition C is that, at the time when the gametes are first stored, C does not have capacity (within the meaning of section 2(4) of the Age of Legal Capacity (Scotland) Act 1991) to consent to the storage of the gametes.", and
   (b)   in sub-paragraph (5), for "becoming competent to deal with the issue of consent to the storage of the gametes" substitute "acquiring such capacity".

10

(1) The gametes of a person ("P") may be kept in storage without P's consent if the following conditions are met.

(2) Condition A is that the gametes are lawfully taken from or provided by P after P has attained the age of 16 years.

(3) Condition B is that, before the gametes are first stored, a registered medical practitioner certifies in writing that P is expected to undergo medical treatment and that in the opinion of the registered medical practitioner—

   (a)   the treatment is likely to cause a significant impairment of P's fertility,
   (b)   P lacks capacity to consent to the storage of the gametes,
   (c)   P is likely at some time to have that capacity, and
   (d)   the storage of the gametes is in P's best interests.

(4) Condition C is that, at the time when the gametes are first stored, P lacks capacity to consent to their storage.

(5) Condition D is that P has not subsequently, at a time when P has capacity to give a consent under this Schedule—

   (a)   given consent to the storage of the gametes, or
   (b)   given written notice to the person keeping the gametes that P does not wish them to continue to be stored.

(6) In relation to Scotland—

(a)   references in sub-paragraphs (3) and (4) to P lacking capacity to consent are to be read as references to P being incapable, within the meaning of section 1(6) of the Adults with Incapacity (Scotland) Act 2000, of giving such consent,

(b)   the references in sub-paragraphs (3) and (5) to P having capacity are to be read as references to P not being so incapable, and

(c)   that Act applies to the storage of gametes under this paragraph to the extent specified in section 84A of that Act.

11

A person's gametes must not be kept in storage by virtue of paragraph 9 or 10 after the person's death.

Creation, use and storage of human admixed embryos

13

After paragraph 11 (as inserted by paragraph 12 above) insert—

Creation, use and storage of human admixed embryos

12

(1) A person's gametes or human cells must not be used to bring about the creation of any human admixed embryo in vitro unless there is an effective consent by that person to any human admixed embryo, the creation of which may be brought about with the use of those gametes or human cells, being used for the purposes of any project of research.

(2) A human admixed embryo the creation of which was brought about in vitro must not be received by any person unless there is an effective consent by each relevant person in relation to the human admixed embryo to the use of the human admixed embryo for the purposes of any project of research.

(3) A human admixed embryo the creation of which was brought about in vitro must not be used for the purposes of a project of research unless—

(a)   there is an effective consent by each relevant person in relation to the human admixed embryo to the use of the human admixed embryo for that purpose, and

(b)   the human admixed embryo is used in accordance with those consents.

(4) If the Authority is satisfied that the parental consent conditions in paragraph 15 are met in relation to the proposed use under a licence of the human cells of a person who has not attained the age of 18 years ("C"), the Authority may in the licence authorise the application of sub-paragraph (5) in relation to C.

(5) Where the licence authorises the application of this subparagraph, the effective consent of a person having parental responsibility for C—

(a)   to the use of C's human cells to bring about the creation of a human admixed embryo in vitro for use for the purposes of a project of research, or

(b)   to the use for those purposes of a human admixed embryo in relation to which C is a relevant person by reason only of the use of C's human cells, is to be treated for the purposes of sub-paragraphs (1) to (3) as the effective consent of C.

(6) If C attains the age of 18 years or the condition in paragraph 15(3) ceases to be met in relation to C, paragraph 4 has effect in relation to C as if any effective consent previously given under subparagraphs (1) to (3) by a person having parental responsibility for C had been given by C but, subject to that, sub-paragraph (5) ceases to apply in relation to C.

(7) Sub-paragraphs (1) to (3) have effect subject to paragraphs 16 and 20.

13

(1) A human admixed embryo the creation of which was brought about in vitro must not be kept in storage unless—

(a)   there is an effective consent by each relevant person in relation to the human admixed embryo to the storage of the human admixed embryo, and

(b)   the human admixed embryo is stored in accordance with those consents.

(2) Where a licence authorises the application of paragraph 12(5) in relation to a person who has not attained the age of 18 years ("C"), the effective consent of a person having parental responsibility for C to the storage of a human admixed embryo in relation to which C is a relevant person by reason only of the use of C's human cells is to be treated for the purposes of sub-paragraph (1) as the effective consent of C.

(3) If C attains the age of 18 years or the condition in paragraph 15(3) ceases to be met in relation to C, paragraph 4 has effect in relation to C as if any effective consent previously given under subparagraph (1) by a person having parental responsibility for C had been given by C but, subject to that, sub-paragraph (2) ceases to apply in relation to C.

(4) Sub-paragraph (1) has effect subject to paragraphs 16 and 20.

14

For the purposes of paragraphs 12 and 13, each of the following is a relevant person in relation to a human admixed embryo the creation of which was brought about in vitro ("human admixed embryo A")—

(a)   each person whose gametes or human cells were used to bring about the creation of human admixed embryo A,

(b)   each person whose gametes or human cells were used to bring about the creation of any embryo, the creation of which was brought about in vitro, which was used to bring about the creation of human admixed embryo A, and

(c)   each person whose gametes or human cells were used to bring about the creation of any other human admixed embryo, the creation of which was brought about in vitro, which was used to bring about the creation of human admixed embryo A.

Cases where human cells etc can be used without consent of person providing them

14

After paragraph 14 (as inserted by paragraph 13 above) insert—

Parental consent conditions

15

(1) In relation to a person who has not attained the age of 18 years ("C"), the parental consent conditions referred to in paragraphs 6(3A) and 12(4) are as follows.

(2) Condition A is that C suffers from, or is likely to develop, a serious disease, a serious physical or mental disability or any other serious medical condition.

(3) Condition B is that either—

(a)   C is not competent to deal with the issue of consent to the use of C's human cells to bring about the creation in vitro of an embryo or human admixed embryo for use for the purposes of a project of research, or

(b)   C has attained the age of 16 years but lacks capacity to consent to such use of C's human cells.

(4) Condition C is that any embryo or human admixed embryo to be created in vitro is to be used for the purposes of a project of research which is intended to increase knowledge about—

(a)   the disease, disability or medical condition mentioned in sub-paragraph (2) or any similar disease, disability or medical condition, or

(b)   the treatment of, or care of persons affected by, that disease, disability or medical condition or any similar disease, disability or medical condition.

(5) Condition D is that there are reasonable grounds for believing that research of comparable effectiveness cannot be carried out if the only human cells that can be used to bring about the creation in vitro of embryos or human admixed embryos for use for the purposes of the project are the human cells of persons who—

(a)   have attained the age of 18 years and have capacity to consent to the use of their human cells to bring about the creation in vitro of an embryo or human admixed embryo for use for the purposes of the project, or

(b)   have not attained that age but are competent to deal with the issue of consent to such use of their human cells.

(6) In relation to Scotland, sub-paragraphs (1) to (5) are to be read with the following modifications—

(a)   for sub-paragraph (3) substitute—
"(3) Condition B is that C does not have capacity (within the meaning of section 2(4ZB) of the Age of Legal Capacity (Scotland) Act 1991) to consent to the use of C's human cells to bring about the creation in vitro of an embryo or human admixed embryo for use for the purposes of a project of research.",

(b)   in sub-paragraph (5)(a), for "have capacity to consent" substitute "are not incapable (within the meaning of section 1(6) of the Adults with Incapacity (Scotland) Act 2000) of giving consent", and

(c) in sub-paragraph (5)(b), for "are competent to deal with the issue of" substitute "have capacity (within the meaning of section 2(4ZB) of the Age of Legal Capacity (Scotland) Act 1991) to".

Adults lacking capacity: exemption relating to use of human cells etc

16

(1) If, in relation to the proposed use under a licence of the human cells of a person who has attained the age of 18 years ("P"), the Authority is satisfied—

(a) that the conditions in paragraph 17 are met,
(b) that paragraphs (1) to (4) of paragraph 18 have been complied with, and
(c) that the condition in paragraph 18(5) is met, the Authority may in the licence authorise the application of this paragraph in relation to P.

(2) Where a licence authorises the application of this paragraph, this Schedule does not require the consent of P—

(a) to the use (whether during P's life or after P's death) of P's human cells to bring about the creation in vitro of an embryo or human admixed embryo for use for the purposes of a project of research,
(b) to the storage or the use for those purposes (whether during P's life or after P's death) of an embryo or human admixed embryo in relation to which P is a relevant person by reason only of the use of P's human cells.

(3) This paragraph has effect subject to paragraph 19.

Consent to use of human cells etc not required: adult lacking capacity

17

(1) The conditions referred to in paragraph 16(1)(a) are as follows.

(2) Condition A is that P suffers from, or is likely to develop, a serious disease, a serious physical or mental disability or any other serious medical condition.

(3) Condition B is that P lacks capacity to consent to the use of P's human cells to bring about the creation in vitro of an embryo or human admixed embryo for use for the purposes of a project of research.

(4) Condition C is that the person responsible under the licence has no reason to believe that P had refused such consent at a time when P had that capacity.

(5) Condition D is that it appears unlikely that P will at some time

have that capacity.

(6) Condition E is that any embryo or human admixed embryo to be created in vitro is to be used for the purposes of a project of research which is intended to increase knowledge about—

(a) the disease, disability or medical condition mentioned in sub-paragraph (2) or any similar disease, disability or medical condition, or
(b) the treatment of, or care of persons affected by, that disease, disability or medical condition or any similar disease, disability or medical condition.

(7) Condition F is that there are reasonable grounds for believing that research of comparable effectiveness cannot be carried out if the only human cells that can be

used to bring about the creation in vitro of embryos or human admixed embryos for use for the purposes of the project are the human cells of persons who—

(a) have attained the age of 18 years and have capacity to consent to the use of their human cells to bring about the creation in vitro of an embryo or human admixed embryo for use for the purposes of the project, or

(b) have not attained that age but are competent to deal with the issue of consent to such use of their human cells.

(8) In this paragraph and paragraph 18 references to the person responsible under the licence are to be read, in a case where an application for a licence is being made, as references to the person who is to be the person responsible.

(9) In relation to Scotland—

(a) references in sub-paragraphs (3) to (5) to P lacking, or having, capacity to consent are to be read respectively as references to P being, or not being, incapable (within the meaning of section 1(6) of the Adults with Incapacity (Scotland) Act 2000) of giving such consent, and

(b) sub-paragraph (7) is to be read with the following modifications—

(i) in paragraph (a), for "have capacity to consent" substitute "are not incapable (within the meaning of section 1(6) of the Adults with Incapacity (Scotland) Act 2000) of giving consent", and

(ii) in paragraph (b), for "are competent to deal with the issue of" substitute "have capacity (within the meaning of section 2(4ZB) of the Age of Legal Capacity (Scotland) Act 1991) to".

Consulting carers etc in case of adult lacking capacity

18

(1) This paragraph applies in relation to a person who has attained the age of 18 years ("P") where the person responsible under the licence ("R") wishes to use P's human cells to bring about the creation in vitro of an embryo or human admixed embryo for use for the purposes of a project of research, in a case where P lacks capacity to consent to their use.

(2) R must take reasonable steps to identify a person who—

(a) otherwise than in a professional capacity or for remuneration, is engaged in caring for P or is interested in P's welfare, and

(b) is prepared to be consulted by R under this paragraph of this Schedule.

(3) If R is unable to identify such a person R must nominate a person who—

(a) is prepared to be consulted by R under this paragraph of this Schedule, but

(b) has no connection with the project.

(4) R must provide the person identified under sub-paragraph (2) or nominated under sub-paragraph (3) ("F") with information about the proposed use of human cells to bring about the creation in vitro of embryos or human admixed embryos for use for the purposes of the project and ask F what, in F's opinion, P's wishes and feelings about the use of P's human cells for that purpose would be likely to be if P had capacity in relation to the matter.

(5) The condition referred to in paragraph 16(1)(c) is that, on being consulted, F has not advised R that in F's opinion P's wishes and feelings would be likely to lead P to decline to consent to the use of P's human cells for that purpose.

(6) In relation to Scotland, the references in sub-paragraphs (1) and (4) to P lacking, or having, capacity to consent are to be read respectively as references to P being, or not being, incapable (within the meaning of section 1(6) of the Adults with Incapacity (Scotland) Act 2000) of giving such consent.

Effect of acquiring capacity

19

(1) Paragraph 16 does not apply to the use of P's human cells to bring about the creation in vitro of an embryo or human admixed embryo if, at a time before the human cells are used for that purpose, P—

    (a)   has capacity to consent to their use, and

    (b)   gives written notice to the person keeping the human cells that P does not wish them to be used for that purpose.

(2) Paragraph 16 does not apply to the storage or use of an embryo or human admixed embryo whose creation in vitro was brought about with the use of P's human cells if, at a time before the embryo or human admixed embryo is used for the purposes of the project of research, P—

    (a)   has capacity to consent to the storage or use, and

    (b)   gives written notice to the person keeping the human cells that P does not wish them to be used for that purpose.

(3) In relation to Scotland, the references in sub-paragraphs (1)(a) and (2)(a) to P having capacity to consent are to be read as references to P not being incapable (within the meaning of section 1(6) of the Adults with Incapacity (Scotland) Act 2000) of giving such consent.

Use of cells or cell lines in existence before relevant commencement date

20

(1) Where a licence authorises the application of this paragraph in relation to qualifying cells, this Schedule does not require the consent of a person ("P")—

    (a)   to the use of qualifying cells of P to bring about the creation in vitro of an embryo or human admixed embryo for use for the purposes of a project of research, or

    (b)   to the storage or the use for those purposes of an embryo or human admixed embryo in relation to which P is a relevant person by reason only of the use of qualifying cells of P.

(2) "Qualifying cells" are human cells which—

    (a)   were lawfully stored for research purposes immediately before the commencement date, or

    (b)   are derived from human cells which were lawfully stored for those purposes at that time.

(3) The "commencement date" is the date on which paragraph 9(2)(a) of Schedule 3 to the Human Fertilisation and Embryology Act 2008 (requirement for consent to use of human cells to create an embryo) comes into force.

Conditions for grant of exemption in paragraph 20

21

(1) A licence may not authorise the application of paragraph 20 unless the Authority is satisfied—

  (a)   that there are reasonable grounds for believing that scientific research will be adversely affected to a significant extent if the only human cells that can be used to bring about the creation *in vitro* of embryos or human admixed embryos for use for the purposes of the project of research are—

   (i)   human cells in respect of which there is an effective consent to their use to bring about the creation in vitro of embryos or human admixed embryos for use for those purposes, or

   (ii)   human cells which by virtue of paragraph 16 can be used without such consent, and

  (b)   that any of the following conditions is met in relation to each of the persons whose human cells are qualifying cells which are to be used for the purposes of the project of research.

(2) Condition A is that—

  (a)   it is not reasonably possible for the person responsible under the licence ("R") to identify the person falling within sub-paragraph (1)(b) ("P"), and

  (b)   where any information that relates to P (without identifying P or enabling P to be identified) is available to R, that information does not suggest that P would have objected to the use of P's human cells to bring about the creation in vitro of an embryo or human admixed embryo for use for the purposes of the project.

(3) Condition B is that—

  (a)   the person falling within sub-paragraph (1)(b) ("P") is dead or the person responsible under the licence ("R") believes on reasonable grounds that P is dead,

  (b)   the information relating to P that is available to R does not suggest that P would have objected to the use of P's human cells to bring about the creation in vitro of an embryo or human admixed embryo for use for the purposes of the project, and

  (c)   a person who stood in a qualifying relationship to P immediately before P died (or is believed to have died) has given consent in writing to the use of P's human cells to bring about the creation in vitro of an embryo or human admixed embryo for use for the purposes of the project.

(4) Condition C is that—

  (a)   the person responsible under the licence ("R") has taken all reasonable steps to contact—

   (i)   the person falling within sub-paragraph (1)(b) ("P"), or

(ii)   in a case where P is dead or R believes on reasonable grounds that P is dead, persons who could give consent for the purposes of subparagraph (3)(c),

but has been unable to do so, and

(b)   the information relating to P that is available to R does not suggest that P would have objected to the use of P's human cells to bring about the creation in vitro of an embryo or human admixed embryo for use for the purposes of the project.

(5) The HTA consent provisions apply in relation to consent for the purposes of sub-paragraph (3)(c) as they apply in relation to consent for the purposes of section 3(6)(c) of the Human Tissue Act 2004; and for the purposes of this sub-paragraph the HTA consent provisions are to be treated as if they extended to Scotland.

(6) In sub-paragraph (5) "the HTA consent provisions" means subsections (4), (5), (6), (7) and (8)(a) and (b) of section 27 of the Human Tissue Act 2004.

(7) In this paragraph references to the person responsible under the licence are to be read, in a case where an application for a licence is being made, as references to the person who is to be the person responsible.

(8) Paragraphs 1 to 4 of this Schedule do not apply in relation to a consent given for the purposes of sub-paragraph (3)(c).

Interpretation

15

After paragraph 21 (as inserted by paragraph 14 above) insert—

Interpretation

22

(1) In this Schedule references to human cells are to human cells

which are not—

(a)   cells of the female or male germ line, or
(b)   cells of an embryo.

(2) References in this Schedule to an embryo or a human admixed embryo which was used to bring about the creation of an embryo ("embryo A") or a human admixed embryo ("human admixed embryo A") include an embryo or, as the case may be, a human admixed embryo which was used to bring about the creation of—

(a)   an embryo or human admixed embryo which was used to bring about the creation of embryo A or human admixed embryo A, and
(b)   the predecessor of that embryo or human admixed embryo mentioned in paragraph (a), and
(c)   the predecessor of that predecessor, and so on.

(3) References in this Schedule to an embryo or a human admixed embryo whose creation may be brought about using an embryo or a human admixed embryo are to be read in accordance with subparagraph (2).

(4) References in this Schedule (however expressed) to the use of human cells to bring about the creation of an embryo or a human admixed embryo include the use of human cells to alter the embryo or, as the case may be, the human admixed embryo.

(5) References in this Schedule to parental responsibility are—

    (a)   in relation to England and Wales, to be read in accordance with the Children Act 1989,

    (b)   in relation to Northern Ireland, to be read in accordance with the Children (Northern Ireland) Order 1995, and

    (c)   in relation to Scotland, to be read as references to parental responsibilities and parental rights within the meaning of the Children (Scotland) Act 1995.

(6) References in this Schedule to capacity are, in relation to England and Wales, to be read in accordance with the Mental Capacity Act 2005.

(7) References in this Schedule to the age of 18 years are, in relation to Scotland, to be read as references to the age of 16 years.

Schedule 4

Section 14

Schedule Inserted in the 1990 Act as Schedule 3ZA

"Schedule 3ZA
Circumstances in which Offer of Counselling Required as Condition of Licence for Treatment

PART 1
KINDS OF TREATMENT IN RELATION TO WHICH COUNSELLING MUST BE OFFERED

1

The treatment services involve the use of the gametes of any person and that person's consent is required under paragraph 5 of Schedule 3 for the use in question.

2

The treatment services involve the use of any embryo the creation of which was brought about in vitro.

3

The treatment services involve the use of an embryo taken from a woman and the consent of the woman from whom the embryo was taken was required under paragraph 7 of Schedule 3 for the use in question.

PART 2
EVENTS IN CONNECTION WITH WHICH COUNSELLING MUST BE OFFERED

4

A man gives the person responsible a notice under paragraph (a) of subsection (1) of section 37 of the Human Fertilisation and Embryology Act 2008 (agreed fatherhood conditions) in a case where the woman for whom the treatment services are provided has previously given a notice under paragraph (b) of that subsection referring to the man.

5

The woman for whom the treatment services are provided gives the person responsible a notice under paragraph (b) of that subsection in a case where the man to whom the notice relates has previously given a notice under paragraph (a) of that subsection.

6

A woman gives the person responsible notice under paragraph (a) of subsection (1) of section 44 of that Act (agreed female parenthood conditions) in a case where the woman for whom the treatment services are provided has previously given a notice under paragraph (b) of that subsection referring to her.

7

The woman for whom the treatment services are provided gives the person responsible a notice under paragraph (b) of that subsection in a case where the other woman to whom the notice relates has previously given a notice under paragraph (a) of that subsection."

Schedule 5

Section 28

Schedule Inserted in the 1990 Act as Schedule 3B

"Schedule 3B
Inspection, Entry, Search and Seizure

Inspection of statutory records

1

(1) A duly authorised person may require a person to produce for inspection any records which the person is required to keep by, or by virtue of, this Act.

(2) Where records which a person is so required to keep are stored in any electronic form, the power under sub-paragraph (1) includes power to require the records to be made available for inspection—

    (a)   in a visible and legible form, or

(b)   in a form from which they can be readily produced in a visible and legible form.

(3) A duly authorised person may inspect and take copies of any records produced for inspection in pursuance of a requirement under this paragraph.

Arranging inspections

2

(1) Where a person—

(a)   makes an enquiry to the Authority which concerns the making of a relevant application by that person, or

(b)   has made a relevant application to the Authority which the Authority has not yet considered, the Authority may arrange for a duly authorised person to inspect any of the premises mentioned in sub-paragraph (3).

(2) For the purposes of sub-paragraph (1) a "relevant application" means—

(a)   an application for authorisation for a person to carry on an activity governed by this Act which the person is not then authorised to carry on, or

(b)   an application for authorisation for a person to carry on any such activity on premises where the person is not then authorised to carry it on.

(3) The premises referred to in sub-paragraph (1) are—

(a)   the premises where any activity referred to in subparagraph (2) is to be carried on;

(b)   any premises that will be relevant third party premises for the purposes of any application.

(4) The power in sub-paragraph (1) is exercisable for purposes of the Authority's functions in relation to licences and third party agreements.

Entry and inspection of premises

3

(1) A duly authorised person may at any reasonable time enter and inspect any premises to which a licence relates or relevant third party premises.

(2) The power in sub-paragraph (1) is exercisable for purposes of the Authority's functions in relation to licences and third party agreements.

4

(1) Subject to sub-paragraph (2), the Authority shall arrange for any premises to which a licence relates to be inspected under paragraph 3 by a duly authorised person at intervals not exceeding two years.

(2) The Authority need not comply with sub-paragraph (1) where the premises in question have been inspected in pursuance of paragraph 2 or 3 at any point within the previous two years.

Entry and search in connection with suspected offence

5

(1) If a justice of the peace is satisfied on sworn information or, in Northern Ireland, on a complaint on oath that there are reasonable grounds for believing—

    (a)   that an offence under this Act is being, or has been committed on any premises, and

    (b)   that any of the conditions in sub-paragraph (2) is met in relation to the premises, the justice of the peace may by signed warrant authorise a duly authorised person, together with any constables, to enter the premises, if need be by force, and search them.

(2) The conditions referred to are—

    (a)   that entry to the premises has been, or is likely to be, refused and notice of the intention to apply for a warrant under this paragraph has been given to the occupier;

    (b)   that the premises are unoccupied;

    (c)   that the occupier is temporarily absent;

    (d)   that an application for admission to the premises or the giving of notice of the intention to apply for a warrant under this paragraph would defeat the object of entry.

(3) A warrant under this paragraph shall continue in force until the end of the period of 31 days beginning with the day on which it is issued.

(4) In relation to Scotland—

    (a)   any reference in sub-paragraph (1) to a justice of the peace includes a reference to a sheriff, and

    (b)   the reference in that sub-paragraph to "on sworn information" is to be read as a reference to "by evidence on oath".

Execution of warrants

6

(1) Entry and search under a warrant under paragraph 5 is unlawful if any of sub-paragraphs (2) to (4) and (6) is not complied with.

(2) Entry and search shall be at a reasonable time unless the person executing the warrant thinks that the purpose of the search may be frustrated on an entry at a reasonable time.

(3) If the occupier of the premises to which the warrant relates is present when the person executing the warrant seeks to enter them, the person executing the warrant shall—

    (a)   produce the warrant to the occupier, and

    (b)   give the occupier—

        (i)   a copy of the warrant, and

        (ii)   an appropriate statement.

(4) If the occupier of the premises to which the warrant relates is not present when the person executing the warrant seeks to enter them, but some other person is present who appears to the person executing the warrant to be in charge of the premises, the person executing the warrant shall—

(a)   produce the warrant to that other person,

(b)   give that other person—

   (i)   a copy of the warrant, and

   (ii)   an appropriate statement, and

(c)   leave a copy of the warrant in a prominent place on the premises.

(5) In sub-paragraphs (3)(b)(ii) and (4)(b)(ii), the references to an appropriate statement are to a statement in writing containing such information relating to the powers of the person executing the warrant and the rights and obligations of the person to whom the statement is given as may be prescribed by regulations made by the Secretary of State.

(6) If the premises to which the warrant relates are unoccupied, the person executing the warrant shall leave a copy of it in a prominent place on the premises.

(7) Where the premises in relation to which a warrant under paragraph 5 is executed are unoccupied or the occupier is temporarily absent, the person executing the warrant shall when leaving the premises, leave them as effectively secured as the person found them.

Seizure in the course of inspection or search

7

(1) A duly authorised person entering and inspecting premises under paragraph 3 may seize anything on the premises which the duly authorised person has reasonable grounds to believe may be required for—

(a)   the purposes of the Authority's functions relating to the grant, revocation, variation or suspension of licences, or

(b)   the purpose of taking appropriate control measures in the event of a serious adverse event or serious adverse reaction.

(2) A duly authorised person entering or searching premises under a warrant under paragraph 5 may seize anything on the premises which the duly authorised person has reasonable grounds to believe may be required for the purpose of being used in evidence in any proceedings for an offence under this Act.

(3) Where a person has power under sub-paragraph (1) or (2) to seize anything, that person may take such steps as appear to be necessary for preserving that thing or preventing interference with it.

(4) The power under sub-paragraph (1) or (2) includes power to retain anything seized in exercise of the power for so long as it may be required for the purpose for which it was seized.

(5) Where by virtue of sub-paragraph (1) or (2) a person ("P") seizes anything, P shall leave on the premises from which the thing was seized a statement giving particulars of what P has seized and stating that P has seized it.

Supplementary provision

8

(1) Power under this Schedule to enter and inspect or search any premises includes power to take such other persons and equipment as the person exercising the power reasonably considers necessary.

(2) Power under this Schedule to inspect or search any premises includes, in particular—

    (a)   power to inspect any equipment found on the premises,

    (b)   power to inspect and take copies of any records found on the premises, and

    (c)   in the case of premises to which a licence relates or premises which are relevant third party premises in relation to a licence, power to observe the carrying-on of the licensed activity on the premises.

(3) Any power under this Schedule to enter, inspect or search premises includes power to require any person to afford such facilities and assistance with respect to matters under that person's control as are necessary to enable the power of entry, inspection or search to be exercised.

9

(1) A person's right to exercise a power under this Schedule is subject to production of evidence of the person's entitlement to exercise it, if required.

(2) As soon as reasonably practicable after having inspected premises in pursuance of arrangements made under paragraph 2 or after having exercised a power under this Schedule to inspect or search premises, the duly authorised person shall—

    (a)   prepare a written report of the inspection, or as the case may be, the inspection and search, and

    (b)   if requested to do so by the appropriate person, give the appropriate person a copy of the report.

(3) In sub-paragraph (2), the "appropriate person" means—

    (a)   in relation to premises to which a licence relates, the person responsible, or

    (b)   in relation to any other premises, the occupier.

Enforcement

10

A person who—

    (a)   fails without reasonable excuse to comply with a requirement under paragraph 1(1) or 8(3), or

    (b)   intentionally obstructs the exercise of any right under this Schedule,

is guilty of an offence and liable on summary conviction to a fine not exceeding level 5 on the standard scale.

Interpretation

11

In this Schedule—

    (a)   "duly authorised person", in the context of any provision, means a person authorised by the Authority to act for the purposes of that provision, and

(b)   "licensed activity", in relation to a licence, means the activity which the licence authorises to be carried on."

Schedule 6

Section 56

Amendments Relating to Parenthood in Cases Involving Assisted Reproduction

PART 1
GENERAL

Population (Statistics) Act 1938 (c. 12)

1

(1) In the Schedule to the Population (Statistics) Act 1938 (particulars which may be required), in paragraph 1 (which relates to the registration of a birth)—

(a)   in paragraph (b), after "child," insert "or as a parent of the child by virtue of section 42 or 43 of the Human Fertilisation and Embryology Act 2008,", and

(b)   in paragraph (c)—

    (i)   in sub-paragraph (i), after "marriage" insert "or of their formation of a civil partnership", and

    (ii)   at the beginning of each of sub-paragraphs (ii) and (iii) insert "where the parents are married,".

(2) Sub-paragraph (1)(b)(ii) does not extend to Scotland.

Births and Deaths Registration Act 1953 (c. 20)

2

In section 1 of the Births and Deaths Registration Act 1953 (particulars of births to be registered) after subsection (2) insert—

> (3) In the case of a child who has a parent by virtue of section 42 or 43 of the Human Fertilisation and Embryology Act 2008, the reference in subsection (2)(a) to the father of the child is to be read as a reference to the woman who is a parent by virtue of that section.

3

In section 2 of the Births and Deaths Registration Act 1953 (information concerning birth to be given to registrar within 42 days), renumber the existing provision as subsection (1) of the section and at the end insert—

> (2) In the case of a child who has a parent by virtue of section 42 or 43 of the Human Fertilisation and Embryology Act 2008, the references in subsection (1) to the father of the child are to be read as references to the woman who is a parent by virtue of that section.

4

In section 9(4) of the Births and Deaths Registration Act 1953 (giving of information to a person other than the registrar), after "that section," insert

> or under paragraph (b), (c) or (d) of subsection (1B) of that section.

5

(1) Section 10 of the Births and Deaths Registration Act 1953 (registration of father where parents not married) is amended as follows.

(2) For the heading to the section substitute "Registration of father where parents not married or of second female parent where parents not civil partners".

(3) After subsection (1A) insert—

> (1B) Notwithstanding anything in the foregoing provisions of this Act and subject to section 10ZA of this Act, in the case of a child to whom section 1(3) of the Family Law Reform Act 1987 does not apply no woman shall as a parent of the child by virtue of section 43 of the Human Fertilisation and Embryology Act 2008 be required to give information concerning the birth of the child, and the registrar shall not enter in the register the name of any woman as a parent of the child by virtue of that section except—
>
> > (a)   at the joint request of the mother and the person stating herself to be the other parent of the child (in which case that person shall sign the register together with the mother); or
> >
> > (b)   at the request of the mother on production of—
> > > (i)   a declaration in the prescribed form made by the mother stating that the person to be registered ("the woman concerned") is a parent of the child by virtue of section 43 of the Human Fertilisation and Embryology Act 2008; and
> > > (ii) a statutory declaration made by the woman concerned stating herself to be a parent of the child by virtue of section 43 of that Act; or
> >
> > (c)   at the request of the woman concerned on production of—
> > > (i)   a declaration in the prescribed form made by the woman concerned stating herself to be a parent of the child by virtue of section 43 of the Human Fertilisation and Embryology Act 2008; and
> > > (ii) a statutory declaration made by the mother stating that the woman concerned is a parent of the child by virtue of section 43 of that Act; or
> >
> > (d)   at the request of the mother or the woman concerned on production of—
> > > (i)   a copy of any agreement made between them under section 4ZA(1)(b) of the Children Act 1989 in relation to the child; and
> > > (ii) a declaration in the prescribed form by the person making the request stating that the agreement was made in compliance with section 4ZA of that Act and has not been brought to an end by an order of a court; or

(e) at the request of the mother or the woman concerned on production of—
   (i) a certified copy of an order under section 4ZA of the Children Act 1989 giving the woman concerned parental responsibility for the child; and
   (ii) a declaration in the prescribed form by the person making the request stating that the order has not been brought to an end by an order of a court; or
(f) at the request of the mother or the woman concerned on production of—
   (i) a certified copy of an order under paragraph 1 of Schedule 1 to the Children Act 1989 which requires the woman concerned to make any financial provision for the child and which is not an order falling within paragraph 4(3) of that Schedule; and
   (ii) a declaration in the prescribed form by the person making the request stating that the order has not been discharged by an order of a court.

(4) After subsection (2) insert—

(2A) Where, in the case of a child to whom section 1(3) of the Family Law Reform Act 1987 does not apply, a person stating herself to be a parent of the child by virtue of section 43 of the Human Fertilisation and Embryology Act 2008 makes a request to the registrar in accordance with any of paragraphs (c) to (f) of subsection (1B)—

(a) she shall be treated as a qualified informant concerning the birth of the child for the purposes of this Act; and
(b) the giving of information concerning the birth of the child by that person and the signing of the register by her in the presence of the registrar shall act as a discharge of any duty of any other qualified informant under section 2 of this Act."

6 For section 10ZA of the Births and Deaths Registration Act 1953 substitute—

10ZA Registration of father or second female parent by virtue of certain provisions of Human Fertilisation and Embryology Act 2008

(1) Notwithstanding anything in the foregoing provisions of this Act, the registrar shall not enter in the register—

(a) as the father of a child, the name of a man who is to be treated for that purpose as the father of the child by virtue of section 39(1) or 40(1) or (2) of the Human Fertilisation and Embryology Act 2008 (circumstances in which man to be treated as father of child for purposes of registration of birth where fertility treatment undertaken after his death); or
(b) as a parent of the child, the name of a woman who is to be treated for that purpose as a parent of the child by virtue of section 46(1) or (2) of that Act (circumstances in which woman to be treated as parent of child for purposes of registration of birth where fertility treatment undertaken after her death), unless the condition in subsection (2) below is satisfied.

(2) The condition in this subsection is satisfied if—

(a)   the mother requests the registrar to make such an entry in the register and produces the relevant documents; or

(b)   in the case of the death or inability of the mother, the relevant documents are produced by some other person who is a qualified informant.

(3) In this section "the relevant documents" means—

(a)   the consent in writing and election mentioned in section 39(1), 40(1) or (2) or 46(1) or (2) (as the case requires) of the Human Fertilisation and Embryology Act 2008;

(b)   a certificate of a registered medical practitioner as to the medical facts concerned; and

(c)   such other documentary evidence (if any) as the registrar considers appropriate.

7

(1) Section 10A of the Births and Deaths Registration Act 1953 (re-registration where parents not married) is amended as follows.

(2) For the heading to the section substitute "Re-registration where parents neither married nor civil partners".

(3) In subsection (1)—

(a)   after "as the father of the child" insert "(or as a parent of the child by virtue of section 42, 43 or 46(1) or (2) of the Human Fertilisation and Embryology Act 2008)", and

(b)   for paragraph (ff) substitute—

(ff)   in the case of a man who is to be treated as the father of the child by virtue of section 39(1) or 40(1) or (2) of the Human Fertilisation and Embryology Act 2008, if the condition in section 10ZA(2) of this Act is satisfied; or.

(4) After subsection (1A) insert—

(1B) Where there has been registered under this Act the birth of a child to whom section 1(3) of the Family Law Reform Act 1987 does not apply, but no person has been registered as a parent of the child by virtue of section 42, 43 or 46(1) or (2) of the Human Fertilisation and Embryology Act 2008 (or as the father of the child), the registrar shall re-register the birth so as to show a woman ("the woman concerned") as a parent of the child by virtue of section 43 or 46(1) or (2) of that Act—

(a)   at the joint request of the mother and the woman concerned; or

(b)   at the request of the mother on production of—

(i)   a declaration in the prescribed form made by the mother stating that the woman concerned is a parent of the child by virtue of section 43 of the Human Fertilisation and Embryology Act 2008; and

(ii)   a statutory declaration made by the woman concerned stating herself to be a parent of the child by virtue of section 43 of that Act; or

(c)   at the request of the woman concerned on production of—

        (i)   a declaration in the prescribed form made by the woman concerned stating herself to be a parent of the child by virtue of section 43 of the Human Fertilisation and Embryology Act 2008; and

        (ii)   a statutory declaration made by the mother stating that the woman concerned is a parent of the child by virtue of section 43 of that Act; or

  (d)   at the request of the mother or the woman concerned on production of—

        (i)   a copy of an agreement made between them under section 4ZA(1)(b) of the Children Act 1989 in relation to the child; and

        (ii)   a declaration in the prescribed form by the person making the request stating that the agreement was made in compliance with section 4ZA of that Act and has not been brought to an end by an order of a court; or

  (e)   at the request of the mother or the woman concerned on production of—

        (i)   a certified copy of an order under section 4ZA of the Children Act 1989 giving the woman concerned parental responsibility for the child; and

        (ii)   a declaration in the prescribed form by the person making the request stating that the order has not been brought to an end by an order of a court; or

  (f)   at the request of the mother or the woman concerned on production of—

        (i)   a certified copy of an order under paragraph 1 of Schedule 1 to the Children Act 1989 which requires the woman concerned to make any financial provision for the child and which is not an order falling within paragraph 4(3) of that Schedule; and

        (ii)   a declaration in the prescribed form by the person making the request stating that the order has not been discharged by an order of a court; or

  (g)   in the case of a woman who is to be treated as a parent of the child by virtue of section 46(1) or (2) of the Human Fertilisation and Embryology Act 2008, if the condition in section 10ZA(2) of this Act is satisfied.

(5) In subsection (2), for paragraphs (b) to (c) substitute—

  (b)   in the case of any of the following requests—

        (i)   a request under subsection (1)(a) or (b) or subsection (1B)(a) or (b);

        (ii)   a request under subsection (1)(d), (e), (f) or (g) or subsection (1B)(d), (e) or (f) made by the mother of the child,

the mother shall also sign the register;

  (bb) in a case within subsection (1)(ff) or (1B)(g), the mother or (as the case may be) the qualified informant shall also sign the register;

  (c)   in the case of a request made under subsection (1)(a) or (c) or a request made under subsection (1)(d), (e), (f) or (g) by the person requesting to be registered as the father of the child, that person shall also sign the register;

(cc)   in the case of a request made under subsection (1B)(a) or (c) or a request made under subsection (1B)(d), (e) or (f) by a woman requesting to be registered as a parent of the child by virtue of section 43 of the Human Fertilisation and Embryology Act 2008, that woman shall also sign the register;.

8

In section 13 of the Births and Deaths Registration Act 1953 (registration of name of child or alteration of name) after subsection (1) insert—

(1ZA) In the case of a child who has a parent by virtue of section 42 or 43 of the Human Fertilisation and Embryology Act 2008, the reference in subsection (1)(b) to the father of the child is to be read as a reference to the woman who is a parent of the child by virtue of that section.

9

(1) Section 14 of the Births and Deaths Registration Act 1953 (re-registration of births of legitimated persons) is amended as follows.

(2) In subsection (1), in the proviso—

(a)   in paragraph (a), after "legitimated person" insert ", or herself to be a parent of the legitimated person by virtue of section 43 of the Human Fertilisation and Embryology Act 2008,", and

(b)   in paragraph (b), after "the paternity of the legitimated person" insert

(or, as the case may be, the parentage of the legitimated person by virtue of section 43 of that Act).

(3) In subsection (2)—

(a)   after "the marriage of his parents" insert "or on their becoming civil partners of each other", and

(b)   after "the date of the marriage" insert "or of the formation of the civil partnership".

10

(1) Section 29A of the Births and Deaths Registration Act 1953 (alternative procedure for certain corrections) is amended as follows.

(2) In subsection (1) for the words from "the father" to the end substitute "—

(a)   the father of the person to whose birth or death the entry relates; or

(b)   a parent of that person (having been so registered on the basis of being such a parent by virtue of 42, 43 or 46(1) or (2) of the Human Fertilisation and Embryology Act 2008)."

(3) In subsection (3), after "not the father" insert "or, as the case may be, that the person shown as a parent was not such a parent by virtue of 42, 43 or 46(1) or (2) of the Human Fertilisation and Embryology Act 2008".

Registration of Births, Deaths and Marriages (Special Provisions) Act 1957 (c. 58)

11

(1) Section 3A of the Births, Deaths and Marriages (Special Provisions) Act 1957 (alternative procedure for certain corrections) is amended as follows.

(2) In subsection (1) for the words from "the father" to the end substitute "—

   (a)   the father of the person to whose birth or death the entry relates, or

   (b)   a parent of that person (having been so registered on the basis of being such a parent by virtue of 42, 43 or 46(1) or (2) of the Human Fertilisation and Embryology Act 2008)."

(3) In subsection (3), after "not the father" insert "or, as the case may be, that the person shown as a parent was not such a parent by virtue of 42, 43 or 46(1) or (2) of the Human Fertilisation and Embryology Act 2008".

12

At the end of section 5 of the Registration of Births, Deaths and Marriages (Special Provisions) Act 1957 (registration of births of legitimated persons in the service departments registers) insert—

   (3) In relation to a person who has a parent by virtue of section 43 of the Human Fertilisation and Embryology Act 2008—

   (a)   any reference to the person's father is a reference to the woman who is a parent by virtue of that section,

   (b)   the reference in subsection (1) to the subsequent marriage of the person's parents is a reference to their subsequent formation of a civil partnership, and

   (c)   the reference in that subsection to paternity is a reference to parentage by virtue of section 43 of that Act.

Family Law Reform Act 1969 (c. 46)

13

In section 25 of the Family Law Reform Act 1969 (interpretation of Part 3), in the definition of "excluded"—

   (a)   for "and to" substitute ", to", and

   (b)   after "1990" insert "and to sections 33 to 47 of the Human Fertilisation and Embryology Act 2008".

Congenital Disabilities (Civil Liability) Act 1976 (c. 28)

14

In section 1 of the Congenital Disabilities (Civil Liability) Act 1976 (civil liability to child born disabled), after subsection (4) insert—

   (4A) In the case of a child who has a parent by virtue of section 42 or 43 of the Human Fertilisation and Embryology Act 2008, the reference in subsection (4) to the child's father includes a reference to the woman who is a parent by virtue of that section.

15

In section 4 of the Congenital Disabilities (Civil Liability) Act 1976 (interpretation and other supplementary provisions), at the end of subsection (4A) insert "or sections 33 to 47 of the Human Fertilisation and Embryology Act 2008."

Legitimacy Act 1976 (c. 31)

16

After section 2 of the Legitimacy Act 1976 (legitimation by subsequent marriage of parents) insert—

2A Legitimation by subsequent civil partnership of parents

Subject to the following provisions of this Act, where—

    (a)   a person ("the child") has a parent ("the female parent") by virtue of section 43 of the Human Fertilisation and Embryology Act 2008 (treatment provided to woman who agrees that second woman to be parent),

    (b)   at the time of the child's birth, the female parent and the child's mother are not civil partners of each other,

    (c)   the female parent and the child's mother subsequently enter into a civil partnership, and

    (d)   the female parent is at the date of the formation of the civil partnership domiciled in England and Wales,

the civil partnership shall render the child, if living, legitimate from the date of the formation of the civil partnership.

17

In section 3 of the Legitimacy Act 1976 (legitimation by extraneous law), renumber the existing provision as subsection (1) of the section and at the end insert—

(2) Subject to the following provisions of this Act, where—

    (a)   a person ("the child") has a parent ("the female parent") by virtue of section 43 of the Human Fertilisation and Embryology Act 2008 (treatment provided to woman who agrees that second woman to be parent),

    (b)   at the time of the child's birth, the female parent and the child's mother are not civil partners of each other,

    (c)   the female parent and the child's mother subsequently enter into a civil partnership, and

    (d)   the female parent is not at the time of the formation of the civil partnership domiciled in England and Wales but is domiciled in a country by the law of which the child became legitimated by virtue of the civil partnership, the child, if living, shall in England and Wales be recognised as having been so legitimated from the date of the formation of the civil partnership notwithstanding that, at the time of the child's birth, the female parent was domiciled in a country the law of which did not permit legitimation by subsequent civil partnership.

18

In section 9 of the Legitimacy Act 1976 (re-registration of birth of legitimated persons)—

(a) in subsection (1), after "marriage" insert "or of the formation of the civil partnership", and

(b) in subsection (3), after "marriage" insert "or civil partnership".

19

In section 10 of the Legitimacy Act 1976 (interpretation), in the definition of "legitimated person", in paragraph (a), after "section 2" insert ", 2A".

Magistrates' Courts Act 1980 (c. 43)

20

In section 65 of the Magistrates' Courts Act 1980 (meaning of family proceedings), in subsection (1), for paragraph (na) substitute—

(na) section 54 of the Human Fertilisation and Embryology Act 2008;.

Supreme Court Act 1981 (c. 54)

21

In Schedule 1 to the Supreme Court Act 1981 (distribution of business in High Court), in paragraph 3(f), for sub-paragraph (iv) substitute—

(iv) section 54 of the Human Fertilisation and Embryology Act 2008.

British Nationality Act 1981 (c. 61)

22

In section 50 of the British Nationality Act 1981 (interpretation) in subsection (9A) (a child's father) for paragraphs (b) and (c) substitute—

(b) where a person is treated as the father of the child under section 28 of the Human Fertilisation and Embryology Act 1990 or section 35 or 36 of the Human Fertilisation and Embryology Act 2008, that person, or

(ba) where a person is treated as a parent of the child under section 42 or 43 of the Human Fertilisation and Embryology Act 2008, that person, or

(c) where none of paragraphs (a) to (ba) applies, a person who satisfies prescribed requirements as to proof of paternity.

Family Law Act 1986 (c. 55)

23

In section 56 of the Family Law Act 1986 (declarations of parentage, legitimacy or legitimation), in subsection (5)(a), after "section 2" insert ", 2A"

Family Law Reform Act 1987 (c. 42)

24

(1) Section 1 of the Family Law Reform Act 1987 (general principle) is amended as follows.

(2) In subsection (3) (children whose father and mother are to be taken to have been married to each other at the time of the child's birth) after paragraph (b) insert—

> (ba) has a parent by virtue of section 42 of the Human Fertilisation and Embryology Act 2008 (which relates to treatment provided to a woman who is at the time of treatment a party to a civil partnership or, in certain circumstances, a void civil partnership);
>
> (bb) has a parent by virtue of section 43 of that Act (which relates to treatment provided to woman who agrees that second woman to be parent) who—
>> (i)   is the civil partner of the child's mother at the time of the child's birth, or
>> (ii)   was the civil partner of the child's mother at any time during the period beginning with the time mentioned in section 43(b) of that Act and ending with the child's birth;".

(3) After subsection (4) insert—

> (5) A child whose parents are parties to a void civil partnership shall, subject to subsection (6), be treated as falling within subsection (3)(bb) if at the time when the parties registered as civil partners of each other both or either of the parties reasonably believed that the civil partnership was valid.

> (6) Subsection (5) applies only where the woman who is a parent by virtue of section 43 was domiciled in England and Wales at the time of the birth or, if she died before the birth, was so domiciled immediately before her death.

> (7) Subsection (5) applies even though the belief that the civil partnership was valid was due to a mistake as to law.

> (8) It shall be presumed for the purposes of subsection (5), unless the contrary is shown, that one of the parties to a void civil partnership reasonably believed at the time of the formation of the civil partnership that the civil partnership was valid.

25

(1) Section 18 of the Family Law Reform Act 1987 (succession on intestacy) is amended as follows.

(2) After subsection (2) insert—

"(2A) In the case of a person who has a parent by virtue of section 43 of the Human Fertilisation and Embryology Act 2008 (treatment provided to woman who agrees that second woman to be parent), the second and third references in subsection (2) to the person's father are to be read as references to the woman who is a parent of the person by virtue of that section."

(3) In subsection (3), for "section 50(1) of that Act" substitute "section 50(1) of the Administration of Estates Act 1925".

Children Act 1989 (c. 41)

26

(1) Section 2 of the Children Act 1989 (parental responsibility for children) is amended as follows.

(2) After subsection (1) insert—

(1A) Where a child—

    (a)   has a parent by virtue of section 42 of the Human Fertilisation and Embryology Act 2008; or

    (b)   has a parent by virtue of section 43 of that Act and is a person to whom section 1(3) of the Family Law Reform Act 1987 applies, the child's mother and the other parent shall each have parental responsibility for the child.

(3) After subsection (2) insert—

(2A) Where a child has a parent by virtue of section 43 of the Human Fertilisation and Embryology Act 2008 and is not a person to whom section 1(3) of the Family Law Reform Act 1987 applies—

    (a)   the mother shall have parental responsibility for the child;

    (b)   the other parent shall have parental responsibility for the child if she has acquired it (and has not ceased to have it) in accordance with the provisions of this Act.

27

After section 4 of the Children Act 1989 insert—

4ZA Acquisition of parental responsibility by second female parent

(1) Where a child has a parent by virtue of section 43 of the Human Fertilisation and Embryology Act 2008 and is not a person to whom section 1(3) of the Family Law Reform Act 1987 applies, that parent shall acquire parental responsibility for the child if—

    (a)   she becomes registered as a parent of the child under any of the enactments specified in subsection (2);

    (b)   she and the child's mother make an agreement providing for her to have parental responsibility for the child; or

    (c)   the court, on her application, orders that she shall have parental responsibility for the child.

(2) The enactments referred to in subsection (1)(a) are—

(a) paragraphs (a), (b) and (c) of section 10(1B) and of section 10A(1B) of the Births and Deaths Registration Act 1953;

(b) paragraphs (a), (b) and (d) of section 18B(1) and sections 18B(3)(a) and 20(1)(a) of the Registration of Births, Deaths and Marriages (Scotland) Act 1965; and

(c) sub-paragraphs (a), (b) and (c) of Article 14ZA(3) of the Births and Deaths Registration (Northern Ireland) Order 1976.

(3) The Secretary of State may by order amend subsection (2) so as to add further enactments to the list in that subsection.

(4) An agreement under subsection (1)(b) is also a "parental responsibility agreement", and section 4(2) applies in relation to such an agreement as it applies in relation to parental responsibility agreements under section 4.

(5) A person who has acquired parental responsibility under subsection (1) shall cease to have that responsibility only if the court so orders.

(6) The court may make an order under subsection (5) on the application—

(a) of any person who has parental responsibility for the child; or

(b) with the leave of the court, of the child himself, subject, in the case of parental responsibility acquired under subsection (1)(c), to section 12(4).

(7) The court may only grant leave under subsection (6)(b) if it is satisfied that the child has sufficient understanding to make the proposed application.

28

(1) Section 12 of the Children Act 1989 (residence orders and parental responsibility) is amended as follows.

(2) After subsection (1) insert—

(1A) Where the court makes a residence order in favour of a woman who is a parent of a child by virtue of section 43 of the Human Fertilisation and Embryology Act 2008 it shall, if that woman would not otherwise have parental responsibility for the child, also make an order under section 4ZA giving her that responsibility.

(3) In subsection (4)—

(a) after "(1)" insert "or (1A)",

(b) after "4" insert "or 4ZA", and

(c) for "father" substitute "parent".

29

In section 91 of the Children Act 1989 (effect and duration of orders)—

(a) in subsection (7), after "4(1)," insert "4ZA(1),", and

(b) in subsection (8)(a), after "4" insert ", 4ZA".

30

In section 104 of the Children Act 1989 (regulations and orders)—

(a) in subsection (2), after "4(1B)," insert "4ZA(3),", and

(b) in subsection (3), after "4(1B)" insert ", 4ZA(3)".

31

In section 105 of the Children Act 1989 (interpretation), in subsection (1), in the definition of "parental responsibility agreement", after "sections 4(1)" insert ", 4ZA(4)".

32

(1) Schedule 1 to the Children Act 1989 (financial provision for children) is amended as follows.

(2) At the end of paragraph 4 insert—

> (5) In the case of a child who has a parent by virtue of section 42 or 43 of the Human Fertilisation and Embryology Act 2008, any reference in sub-paragraph (2), (3) or (4) to the child's father is a reference to the woman who is a parent of the child by virtue of that section.

(3) At the end of paragraph 10 insert—

> (8) In the case of a child who has a parent by virtue of section 42 or 43 of the Human Fertilisation and Embryology Act 2008, the reference in sub-paragraph (1)(a) to the child's father is a reference to the woman who is a parent of the child by virtue of that section.

Human Fertilisation and Embryology Act 1990 (c. 37)

33

(1) Section 32 of the 1990 Act (information to be provided to Registrar General) is amended as follows.

(2) In subsection (1)—

(a) for "man" substitute "person", and
(b) for "father" substitute "parent".

(3) In subsection (2), for the words from "that the man" to "section 28 of this Act" substitute "that the person may be a parent of the child by virtue of any of the relevant statutory provisions".

(4) After subsection (2) insert—

> (2A) In subsection (2) "the relevant statutory provisions" means—
>
> (a) section 28 of this Act, and
> (b) sections 35 to 47 of the Human Fertilisation and Embryology Act 2008.

34

In section 34 of the 1990 Act (disclosure in the interests of justice), in subsection (1), after "of this Act" insert "or sections 33 to 47 of the Human Fertilisation and Embryology Act 2008.

35

(1) Section 35 of the 1990 Act (disclosure of information in the interests of justice: congenital disabilities etc) is amended as follows.

(2) In subsections (1) and (2), for "sections 27 to 29 of this Act" substitute "the relevant statutory provisions".

(3) After subsection (2) insert—

> (2A) In subsections (1) and (2) "the relevant statutory provisions" means—
>
> > (a)   sections 27 to 29 of this Act, and
> > (b)   sections 33 to 47 of the Human Fertilisation and Embryology Act 2008.

Child Support Act 1991 (c. 48)

36

In section 26 of the Child Support Act 1991 (disputes about parentage), in subsection (2), for Cases B and B1 substitute—

> **CASE B**
>
> Where the alleged parent is a parent of the child in question by virtue of an order under section 30 of the Human Fertilisation and Embryology Act 1990 or section 54 of the Human Fertilisation and Embryology Act 2008 (parental orders).
>
> **CASE B1**
>
> Where the Secretary of State is satisfied that the alleged parent is a parent of the child in question by virtue of section 27 or 28 of the Human Fertilisation and Embryology Act 1990 or any of sections 33 to 46 of the Human Fertilisation and Embryology Act 2008 (which relate to children resulting from assisted reproduction).

Family Law Act 1996 (c. 27)

37

In section 63 of the Family Law Act 1996 (definition of family proceedings), in subsection (2), for paragraph (h) substitute—

> (h)   section 54 of the Human Fertilisation and Embryology Act 2008;.

Access to Justice Act 1999 (c. 22)

38

In Schedule 2 to the Access to Justice Act 1999 (community legal services: excluded services), in paragraph 2(3), for paragraph (f) substitute—

> (f)   under section 54 of the Human Fertilisation and Embryology Act 2008,.

Adoption and Children Act 2002 (c. 38)

39

(1) Section 51 of the Adoption and Children Act 2002 (adoption by one person) is amended as follows.

(2) In subsection (4), for paragraph (b) substitute—

    (b)   by virtue of the provisions specified in subsection (5), there is no other parent, or.

(3) After subsection (4) insert—

    (5) The provisions referred to in subsection (4)(b) are—

        (a)   section 28 of the Human Fertilisation and Embryology Act 1990 (disregarding subsections (5A) to (5I) of that section), or

        (b)   sections 34 to 47 of the Human Fertilisation and Embryology Act 2008 (disregarding sections 39, 40 and 46 of that Act).

Mental Capacity Act 2005 (c. 9)

40

In section 27 of the Mental Capacity Act 2005 (family relationships), in subsection (1), after paragraph (h) insert—

    (i)   giving a consent under the Human Fertilisation and Embryology Act 2008.

PART 2
ENACTMENTS RELATING ONLY TO SCOTLAND

Children and Young Persons (Scotland) Act 1937 (c. 37)

41

In section 110(1) of the Children and Young Persons (Scotland) Act 1937 (interpretation), in the definition of "parental responsibilities"—

    (a)   the words from "a father" to the end become paragraph (a), and
    (b)   after that paragraph insert—

        (b)   a second female parent would have as a parent but for the operation of section 3(1)(d) of that Act.

Registration of Births, Deaths and Marriages (Scotland) Act 1965 (c. 49)

42

In section 14 of the Registration of Births, Deaths and Marriages (Scotland) Act 1965 (duty to give information of particulars of birth), after subsection (4) insert—

    (4A) In the case of a child who has a parent by virtue of section 42 of the Human Fertilisation and Embryology Act 2008, the references in subsections (1) and (2) to the father of the child are to be read as references to the woman who is a parent by virtue of that section.

43

For section 18ZA of the Registration of Births, Deaths and Marriages (Scotland) Act 1965 substitute—

18ZA Registration of father or second female parent by virtue of certain provisions of the Human Fertilisation and Embryology Act 2008

(1) The registrar shall not enter in the register—

(a) as the father of a child the name of a man who is to be treated for that purpose as the father of the child by virtue of section 39(1) or 40(1) or (2) of the Human Fertilisation and Embryology Act 2008 (circumstances in which man to be treated as father of child for purpose of registration of birth where fertility treatment undertaken after his death); or

(b) as a parent of the child, the name of a woman who is to be treated for that purpose as a parent of the child by virtue of section 46(1) or (2) of that Act (circumstances in which woman to be treated as parent of child for purposes of registration of birth where fertility treatment undertaken after her death), unless the condition in subsection (2) below is satisfied.

(2) The condition in this subsection is satisfied if—

(a) the mother requests the registrar to make such an entry in the register and produces the relevant documents; or

(b) in the case of the death or inability of the mother, the relevant documents are produced by some other person who is a qualified informant.

(3) In this section "the relevant documents" means—

(a) the consent in writing and election mentioned in section 39(1), 40(1) or (2) or 46(1) or (2) (as the case requires) of the Human Fertilisation and Embryology Act 2008;

(b) a certificate of a registered medical practitioner as to the medical facts concerned; and

(c) such other documentary evidence (if any) as the registrar considers appropriate.

44

After section 18A of the Registration of Births, Deaths and Marriages (Scotland) Act 1965 insert—

18B Births of children where second female parent by virtue of section 43 of the Human Fertilisation and Embryology Act 2008

(1) No woman shall as a parent of a child by virtue of section 43 of the Human Fertilisation and Embryology Act 2008 ("the woman concerned") be required, as a parent of the child, to give information concerning the birth of the child and, save as provided in section 20 of this Act, the district registrar for the registration district shall not enter in the birth registration form concerning the birth the name and surname of any woman as a parent of the child by virtue of section 43 of that Act of 2008 except—

(a)   at the joint request of the mother and the woman concerned (in which case the woman concerned shall attest, in the prescribed manner, the birth registration form together with the mother); or

(b)   at the request of the mother on production of—

    (i)   a declaration in the prescribed form made by the mother stating that the woman concerned is a parent of the child by virtue of section 43 of the Human Fertilisation and Embryology Act 2008; and

    (ii)   a statutory declaration made by the woman concerned acknowledging herself to be a parent of the child by virtue of section 43 of that Act; or

(c)   at the request of the mother on production of a decree by a competent court finding or declaring the woman concerned to be a parent of the child by virtue of section 43 of that Act; or

(d)   at the request of the woman concerned on production of—

    (i)   a declaration in the prescribed form made by the woman concerned acknowledging herself to be a parent of the child by virtue of section 43 of that Act; and

    (ii)   a statutory declaration made by the mother stating that the woman concerned is a parent of the child by virtue of section 43 of that Act.

(2) Where a person acknowledging herself to be a parent of the child by virtue of section 43 of the Human Fertilisation and Embryology Act 2008 makes a request to the district registrar for the registration district in accordance with paragraph (d) of subsection (1) of this section, she shall be treated as a qualified informant concerning the birth of the child for the purposes of this Act; and the giving of information concerning the birth of the child by that person and the attesting of the birth registration form concerning the birth by her in the presence of the registrar shall act as a discharge of any duty of any other qualified informant under section 14 of this Act.

(3) In any case where the name and surname of a woman who is a parent of a child by virtue of section 43 of the Human Fertilisation and Embryology Act 2008 has not been entered in the birth registration form concerning the birth, the Registrar General may record that name and surname by causing an appropriate entry to be made in the Register of Corrections Etc—

(a)   if there is produced to him a declaration and a statutory declaration such as are mentioned in paragraph (b) or (d) of subsection (1) of this section; or

(b)   if, where the mother is dead or cannot be found or is incapable of making a request under subsection (1)(b) or (c) of this section, or a declaration under subsection (1)(b)(i) or a statutory declaration under subsection (1)(d)(ii) of this section, the Registrar General is ordered so to do by the sheriff upon application made to the sheriff by the person acknowledging herself to be a parent of the child by virtue of section 43 of the Human Fertilisation and Embryology Act 2008.

45

In section 20 of the Registration of Births, Deaths and Marriages (Scotland) Act 1965—

(a)   after subsection (1)(c) insert ", or

(d)   the entry relating to the child in the register of births has been made so as to imply that the person, other than the mother, recorded as a parent of the child is so by virtue of section 43 of the Human Fertilisation and Embryology Act 2008 and the mother and that person have subsequently become parties to a civil partnership with each other and subject to subsection (1B) below, and

(b)   in subsection (1B)—
   (i)   after "(c)" insert "or (d)",
   (ii)   after "paternity" insert "or parentage", and
   (iii)   after "18" insert "or 18B".

Family Law (Scotland) Act 1985 (c. 37)

46

In section 9(1)(c)(ii) of the Family Law (Scotland) Act 1985 (court to consider burden of caring for child following dissolution of civil partnership), after "family" insert "or in respect of whom they are, by virtue of sections 33 and 42 of the Human Fertilisation and Embryology Act 2008, the parents".

47

In section 27(1) of the Family Law (Scotland) Act 1985 (interpretation), in the definition of "family", at the end insert "or in respect of whom they are, by virtue of sections 33 and 42 of the Human Fertilisation and Embryology Act 2008, the parents;".

Children (Scotland) Act 1995 (c. 36)

48

In section 1(1) of the Children (Scotland) Act 1995 (parental responsibilities), after "3(1)(b)" insert ", and (d)".

49

In section 2(1) of the Children (Scotland) Act 1995 (parental rights), after "3(1)(b)" insert ", and (d)".

50

(1) Section 3 of the Children (Scotland) Act 1995 (provisions relating both to parental responsibilities and parental rights) is amended as follows.

(2) After subsection (1)(b), insert—

(c)   without prejudice to any arrangements which may be made under subsection (5) below, where a child has a parent by virtue of section 42 of the Human Fertilisation and Embryology Act 2008, that parent has parental responsibilities and parental rights in relation to the child;

(d)   without prejudice to any arrangements which may be made under subsection (5) below and subject to any agreement which may be made under section 4A(1) of this Act, where a child has a parent by virtue of section 43 of the Human Fertilisation and Embryology Act 2008, that parent has parental responsibilities and parental rights in relation to the child if she is registered as a parent of the child under any of the enactments mentioned in subsection (3A).

(3) After subsection (3), insert—

(3A) Those enactments are—

(a) paragraphs (a), (b) and (d) of section 18B(1) and section 18B(3)(a) of the Registration of Births, Deaths and Marriages (Scotland) Act 1965;

(b) paragraphs (a), (b) and (c) of section 10(1B) and of section 10A(1B) of the Births and Deaths Registration Act 1953;

(c) sub-paragraphs (a), (b) and (c) of Article 14ZA(3) of the Births and Deaths Registration (Northern Ireland) Order 1976."

(4) In subsection (5), for "section 4(1)" substitute "sections 4(1) and 4A(1).

51

After section 4 of the Children (Scotland) Act 1995 insert—

4A Acquisition of parental responsibilities and parental rights by second female parent by agreement with mother

(1) Where—

(a) a child's mother has not been deprived of some or all of the parental responsibilities and parental rights in relation to the child; and

(b) the child has a parent by virtue of section 43 of the Human Fertilisation and Embryology Act 2008 and that parent is not registered as such under any of the enactments mentioned in section 3(3A), the mother and the other parent may by agreement provide that, as from the appropriate date, the other parent shall have the parental responsibilities and rights (in the absence of any order under section 11 of this Act affecting responsibilities and rights) as if the other parent were treated as a parent by virtue of section 42 of that Act of 2008.

(2) Section 4(2), (3) and (4) applies in relation to an agreement under subsection (1) of this section as it applies in relation to an agreement under subsection (1) of section 4.

52

(1) Section 11 of the Children (Scotland) Act 1995 (court orders relating to parental responsibilities) is amended as follows.

(2) In subsection (4)(c)—

(a) for "subsection (9) of section 30 of the Human Fertilisation and Embryology Act 1990 (provision for enactments about adoption to have effect with modifications)" substitute "section 55(1) of the Human Fertilisation and Embryology Act 2008 (parental orders: supplementary provision)", and

(b) for "subsection (1) of that section" substitute "section 54 of that Act".

(3) In subsection (11), after "4(2)" insert "or 4A(2)".

53

In section 12(4)(b) of the Children (Scotland) Act 1995 (meaning of "child of the family" in civil partnership cases)—

    (a)   the words from "who" to the end become sub-paragraph (i), and
    (b)   after that sub-paragraph insert "; or
        (ii)   whose parents are the partners (being parents by virtue of sections 33 and 42 of the Human Fertilisation and Embryology Act 2008)."

54

In section 15(1) of the Children (Scotland) Act 1995 (interpretation of Part 1), in the definition of "parent"—

    (a)   after "1990" insert "and Part 2 of the Human Fertilisation and Embryology Act 2008", and
    (b)   for "subsection (9) of the said section 30" substitute "section 55(1) of that Act of 2008".

Criminal Law (Consolidation) (Scotland) Act 1995 (c. 39)

55

In section 1(1) of the Criminal Law (Consolidation) (Scotland) Act 1995 (offence of incest), at the end of the table set out at the end of that subsection insert—

"3 Relationships by virtue of Part 2 of the Human Fertilisation and Embryology Act 2008	
Mother	Father
Daughter	Son
Second female parent by virtue of section 42 or 43 of that Act"	

Adoption and Children (Scotland) Act 2007 (asp 4)

56

(1) Section 30 of the Adoption and Children (Scotland) Act 2007 (adoption by one person) is amended as follows.

(2) In subsection (7), for paragraph (c) substitute—

    (c)   by virtue of the provisions specified in subsection (7A), there is no other parent, or.

(3) After subsection (7) insert—

(7A) The provisions referred to in subsection (7)(c) are—

   (a)   section 28 of the Human Fertilisation and Embryology Act 1990 (disregarding subsections (5A) to (5I) of that section), or

   (b)   sections 34 to 47 of the Human Fertilisation and Embryology Act 2008 (disregarding sections 39, 40 and 46 of that Act).

PART 3
ENACTMENTS RELATING ONLY TO NORTHERN IRELAND

Legitimacy Act (Northern Ireland) 1928 (c. 5 (N.I.))

57

(1) Section 1 of the Legitimacy Act (Northern Ireland) 1928 (legitimation by subsequent marriage of parents) is amended as follows.

(2) In the heading, after "marriage" insert "or civil partnership".

(3) After subsection (1) insert—

   (1A) Subject to subsection (3), where—

   (a)   a person ("the child") has a parent ("the female parent") by virtue of section 43 of the Human Fertilisation and Embryology Act 2008 (treatment provided to woman who agrees that second woman to be parent);

   (b)   at the time of the child's birth, the female parent and the child's mother are not civil partners of each other;

   (c)   the female parent and the child's mother subsequently enter into a civil partnership; and

   (d)   the female parent is at the date of the formation of the civil partnership domiciled in Northern Ireland, the civil partnership shall render the child, if living, legitimate from the date of the formation of the civil partnership.

58

(1) Section 8 of the Legitimacy Act (Northern Ireland) 1928 (provisions as to persons legitimated by extraneous law) is amended as follows.

(2) After subsection (1) insert—

   (1A) Where—

   (a)   a person ("the child") has a parent ("the female parent") by virtue of section 43 of the Human Fertilisation and Embryology Act 2008 (treatment provided to woman who agrees that second woman to be parent);

   (b)   at the time of the child's birth, the female parent and the child's mother are not civil partners of each other;

   (c)   the female parent and the child's mother subsequently enter into a civil partnership; and

   (d)   the female parent is at the time of the formation of the civil partnership domiciled in a country, other than Northern Ireland, by the law of which the child became legitimated by virtue of the civil partnership; the child, if living, shall in Northern Ireland be recognised as having been so legitimated from the date of the formation of the civil partnership notwithstanding that, at the time of the child's birth, the female parent was not domiciled in a country the law of which permitted legitimation by subsequent civil partnership.

59

In section 11 of the Legitimacy Act (Northern Ireland) 1928 (interpretation), in the definition of "date of legitimation", after "date of the marriage" insert

or of the formation of the civil partnership.

Births and Deaths Registration (Northern Ireland) Order 1976 (S.I. 1976/1041 (N.I. 14))

60

(1) Article 10 of the Births and Deaths Registration (Northern Ireland) Order 1976 (registration of births) is amended as follows.

(2) In paragraph (4) for "Article 14" substitute "Articles 14 and 14ZA".

(3) After paragraph (4) insert—

(4A) In the case of a child who has a parent by virtue of section 42 or 43 of the Human Fertilisation and Embryology Act 2008, the references in paragraphs (3)(a) and (4) to the father of the child are to be read as references to the woman who is a parent by virtue of that section.

61

After Article 14 of the Births and Deaths Registration (Northern Ireland) Order 1976 insert—

14ZA Registration of second female parent where parents not civil partners

(1) This Article applies, subject to Article 14A, in the case of a child who—

    (a)   has a parent by virtue of section 43 of the Human Fertilisation and Embryology Act 2008; but

    (b)   is a person to whom Article 155(3) of the Children (Northern Ireland) Order 1995 (persons to be covered by references to a person whose mother and father were married to each other at the time of the person's birth) does not apply.

(2) The woman who is a parent by virtue of section 43 of the Human Fertilisation and Embryology Act 2008 shall not as such be under any duty to give any information under this Part concerning the birth of the child.

(3) A registrar shall not enter the name of any person as a parent of the child by virtue of that section unless—

    (a)   the mother and the person stating herself to be the other parent of the child jointly request the registrar to do so and in that event the mother and that person shall sign the register in the presence of each other; or

    (b)   the mother requests the registrar to do so and produces—

(i) a declaration in the prescribed form made by her stating that the person to be registered ("the woman concerned") is a parent of the child by virtue of section 43 of the Human Fertilisation and Embryology Act 2008; and

(ii) a statutory declaration made by the woman concerned stating herself to be a parent of the child by virtue of section 43 of that Act; or

(c) the woman concerned requests the registrar to do so and produces—

(i) a declaration in the prescribed form made by the woman concerned stating herself to be a parent of the child by virtue of section 43 of the Human Fertilisation and Embryology Act 2008; and

(ii) a statutory declaration made by the mother stating that the woman concerned is a parent of the child by virtue of section 43 of that Act; or

(d) the mother or the woman concerned requests the registrar to do so and produces—

(i) a copy of a parental responsibility agreement made between them in relation to the child; and

(ii) a declaration in the prescribed form by the person making the request stating that the agreement was made in compliance with Article 7 of the Children (Northern Ireland) Order 1995 and has not been brought to an end by an order of a court; or

(e) the mother or the woman concerned requests the registrar to do so and produces—

(i) a certified copy of an order under Article 7 of the Children (Northern Ireland) Order 1995 giving the woman concerned parental responsibility for the child; and

(ii) a declaration in the prescribed form by the person making the request stating that the order has not been brought to an end by an order of a court; or

(f) the mother or the woman concerned requests the registrar to do so and produces—

(i) a certified copy of an order under paragraph 2 of Schedule 1 to the Children (Northern Ireland) Order 1995 which requires the woman concerned to make any financial provision for the child and which is not an order falling within paragraph 5(3) of that Schedule; and

(ii) a declaration in the prescribed form by the person making the request stating that the order has not been discharged by an order of a court.

(4) Where, in the case of a child to whom Article 155(3) of the Children (Northern Ireland) Order 1995 does not apply, a person stating herself to be a parent of the child by virtue of section 43 of the Human Fertilisation and Embryology Act 2008 makes a request to the registrar in accordance with any of sub-paragraphs (c) to (f) of paragraph (3)—

(a) she shall be treated as a qualified informant concerning the birth of the child for the purposes of this Part; and

(b) on the giving of the required information concerning the birth of the child by that person and the signing of the register by her in the presence of the registrar every other qualified informant shall cease to be under the duty imposed by Article 10(4).

62

For Article 14A of the Births and Deaths Registration (Northern Ireland) Order 1976 substitute—

> **14A Registration of father or second female parent by virtue of certain provisions of Human Fertilisation and Embryology Act 2008**
>
> (1) A registrar shall not enter in the register—
>
> (a)　as the father of a child, the name of a man who is to be treated for that purpose as the father of the child by virtue of section 39(1)or 40(1) or (2) of the Human Fertilisation and Embryology Act 2008 (circumstances in which man to be treated as father of child for purposes of registration of birth where fertility treatment undertaken after his death); or
>
> (b)　as a parent of the child, the name of a woman who is to be treated for that purpose as a parent of the child by virtue of section 46(1) or (2) of that Act (circumstances in which woman to be treated as parent of child for purposes of registration of birth where fertility treatment undertaken after her death); unless the condition in paragraph (2) below is satisfied.
>
> (2) The condition in this paragraph is satisfied if—
>
> (a)　the mother requests the registrar to make such an entry in the register and produces the relevant documents; or
>
> (b)　in the case of the death or inability of the mother, the relevant documents are produced by some other person who is a qualified informant.
>
> (3) In this Article "the relevant documents" means—
>
> (a)　the consent in writing and election mentioned in section 39(1), 40(1) or (2) or 46(1) or (2) (as the case requires) of the Human Fertilisation and Embryology Act 2008;
>
> (b)　a certificate of a registered medical practitioner as to the medical facts concerned; and
>
> (c)　such other documentary evidence (if any) as the registrar considers appropriate.

63

(1) Article 18 of the Births and Deaths Registration (Northern Ireland) Order 1976 (re-registration of births) is amended as follows.

(2) In paragraph (1)—

(a)　in sub-paragraph (b), after "child" insert "who has a father and",

(b)　after sub-paragraph (b) insert—

> (ba)　in the case of a child who has a parent by virtue of section 43 of the Human Fertilisation and Embryology Act 2008 and to whom Article 155(3) of the Children (Northern Ireland) Order 1995 does not apply—

  (i)   the birth was registered as if Article 155(3) of that Order did apply to the child; or

  (ii)   no particulars relating to a parent of the child by virtue of section 42, 43 or 46(1) or (2) of that Act have been entered in the register; or, and

(c)   for sub-paragraph (c) substitute—

  (c)   in the case of a person who is to be treated—

  (i)   as the father of the child by virtue of section 39(1) or 40(1) or (2) of the Human Fertilisation and Embryology Act 2008; or

  (ii)   as a parent of the child by virtue of section 46(1) or (2) of that Act; the condition in Article 14A(2) is satisfied.

(3) At the end of paragraph (1A) insert "and re-registration under subparagraph (ba)(ii) shall not be authorised otherwise than in accordance with Article 14ZA(3)".

64

(1) Article 19 of the Births and Deaths Registration (Northern Ireland) Order 1976 (re-registration of births of legitimated persons) is amended as follows.

(2) In paragraph (3)—

  (a)   after sub-paragraph (a) insert—

  (aa)   the name of a person acknowledging herself to be a parent of the legitimated person by virtue of section 43 of the Human Fertilisation and Embryology Act 2008 has been entered in the register in pursuance of Article 14ZA or 18 of this Order; or, and

  (b)   after sub-paragraph (b) insert—

  (ba)   the parentage by virtue of section 43 of the Human Fertilisation and Embryology Act 2008 of the legitimated person has been established by a decree of a court of competent jurisdiction; or

(3) In paragraph (4), after "marriage" insert "or the formation of the civil partnership".

(4) In paragraph (5)—

  (a)   after "marriage" insert "or civil partnership", and

  (b)   after "date of the marriage" insert "or the formation of the civil partnership".

65

In Article 20 of the Births and Deaths Registration (Northern Ireland) Order 1976 (registration of births of legitimated person), in paragraph (2), for "subparagraph (a)" substitute "sub-paragraphs (a) and (aa)".

66

In Article 37 of the Births and Deaths Registration (Northern Ireland) Order 1976 (registration or alteration of child's name), in paragraph (7)—

(a) after sub-paragraph (a) insert—

(aa) in the case of a child who has a parent by virtue of section 42 or 43 of the Human Fertilisation and Embryology Act 2008, the mother and other parent of the child if Article 155(3) of the Children (Northern Ireland) Order 1995 applies to the child or if it does not apply but the other parent has parental responsibility for the child; and

(b) for sub-paragraph (b) substitute—

(b) the mother of the child if—
(i) in the case of a child who has a father, the child's parents were not married to each other at the time of the birth and the father does not have parental responsibility for the child; and
(ii) in the case of a child who has a parent by virtue of section 43 of the Human Fertilisation and Embryology Act 2008, Article 155(3) of the Children (Northern Ireland) Order 1995 does not apply to the child and the parent by virtue of that section of that Act does not have parental responsibility for the child;.

Family Law Reform (Northern Ireland) Order 1977 (S.I. 1977/1250 (N.I. 17))

67

In Article 13 of the Family Law Reform (Northern Ireland) Order 1977 (interpretation of Part 3), in the definition of "excluded", after "1990" insert

and to sections 33 to 47 of the Human Fertilisation and Embryology Act 2008.

Adoption (Northern Ireland) Order 1987 (S.I. 1987/2203 (N.I. 22))

68

(1) Article 15 of the Adoption (Northern Ireland) Order 1987 (adoption by one person) is amended as follows.

(2) In paragraph (3)(a), for the words from "or, by virtue of" to "other parent" substitute "or, by virtue of the provisions specified in paragraph (3A), there is no other parent".

(3) After paragraph (3) insert—

(3A) The provisions referred to in paragraph (3)(a) are—

(a) section 28 of the Human Fertilisation and Embryology Act 1990 (disregarding subsections (5A) to (5I) of that section), or
(b) sections 34 to 47 of the Human Fertilisation and Embryology Act 2008 (disregarding sections 39, 40 and 46 of that Act).

Child Support (Northern Ireland) Order 1991 (SI 1991/2628 (NI 23))

69

In Article 27 of the Child Support (Northern Ireland) Order 1991 (disputes about parentage), in paragraph (2), for Cases B and B1 substitute—

> **"CASE B**
>
> Where the alleged parent is a parent of the child in question by virtue of an order under section 30 of the Human Fertilisation and Embryology Act 1990 or section 54 of the Human Fertilisation and Embryology Act 2008 (parental orders).
>
> **CASE B1**
>
> Where the Department is satisfied that the alleged parent is a parent of the child in question by virtue of section 27 or 28 of the Human Fertilisation and Embryology Act 1990 or any of sections 33 to 46 of the Human Fertilisation and Embryology Act 2008 (which relate to children resulting from assisted reproduction)."

Children (Northern Ireland) Order 1995 (SI 1995/755 (NI 2))

70

In Article 2 of the Children (Northern Ireland) Order 1995, in paragraph (2), in the definition of "parental responsibility agreement", for "Article 7(1)(b)" substitute "Article 7(1ZB)".

71

(1) Article 5 of the Children (Northern Ireland) Order 1995 (parental responsibility for children) is amended as follows.

(2) After paragraph (1) insert—

> "(1A) Where a child—
>
> (a)   has a parent by virtue of section 42 of the Human Fertilisation and Embryology Act 2008; or
>
> (b)   has a parent by virtue of section 43 of that Act and is a person to whom Article 155(3) applies, the child's mother and the other parent shall each have parental responsibility for the child."

(3) After paragraph (2) insert—

> (2A) Where a child has a parent by virtue of section 43 of the Human Fertilisation and Embryology Act 2008 and is not a person to whom Article 155(3) applies—
>
> (a)   the mother shall have parental responsibility for the child;
>
> (b)   the other parent shall have parental responsibility for the child if she has acquired it (and has not ceased to have it) in accordance with the provisions of this Order.

72

(1) Article 7 of the Children (Northern Ireland) Order 1995 (acquisition of parental responsibility) is amended as follows.

(2) In paragraph (1)(b), omit "(a "parental responsibility agreement")".

(3) After paragraph (1) insert—

(1ZA) Where a child has a parent by virtue of section 43 of the Human Fertilisation and Embryology Act 2008 and is not a person to whom Article 155(3) applies, that parent shall acquire parental responsibility for the child if—

    (a)   she becomes registered as a parent of the child;

    (b)   she and the child's mother make an agreement providing for her to have parental responsibility for the child; or

    (c)   the court, on her application, orders that she shall have parental responsibility for the child.

(1ZB) An agreement under paragraph (1)(b) or (1ZA)(b) is known as a "parental responsibility agreement".

(4) After paragraph (2) insert—

(2A) In paragraph (1)(a) "registered" means registered under—

    (a)   Article 14(3)(a), (b) or (c)of the Births and Deaths Registration (Northern Ireland) Order 1976;

    (b)   paragraph (a), (b) or (c) of section 10(1) or 10A(1) of the Births and Deaths Registration Act 1953; or

    (c)   paragraph (a), (b)(i) or (c) of section 18(1) of the Registration of Births, Deaths and Marriages (Scotland) Act 1965.

(2B) In paragraph (1ZA)(a) "registered" means registered under—

(a) Article 14ZA(3)(a), (b) or (c) of the Births and Deaths Registration (Northern Ireland) Order 1976;

    (b)   paragraph (a), (b) or (c) of section 10(1B) and of section 10A(1B) of the Births and Deaths Registration Act 1953; or

    (c)   paragraph (a), (b) or (d) of section 18B(1) of, or sections 18B(3)(a) and 20(1)(a) of, the Registration of Births, Deaths and Marriages (Scotland) Act 1965.

(5) In paragraph (3), omit the words from "and "registered"" to the end.

(6) In paragraph (3A), after "paragraph (1)" insert ", (1ZA)".

(7) In paragraph (4)—

    (a)   for "the father" substitute "a parent", and

    (b)   after "paragraph (1)(c)" insert "or (1ZA)(c)".

73

In Article 8 of the Children (Northern Ireland) Order 1995 (residence, contact and other orders with respect to children), in paragraph (4), for subparagraph (g) substitute—

(g)   section 54 of the Human Fertilisation and Embryology Act 2008;.

74

(1) Article 12 of the Children (Northern Ireland) Order 1995 (residence orders and parental responsibility) is amended as follows.

(2) After paragraph (1) insert—

(1A) Where the court makes a residence order in favour of a person who is a parent of a child by virtue of section 43 of the Human Fertilisation and Embryology Act 2008 it shall, if that person would not otherwise have parental responsibility for the child, also make an order under Article 7(1ZA) giving her that responsibility.

(3) In paragraph (4)—

(a)   after "(1)" insert "or (1A)", and
(b)   for "father" substitute "parent".

75

(1) Article 155 of the Children (Northern Ireland) Order 1995 (parents not being married to each other to have no effect in law on relationships) is amended as follows.

(2) In paragraph (3), after sub-paragraph (b) insert—

(ba) has a parent by virtue of section 42 of the Human Fertilisation and Embryology Act 2008 (which relates to treatment provided to a woman who is at the time of treatment a party to a civil partnership or, in certain circumstances, a void civil partnership);
(bb) has a parent by virtue of section 43 of that Act (which relates to treatment provided to woman who agrees that second woman to be parent) who—
(i)   is the civil partner of the child's mother at the time of the child's birth, or
(ii) was the civil partner of the child's mother at any time during the period beginning with the time mentioned in section 43(b) of that Act and ending with the child's birth;.

(3) After paragraph (4) insert—

(4A) A child whose parents are parties to a void civil partnership shall, subject to paragraph (4B), be treated as falling within paragraph (3)(bb) if at the time when the parties registered as civil partners of each other both or either of the parties reasonably believed that the civil partnership was valid.

(4B) Paragraph (4A) applies only where the woman who is a parent by virtue of section 43 was domiciled in Northern Ireland at the time of the birth or, if she died before the birth, was so domiciled immediately before her death.

(4C) Paragraph (4A) applies even though the belief that the civil partnership was valid was due to a mistake as to law.

(4D) It shall be presumed for the purposes of paragraph (4A), unless the contrary is shown, that one of the parties to a void civil partnership reasonably believed at the time of the formation of the civil partnership that the civil partnership was valid.

76

In Article 179 of the Children (Northern Ireland) Order 1995 (effect and duration of orders etc), in paragraph (7), after "7(1)" insert ", (1ZA)".

77

(1) Schedule 1 to the Children (Northern Ireland) Order 1995 (financial provision for children) is amended as follows.

(2) At the end of paragraph 5 insert—

> (5) In the case of a child who has a parent by virtue of section 42 or 43 of the Human Fertilisation and Embryology Act 2008, any reference in sub-paragraph (2), (3) or (4) to the child's father is a reference to the woman who is a parent of the child by virtue of that section.

(3) At the end of paragraph 12 insert—

> (8) In the case of a child who has a parent by virtue of section 42 or 43 of the Human Fertilisation and Embryology Act 2008, the reference in sub-paragraph (1)(a) to the child's father is a reference to the woman who is a parent of the child by virtue of that section.

78

(1) Paragraph 1 of Schedule 6 to the Children (Northern Ireland) Order 1995 (succession on intestacy where parents not married to each other) is amended as follows.

(2) At the end of sub-paragraph (2) insert—

> (2A) In the case of a person who has a parent by virtue of section 43 of the Human Fertilisation and Embryology Act 2008 (treatment provided to woman who agrees that second woman to be parent), the second and third references in paragraph (2) to the person's father are to be read as references to the woman who is a parent of the person by virtue of that section."

> (3) In sub-paragraph (3) for "section 19(1) of that Act" substitute "section 19(1) of the Administration of Estates Act (Northern Ireland) 1955.

Family Homes and Domestic Violence (Northern Ireland) Order 1998
(SI 1998/1071 (NI 6))

79

In Article 2 of the Family Homes and Domestic Violence (Northern Ireland) Order 1998 (interpretation), in paragraph (3), for sub-paragraph (f) substitute—

> (f)   section 54 of the Human Fertilisation and Embryology Act 2008;.

Schedule 7

Section 65

Minor and Consequential Amendments

Congenital Disabilities (Civil Liability) Act 1976 (c. 28)

1

In section 4 of the Congenital Disabilities (Civil Liability) Act 1976 (interpretation), in subsection (2), for "section 1 of the Human Fertilisation and Embryology Act 1990" substitute "section 1(1) of the Human Fertilisation and Embryology Act 1990 and any regulations under section 1(6) of that Act.

Human Fertilisation and Embryology Act 1990 (c. 37)

2

In section 2 of the 1990 Act (other terms)—

    (a)   in subsection (1), in the definition of "store", for "or embryos" substitute ", embryos or human admixed embryos", and

    (b)   in subsection (2), for "or gametes" substitute ", gametes or human admixed embryos".

3

In section 7 of the 1990 Act (reports to Secretary of State) for subsection (1) substitute—

    (1) The Authority shall prepare—

        (a)   a report for the period beginning with the 1 August preceding the relevant commencement date (or if that date is a 1 August, beginning with that date) and ending with the next 31 March, and

        (b)   a report for each succeeding period of 12 months ending with 31 March.

    (1A) In subsection (1)(a) "the relevant commencement date" means the day on which paragraph 3 of Schedule 7 to the Human Fertilisation and Embryology Act 2008 comes into force.

    (1B) The Authority shall send each report to the Secretary of State as soon as practicable after the end of the period for which it is prepared.

4

Omit section 10 of the 1990 Act (licensing procedure).

5

In section 13A of the 1990 Act (conditions of licences for non-medical fertility services), omit subsection (4).

6

In section 14A of the 1990 Act (conditions of licences: human application), in subsection (1)—

    (a)   omit the "and" at the end of paragraph (a), and

    (b)   at the end of paragraph (b) insert ", and

    (c)   every licence under paragraph 3 of that Schedule, so far as authorising activities in connection with the derivation from embryos of stem cells that are intended for human application."

7

In section 15 of the 1990 Act (conditions of research licences) after subsection (4) insert—

> (5) If by virtue of paragraph 20 of Schedule 3 (existing cells or cell lines) qualifying cells, as defined by paragraph 20(2) of that Schedule, of a person ("P") are used to bring about the creation in vitro of an embryo or human admixed embryo without P's consent, steps shall be taken to ensure that the embryo or human admixed embryo cannot subsequently be attributed to P.

8

Omit section 22 of the 1990 Act (temporary suspension of licence).

9

In section 23 of the 1990 Act (directions: general)—

    (a)   in subsection (5), for paragraph (a) substitute—

>   (a)   in respect of any licence (including a licence which has ceased to have effect), by serving notice of the directions on the person—
>
>   (i)   who is the person responsible or the holder of the licence, if different, or
>
>   (ii)   who was the person responsible or the holder of the licence, if different, and

    (b)   omit subsection (6).

10

(1) Section 31A of the 1990 Act (the Authority's register of licences) is amended as follows.

(2) In subsection (1)—

    (a)   omit the "and" at the end of paragraph (a), and

    (b)   at the end of paragraph (b) insert ", and

    (c)   every licence under paragraph 3 of Schedule 2 authorising activities in connection with the derivation from embryos of stem cells that are intended for human application.".

(3) In subsection (2)(c), for ", if applicable, the nominal licensee" substitute "the name of the holder of the licence (if different)".

11

In section 32 of the 1990 Act (information to be provided to Registrar General), in subsection (3), for "33" substitute "33A".

12

In section 34 of the 1990 Act (disclosure in the interests of justice), in subsection (1), for "section 31(2)(b)" substitute "section 31(2)(c) to (e)".

13

In section 47 of the 1990 Act (index)—

(a) in the first column, after "embryo" insert "(except in section 4A or in the term "human admixed embryo")",

(b) in the first column, after "gametes, eggs or sperm", insert "(except in section 4A)",

(c) in the first column, in the entry relating to "store", after "embryos" insert ", human admixed embryos",

(d) at the appropriate places insert—

"Appeals committee	Section 20A(2)"
"Human admixed embryo	Section 4A(6)"
"Nuclear DNA (in relation to an embryo)	Section 2(1)", and

(e) omit the entries relating to "licence committee" and "nominal licensee".

14

In section 48 of the 1990 Act (application to Northern Ireland) for "sections 33(6)(h) and" substitute "sections 33A(2)(r) and".

15

In Schedule 1 to the 1990 Act (the Authority: supplementary provision)—

(a) in paragraph 9(1), for "The" substitute "Subject to any provision of this Act, the",

(b) in paragraph 10(3), omit "or any licence committee", and

(c) after paragraph 14, insert—

Application of Statutory Instruments Act 1946

15

The Statutory Instruments Act 1946 applies to any power to make orders or regulations conferred by an Act on the Authority as if the Authority were a Minister of the Crown.

Age of Legal Capacity (Scotland) Act 1991 (c. 50)

16

In section 2 of the Age of Legal Capacity (Scotland) Act 1991, after subsection (4) (which provides for an exception to the general rule about the age of legal capacity in relation to surgical, medical or dental procedure or treatment) insert—

> (4ZA) For the purposes of subsection (4), the storage of gametes in accordance with the Human Fertilisation and Embryology Act 1990 is to be treated as a medical procedure.

> (4ZB) A person under the age of 16 years shall have legal capacity to consent to the use of the person's human cells in accordance with Schedule 3 to the Human Fertilisation and Embryology Act 1990 for the purposes of a project of research where the person is capable of understanding the nature of the research; and in this subsection "human cells" has the same meaning as in that Schedule.

17 Children (Scotland) Act 1995 (c.36)

In section 15 of the Children (Scotland) Act 1995 (interpretation of Part 1), after subsection (6) insert—

> (7) No provision in this Part of this Act shall permit a person to give a consent to the storage of gametes under the Human Fertilisation and Embryology Act 1990 on behalf of a child.

Adults with Incapacity (Scotland) Act 2000 (asp 2)

18

After section 84 of the Adults with Incapacity (Scotland) Act 2000 insert—

> **"84A Application to storage of gametes without adult's consent where adult is incapable**

> (1) The storage of gametes under paragraph 10 of Schedule 3 to the Human Fertilisation and Embryology Act 1990 (storage of gametes without patient's consent where patient is incapable) is to be treated as an intervention in the affairs of an adult under this Act.

> (2) Sections 2 to 5, 8, 11, 14 and 85 of this Act apply to a registered medical practitioner's decision under that paragraph as they apply to decisions taken for the purposes of this Act.

> (3) Section 52 of this Act applies to a practitioner's decision under that paragraph as it applies to decisions taken for the purposes of section 47 of this Act.

> (4) Part 5 of this Act (other than section 52) does not apply to the storage of gametes under that paragraph.

> (5) Section 83 of this Act applies to a practitioner's decision under that paragraph as if the practitioner were exercising powers under this Act.

> (6) Nothing in this section authorises any person, other than the person whose gametes are to be stored, to consent to the storage of the gametes.

84B Application to use of human cells to create an embryo in vitro without adult's consent

(1) The use of an adult's human cells to bring about the creation in vitro of an embryo or human admixed embryo for use for the purposes of a project of research—

    (a)   without the adult's consent, and

    (b)   where the adult is incapable, is to be treated as an intervention in the affairs of an adult under this Act.

(2) Sections 2 to 5, 8, 11, 14 and 85 of this Act apply to decisions made under paragraphs 16 and 18 of Schedule 3 to the Human Fertilisation and Embryology Act 1990 (when consent to the use of human cells is not required due to adult being incapable of consenting) as they apply to decisions taken for the purposes of this Act.

(3) Section 51 of this Act does not apply to the use of an adult's human cells to bring about the creation in vitro of an embryo or human admixed embryo for use for the purposes of a project of research.

(4) Section 83 of this Act applies to a decision made under paragraphs 16 and 18 of Schedule 3 to the Human Fertilisation and Embryology Act 1990 as if the person making the decision were exercising powers under this Act.

(5) Expressions used in this section and in Schedule 3 to the Human Fertilisation and Embryology Act 1990 have the same meaning in this section as in that Schedule.

19 Criminal Justice and Police Act 2001 (c. 16)

In section 57 of the Criminal Justice and Police Act 2001 (retention of seized items), in subsection (1)(k), for "section 40(4) of" substitute "paragraph 7(4) of Schedule 3B to".

20

In section 66 of the Criminal Justice and Police Act 2001 (general interpretation of Part 2)—

    (a)   in subsection (4), after paragraph (j) insert—

        (ja)   paragraph 5 of Schedule 3B to the Human Fertilisation and Embryology Act 1990.",

    (b)   in subsection (5), omit paragraph (g).

21

In Schedule 1 to the Criminal Justice and Police Act 2001 (powers of seizure) for paragraph 52 substitute—

52

Each of the powers of seizure conferred by the provisions of paragraph 7(1) and (2) of Schedule 3B to the Human Fertilisation and Embryology Act 1990.

22 Human Tissue Act 2004 (c. 30)

In section 1 of the Human Tissue Act 2004 (authorisation of activities for scheduled purposes)—

(a)   after subsection (9) insert—

(9A) Subsection (1)(f) does not apply to the use of relevant material for the purpose of research where the use of the material requires consent under paragraph 6(1) or 12(1) of Schedule 3 to the Human Fertilisation and Embryology Act 1990 (use of human cells to create an embryo or a human admixed embryo) or would require such consent but for paragraphs 16 and 20 of that Schedule., and

(b)   after subsection (10) insert—

(10A) In the case of an activity in relation to which subsection (8) has effect, subsection (10)(c) is to be read subject to any requirements imposed by Schedule 3 to the Human Fertilisation and Embryology Act 1990 in relation to the activity.

23

In section 14 of the Human Tissue Act 2004 (remit of the Human Tissue Authority), after subsection (2) insert—

(2ZA) The activities within the remit of the Authority do not include the use, for a scheduled purpose, of relevant material where the use of the material requires consent under paragraph 6(1) or 12(1) of Schedule 3 to the Human Fertilisation and Embryology Act 1990 (use of human cells to create an embryo or a human admixed embryo) or would require such consent but for paragraphs 16 and 20 of that Schedule.

24

In section 54 of the Human Tissue Act 2004 (general interpretation), for subsection (6), substitute—

(6) In this Act "embryo" and "gametes" have the same meaning as they have by virtue of section 1(1), (4) and (6) of the Human Fertilisation and Embryology Act 1990 in the other provisions of that Act (apart from section 4A).

25 Mental Capacity Act 2005 (c. 9)

In section 30 of the Mental Capacity Act 2005 (research), after subsection (3) insert—

(3A) Research is not intrusive to the extent that it consists of the use of a person's human cells to bring about the creation in vitro of an embryo or human admixed embryo, or the subsequent storage or use of an embryo or human admixed embryo so created.

(3B) Expressions used in subsection (3A) and in Schedule 3 to the Human Fertilisation and Embryology Act 1990 (consents to use or storage of gametes, embryos or human admixed embryos etc) have the same meaning in that subsection as in that Schedule.

Schedule 8

Section 66

Repeals and Revocations

PART 1
REPEALS

Short title and chapter	Extent of repeal
Surrogacy Arrangements Act 1985 (c. 49)	In section 2(1)(a), the words "or take part in".
Human Fertilisation and Embryology Act 1990 (c. 37)	In section 3(3), paragraph (d) and the word "or" immediately before it.
	In section 4(1), paragraph (c) and the word "or" immediately before it.
	In section 8(1), the word "and" immediately after paragraph (c).
	Section 10.
	In section 12—
	(a) in subsection (1)(c), the words "or nonmedical fertility services", and
	(b) in subsection (2), the word "and" at the end of paragraph (a).
	Section 13A(4).
	In section 14(5), the words "or, as the case may be, five years".
	In section 14A(1), the word "and" at the end of paragraph (a).
	Section 16(6) and (7).
	Section 17(3).
Human Fertilisation and Embryology Act 1990 (c. 37)— cont.	Section 22.
	Section 23(6).

	Section 30.
	In section 31A(1), the word "and" at the end of paragraph (a).
	Sections 39 and 40.
	In section 41—
	(a) subsection (2A),
	(b) in subsection (4), the words ", other than an offence to which subsection (4B) applies,",
	(c) subsections (4A), (4B) and (6), and
	(d) in subsection (9), the words "(6),".
	In section 47, in the index, the entries relating to "licence committee" and "nominal licensee".
	In Schedule 1—
	(a) in paragraph 5(5), paragraph (b) and the word "or" immediately after paragraph (b), and
	(b) in paragraph 10(3), the words "or any licence committee".
	In Schedule 2, in paragraph 1(1)(d), the words from "or" onwards.
Human Fertilisation and Embryology (Disclosure of Information) Act 1992 (c. 54)	The whole Act.
Criminal Justice and Police Act 2001 (c. 16)	Section 66(5)(g). In Schedule 2, paragraph 16(2)(e).
Human Reproductive Cloning Act 2001 (c. 23)	The whole Act.
Family Law Act (Northern Ireland) 2001 (c. 12 (NI))	Section 1(4).

Human Fertilisation and Embryology (Deceased Fathers) Act 2003 (c. 24)	In the Schedule, paragraphs 3, 5, 7, 9, 10, 12 and 18.

PART 2
REVOCATIONS

Title	Extent of revocation
Children (Northern Ireland) Order 1995 (SI 1995/755 (NI 2))	In Article 7— (a) in paragraph (1)(b), the words "(a "parental responsibility agreement")", and
	(b) in paragraph (3), the words from "and "registered"" to the end.
Human Fertilisation and Embryology (Research Purposes) Regulations 2001 (SI 2001/188)	The whole instrument.

Appendix 2

HUMAN FERTILISATION AND EMBRYOLOGY ACT 1990 (AS AMENDED)

ARRANGEMENT OF SECTIONS

Principal terms used

Principal terms used

1 Meaning of 'embryo', 'gamete' and associated expressions

(1) In this Act, except where otherwise stated –

(a)   embryo means a live human embryo where fertilisation is complete, and
(b)   references to an embryo include an egg in the process of fertilisation,

and, for this purpose, fertilisation is not complete until the appearance of a two cell zygote.

[(1) In this Act (except in section 4A or in the term "human admixed embryo")—

(a) embryo means a live human embryo and does not include a human admixed embryo (as defined by section 4A(6)), and

(b) references to an embryo include an egg that is in the process of fertilisation or is undergoing any other process capable of resulting in an embryo.]

(2) This Act, so far as it governs bringing about the creation of an embryo, applies only to bringing about the creation of an embryo outside the human body; and in this Act –

(a) references to embryos the creation of which was brought about in vitro (in their application to those where fertilisation is complete) are to those where fertilisation began outside the human body whether or not it was completed there, and

[(a) references to embryos the creation of which was brought about in vitro (in their application to those where fertilisation or any other process by which an embryo is created is complete) are to those where fertilisation or any other process by which the embryo was created began outside the human body whether or not it was completed there, and]

(b) references to embryos taken from a woman do not include embryos whose creation was brought about *in vitro*.

(3) This Act, so far as it governs the keeping or use of an embryo, applies only to keeping or using an embryo outside the human body.

(4) References in this Act to gametes, eggs or sperm, except where otherwise stated, are to live human gametes, eggs or sperm but references below in this Act to gametes or eggs do not include eggs in the process of fertilisation.

[(4) In this Act (except in section 4A)—

(a) references to eggs are to live human eggs, including cells of the female germ line at any stage of maturity, but (except in subsection (1)(b)) not including eggs that are in the process of fertilisation or are undergoing any other process capable of resulting in an embryo,

(b) references to sperm are to live human sperm, including cells of the male germ line at any stage of maturity, and

(c) references to gametes are to be read accordingly.]

(5) For the purposes of this Act, sperm is to be treated as partner-donated sperm if the donor of the sperm and the recipient of the sperm declare that they have an intimate physical relationship.

[(6) If it appears to the Secretary of State necessary or desirable to do so in the light of developments in science or medicine, regulations may provide that in this Act (except in section 4A) "embryo", "eggs", "sperm" or "gametes" includes things specified in the regulations which would not otherwise fall within the definition.

(7) Regulations made by virtue of subsection (6) may not provide for anything containing any nuclear or mitochondrial DNA that is not human to be treated as an embryo or as eggs, sperm or gametes.]

Amendment: SI 2007/1522.

Prospective Amendment: Subsection prospectively repealed and substituted, words in square brackets prospectively substituted; Sub-s (2), para (a) prospectively substituted, Sub-s (4) prospectively substituted, Subsections, (6), (7) prospectively inserted by the Human Fertilisation and Embryology Act 2008, s 1(1)–(5), with effect from a date to be appointed.

1A Reference to Directives

In this Act –

'the first Directive' means Directive 2004/23/EC of the European Parliament and of the Council of 31 March 2004 on setting standards of quality and safety for the donation, procurement, testing, processing, preservation, storage and distribution of human tissues and cells,

'the second Directive' means Commission Directive 2006/17/EC of 8 February 2006 implementing Directive 2004/23/EC of the European Parliament and of the Council as regards certain technical requirements for the donation, procurement and testing of human tissues and cells, and

'the third Directive' means Commission Directive 2006/86/EC of 24 October 2006 implementing Directive 2004/23/EC of the European Parliament and of the Council as regards traceability requirements, notification of serious adverse reactions and events and certain technical requirements for the coding, processing, preservation, storage and distribution of human tissues and cells.

Amendment: SI 2007/1522.

2 Other terms

(1) In this Act –

'the Authority' means the Human Fertilisation and Embryology Authority established under section 5 of this Act,

'basic partner treatment services' means treatment services that are provided for a woman and a man together without using –

(a) the gametes of any other person, or
(b) embryos created outside the woman's body,

'competent authority', in relation to an EEA state other than the United Kingdom or in relation to Gibraltar, means an authority designated in accordance with the law of that state or territory as responsible for implementing the requirements of the first, second and third Directives,

'directions' means directions under section 23 of this Act,

'distribution', in relation to gametes or embryos intended for human application, means transportation or delivery, and related terms are to be interpreted accordingly,

'human application' means use in a human recipient,

'licence' means a licence under Schedule 2 of this Act and, in relation to a licence, 'the person responsible' has the meaning given by section 17 of this Act, 'non-medical fertility services' means any services that are provided, in the course of a business, for the purpose of assisting women to carry children, but are not medical, surgical or obstetric services,

['nuclear DNA', in relation to an embryo, includes DNA in the pronucleus of the embryo,]

'processing', in relation to gametes or embryos intended for human application, means any operation involved in their preparation, manipulation or packaging, and related terms are to be interpreted accordingly,

'procurement', in relation to gametes or embryos intended for human application, means any process by which they are made available, and related terms are to be interpreted accordingly,

'serious adverse event' means –

(a)   any untoward occurrence which may be associated with the procurement, testing, processing, storage or distribution of gametes or embryos intended for human application and which, in relation to a donor of gametes or a person who receives treatment services or non-medical fertility services –

  (i)   might lead to the transmission of a communicable disease, to death, or life-threatening, disabling or incapacitating conditions, or

  (ii)   might result in, or prolong, hospitalisation or illness, or

(b)   any type of gametes or embryo misidentification or mix-up,

'serious adverse reaction' means an unintended response, including a communicable disease, in a donor of gametes intended for human application or a person who receives treatment services or non-medical fertility services, which may be associated with the procurement or human application of gametes or embryos and which is fatal, life-threatening, disabling, incapacitating or which results in, or prolongs, hospitalisation or illness,

'store', in relation to gametes *or embryos* [, embryos or human admixed embryos], means preserve, whether by cryopreservation or in any other way, and 'storage' and 'stored' are to be interpreted accordingly,

'traceability' means the ability –

(a)   to identify and locate gametes and embryos during any step from procurement to use for human application or disposal,

(b)   to identify the donor and recipient of particular gametes or embryos,

(c)   to identify any person who has carried out any activity in relation to particular gametes or embryos, and

(d)   to identify and locate all relevant data relating to products and materials coming into contact with particular gametes or embryos and which can affect their quality or safety, and

'treatment services' means medical, surgical or obstetric services provided to the public or a section of the public for the purpose of assisting women to carry children.

(2) References in this Act to keeping, in relation to embryos *or gametes* [, gametes or human admixed embryos], include keeping while preserved in storage.

(2A) For the purposes of this Act, a person who, from any premises, controls the provision of services for transporting gametes or embryos is to be taken to distribute gametes or embryos on those premises.

(2B) In this Act, any reference to a requirement of a provision of the first, second or third Directive is a reference to a requirement which that provision requires to be imposed.

(3) For the purposes of this Act, a women is not to be treated as carrying a child until the embryo has become implanted.

Amendments: SI 2007/1522.

Prospective Amendments: Definition prospectively inserted; words in italics repealed and subsequent words in square brackets prospectively substituted by the Human Fertilisation and Embryology Act 2008, s 2, s 65, Sch 7, para 2(b) with effect from a date to be appointed.

2A Third party agreements

(1) For the purposes of this Act, a 'third party agreement' is an agreement in writing between a person who holds a licence and another person which is made in accordance with any licence conditions imposed by the Authority for the purpose of securing compliance with the requirements of Article 24 of the first Directive (relations between tissue establishments and third parties) and under which the other person –

    (a)   procures, tests or processes gametes or embryos (or both), on behalf of the holder of the licence, or

    (b)   supplies to the holder of the licence any goods or services (including distribution services) which may affect the quality or safety of gametes or embryos.

(2) In this Act –

    'relevant third party premises', in relation to a licence, means any premises (other than premises to which the licence relates) –

    (a)   on which a third party procures, tests, processes or distributes gametes or embryos on behalf of any person in connection with activities carried out by that person under a licence, or

    (b)   from which a third party provides any goods or services which may affect the quality or safety of gametes or embryos to any person in connection with activities carried out by that person under a licence;

    'third party' means a person with whom a person who holds a licence has a third party agreement.

(3) References in this Act to the persons to whom a third party agreement applies are to –

    (a)   the third party,

- (b) any person designated in the third party agreement as a person to whom the agreement applies, and
- (c) any person acting under the direction of a third party or of any person so designated.

Amendment: SI 2007/1522.

Activities governed by the Act

3 Prohibitions in connection with embryos

(1) No person shall bring about the creation of an embryo except in pursuance of a licence.

(1A) No person shall keep or use an embryo except –

- (a) in pursuance of a licence, or
- (b) in the case of –
    - (i) the keeping, without storage, of an embryo intended for human application, or
    - (ii) the processing, without storage, of such an embryo,

in pursuance of a third party agreement.

(1B) No person shall procure or distribute an embryo intended for human application except in pursuance of a licence or a third party agreement.

(2) No person shall place in a woman –

- *(a) a live embryo other than a human embryo, or*
- *(b) any live gametes other than human gametes.*

[(2) No person shall place in a woman—

- (a) an embryo other than a permitted embryo (as defined by section 3ZA), or
- (b) any gametes other than permitted eggs or permitted sperm (as so defined).]

(3) A licence cannot authorise –

- (a) keeping or using an embryo after the appearance of the primitive streak,
- (b) placing an embryo in any animal, [or]
- (c) keeping or using an embryo in any circumstances in which regulations prohibit its keeping or use, *or*
- *(d) replacing a nucleus of a cell of an embryo with a nucleus taken from a cell of any person, embryo or subsequent development of an embryo.*

(4) For the purposes of subsection (3)(a) above, the primitive streak is to be taken to have appeared in an embryo not later than the end of the period of 14 days *beginning with the day when the gametes are mixed* [the day on which the process of creating the embryo began], not counting any time during which the embryo is stored.

Amendment: SI 2007/1522.

Prospective Amendment: Subsections substituted; para (3)(d) prospectively repealed; words in italics prospectively repealed and subsequent words in square brackets inserted by the Human Fertilisation and Embryology Act 2008, s 3(1), (2); (4) with effect from a date to be appointed.

[3ZA Permitted eggs, permitted sperm and permitted embryos]

[(1) This section has effect for the interpretation of section 3(2).

(2) A permitted egg is one—

    (a)   which has been produced by or extracted from the ovaries of a woman, and

    (b)   whose nuclear or mitochondrial DNA has not been altered.

(3) Permitted sperm are sperm—

    (a)   which have been produced by or extracted from the testes of a man, and

    (b)   whose nuclear or mitochondrial DNA has not been altered.

(4) An embryo is a permitted embryo if—

    (a)   it has been created by the fertilisation of a permitted egg by permitted sperm,

    (b)   no nuclear or mitochondrial DNA of any cell of the embryo has been altered, and

    (c)   no cell has been added to it other than by division of the embryo's own cells.

(5) Regulations may provide that—

    (a)   an egg can be a permitted egg, or

    (b)   an embryo can be a permitted embryo,

even though the egg or embryo has had applied to it in prescribed circumstances a prescribed process designed to prevent the transmission of serious mitochondrial disease.

(6) In this section—

    (a)   'woman' and "man" include respectively a girl and a boy (from birth), and

    (b)   'prescribed' means prescribed by regulations.]

Prospective Amendment: Section prospectively inserted by the Human Fertilisation and Embryology Act 2008, s 3(1), (5) with effect from a date to be appointed.

3A Prohibition in connection with germ cells

(1) No person shall, for the purpose of providing fertility services for any woman, use female germ cells taken from or derived from an embryo or a foetus or use embryos created by using such cells.

(2) In this section –

    'female germ cells' means cells of the female germ line and includes such cells at any stage of maturity and accordingly includes eggs; and 'fertility services' means medical, surgical or obstetric services provided for the purpose of assisting women to carry children.

Amendment: Section inserted by Criminal Justice and Public Order Act 1994, s 156(1), (2).

4 Prohibitions in connection with gametes

(1) No person shall –

- (a)   store any gametes, or
- (b)   in the course of providing treatment services for any woman, use –
    - (i)   any sperm, other than partner-donated sperm which has been neither processed nor stored,
    - (ii)   the woman's eggs after processing or storage, or
    - (iii)   the eggs of any other woman, *or*
- *(c)   mix gametes with the live gametes of any animal,*

except in pursuance of a licence.

(1A) No person shall procure, test, process or distribute any gametes intended for human application except in pursuance of a licence or a third party agreement.

(2) A licence cannot authorise storing or using gametes in any circumstances in which regulations prohibit their storage or use.

(3) No person shall place sperm and eggs in a woman in any circumstances specified in regulations except in pursuance of a licence.

(4) Regulations made by virtue of subsection (3) above may provide that, in relation to licences only to place sperm and eggs in a woman in such circumstances, sections 12 to 22 of this Act shall have effect with such modifications as may be specified in the regulations.

(5) Activities regulated by this section or section 3 [or 4A]of this Act are referred to in this Act as 'activities governed by this Act'.

Amendments: SI 2007/1522.

Prospective Amendments: Sub-s (1): para (c) and word 'or' immediately preceding it prospectively repealed by the Human Fertilisation and Embryology Act 2008, s 4(1)(a)(i), (ii); Sub-s (5), words 'or 4A' in square brackets prospectively inserted by the Human Fertilisation and Embryology Act 2008, s 4(1)(b) with effect from a date to be appointed.

[4A Prohibitions in connection with genetic material not of human origin]

[(1) No person shall place in a woman—

- (a)   a human admixed embryo,
- (b)   any other embryo that is not a human embryo, or
- (c)   any gametes other than human gametes.

(2) No person shall—

- (a)   mix human gametes with animal gametes,
- (b)   bring about the creation of a human admixed embryo, or

(c)   keep or use a human admixed embryo

except in pursuance of a licence.

(3) A licence cannot authorise keeping or using a human admixed embryo after the earliest of the following—

(a)   the appearance of the primitive streak, or
(b)   he end of the period of 14 days beginning with the day on which the process of creating the human admixed embryo began, but not counting any time during which the human admixed embryo is stored.

(4) A licence cannot authorise placing a human admixed embryo in an animal.

(5) A licence cannot authorise keeping or using a human admixed embryo in any circumstances in which regulations prohibit its keeping or use.

(6) For the purposes of this Act a human admixed embryo is—

(a)   an embryo created by replacing the nucleus of an animal egg or of an animal cell, or two animal pronuclei, with—
   (i)   two human pronuclei,
   (ii)   one nucleus of a human gamete or of any other human cell, or
   (iii) one human gamete or other human cell,
(b)   any other embryo created by using—
   (i)   human gametes and animal gametes, or
   (ii)   one human pronucleus and one animal pronucleus,
(c)   a human embryo that has been altered by the introduction of any sequence of nuclear or mitochondrial DNA of an animal into one or more cells of the embryo,
(d)   a human embryo that has been altered by the introduction of one or more animal cells, or
(e)   any embryo not falling within paragraphs (a) to (d) which contains both nuclear or mitochondrial DNA of a human and nuclear or mitochondrial DNA of an animal ("animal DNA") but in which the animal DNA is not predominant.

(7) In subsection (6)—

(a)   references to animal cells are to cells of an animal or of an animal embryo, and
(b)   references to human cells are to cells of a human or of a human embryo.

(8) For the purposes of this section an "animal" is an animal other than man.

(9) In this section "embryo" means a live embryo, including an egg that is in the process of fertilisation or is undergoing any other process capable of resulting in an embryo.

(10) In this section—

(a)   references to eggs are to live eggs, including cells of the female germ line at any stage of maturity, but (except in subsection (9)) not including eggs that are in the process of fertilisation or are undergoing any other process capable of resulting in an embryo, and

(b)   references to gametes are to eggs (as so defined) or to live sperm, including cells of the male germ line at any stage of maturity.

(11) If it appears to the Secretary of State necessary or desirable to do so in the light of developments in science or medicine, regulations may—

(a)   amend (but not repeal) paragraphs (a) to (e) of subsection (6);

(b)   provide that in this section "embryo", "eggs" or "gametes" includes things specified in the regulations which would not otherwise fall within the definition.

(12) Regulations made by virtue of subsection (11)(a) may make any amendment of subsection (7) that appears to the Secretary of State to be appropriate in consequence of any amendment of subsection (6).]

Prospective Amendment: Prospectively inserted by the Human Fertilisation and Embryology Act 2008, s 4(2) with effect from a date to be appointed.

The Human Fertilisation and Embryology Authority, its functions and procedure

5 The Human Fertilisation and Embryology Authority

(1) There shall be a body corporate called the Human Fertilisation and Embryology Authority.

(2) The Authority shall consist of –

(a)   a chairman and deputy chairman, and

(b)   such number of other members as the Secretary of State appoints.

(3) Schedule 1 to this Act (which deals with the membership of the Authority, etc) shall have effect.

6 Accounts and audit

(1) The Authority shall keep proper accounts and proper records in relation to the accounts and shall prepare for each accounting year a statement of accounts.

(2) The annual statement of accounts shall comply with any direction given by the Secretary of State, with the approval of the Treasury, as to the information to be contained in the statement, the way in which the information is to be presented or the methods and principles according to which the statement is to be prepared.

(3) Not later than five months after the end of an accounting year, the Authority shall send a copy of the statement of accounts for that year to the Secretary of State and to the Comptroller and Auditor General.

(4) The Comptroller and Auditor General shall examine, certify and report on every statement of accounts received by him under subsection (3) above and shall lay a copy of the statement and of his report before each House of Parliament.

(5) The Secretary of State and the Comptroller and Auditor General may inspect any records relating to the accounts.

(6) In this section 'accounting year' means the period beginning with the day when the Authority is established and ending with the following 31st March, or any later period of twelve months ending with the 31st March.

7 Reports to Secretary of State

(1) The Authority shall prepare a report for the first twelve months of its existence, and a report for each succeeding period of twelve months, and shall send each report to the Secretary of State as soon as practicable after the end of the period for which it is prepared.

[(1) The Authority shall prepare—

    (a)   a report for the period beginning with the 1 August preceding the relevant commencement date (or if that date is a 1 August, beginning with that date) and ending with the next 31 March, and

    (b)   a report for each succeeding period of 12 months ending with 31 March.

(1A) In subsection (1)(a) "the relevant commencement date" means the day on which paragraph 3 of Schedule 7 to the Human Fertilisation and Embryology Act 2008 comes into force.

(1B) The Authority shall send each report to the Secretary of State as soon as practicable after the end of the period for which it is prepared.]

(2) A report prepared under this section for any period shall deal with the activities of the Authority in the period and the activities the Authority proposes to undertake in the succeeding period of twelve months.

(3) The Secretary of State shall lay before each House of Parliament a copy of every report received by him under this section.

Prospective Amendment: Sub-s (1) prospectively substituted, by subsequent sub-ss (1), (1A), (1B), by the Human Fertilisation and Embryology Act 2008, s 65, Sch 7, para 3. With effect from a date to appointed.

8 General functions of the Authority

[(1)] The Authority shall –

    (a)   keep under review information about embryos and any subsequent development of embryos and about the provision of treatment services and activities governed by this Act, and advise the Secretary of State, if he asks it to do so, about those matters,

    (b)   publicise the services provided to the public by the Authority or provided in pursuance of licences,

    (c)   provide, to such extent as it considers appropriate, advice and information for persons to whom licences apply or who are receiving treatment services or providing gametes or embryos for use for the purposes of activities governed by this Act, or may wish to do so, *and*

[(ca) maintain a statement of the general principles which it considers should be followed—
    (i)   in the carrying-on of activities governed by this Act, and
    (ii)   in the carrying-out of its functions in relation to such activities,
(cb) promote, in relation to activities governed by this Act, compliance with—
    (i)   requirements imposed by or under this Act, and
    (ii)   the code of practice under section 25 of this Act, and]
(d)   perform such other functions as may be specified in regulations.

[(2) The Authority may, if it thinks fit, charge a fee for any advice provided under subsection (1)(c).]

Prospective Amendment: Prospectively inserted by Human Fertilisation Act 2008, s 6(1), (2) (a) (b) with effect from a date to be appointed.

[8ZA Duties in relation to carrying out its functions]

[(1) The Authority must carry out its functions effectively, efficiently and economically.

(2) In carrying out its functions, the Authority must, so far as relevant, have regard to the principles of best regulatory practice (including the principles under which regulatory activities should be transparent, accountable, proportionate, consistent and targeted only at cases in which action is needed).]

Prospective Amendment: Prospectively inserted by the Human Fertilisation and Embryology Act 2008, s 7 with effect from a date to be appointed.

8A Duty of Authority to communicate with competent authorities of other EEA states

The Authority shall communicate to the competent authorities of EEA states other than the United Kingdom or of Gibraltar, and to the European Commission, such information in relation to serious adverse events and serious adverse reactions as is necessary for the purpose of enabling appropriate action to be taken, including where necessary the withdrawal from use of gametes and embryos that are intended for human application but are known or suspected to be unsuitable for such application.

Amendment: SI 2007/1522.

[8B Agency arrangements and provision of services]

[(1) Arrangements may be made between the Authority and a government department, a public authority or the holder of a public office ("the other authority") for—

(a)   any functions of the Authority to be exercised by, or by members of the staff of, the other authority, or
(b)   the provision by the other authority of administrative, professional or technical services to the Authority.

(2) Arrangements under subsection (1)(a) do not affect responsibility for the carrying-out of the Authority's functions.

(3) Subsection (1)(a) does not apply to any function of making subordinate legislation (within the meaning of the Interpretation Act 1978).]

Prospective Amendment: Prospectively inserted by the Human Fertilisation and Embryology Act 2008, s 8 with effect from a date to be appointed.

[8C Contracting out functions of Authority]

[(1) This section applies to any function of the Authority other than—

(a) any function which, by virtue of any enactment, may be exercised only by members of the Authority,

(b) a function excluded from this section by subsection (2), or

(c) a function excluded from this section by the Secretary of State by order.

(2) A function is excluded from this section if—

(a) it relates to the grant, revocation or variation of any licence,

(b) it is a power or right of entry, search or seizure into or of any property, or

(c) it is a function of making subordinate legislation (within the meaning of the Interpretation Act 1978).

(3) The Authority may make arrangements with any person ("the authorised person") for the exercise by that person, or by the employees of that person, of any function of the Authority to which this section applies.

(4) Any arrangements made by the Authority under this section—

(a) may be revoked at any time by the Authority, and

(b) do not prevent the Authority from exercising any function to which the arrangements relate.

(5) Subject to subsection (6), anything done or omitted to be done by or in relation to the authorised person (or an employee of the authorised person) in, or in connection with, the exercise or purported exercise of any function to which the arrangements relate is to be treated for all purposes as done or omitted to be done by or in relation to the Authority.

(6) Subsection (5) does not apply—

(a) for the purposes of so much of any contract between the authorised person and the Authority as relates to the exercise of the function, or

(b) for the purposes of any criminal proceedings brought in respect of anything done or omitted to be done by the authorised person (or any employee of the authorised person).

(7) Section 38A(2) of this Act (which relates to the keeping of embryos, human admixed embryos and gametes) applies in relation to the authorised person or any employee of the authorised person, when exercising functions of the

Authority, as it applies in relation to any member or employee of the Authority exercising functions as member or employee.]

Prospective Amendment: Prospectively inserted by the Human Fertilisation and Embryology Act 2008, s 8 with effect from a date to be appointed.

[8D Disclosure of information where functions of Authority exercised by others]

[(1) This section applies to—

(a)   the Authority,
(b)   any public authority or other person exercising functions of the Authority by virtue of section 8B,
(c)   any member of staff of any person falling within paragraph (b),
(d)   any person exercising functions of the Authority by virtue of section 8C,
(e)   an employee of any person falling within paragraph (d), or
(f)   any person engaged by the Authority to provide services to the Authority.

(2) No obligation of confidence is to prevent the disclosure of information by a person to whom this section applies to another such person if the disclosure is necessary or expedient for the purposes of the exercise of any function of the Authority.]

Prospective Amendment: Prospectively inserted by the Human Fertilisation and Embryology Act 2008, s 8 with effect from a date to be appointed.

[8E Power to assist other public authorities

(1) The Authority may if it thinks it appropriate to do so provide assistance to any other public authority in the United Kingdom for the purpose of the exercise by that authority of its functions.

(2) Assistance provided by the Authority under this section may be provided on such terms, including terms as to payment, as it thinks fit.]

Prospective Amendment: Subsection prospectively inserted by the Human Fertilisation and Embryology Act 2008, s 8 with effect from a date to be appointed.

9 Licence committees and other committees

(1) The Authority shall maintain one or more committees to discharge the Authority's functions relating to the grant, variation, suspension and revocation of licences, and a committee discharging those functions is referred to in this Act as a 'licence committee'.

(2) The Authority may provide for the discharge of any of its other functions by committees or by members or employees of the Authority.

(3) A committee (other than a licence committee) may appoint sub-committees.

(4) Persons, committees or sub-committees discharging functions of the Authority shall do so in accordance with any general directions of the Authority.

(5) A licence committee shall consist of such number of persons as may be specified in or determined in accordance with regulations, all being members of the Authority, and shall include at least one person who is not authorised to carry on or participate in any activity under the authority of a licence and would not be so authorised if outstanding applications were granted.

(6) A committee (other than a licence committee) or a sub-committee may include a minority of persons who are not members of the Authority.

(7) Subject to subsection (10) below, a licence committee, before considering an application for authority –

(a) *for a person to carry on an activity governed by this Act which he is not then authorised to carry on, or*

(b) *for a person to carry on any such activity on premises where he is not then authorised to carry it on,*

shall arrange for the premises where the activity is to be carried on to be inspected on its behalf, and for a report on the inspection to be made to it.

[(7A) Before considering such an application, the licence committee may also arrange for –

(a) *any premises that will be relevant third party premises for the purposes of the application to be inspected on its behalf, and*

(b) *a report on the inspection to be made to it.*

(8) A licence committee shall arrange for any premises to which a licence relates to be inspected on its behalf at intervals not exceeding two years, and for a report on the inspection to be made to it.

(9) ...

(10) A licence committee need not comply with subsection (7) above where the premises in question have been inspected in pursuance of that subsection or subsection (8) above at some time during the period of two years ending with the date of the application, and the licence committee considers that a further inspection is not necessary.

(10A) A licence committee may arrange for any relevant third party premises to be inspected on its behalf and for a report on the inspection to be made to it.

(11) An inspection in pursuance of subsection (7), (7A), (8) or (10A) above may be carried out by a person who is not a member of a licence committee.]

Prospective Amendment: Subsections prospectively repealed and subsequent subsections in square brackets subsequently inserted by the Human Fertilisation and Embryology Act 2008, s 10 with effect from a date to be appointed.

[9A Power to delegate and establish committees]

[(1) The Authority may delegate a function to a committee, to a member or to staff.

(2) The Authority may establish such committees or sub-committees as it thinks fit (whether to advise the Authority or to exercise a function delegated to it by the Authority).

(3) Subject to any provision made by regulations under section 20A (appeals committees), the members of the committees or sub-committees may include persons who are not members of the Authority.

(4) Subsection (1) has effect subject to any enactment requiring a decision to be taken by members of the Authority or by a committee consisting of members of the Authority.]

Amendments: SI 2007/1522.

Prospective Amendment: Subsections prospectively repealed and subsequent subsections in square brackets subsequently inserted by the Human Fertilisation and Embryology Act 2008, s 10 with effect from a date to be appointed.

10 Licensing procedure

(1) Regulations may make such provision as appears to the Secretary of State to be necessary or desirable about the proceedings of licence committees and of the Authority on any appeal from such a committee.

(2) The regulations may in particular include provision –

   (a)   for requiring persons to give evidence or to produce documents, and
   (b)   about the admissibility of evidence.

Prospective Amendment: Prospectively repealed by the Human Fertilisation and Embryology Act 2008, ss 65, 66, Sch 7, para 4, Sch 8, Pt 1 with effect from a date to be appointed.

Scope of licences

11 Licences for treatment, storage and research

(1) The Authority may grant the following and no other licences –

   (a)   licences under paragraph 1 of Schedule 2 to this Act authorising activities in the course of providing treatment services,
   (aa) licences under paragraph 1A of that Schedule authorising activities in the course of providing non-medical fertility services,
   (b)   licences under that Schedule authorising the storage of gametes *and embryos*[, embryos or human admixed embryos], and,
   (c)   licences under paragraph 3 of that Schedule authorising activities for the purposes of a project of research.

(2) Paragraph 4 of that Schedule has effect in the case of all licences.

Amendment: SI 2007/1522.

Prospective Amendment: Words in italics prospectively repealed and subsequent words in square brackets prospectively substituted by the Human Fertilisation and Embryology Act 2008, s 11 with effect from a date to be appointed.

Licence conditions

12 General conditions

(1) The following shall be conditions of every licence granted under this Act –

    (a)   except to the extent that the activities authorised by the licence fall within paragraph (aa), that those activities shall be carried on only on the premises to which the licence relates and under the supervision of the person responsible,

    (aa) that any activities to which section 3(1A)(b) or (1B) or 4(1A) applies shall be carried on only on the premises to which the licence relates or on relevant third party premises,

    (b)   that any member or employee of the Authority, on production, if so required, of a document identifying the person as such, shall at all reasonable times be permitted to enter those premises and inspect them (which includes inspecting any equipment or records and observing any activity),

    (c)   except in relation to the use of gametes in the course of providing basic partner treatment services or *non-medical fertility services*, that the provisions of Schedule 3 to this Act shall be complied with,

    (d)   that proper records shall be maintained in such form as the Authority may specify in directions,

    (e)   that no money or other benefit shall be given or received in respect of any supply of gametes *or embryos* [, embryos or human admixed embryos] unless authorised by directions,

    (f)   that, where gametes *or embryos* [, embryos or human admixed embryos] are supplied to a person to whom another licence applies, that person shall also be provided with such information as the Authority may specify in directions, and

    (g)   that the Authority shall be provided, in such form and at such intervals as it may specify in directions, with such copies of or extracts from the records, or such other information, as the directions may specify.

[(2) Subsection (3) applies to –

    (a)   every licence under paragraph 1 or 1A of Schedule 2, *and*

    (b)   every licence under paragraph 2 of that Schedule, so far as authorising the storage of gametes or embryos intended for human application [, and

    (c)   every licence under paragraph 3 of that Schedule, so far as authorizing activities in connection with the derivation from embryos of stem cells that are intended for human application.]

(3) It shall be a condition of every licence to which this subsection applies that –

    (a)   such information as is necessary to facilitate the traceability of gametes and embryos, and

    (b)   any information relating to the quality or safety of gametes or embryos, shall be recorded and provided to the Authority upon request.

Amendments: SI 2007/1522.

Prospective Amendment: Words in para (c) prospectively repealed, words in paras (e) and (f) prospectively substituted and paragraph prospectively inserted by the Human Fertilisation and Embryology Act 2008 s 12 (2), (3) with effect from a date to be appointed.

13 Conditions of licences for treatment

(1) The following shall be conditions of every licence under paragraph 1 of Schedule 2 to this Act.

(2) Such information shall be recorded as the Authority may specify in directions about the following –

   (a)   the persons for whom services are provided in pursuance of the licence,
   (b)   the services provided for them,
   (c)   the persons whose gametes are kept or used for the purposes of services provided in pursuance of the licence or whose gametes have been used in bringing about the creation of embryos so kept or used,
   (d)   any child appearing to the person responsible to have been born as a result of treatment in pursuance of the licence,
   (e)   any mixing of egg and sperm and any taking of an embryo from a woman or other acquisition of an embryo, and
   (f)   such other matters as the Authority may specify in directions.

(3) The records maintained in pursuance of the licence shall include any information recorded in pursuance of subsection (2) above and any consent of a person whose consent is required under Schedule 3 to this Act.

(4) No information shall be removed from any records maintained in pursuance of the licence before the expiry of such period as may be specified in directions for records of the class in question.

(5) A woman shall not be provided with treatment services, *[other than basic partner treatment services]*, unless account has been taken of the welfare of any child who may be born as a result of the treatment (including the need of that child for *a father*), and of any other child who may be affected by the birth.

(6) A woman shall not be provided with any treatment services involving –

   (a)   the use of any gametes of any person, if that person's consent is required under paragraph 5 of Schedule 3 to this Act for the use in question,
   (b)   the use of any embryo the creation of which was brought about in vitro, or
   (c)   the use of any embryo taken from a woman, if the consent of the woman from whom it was taken is required under paragraph 7 of that Schedule for the use in question,

unless the woman being treated and, where she is being treated together with a man, the man have been given a suitable opportunity to receive proper counselling about the implications of taking the proposed steps, and have been provided with such relevant information as is proper.

[(6) A woman shall not be provided with treatment services of a kind specified in Part 1 of Schedule 3ZA unless she and any man or woman who is to be treated together with her have been given a suitable opportunity to receive proper counselling about the implications of her being provided with treatment services of that kind, and have been provided with such relevant information as is proper.

(6A) A woman shall not be provided with treatment services after the happening of any event falling within any paragraph of Part 2 of Schedule 3ZA unless (before or after the event) she and the intended second parent have been given a suitable opportunity to receive proper counselling about the implications of the woman being provided with treatment services after the happening of that event, and have been provided with such relevant information as is proper.

(6B) The reference in subsection (6A) to the intended second parent is a reference to—

(a) any man as respects whom the agreed fatherhood conditions in section 37 of the Human Fertilisation and Embryology Act 2008 ("the 2008 Act") are for the time being satisfied in relation to treatment provided to the woman mentioned in subsection(6A), and

(b) any woman as respects whom the agreed female parenthood conditions in section 44 of the 2008 Act are for the time being satisfied in relation to treatment provided to the woman mentioned in subsection (6A).

(6C) In the case of treatment services falling within paragraph 1 of Schedule 3ZA (use of gametes of a person not receiving those services) or paragraph 3 of that Schedule (use of embryo taken from a woman not receiving those services), the information provided by virtue of subsection (6) or (6A) must include such information as is proper about—

(a) the importance of informing any resulting child at an early age that the child results from the gametes of a person who is not a parent of the child, and

(b) suitable methods of informing such a child of that fact.

(6D) Where the person responsible receives from a person ("X") notice under section 37(1)(c) or 44(1)(c) of the 2008 Act of X's withdrawal of consent to X being treated as the parent of any child resulting from the provision of treatment services to a woman ("W"), the person responsible—

(a) must notify W in writing of the receipt of the notice from X, and

(b) no person to whom the licence applies may place an embryo or sperm and eggs in W, or artificially inseminate W, until W has been so notified.

(6E) Where the person responsible receives from a woman ("W") who has previously given notice under section 37(1)(b) or 44(1)(b) of the 2008 Act that she consents to another person ("X") being treated as a parent of any child resulting from the provision of treatment services to W—

(a) notice under section 37(1)(c) or 44(1)(c) of the 2008 Act of the withdrawal of W's consent, or

(b) a notice under section 37(1)(b) or 44(1)(b) of the 2008 Act in respect of a person other than X,

the person responsible must take reasonable steps to notify X in writing of the receipt of the notice mentioned in paragraph (a) or (b).]

(7) Suitable procedures shall be maintained –

(a) for determining the persons providing gametes or from whom embryos are taken for use in pursuance of the licence, and

(b) for the purpose of securing that consideration is given to the use of practices not requiring the authority of a licence as well as those requiring such authority.

[(8) Subsections (9) and (10) apply in determining any of the following—

(a) the persons who are to provide gametes for use in pursuance of the licence in a case where consent is required under paragraph 5 of Schedule 3 for the use in question;

(b) the woman from whom an embryo is to be taken for use in pursuance of the licence, in a case where her consent is required under paragraph 7 of Schedule 3 for the use of the embryo;

(c) which of two or more embryos to place in a woman.

(9) Persons or embryos that are known to have a gene, chromosome or mitochondrion abnormality involving a significant risk that a person with the abnormality will have or develop—

(a) a serious physical or mental disability,

(b) a serious illness, or

(c) any other serious medical condition,

must not be preferred to those that are not known to have such an abnormality.

(10) Embryos that are known to be of a particular sex and to carry a particular risk, compared with embryos of that sex in general, that any resulting child will have or develop—

(a) a gender-related serious physical or mental disability,

(b) a gender-related serious illness, or

(c) any other gender-related serious medical condition, must not be preferred to those that are not known to carry such a risk.

(11) For the purposes of subsection (10), a physical or mental disability, illness or other medical condition is gender-related if—

(a) it affects only one sex, or

(b) it affects one sex significantly more than the other.

(12) No embryo appropriated for the purpose mentioned in paragraph 1(1)(ca) of Schedule 2 (training in embryological techniques) shall be kept or used for the provision of treatment services.

(13) The person responsible shall comply with any requirement imposed on that person by section 31ZD.]

Amendment: SI 2007/1522.

Prospective Amendments: Words prospectively repealed; subsection substituted; subsections (8)–(13) prospectively inserted; Human Fertilisation and Embryology Act 2008, s 14 (1), (2) (a), (4) with effect from a date to be appointed.

13A Conditions of licences for non-medical fertility services

(1) The following shall be conditions of every licence under paragraph 1A of Schedule 2.

(2) The requirements of section 13(2) to (4) and (7) shall be complied with.

(3) A woman shall not be provided with any non-medical fertility services involving the use of sperm other than partner-donated sperm unless the woman being provided with the services has been given a suitable opportunity to receive proper counselling about the implications of taking the proposed steps, and has been provided with such relevant information as is proper.

(4) Donors of sperm, other than partner-donated sperm, shall be provided with such information as the Authority shall specify in directions for the purpose of securing compliance with the requirements of Part A of the Annex to the first Directive (information to be provided on the donation of reproductive cells).

Amendment: SI 2007/1522.

Prospective Amendment: Subsection prospectively repealed by Human Fertilisation and Embryology Act 2008, s 65, Sch 7, para 5, with effect from a date to be appointed.

14 Conditions of storage licences

(1) The following shall be conditions of every licence *authorising the storage of gametes or embryos –* [authorising the storage of gametes, embryos or human admixed embryos.]

> *(a)* *that gametes of a person or an embryo taken from a woman shall be placed in storage only if received from that person or woman or acquired from a person to whom a licence or third party agreement applies and that an embryo the creation of which has been brought about in vitro otherwise than in pursuance of that licence shall be placed in storage only if acquired from a person to whom a licence or third party agreement applies,*
> [(a) that gametes of a person shall be placed in storage only if—
>   (i) received from that person,
>   (ii) acquired in circumstances in which by virtue of paragraph 9 or 10 of Schedule 3 that person's consent to the storage is not required, or
>   (iii) acquired from a person to whom a licence or third party agreement applies,
> (aa) that an embryo taken from a woman shall be placed in storage only if—

(i)   received from that woman, or

(ii)   acquired from a person to whom a licence or third party agreement applies,

(ab)   that an embryo the creation of which has been brought about in *vitro* otherwise than in pursuance of that licence shall be placed in storage only if acquired from a person to whom a licence or third party agreement applies,

(ac)   that a human admixed embryo the creation of which has been brought about in *vitro* otherwise than in pursuance of that licence shall be placed in storage only if acquired from a person to whom a licence under paragraph 2 or 3 of Schedule 2 applies,]

(b)   that gametes or embryos which are or have been stored shall not be supplied to a person otherwise than in the course of providing treatment services unless that person is a person to whom a licence applies

[(ba)   that human admixed embryos shall not be supplied to a person unless that person is a person to whom a licence applies,]

(c)   that no gametes *or embryos* [embryos or human admixed embryos] shall be kept in storage for longer than the statutory storage period and, if stored at the end of the period, shall be allowed to perish, and

(d)   that such information as the Authority may specify in directions as to the persons whose consent is required under Schedule 3 to this Act, the terms of their consent and the circumstances of the storage and as to such other matters as the Authority may specify in directions shall be included in the records maintained in pursuance of the licence.

(2) No information shall be removed from any records maintained in pursuance of such a licence before the expiry of such period as may be specified in directions for records of the class in question.

(3) The statutory storage period in respect of gametes is such period not exceeding ten years as the licence may specify.

(4) The statutory storage period in respect of embryos is such period not exceeding *five years* [ten years] as the licence may specify.

[(4A) The statutory storage period in respect of human admixed embryos is such period not exceeding ten years as the licence may specify.]

(5) Regulations may provide that subsection (3) *or (4)* [(4) or (4a)] above shall have effect as if for ten years *or, as the case may be, five years* there were substituted –

(a)   such shorter period, or

(b)   in such circumstances as may be specified in the regulations, such longer period, as may be specified in the regulations.

Amendment: SI 2007/1522.

Prospective Amendment: Para (a) prospectively substituted by subsequent paras (aa)–(ac); para (ba) prospectively inserted; words in italics prospectively repealed and subsequent words in square brackets substituted; Subsection (4A) prospectively inserted by Human Fertilisation and Embryology Act 2008, s 15(1), (2)(c), with effect from a date to be appointed.

14A Conditions of licences: human application

(1) This section applies to –

(a) every licence under paragraph 1 or 1A of Schedule 2, *and*

(b) every licence under paragraph 2 of that Schedule, so far as authorising storage of gametes or embryos intended for human application[, and

(c) every licence under paragraph 3 of that Schedule, so far as authorising activities in connection with the derivation from embryos of stem cells that are intended for human application.]

(2) A licence to which this section applies may not authorise the storage, procurement, testing, processing or distribution of gametes or embryos unless it contains the conditions required by Schedule 3A.

(3) In relation to any gametes or embryos imported into the United Kingdom from an EEA state other than the United Kingdom or from Gibraltar, compliance with the requirements of the laws or other measures adopted in the relevant state or territory for the purpose of implementing the first, second and third Directives shall be taken to be compliance with the conditions required by Schedule 3A.

(4) Subsection (3) shall not apply to any licence conditions imposed by the Authority which amount to more stringent protective measures for the purposes of Article 4(2) of the first Directive.

Amendment: SI 2007/1522.

Prospective Amendment: Words in italics prospectively repealed; words in square brackets prospectively inserted by Human Fertilisation and Embryology Act 2008 ss 65, 66, Sch 7, para 6(a), Sch 8, Pt 1 with effect from a date to be appointed.

15 Conditions of research licences

(1) The following shall be conditions of every licence under paragraph 3 of Schedule 2 to this Act.

(2) The records maintained in pursuance of the licence shall include such information as the Authority may specify in directions about such matters as the Authority may so specify.

(3) No information shall be removed from any records maintained in pursuance of the licence before the expiry of such period as may be specified in directions for records of the class in question.

(4) No embryo appropriated for the purposes of any project of research shall be kept or used otherwise than for the purposes of such a project

[(5) If by virtue of paragraph 20 of Schedule 3 (existing cells or cell line) qualifying cells, as defined by paragraph 20 (2) of that Schedule, of a person ("P") are used to bring about the creation *in vitro* of an embryo or human admixed embryo P's consent, steps shall be taken to ensure the embryo or human admixed embryo cannot subsequently be attributed to P.]

Prospective Amendment: Subsection prospectively inserted by Human Fertilisation and Embryology Act 2008, ss 65, Sch 7, para 7 with effect from a date to be appointed.

15A Duties of the Authority in relation to serious adverse events and serious adverse reactions

(1) The Authority shall investigate serious adverse events and serious adverse reactions and take appropriate control measures.

(2) In investigating any serious adverse event or serious adverse reaction, the Authority shall, where it is appropriate to do so, arrange for –

(a) any premises to which a licence relates and any relevant third party premises to be inspected on its behalf, and

(b) a report on the inspection to be made to it.

(3) If the Authority receives a request from a competent authority in an EEA state other than the United Kingdom or in Gibraltar to carry out an inspection in relation to a serious adverse event or serious adverse reaction, the Authority must arrange for such an inspection to be carried out, for a report to be made of the inspection and for appropriate control measures to be taken.

Amendment: SI 2007/1522.

Grant, revocation and suspension of licences

16 Grant of licence

(1) Where application is made to the Authority in a form approved for the purpose by it accompanied by the initial fee, a licence may be granted to any person by a licence committee if the requirements of subsection (2) below are met and any additional fee is paid.

[(1) The Authority may on application grant a licence to any person if the requirements of subsection (2) below are met.]

(2) The requirements mentioned in subsection (1) above are –

(a) that the application is for a licence designating an individual as the person under whose supervision the activities to be authorised by the licence are to be carried on,

(b) that either that individual is the applicant or –
   (i)   the application is made with the consent of that individual, and
   (ii) the *licence committee* [Authority] is satisfied that the applicant is a suitable person to hold a licence,

(c) in relation to a licence under paragraph 1 or 1A of Schedule 2 or a licence under paragraph 2 of that Schedule authorising the storage of gametes or embryos intended for human application, [or a licence under paragraph 3 of that Schedule authorising activities in connection with the derivation from embryos of stem cells that are intended for human application], that the individual –
   (i)   possesses a diploma, certificate or other evidence of formal qualifications in the field of medical or biological sciences,

awarded on completion of a university course of study, or other course of study recognised in the United Kingdom as equivalent, or is otherwise considered by the *licence committee* [Authority] to be suitably qualified on the basis of academic qualifications in the field of nursing, and

(ii) has at least two years' practical experience which is directly relevant to the activity to be authorised by the licence,

(ca) in relation to a licence under paragraph 2 of Schedule 2 authorising storage of gametes *or embryos* [embryos or human admixed embryos] not intended for human application or a licence under paragraph 3 of that Schedule,[authorising activities other than in connection with the derivation from embryos of stem cells that are intended for human application] that the *licence committee* [Authority] is satisfied that the qualifications and experience of that individual are such as are required for the supervision of the activities,

(cb) that the *licence committee* [Authority] is satisfied that the character of that individual is such as is required for the supervision of the activities and that the individual will discharge the duty under section 17 of this Act,

(d) that the *licence committee* [Authority] is satisfied that the premises in respect of which the licence is to be granted [and any premises which will be relevant third party premises] are suitable for the activities, and

(e) that all other requirements of this Act in relation to the granting of the licence are satisfied.

(3) The grant of a licence to any person may be by way of renewal of a licence granted to that person, whether on the same or different terms.

(4) Where the *licence committee* [Authority] is of the opinion that the information provided in the application is insufficient to enable it to determine the application, it need not consider the application until the applicant has provided it with such further information as it may require him to provide.

(5) The *licence committee* [Authority] shall not grant a licence unless a copy of the conditions to be imposed by the licence has been shown to, and acknowledged in writing by, the applicant and (where different) the person under whose supervision the activities are to be carried on.

(6) In subsection (1) above 'initial fee' and 'additional fee' mean a fee of such amount as may be fixed from time to time by the Authority with the approval of the Secretary of State and the Treasury, and in determining any such amount, the Authority may have regard to the costs of performing all its functions.

(7) Different fees may be fixed for different circumstances and fees paid under this section are not repayable.

Amendments: SI 2007/1522.

Prospective Amendment: Subsection prospectively substituted ; words 'licence committee' in italics repealed and subsequent word in square brackets substituted; para (c) words from 'or a licence' to 'for human application' in square brackets inserted; words in italics repealed and subsequent words in square brackets substituted; in para (ca) words from 'authorising activities otherwise' to 'for human application' in square brackets inserted; Sub-ss (6), (7): repealed by the Human Fertilisation and Embryology Act 2008, ss 16(1), (6), 66, Sch 8, Pt 1, with effect from a date to be appointed.

17 The person responsible

(1) It shall be the duty of the individual under whose supervision the activities authorised by a licence are carried on (referred to in this Act as the 'person responsible') to secure –

    (a)   that the other persons to whom the licence applies are of such character, and are so qualified by training and experience, as to be suitable persons to participate in the activities authorised by the licence,

    (b)   that proper equipment is used,

    (c)   that proper arrangements are made for the keeping of gametes *and embryos* [embryos and human admixed embryos] and for the disposal of gametes *or embryos* [embryos and human admixed embryos] that have been allowed to perish,

    (d)   that suitable practices are used in the course of the activities,

    (e)   that the conditions of the licence are complied with

    (f)   that conditions of third party agreements relating to the procurement, testing, processing or distribution of gametes or embryos are complied with, and

    (g)   that the Authority is notified and provided with a report analysing the cause and the ensuing outcome of any serious adverse event or serious adverse reaction]

(2) References in this Act to the persons to whom a licence applies are to –

    (a)   the person responsible,

    (b)   any person designated in the licence, or in a notice given to the Authority by the person who holds the licence or the person responsible, as a person to whom the licence applies, and

    (c)   any person acting under the direction of the person responsible or of any person so designated.

(3) References below in this Act to the nominal licensee are to a person who holds a licence under which a different person is the person responsible.

Amendments: SI 2007/1522.

Prospective Amendment: Words in italics prospectively repealed and subsequent words in square brackets substituted; subsection prospectively repealed by Human Fertilisation and Embryology Act 2008, ss 17(1), (2)(a), (3), Sch 8, Pt 1, with effect from a date to be appointed.

18 Revocation and variation of licence

(1) A licence committee may revoke a licence if it is satisfied –

    (a)   *that any information given for the purposes of the application for the grant of the licence was in any material respect false or misleading,*

    (b)   *that the premises to which the licence relates are no longer suitable for the activities authorised by the licence,*

(ba) that any premises which are relevant third party premises in relation to the licence are not suitable for the activities entrusted to the third party by the person who holds the licence[1]

(c) that the person responsible has failed to discharge, or is unable because of incapacity to discharge, the duty under section 17 of this Act or has failed to comply with directions given in connection with any licence, or

(d) that there has been any other material change of circumstances since the licence was granted.

(2) A licence committee may also revoke a licence if –

(a) it ceases to be satisfied that the character of the person responsible is such as is required for the supervision of those activities or that the nominal licensee is a suitable person to hold a licence, or

(b) the person responsible dies or is convicted of an offence under this Act.

(3) Where a licence committee has power to revoke a licence under subsection (1) above it may instead vary any terms of the licence.

(4) A licence committee may, on an application by the person responsible or the nominal licensee, vary or revoke a licence.

(5) A licence committee may, on an application by the nominal licensee, vary the licence so as to designate another individual in place of the person responsible if –

(a) the committee is satisfied that the character, qualifications and experience of the other individual are such as are required for the supervision of the activities authorised by the licence and that the individual will discharge the duty under section 17 of this Act, and

(b) the application is made with the consent of the other individual.

(6) Except on an application under subsection (5) above, a licence can only be varied under this section –

(a) so far as it relates to the activities authorised by the licence, the manner in which they are conducted or the conditions of the licence, or

(b) so as to extend or restrict the premises to which the licence relates.

Amendments: SI 2007/1522.

Prospective Amendment: Section prospectively repealed and substituted, together with s 18A, by the Human Fertilisation and Embryology Act 2008, s 18 with effect from a date to be appointed.

[18 Revocation of licence

(1) The Authority may revoke a licence on application by—

(a) the person responsible, or

(b) the holder of the licence (if different).

(2) The Authority may revoke a licence otherwise than on application under subsection (1) if—

(a)   it is satisfied that any information given for the purposes of the application for the licence was in any material respect false or misleading,

(b)   it is satisfied that the person responsible has failed to discharge, or is unable because of incapacity to discharge, the duty under section 17,

(c)   it is satisfied that the person responsible has failed to comply with directions given in connection with any licence,

(d)   it ceases to be satisfied that the premises specified in the licence are suitable for the licensed activity,

(e)   it ceases to be satisfied that any premises which are relevant third party premises in relation to a licence are suitable for the activities entrusted to the third party by the person who holds the licence,

(f)   it ceases to be satisfied that the holder of the licence is a suitable person to hold the licence,

(g)   it ceases to be satisfied that the person responsible is a suitable person to supervise the licensed activity,

(h)   the person responsible dies or is convicted of an offence under this Act, or

(i)   it is satisfied that there has been any other material change of circumstances since the licence was granted.]

Amendment: Section prospectively substituted, together with s 18A, for this section as originally enacted, by the Human Fertilisation and Embryology Act 2008, s 18 with effect from a date to be appointed.

[18A Variation of licence

(1) The Authority may on application by the holder of the licence vary the licence so as to substitute another person for the person responsible if—

(a)   the application is made with the consent of that other person, and

(b)   the Authority is satisfied that the other person is a suitable person to supervise the licensed activity.

(2) The Authority may vary a licence on application by—

(a)   the person responsible, or

(b)   the holder of the licence (if different).

(3) The Authority may vary a licence without an application under subsection (2) if it has the power to revoke the licence under section 18(2).

(4) The powers under subsections (2) and (3) do not extend to making the kind of variation mentioned in subsection (1).

(5) The Authority may vary a licence without an application under subsection (2) by—

(a)   removing or varying a condition of the licence, or

(b)   adding a condition to the licence.

(6) The powers conferred by this section do not extend to the conditions required by sections 12 to 15 of this Act.]

Prospective Amendment: Prospectively substituted, together with s 18, for that section as originally enacted, by the Human Fertilisation and Embryology Act 2008, s 18, with effect from a date to be appointed.

19 *Procedure for refusal, variation or revocation of licence*

(1) Where a licence committee proposes to refuse a licence or to refuse to vary a licence so as to designate another individual in place of the person responsible, the committee shall give notice of the proposal, the reasons for it and the effect of subsection (3) below to the applicant.

(2) Where a licence committee proposes to vary or revoke a licence, the committee shall give notice of the proposal, the reasons for it and the effect of subsection (3) below to the person responsible and the nominal licensee (but not to any person who has applied for the variation or revocation).

(3) If, within the period of twenty-eight days beginning with the day on which notice of the proposal is given, any person to whom notice was given under subsection (1) or (2) above gives notice to the committee of a wish to make to the committee representations about the proposal in any way mentioned in subsection (4) below, the committee shall, before making its determination, give the person an opportunity to make representations in that way.

(4) The representations may be –

  (a) oral representations made by the person, or another acting on behalf of the person, at a meeting of the committee, and
  (b) written representations made by the person.

(5) A licence committee shall –

  (a) in the case of a determination to grant a licence, give notice of the determination to the person responsible and the nominal licensee,
  (b) in the case of a determination to refuse a licence, or to refuse to vary a licence so as to designate another individual in place of the person responsible, give such notice to the applicant, and
  (c) in the case of a determination to vary or revoke a licence, give such notice to the person responsible and the nominal licensee.

(6) A licence committee giving notice of a determination to refuse a licence or to refuse or vary a licence so as to designate another individual in place of the person responsible, or of a determination to vary or revoke a licence otherwise than on an application by the person responsible or the nominal licensee, shall give in the notice the reasons for its decision.

Prospective Amendment: Section prospectively repealed and substituted, together with ss 19A, 19B, for this section as originally enacted, by the Human Fertilisation and Embryology Act 2008, s 19, with effect from a date to be appointed.

[19 Procedure in relation to licensing decisions

(1) Before making a decision—

(a)   to refuse an application for the grant, revocation or variation of a licence, or

(b)   to grant an application for a licence subject to a condition imposed under paragraph 1(2), 1A(2), 2(2) or 3(6) of Schedule 2, the Authority shall give the applicant notice of the proposed decision and of the reasons for it.

(2) Before making a decision under section 18(2) or 18A(3) or (5) the Authority shall give notice of the proposed decision and of the reasons for it to—

(a)   the person responsible, and

(b)   the holder of the licence (if different).

(3) Where an application has been made under section 18A(2) to vary a licence, but the Authority considers it appropriate to vary the licence otherwise than in accordance with the application, before so varying the licence the Authority shall give notice of its proposed decision and of the reasons for it to—

(a)   the person responsible, and

(b)   the holder of the licence (if different).

(4) A person to whom notice is given under subsection (1), (2) or (3) has the right to require the Authority to give him an opportunity to make representations of one of the following kinds about the proposed decision, namely—

(a)   oral representations by him, or a person acting on his behalf;

(b)   written representations by him.

(5) The right under subsection (4) is exercisable by giving the Authority notice of the exercise of the right before the end of the period of 28 days beginning with the day on which the notice under subsection (1), (2) or (3) was given.

(6) The Authority may by regulations make such additional provision about procedure in relation to the carrying out of functions under sections 18 and 18A and this section as it thinks fit.]

Prospective Amendment: Prospectively substituted, together with ss 19A, 19B, for this section as originally enacted, by the Human Fertilisation and Embryology Act 2008, s 19.with effect from a date to be appointed.

[19A Notification of licensing decisions

(1) In the case of a decision to grant a licence, the Authority shall give notice of the decision to—

(a)   the applicant, and

(b)   the person who is to be the person responsible.

(2) In the case of a decision to revoke a licence, the Authority shall give notice of the decision to—

(a)   the person responsible, and

(b)   the holder of the licence (if different).

(3) In the case of a decision to vary a licence on application under section 18A(1), the Authority shall give notice of the decision to—

(a) the holder of the licence, and
(b) (if different) the person who is to be the person responsible.

(4) In the case of any other decision to vary a licence, the Authority shall give notice of the decision to—

(a) the person responsible, and
(b) the holder of the licence (if different).

(5) In the case of a decision to refuse an application for the grant, revocation or variation of a licence, the Authority shall give notice of the decision to the applicant.

(6) Subject to subsection (7), a notice under subsection (2), (4) or (5) shall include a statement of the reasons for the decision.

(7) In the case of a notice under subsection (2) or (4), the notice is not required to include a statement of the reasons for the decision if the decision is made on an application under section 18(1) or 18A(2).]

Prospective Amendment: Section prospectively substituted, together with ss 19, 19B, for s 19 as originally enacted, by the Human Fertilisation and Embryology Act 2008, s 19 with effect from a date to be appointed.

[19B Applications under this Act

(1) Directions may make provision about—

(a) the form and content of applications under this Act, and
(b) the information to be supplied with such an application.

(2) The Secretary of State may by regulations make other provision about applications under this Act.

(3) Such regulations may, in particular, make provision about procedure in relation to the determination of applications under this Act and may, in particular, include—

(a) provision for requiring persons to give evidence or to produce documents;
(b) provision about the admissibility of evidence.]

Prospective Amendment: Prospectively substituted, together with ss 19, 19B, for s 19 as originally enacted, by the Human Fertilisation and Embryology Act 2008, s 19 with effect from a date to be appointed.

[19C Power to suspend licence

(1) Where the Authority—

(a) has reasonable grounds to suspect that there are grounds for revoking a licence, and
(b) is of the opinion that the licence should immediately be suspended,

it may by notice suspend the licence for such period not exceeding three months as may be specified in the notice.

(2) The Authority may continue suspension under subsection (1) by giving a further notice under that subsection.

(3) Notice under subsection (1) shall be given to the person responsible or where the person responsible has died or appears to be unable because of incapacity to discharge the duty under section 17—

(a)   to the holder of the licence, or
(b)   to some other person to whom the licence applies.

(4) Subject to subsection (5), a licence shall be of no effect while a notice under subsection (1) is in force.

(5) An application may be made under section 18(1) or section 18A(1) or (2) even though a notice under subsection (1) is in force.]

Prospective Amendment: Prospectively inserted by Human Fertilisation and Embryology Act 2008, s 20, with effect from a date to be appointed.

20 *Appeal to Authority against determinations of licence committee*

(1) Where a licence committee determines to refuse a licence or to refuse to vary a licence so as to designate another individual in place of the person responsible, the applicant may appeal to the Authority if notice has been given to the committee and to the Authority before the end of the period of twenty-eight days beginning with the date on which notice of the committee's determination was served on the applicant.

(2) Where a licence committee determines to vary or revoke a licence, any person on whom notice of the determination was served (other than a person who applied for the variation or revocation) may appeal to the Authority if notice has been given to the committee and to the Authority before the end of the period of twenty-eight days beginning with the date on which notice of the committee's determination was served.

(3) An appeal under this section shall be by way of rehearing by the Authority and no member of the Authority who took any part in the proceedings resulting in the determination appealed against shall take any part in the proceedings on appeal.

(4) On the appeal –

(a)   the appellant shall be entitled to appear or be represented,
(b)   the members of the licence committee shall be entitled to appear, or the committee shall be entitled to be represented, and
(c)   the Authority shall consider any written representations received from the appellant or any member of the committee and may take into account any matter that could be taken into account by a licence committee,

and the Authority may make such determination on the appeal as it thinks fit.

(5) The Authority shall give notice of its determination to the appellant and, if it is a determination to refuse a licence or to refuse to vary a licence so as to designate another individual in place of the person responsible or a determination to vary or revoke a licence, shall include in the notice the reasons for the decision.

(6) The functions of the Authority on an appeal under this section cannot be discharged by any committee, member or employee of the Authority and, for the purposes of the appeal, the quorum shall not be less than five.

Prospective Amendment: Section prospectively repealed and substituted, together with ss 20A, 20B, 21, for this section and s 21 as originally enacted, by the Human Fertilisation and Embryology Act 2008, s 21 with effect from a date to be appointed.

[20 Right to reconsideration of licensing decisions

(1) If an application for the grant, revocation or variation of a licence is refused, the applicant may require the Authority to reconsider the decision.

(2) Where the Authority decides to vary or revoke a licence, any person to whom notice of the decision was required to be given (other than a person who applied for the variation or revocation) may require the Authority to reconsider the decision.

(3) The right under subsections (1) and (2) is exercisable by giving the Authority notice of exercise of the right before the end of the period of 28 days beginning with the day on which notice of the decision concerned was given under section 19A.

(4) If the Authority decides —

   (a)   to suspend a licence under section 19C(1), or
   (b)   to continue the suspension of a licence under section 19C(2), any person to whom notice of the decision was required to be given may require the Authority to reconsider the decision.

(5) The right under subsection (4) is exercisable by giving the Authority notice of exercise of the right before the end of the period of 14 days beginning with the day on which notice of the decision concerned was given under section 19C.

(6) The giving of any notice to the Authority in accordance with subsection (5) shall not affect the continuation in force of the suspension of the licence in respect of which that notice was given.

(7) Subsections (1), (2) and (4) do not apply to a decision on reconsideration.]

Prospective Amendment: Section prospectively substituted, together with ss 20A, 20B, 21, for this section and s 21 as originally enacted, by the Human Fertilisation and Embryology Act 2008, s 21 with effect from a date to be appointed.

[20A Appeals committee

(1) The Authority shall maintain one or more committees to carry out its functions in pursuance of notices under section 20.

(2) A committee under subsection (1) is referred to in this Act as an appeals committee.

(3) Regulations shall make provision about the membership and proceedings of appeals committees.

(4) Regulations under subsection (3) may, in particular, provide—

  (a)   for the membership of an appeals committee to be made up wholly or partly of persons who are not members of the Authority, and
  (b)   for the appointment of any person to advise an appeals committee on prescribed matters.

(5) For the purposes of subsection (4) "prescribed" means prescribed by regulations under subsection (3).]

Prospective Amendment: Section prospectively substituted, together with ss 20A, 20B, 21, for this section and s 21 as originally enacted, by the Human Fertilisation and Embryology Act 2008, s 21 with effect from a date to be appointed.

[20B Procedure on reconsideration

(1) Reconsideration shall be by way of a fresh decision.

(2) Regulations shall make provision about the procedure in relation to reconsideration.

(3) Regulations under subsection (2) may, in particular, make provision—

  (a)   entitling a person by whom reconsideration is required, ("the appellant") to require that the appellant or the appellant's representative be given an opportunity to appear before and be heard by the appeals committee dealing with the matter,
  (b)   entitling the person who made the decision which is the subject of reconsideration to appear at any meeting at which such an opportunity is given, and to be heard in person or by a representative,
  (c)   requiring the appeals committee dealing with the matter to consider any written representations received from the appellant or the person who made the decision which is the subject of reconsideration,
  (d)   preventing any person who made the decision which is the subject of reconsideration from sitting as a member of the appeals committee dealing with the matter,
  (e)   requiring persons to give evidence or to produce documents,
  (f)   concerning the admissibility of evidence, and
  (g)   requiring the appellant and any prescribed person to be given notice of the decision on reconsideration and a statement of reasons for the appeals committee's decision.

(4) Regulations under subsection (2) may, in particular, make different provision about the procedure on reconsideration depending upon whether the reconsideration is in pursuance of a notice under section 20(3) or a notice under section 20(5).

(5) Such regulations may, in particular, make provision—

(a) in relation to cases where a person requires reconsideration of a decision to suspend a licence and reconsideration of a decision to continue the suspension of that licence, and

(b) in relation to cases where reconsideration of a decision is required under section 20(2) by only one of two persons by whom it could have been required.

(6) In this section—

(a) "prescribed" means prescribed by regulations under subsection (2), and

(b) "reconsideration" means reconsideration in pursuance of a notice under section 20.]

Prospective Amendment: Section prospectively substituted, together with ss 20A, 20B, 21, for this section and s 21 as originally enacted, by the Human Fertilisation and Embryology Act 2008, s 21 with effect from a date to be appointed.

21 Appeals to High Court or Court of Session

Where the Authority determines under section 20 of this Act –

(a) to refuse a licence or to refuse to vary a licence so as to designate another individual in place of the person responsible, or

(b) to vary or revoke a licence,

any person on whom notice of the determination was served may appeal to the High Court or, in Scotland, the Court of Session on a point of law.

Prospective Amendment: Section prospectively repealed and substituted, together with ss 20, 20A, 20B, for s 20 and this section as originally enacted, by the Human Fertilisation and Embryology Act 2008, s 21 with effect from a date to be appointed.

[21 Appeal on a point of law

A person aggrieved by a decision on reconsideration in pursuance of a notice under section 20 may appeal to the High Court or, in Scotland, the Court of Session on a point of law.]

Prospective Amendment: Section prospectively substituted, together with ss 20, 20A, 20B, for s 20 and this section as originally enacted, by the Human Fertilisation and Embryology Act 2008, s 21, with effect from a date to be appointed.

22 Temporary suspension of licence

(1) Where a licence committee –

(a) has reasonable grounds to suspect that there are grounds for revoking the licence under section 18 of this Act, and

(b) is of the opinion that the licence should immediately be suspended,

it may by notice suspend the licence for such period not exceeding three months as may be specified in the notice.

(2) Notice under subsection (1) above shall be given to the person responsible or, where the person responsible has died or appears to the licence committee to be

unable because of incapacity to discharge the duty under section 17 of this Act, to some other person to whom the licence applies or the nominal licensee and a licence committee may, by a further notice to that person, renew or further renew the notice under subsection (1) above for such further period not exceeding three months as may be specified in the renewal notice.

(3) While suspended under this section a licence shall be of no effect, but application may be made under section 18(5) of this Act by the nominal licensee to designate another individual as the person responsible.

Prospective: Amendment: Section prospectively repealed by the Human Fertilisation and Embryology Act 2008, ss 65, 66, Sch 7, para 8, Sch 8, Pt 1 with effect from a date to be appointed.

Directions and guidance

23 Directions: general

(1) The Authority may from time to time give directions for any purpose for which directions may be given under this Act or directions varying or revoking such directions.

(2) A person to whom any requirement contained in directions is applicable shall comply with the requirement.

(3) Anything done by a person in pursuance of directions is to be treated for the purposes of this Act as done in pursuance of a licence.

(4) Where directions are to be given to a particular person, they shall be given by serving notice of the directions on the person.

(5) In any other case, directions may be given –

(a) *in respect of any licence (including a licence which has ceased to have effect), by serving notice of the directions on the person who is or was the person responsible or the nominal licensee, or*

[(a) in respect of any licence (including a licence which has ceased to have effect by serving notice of the direction on the person

    (i) who is the person responsible or the holder of the licence, if different, or

    (ii) who was the person responsible or the holder of the licence, if different,

(b) if the directions appear to the Authority to be general directions or it appears to the Authority that it is not practicable to give notice in pursuance of paragraph (a) above, by publishing the directions in such way as, in the opinion of the Authority, is likely to bring the directions to the attention of the persons to whom they are applicable.]

(6) This section does not apply to directions under section 9(4) of this Act.

Prospective Amendment: Para (a) prospectively substituted and subsection prospectively repealed by the Human Fertilisation and Embryology Act 2008, s 65, Sch 7, para 9(a) with effect from a date to be appointed.

24 Directions as to particular matters

(1) If, in the case of any information about persons for whom treatment services, other than basic partner treatment services, were provided, the person responsible does not know that any child was born following the treatment, the period specified in directions by virtue of section 13(4) of this Act shall not expire less than 50 years after the information was first recorded.

(2) In the case of every licence under paragraph 1 or 1A of Schedule 2 to this Act, directions shall require information to be recorded and given to the Authority about each of the matters referred to in section 13(2)(a) to (e) of this Act.

(3) In relation to gametes or embryos that are not intended for human application, directions may authorise, in such circumstances and subject to such conditions as may be specified in the directions, the keeping, by or on behalf of a person to whom a licence applies, of gametes or embryos in the course of their carriage to or from any premises.

(3A) In relation to gametes and embryos that are intended for human application, directions may authorise the keeping of gametes or embryos by or on behalf of a person to whom a licence applies, in the course of their carriage –

[(3B) Directions may authorise, in such circumstances and subject to such conditions as may be specified in the directions, the keeping, by or on behalf of a person to whom a licence applies, of human admixed embryos in the course of their carriage to or from any premises.]

 (a) between premises to which licences relate,
 (b) between such premises and relevant third party premises,
 (c) between premises referred to in paragraphs (a) and (b) and tissue establishments accredited, designated, authorised or licensed under the laws, or other measures, of an EEA state other than the United Kingdom or of Gibraltar which implement the first, second and third Directives, or
 (d) between premises referred to in paragraphs (a) and (b) and tissue establishments in a country which is not an EEA state, pursuant to directions given under subsection (4),

in such circumstances and subject to such conditions as may be specified in the directions.

(4) Directions may authorise any person to whom a licence applies to receive gametes *or embryos* [embryos or human admixed embryos] from outside the United Kingdom or to send gametes *or embryos* [embryos or human admixed embryos] outside the United Kingdom in such circumstances and subject to such conditions as may be specified in the directions, and directions made by virtue of this subsection may provide for sections 12 to 14 of this Act to have effect with such modifications as may be specified in the directions.

(4A) In giving any directions under subsection (4) authorising any person to whom a licence applies to import into the United Kingdom from a country which is not an EEA state, or to export from the United Kingdom to such a country, gametes or embryos intended for human application, the Authority shall –

(a) include directions specifying the measures that persons to whom a licence applies shall take to ensure that all such imports or exports meet standards of quality and safety equivalent to those laid down in this Act, and

(b) have regard to ensuring traceability.

[(4B) Regulations may make provision requiring or authorising the giving of directions in relation to particular matters which are specified in the regulations and relate to activities falling within section 4A(2) (activities involving genetic material of animal origin).]

(5) A licence committee may from time to time give such directions as are mentioned in subsection (7) below where a licence has been varied or has ceased to have effect (whether by expiry, suspension, revocation or otherwise).

(6) A licence committee proposing to suspend, revoke or vary a licence may give such directions as are mentioned in subsection (7) below.

(7) The directions referred to in subsections (5) and (6) above are directions given for the purpose of securing the continued discharge of the duties of the person responsible under the licence concerned ('the old licence'), and such directions may, in particular –

(a) require anything kept or information held in pursuance of the old licence to be transferred to the Authority or any other person, or

(b) provide for the discharge of the duties in question by any individual, being an individual whose character, qualifications and experience are, in the opinion of the committee, such as are required for the supervision of the activities authorised by the old licence, and authorise those activities to be carried on under the supervision of that individual,

but cannot require any individual to discharge any of those duties unless the individual has consented in writing to do so.

(8) Directions for the purpose referred to in subsection (7)(a) above shall be given to the person responsible under the old licence, or where that person has died or appears to the licence committee to have become unable because of incapacity to discharge the duties in question, to some other person to whom the old licence applies or applied or to the nominal licensee.

(9) Directions for the purpose referred to in subsection (7)(b) above shall be given to the individual who under the direction is to discharge the duty.

(10) Where a person who holds a licence dies, anything done subsequently by an individual which that individual would have been authorised to do if the licence had continued in force shall, until directions are given by virtue of this section, be treated as authorised by a licence.

[(5A) Directions may make provision for the purpose of dealing with a situation arising in consequence of—

(a)   the variation of a licence, or

(b)   a licence ceasing to have effect.

(5B) Directions under subsection (5A)(a) may impose requirements—

(a)   on the holder of the licence,

(b)   on the person who is the person responsible immediately before or immediately after the variation, or

(c)   on any other person, if that person consents.

(5C) Directions under subsection (5A)(b) may impose requirements—

(a)   on the person who holds the licence immediately before the licence ceases to have effect,

(b)   on the person who is the person responsible at that time, or

(c)   on any other person, if that person consents.

(5D) Directions under subsection (5A) may, in particular, require anything kept, or information held, in pursuance of the licence to be transferred in accordance with the directions.

(5E) Where a licence has ceased to have effect by reason of the death or dissolution of its holder, anything subsequently done by a person before directions are given under subsection (5A) shall, if the licence would have been authority for doing it, be treated as authorised by a licence.]

(11) Where the Authority proposes to give directions specifying any animal for the purposes of paragraph 1(1)(f) or *3(5)* [3 (2)]of Schedule 2 to this Act, it shall report the proposal to the Secretary of State; and the directions shall not be given until the Secretary of State has laid a copy of the report before each House of Parliament.

(12) Directions may require a unique code to be assigned to each donation of gametes and embryos intended for human application received pursuant to a licence.

(13) The Authority may give directions as to the information to be provided to it and any measures to be taken by the person responsible in the event of –

(a)   any occurrence which may adversely influence the quality or safety of gametes or embryos intended for human application,

(b)   any adverse incident which may be linked to the quality or safety of gametes or embryos intended for human application, or

(c)   any misidentification or mix-up of gametes or embryos intended for human application.

(14) In this section, 'issue establishment' has the meaning given by Article 3(o) of the first Directive.

Amendments: SI 2007/1522.

Prospective Amendment: Sub-s (3B) prospectively inserted, words 'or embryos' in italics in both places they occur repealed and subsequent words in square brackets substituted, Sub-s (4B) prospectively inserted, Sub-ss (5)–(10), substituted, by subsequent sub-ss (5A)–(5E), Sub-s (11): reference to '3(5)' in italics repealed and subsequent reference in square brackets substituted with effect from a date to be appointed.

25 Code of practice

(1) The Authority shall maintain a code of practice giving guidance about the proper conduct of activities carried on in pursuance of a licence under this Act and the proper discharge of the functions of the person responsible and other persons to whom the licence applies.

(2) The guidance given by the code shall include guidance for those providing treatment services about the account to be taken of the welfare of children who may be born as a result of treatment services (including a child's need for *a father* [supportive parenting]), and of other children who may be affected by such births.

[(2A) The code shall also give guidance about—

    (a)   the giving of a suitable opportunity to receive proper counselling, and
    (b)   the provision of such relevant information as is proper,

in accordance with any condition that is by virtue of section 13(6) or (6A) a condition of a licence under paragraph 1 of Schedule 2.]

(3) The code may also give guidance about the use of any technique involving the placing of sperm and eggs in a woman.

(4) The Authority may from time to time revise the whole or any part of the code.

(5) The Authority shall publish the code as for the time being in force.

(6) A failure on the part of any person to observe any provision of the code shall not of itself render the person liable to any proceedings, but –

    (a)   *a licence committee* [the Authority] shall, in considering whether there has been any failure to comply with any conditions of a licence and, in particular, conditions requiring anything to be 'proper' or 'suitable', take account of any relevant provision of the code, and
    (b)   *a licence committee* [the Authority] may, in considering, where it has power to do so, whether or not to vary or revoke a licence, take into account any observance of or failure to observe the provisions of the code.

Prospective Amendment: Words in italics prospectively repealed and subsequent words in square brackets prospectively substituted; Sub-s (2A): prospectively inserted by the Human Fertilisation and Embryology Act 2008, s 23(1), (3) with effect from a date to be appointed.

26 Procedure for approval of code

(1) The Authority shall send a draft of the proposed first code of practice under section 25 of this Act to the Secretary of State within twelve months of the commencement of section 5 of this Act.

(2) If the Authority proposes to revise the code or, if the Secretary of State does not approve a draft of the proposed first code, to submit a further draft, the Authority shall send a draft of the revised or, as the case may be, a further draft of the proposed first code to the Secretary of State.

(3) Before preparing any draft, the Authority shall consult such persons as the Secretary of State may require it to consult and such other persons (if any) as it considers appropriate.

(4) If the Secretary of State approves a draft, he shall lay it before Parliament and, if he does not approve it, he shall give reasons to the Authority.

(5) A draft approved by the Secretary of State shall come into force in accordance with directions.

Status

27 Meaning of 'mother'

(1) The woman who is carrying or has carried a child as a result of the placing in her of an embryo or of sperm and eggs, and no other woman, is to be treated as the mother of the child.

(2) Subsection (1) above does not apply to any child to the extent that the child is treated by virtue of adoption as not being the woman's child.

(3) Subsection (1) above applies whether the woman was in the United Kingdom or elsewhere at the time of the placing in her of the embryo or the sperm and eggs.

Amendments: Words substituted: Adoption and Children Act 2002, s 139(1), Sch 3, paras 76, 77.

Prospective Amendments: Section prospectively repealed for certain purposes by Human Fertilisation and Embryology Act 2008, s 57(2) with effect from a date to be appointed.

28 *Meaning of 'father'*

(1)[Subject to subsections (5A) to (5I) below, this section applies in the case of a child who is being or has been carried by a woman as the result of the placing in her of an embryo or of sperm and eggs or her artificial insemination.

(2) If –

   (a)   at the time of the placing in her of the embryo or the sperm and eggs or of her insemination, the woman was a party to a marriage, and
   (b)   the creation of the embryo carried by her was not brought about with the sperm of the other party to the marriage,

then, subject to subsection (5) below, the other party to the marriage shall be treated as the father of the child unless it is shown that he did not consent to the placing in her of the embryo or the sperm and eggs or to her insemination (as the case may be).

(3) If no man is treated, by virtue of subsection (2) above, as the father of the child but –

(a)   the embryo or the sperm and eggs were placed in the woman, or she was artificially inseminated, in the course of treatment services provided for her and a man together by a person to whom a licence applies, and

(b)   the creation of the embryo carried by her was not brought about with the sperm of that man,

then, subject to subsection (5) below, that man shall be treated as the father of the child.

(4)   Where a person is treated as the father of the child by virtue of subsection (2) or (3) above, no other person is to be treated as the father of the child.

(5)   Subsections (2) and (3) above do not apply –

(a)   in relation to England and Wales and Northern Ireland, to any child who, by virtue of the rules of common law, is treated as the legitimate child of the parties to a marriage,

(b)   in relation to Scotland, to any child who, by virtue of any enactment or other rule of law, is treated as the child of the parties to a marriage, or

(c)   to any child to the extent that the child is treated by virtue of adoption as not being the man's child.

[(5A)   If –

(a)   a child has been carried by a woman as the result of the placing in her of an embryo or of sperm and eggs or her artificial insemination,

(b)   the creation of the embryo carried by her was brought about by using the sperm of a man after his death, or the creation of the embryo was brought about using the sperm of a man before his death but the embryo was placed in the woman after his death,

(c)   the woman was a party to a marriage with the man immediately before his death,

(d)   the man consented in writing (and did not withdraw the consent) –

(i)   to the use of his sperm after his death which brought about the creation of the embryo carried by the woman or (as the case may be) to the placing in the woman after his death of the embryo which was brought about using his sperm before his death, and

(ii)   to being treated for the purpose mentioned in subsection (5I) below as the father of any resulting child,

(e)   the woman has elected in writing not later than the end of the period of 42 days from the day on which the child was born for the man to be treated for the purpose mentioned in subsection (5I) below as the father of the child, and

(f)   no-one else is to be treated as the father of the child by virtue of subsection (2) or (3) above or by virtue of adoption or the child being treated as mentioned in paragraph (a) or (b) of subsection (5) above,

then the man shall be treated for the purpose mentioned in subsection (5I) below as the father of the child.

(5B)   If –

(a) a child has been carried by a woman as the result of the placing in her of an embryo or of sperm and eggs or her artificial insemination,

(b) the creation of the embryo carried by her was brought about by using the sperm of a man after his death, or the creation of the embryo was brought about using the sperm of a man before his death but the embryo was placed in the woman after his death,

(c) the woman was not a party to a marriage with the man immediately before his death but treatment services were being provided for the woman and the man together before his death either by a person to whom a licence applies or outside the United Kingdom,

(d) the man consented in writing (and did not withdraw the consent) –

    (i) to the use of his sperm after his death which brought about the creation of the embryo carried by the woman or (as the case may be) to the placing in the woman after his death of the embryo which was brought about using his sperm before his death, and

    (ii) to being treated for the purpose mentioned in subsection (5I) below as the father of any resulting child,

(e) the woman has elected in writing not later than the end of the period of 42 days from the day on which the child was born for the man to be treated for the purpose mentioned in subsection (5I) below as the father of the child, and

(f) no-one else is to be treated as the father of the child by virtue of subsection (2) or (3) above or by virtue of adoption or the child being treated as mentioned in paragraph (a) or (b) of subsection (5) above,

then the man shall be treated for the purpose mentioned in subsection (5I) below as the father of the child.

(5C) If –

(a) a child has been carried by a woman as the result of the placing in her of an embryo,

(b) the embryo was created at a time when the woman was a party to a marriage,

(c) the creation of the embryo was not brought about with the sperm of the other party to the marriage,

(d) the other party to the marriage died before the placing of the embryo in the woman,

(e) the other party to the marriage consented in writing (and did not withdraw the consent) –

    (i) to the placing of the embryo in the woman after his death, and

    (ii) to being treated for the purpose mentioned in subsection (5I) below as the father of any resulting child,

(f) the woman has elected in writing not later than the end of the period of 42 days from the day on which the child was born for the other party to the marriage to be treated for the purpose mentioned in subsection (5I) below as the father of the child, and

(g) no-one else is to be treated as the father of the child by virtue of subsection (2) or (3) above or by virtue of adoption or the child being treated as mentioned in paragraph (a) or (b) of subsection (5) above, then the other party to the marriage shall be treated for the purpose mentioned in subsection (5I) below as the father of the child.

(5D) If –

(a) a child has been carried by a woman as the result of the placing in her of an embryo,

(b) the embryo was not created at a time when the woman was a party to a marriage but was created in the course of treatment services provided for the woman and a man together either by a person to whom a licence applies or outside the United Kingdom,

(c) the creation of the embryo was not brought about with the sperm of that man,

(d) the man died before the placing of the embryo in the woman,

(e) the man consented in writing (and did not withdraw the consent) –
(i) to the placing of the embryo in the woman after his death, and
(ii) to being treated for the purpose mentioned in subsection (5I) below as the father of any resulting child,

(f) the woman has elected in writing not later than the end of the period of 42 days from the day on which the child was born for the man to be treated for the purpose mentioned in subsection (5I) below as the father of the child, and

(g) no-one else is to be treated as the father of the child by virtue of subsection (2) or (3) above or by virtue of adoption or the child being treated as mentioned in paragraph (a) or (b) of subsection (5) above,

then the man shall be treated for the purpose mentioned in subsection (5I) below as the father of the child.

(5E) In the application of subsections (5A) to (5D) above to Scotland, for any reference to a period of 42 days there shall be substituted a reference to a period of 21 days.

(5F) The requirement under subsection (5A), (5B), (5C) or (5D) above as to the making of an election (which requires an election to be made either on or before the day on which the child was born or within the period of 42 or, as the case may be, 21 days from that day) shall nevertheless be treated as satisfied if the required election is made after the end of that period but with the consent of the Registrar General under subsection (5G) below.

(5G) The Registrar General may at any time consent to the making of an election after the end of the period mentioned in subsection (5F) above if, on an application made to him in accordance with such requirements as he may specify, he is satisfied that there is a compelling reason for giving his consent to the making of such an election.

(5H) In subsections (5F) and (5G) above 'the Registrar General' means the Registrar General for England and Wales, the Registrar General of Births, Deaths and Marriages for Scotland or (as the case may be) the Registrar General for Northern Ireland.

(5I) The purpose referred to in subsections (5A) to (5D) above is the purpose of enabling the man's particulars to be entered as the particulars of the child's father in (as the case may be) a register of live-births or still-births kept under the Births and Deaths Registration Act 1953 or the Births and Deaths Registration (Northern Ireland) Order 1976 or a register of births or still-births kept under the Registration of Births, Deaths and Marriages (Scotland) Act 1965.

(6) Where –

(a) the sperm of a man who had given such consent as is required by paragraph 5 of Schedule 3 to this Act was used for a purpose for which such consent was required, or

(b) the sperm of a man, or any embryo the creation of which was brought about with his sperm, was used after his death,

he is not, subject to subsections (5A) and (5B) above, to be treated as the father of the child.

(7) The references in subsection (2) above and subsections (5A) to (5D) above to the parties to a marriage at the time there referred to –

(a) are to the parties to a marriage subsisting at that time, unless a judicial separation was then in force, but

(b) include the parties to a void marriage if either or both of them reasonably believed at that time that the marriage was valid; and for the purposes of this subsection it shall be presumed, unless the contrary is shown, that one of them reasonably believed at that time that the marriage was valid.

(8) This section applies whether the woman was in the United Kingdom or elsewhere at the time of the placing in her of the embryo or the sperm and eggs or her artificial insemination.

(9) In subsection (7)(a) above, 'judicial separation' includes a legal separation obtained in a country outside the British Islands and recognised in the United Kingdom.

Amendments: Inserted: Human Fertilisation and Embryology (Deceased Fathers) Act 2003, s 2(1); Words substituted: Adoption and Children Act 2002, s 139(1), Sch 3, paras 76, 78.

Prospective Amendments: Prospectively repealed for certain purposes by Human Fertilisation and Embryology Act 2008, s 57(2) with effect from a date to be appointed.

29 Effect of sections 27 and 28

(1) Where by virtue of section 27 or 28 of this Act a person is to be treated as the mother or father of a child, that person is to be treated in law as the mother or, as the case may be, father of the child for all purposes.

(2) Where by virtue of section 27 or 28 of this Act a person is not to be treated as the mother or father of a child, that person is to be treated in law as not being the mother or, as the case may be, father of the child for any purpose.

(3) Where subsection (1) or (2) above has effect, references to any relationship between two people in any enactment, deed or other instrument or document (whenever passed or made) are to be read accordingly.

(3A) Subsections (1) to (3) above do not apply in relation to the treatment in law of a deceased man in a case to which section 28(5A), (5B), (5C) or (5D) of this Act applies.

(3B) Where subsection (5A), (5B), (5C) or (5D) of section 28 of this Act applies, the deceased man –

> *(a)   is to be treated in law as the father of the child for the purpose referred to in that subsection, but*
> *(b)   is to be treated in law as not being the father of the child for any other purpose.*

(3C) Where subsection (3B) above has effect, references to any relationship between two people in any enactment, deed or other instrument or document (whenever passed or made) are to be read accordingly.

(3D) In subsection (3C) above 'enactment' includes an enactment comprised in, or in an instrument made under, an Act of the Scottish Parliament or Northern Ireland legislation.

(4) In relation to England and Wales and Northern Ireland, nothing in the provisions of section 27(1) or 28(2) to (4) or (5A) to (5I) read with this section, affects –

> *(a)   the succession to any dignity or title of honour or renders any person capable of succeeding to or transmitting a right to succeed to any such dignity or title, or*
> *(b)   the devolution of any property limited (expressly or not) to devolve (as nearly as the law permits) along with any dignity or title of honour.*

(5) In relation to Scotland –

> *(a)   those provisions do not apply to any title, coat of arms, honour or dignity transmissible on the death of the holder thereof or affect the succession thereto or the devolution thereof, and*
> *(b)   where the terms of any deed provide that any property or interest in property shall devolve along with a title, coat of arms, honour or dignity, nothing in those provisions shall prevent that property or interest from so devolving.*

Amendments: Subsections inserted: Human Fertilisation and Embryology (Deceased Fathers) Act 2003, s 1(2). Words inserted: Human Fertilisation and Embryology (Deceased Fathers) Act 2003, s 2(1), Schedule, para 16.

Prospective Amendments: Section prospectively repealed for certain purposes by Human Fertilisation and Embryology Act 2008, s 57(2) with effect from a date to be appointed.

30 Parental orders in favour of gamete donors

(1) The court may make an order providing for a child to be treated in law as the child of the parties to a marriage (referred to in this section as 'the husband' and 'the wife') if –

   (a)   the child has been carried by a woman other than the wife as the result of the placing in her of an embryo or sperm and eggs or her artificial insemination,

   (b)   the gametes of the husband or the wife, or both, were used to bring about the creation of the embryo, and

   (c)   the conditions in subsections (2) to (7) below are satisfied.

(2) The husband and the wife must apply for the order within six months of the birth of the child or, in the case of a child born before the coming into force of this Act, within six months of such coming into force.

(3) At the time of the application and of the making of the order –

   (a)   the child's home must be with the husband and the wife, and

   (b)   the husband or the wife, of both of them, must be domiciled in a part of the United Kingdom or in the Channel Islands or the Isle of Man.

(4) At the time of the making of the order both the husband and the wife must have attained the age of eighteen.

(5) The court must be satisfied that both the father of the child (including a person who is the father by virtue of section 28 of this Act), where he is not the husband, and the woman who carried the child have freely, and with full understanding of what is involved, agreed unconditionally to the making of the order.

(6) Subsection (5) above does not require the agreement of a person who cannot be found or is incapable of giving agreement and the agreement of the woman who carried the child is ineffective for the purposes of that subsection if given by her less than six weeks after the child's birth.

(7) The court must be satisfied that no money or other benefit (other than for expenses reasonably incurred) has been given or received by the husband or the wife for or in consideration of –

   (a)   the making of the order,

   (b)   any agreement required by subsection (5) above,

   (c)   the handing over of the child to the husband and the wife, or

   (d)   the making of any arrangements with a view to the making of the order,

unless authorised by the court.

(8) For the purposes of an application under this section –

   (a)   in relation to England and Wales, section 92(7) to (10) of, and Part I of Schedule 11 to, the Children Act 1989 (jurisdiction of courts) shall apply for the purposes of this section to determine the meaning of 'the court' as they apply for the purposes of that Act and proceedings on the application shall be 'family proceedings' for the purposes of that Act,

(*b*)   in relation to Scotland, 'the court' means the Court of Session or the sheriff court of the sheriffdom within which the child is, and

(*c*)   in relation to Northern Ireland, 'the court' means the High Court or any county court within whose division the child is.

(*9*) Regulations may provide –

(*a*)   for any provision of the enactments about adoption to have effect, with such modifications (if any) as may be specified in the regulations, in relation to orders under this section, and applications for such orders, as it has effect in relation to adoption, and applications for adoption orders, and

(*b*)   for references in any enactment to adoption, an adopted child or an adoptive relationship to be read (respectively) as references to the effect of an order under this section, a child to whom such an order applies and a relationship arising by virtue of the enactments about adoption, as applied by the regulations, and for similar expressions in connection with adoption to be read accordingly,

and the regulations may include such incidental or supplemental provision as appears to the Secretary of State necessary or desirable in consequence of any provision made by virtue of paragraph (a) or (b) above.

(*10*) In this section 'the enactments about adoption' means the Adoption Act 1976,[Adoption and Children Act 2002], the Adoption (Scotland) Act 1978 and the Adoption (Northern Ireland) Order 1987 [and the Adoption and Children (Scotland) Act 2007 (asp 4)].

(*11*) Subsection (1)(a) above applies whether the woman was in the United Kingdom or elsewhere at the time of the placing in her of the embryo or the sperm and eggs or her artificial insemination.

Prospective Amendment: Section prospectively repealed by the Human Fertilisation and Embryology Act 2008, ss 57(3), 66, Sch 8, Pt 1 with effect from a date to be appointed.

Information

31 The Authority's register of information

(*1*) The Authority shall keep a register which shall contain any information obtained by the Authority which falls within subsection (2) below.

(*2*) Information falls within this subsection if it relates to –

[(*a*) the provision for any identifiable individual of treatment services other than basic partner treatment services,

(*aa*) the procurement or distribution, in the course of providing non-medical fertility services for any identifiable individual, of any sperm (other than partner-donated sperm which has not been stored),

(*b*)   the keeping of the gametes of any identifiable individual or of an embryo taken from any identifiable woman,

[(*ba*)the use, otherwise than for the purposes of basic partner treatment services, of gametes of an identifiable individual, or *(bb)* *the use of an embryo taken from any identifiable woman,*

or if it shows that any identifiable individual [is a relevant individual.

(3) *A person who has attained the age of eighteen ('the applicant') may by notice to the Authority require the Authority to comply with a request under subsection (4) below, and the Authority shall do so if –*

(a) *the information contained in the register shows that the applicant[is a relevant individual, and*

(b) *the applicant has been given a suitable opportunity to receive proper counselling about the implications of compliance with the request.*

(4) *The applicant may request the Authority to give the applicant notice stating whether or not the information contained in the register shows that a person other than a parent of the applicant would or might, but for sections 27 to 29 of this Act, be a parent of the applicant and, if it does show that –*

(a) *giving the applicant so much of that information as relates to the person concerned as the Authority is required by regulations to give (but no other information), or*

(b) *stating whether or not that information shows that, but for sections 27 to 29 of this Act, the applicant, and a person specified in the request as a person whom the applicant proposes to marry, would or might be related.*

(5) *Regulations cannot require the Authority to give any information as to the identity of a person whose gametes have been used or from whom an embryo has been taken if a person to whom a licence applied was provided with the information at a time when the Authority could not have been required to give information of the kind in question.*

(6) *A person who has not attained the age of eighteen ('the minor') may by notice to the Authority specifying another person ('the intended spouse') as a person whom the minor proposes to marry require the Authority to comply with a request under subsection (7) below, and the Authority shall do so if –*

(a) *the information contained in the register shows that the minor[is a relevant individual, and*

(b) *the minor has been given a suitable opportunity to receive proper counselling about the implications of compliance with the request.*

(7) *The minor may request the Authority to give the minor notice stating whether or not the information contained in the register shows that, but for sections 27 to 29 of this Act, the minor and the intended spouse would or might be related.*

(8) *In this section 'relevant individual' means an individual who was, or may have been, born in consequence of –*

(a) *treatment services other than basic partner treatment services, or*

(b) *the procurement or distribution, in the course of providing non-medical fertility services, of any sperm (other than partner-donated sperm which has not been stored).*

Amendment: Paragraphs substituted and inserted, words substituted and repealed and subsection inserted: SI 2007/1522.

Prospective Amendment: Section prospectively repealed and substituted, Human Fertilisation and Embryology Act 2008, s 24 with effect from a date to be appointed.

[31 Register of information

(1) The Authority shall keep a register which is to contain any information which falls within subsection (2) and which—

    (a)   immediately before the coming into force of section 24 of the Human Fertilisation and Embryology Act 2008, was contained in the register kept under this section by the Authority, or

    (b)   is obtained by the Authority.

(2) Subject to subsection (3), information falls within this subsection if it relates to—

    (a)   the provision for any identifiable individual of treatment services other than basic partner treatment services,

    (b)   the procurement or distribution of any sperm, other than sperm which is partner-donated sperm and has not been stored, in the course of providing non-medical fertility services for any identifiable individual,

    (c)   the keeping of the gametes of any identifiable individual or of an embryo taken from any identifiable woman,

    (d)   the use of the gametes of any identifiable individual other than their use for the purpose of basic partner treatment services, or

    (e)   the use of an embryo taken from any identifiable woman, or if it shows that any identifiable individual is a relevant individual.

(3) Information does not fall within subsection (2) if it is provided to the Authority for the purposes of any voluntary contact register as defined by section 31ZF(1).

(4) In this section "relevant individual" means an individual who was or may have been born in consequence of—

    (a)   treatment services, other than basic partner treatment services, or

    (b)   the procurement or distribution of any sperm (other than partner-donated sperm which has not been stored) in the course of providing non-medical fertility services.

Prospective Amendment: Section prospectively substituted, together with ss 31ZA–31ZG, for this section as originally enacted, by the Human Fertilisation and Embryology Act 2008, s 24 with effect from a date to be appointed.

31ZA Request for information as to genetic parentage etc

(1) A person who has attained the age of 16 ("the applicant") may by notice to the Authority require the Authority to comply with a request under subsection (2).

(2) The applicant may request the Authority to give the applicant notice stating whether or not the information contained in the register shows that a person ("the donor") other than a parent of the applicant would or might, but for the relevant statutory provisions, be the parent of the applicant, and if it does show that—

    (a)   giving the applicant so much of that information as relates to the donor as the Authority is required by regulations to give (but no other information), or

    (b)   stating whether or not that information shows that there are other persons of whom the donor is not the parent but would or might, but for the relevant statutory provisions, be the parent and if so—

        (i)   the number of those other persons,

        (ii)   the sex of each of them, and

        (iii)   the year of birth of each of them.

(3) The Authority shall comply with a request under subsection (2) if—

    (a)   the information contained in the register shows that the applicant is a relevant individual, and

    (b)   the applicant has been given a suitable opportunity to receive proper counselling about the implications of compliance with the request.

(4) Where a request is made under subsection (2)(a) and the applicant has not attained the age of 18 when the applicant gives notice to the Authority under subsection (1), regulations cannot require the Authority to give the applicant any information which identifies the donor.

(5) Regulations cannot require the Authority to give any information as to the identity of a person whose gametes have been used or from whom an embryo has been taken if a person to whom a licence applied was provided with the information at a time when the Authority could not have been required to give information of the kind in question.

(6) The Authority need not comply with a request made under subsection (2)(b) by any applicant if it considers that special circumstances exist which increase the likelihood that compliance with the request would enable the applicant—

    (a)   to identify the donor, in a case where the Authority is not required by regulations under subsection (2)(a) to give the applicant information which identifies the donor, or

    (b)   to identify any person about whom information is given under subsection (2)(b).

(7) In this section—

    "relevant individual" has the same meaning as in section 31;

    "the relevant statutory provisions" means sections 27 to 29 of this Act and sections 33 to 47 of the Human Fertilisation and Embryology Act 2008.

Prospective Amendment: Section prospectively substituted together with ss 31ZA–31ZG, for this section as originally enacted, by the Human Fertilisation and Embryology Act 2008, s 24 with effect from a date to be appointed.

[31ZB Request for information as to intended spouse etc

[(1) Subject to subsection (4), a person ("the applicant") may by notice to the Authority require the Authority to comply with a request under subsection (2).

(2) The applicant may request the Authority to give the applicant notice stating whether or not information contained in the register shows that, but for the relevant statutory provisions, the applicant would or might be related to a person specified in the request ("the specified person") as—

    (a)   a person whom the applicant proposes to marry,

    (b)   a person with whom the applicant proposes to enter into a civil partnership, or

    (c)   a person with whom the applicant is in an intimate physical relationship or with whom the applicant proposes to enter into an intimate physical relationship.

(3) Subject to subsection (5), the Authority shall comply with a request under subsection (2) if—

    (a)   the information contained in the register shows that the applicant is a relevant individual,

    (b)   the Authority receives notice in writing from the specified person consenting to the request being made and that notice has not been withdrawn, and

    (c)   the applicant and the specified person have each been given a suitable opportunity to receive proper counselling about the implications of compliance with the request.

(4) A request may not be made under subsection (2)(c) by a person who has not attained the age of 16.

(5) Where a request is made under subsection (2)(c) and the specified person has not attained the age of 16 when the applicant gives notice to the Authority under subsection (1), the Authority must not comply with the request.

(6) Where the Authority is required under subsection (3) to comply with a request under subsection (2), the Authority must take all reasonable steps to give the applicant and the specified person notice stating whether or not the information contained in the register shows that, but for the relevant statutory provisions, the applicant and the specified person would or might be related.

(7) In this section—

    "relevant individual" has the same meaning as in section 31;
    "the relevant statutory provisions" has the same meaning as in section 31ZA.]

Prospective Amendment: Section prospectively substituted together with ss 31ZA–31ZG, for this section as originally enacted, by the Human Fertilisation and Embryology Act 2008, s 24 with effect from a date to be appointed.

[31ZC Power of Authority to inform donor of request for information

(1) Where—

    (a)   the Authority has received from a person ("the applicant") a notice containing a request under subsection (2)(a) of section 31ZA, and

    (b)   compliance by the Authority with its duty under that section has involved or will involve giving the applicant information relating to a person other than the parent of the applicant who would or might, but for the relevant statutory provisions, be a parent of the applicant ("the donor"), the Authority may notify the donor that a request under section 31ZA(2)(a) has been made, but may not disclose the identity of the applicant or any information relating to the applicant.

(2) In this section "the relevant statutory provisions" has the same meaning as in section 31ZA.]

Prospective Amendment: Section prospectively substituted, together with ss 31ZA–31ZG, for this section as originally enacted, by the Human Fertilisation and Embryology Act 2008, s 24 with effect from a date to be appointed.

[31ZD Provision to donor of information about resulting children

(1) This section applies where a person ("the donor") has consented under Schedule 3 (whether before or after the coming into force of this section) to—

    (a)   the use of the donor's gametes, or an embryo the creation of which was brought about using the donor's gametes, for the purposes of treatment services provided under a licence, or

    (b)   the use of the donor's gametes for the purposes of non-medical fertility services provided under a licence.

(2) In subsection (1)—

    (a)   "treatment services" do not include treatment services provided to the donor, or to the donor and another person together, and

    (b)   "non-medical fertility services" do not include any services involving partner-donated sperm.

(3) The donor may by notice request the appropriate person to give the donor notice stating—

    (a)   the number of persons of whom the donor is not a parent but would or might, but for the relevant statutory provisions, be a parent by virtue of the use of the gametes or embryos to which the consent relates,

    (b)   the sex of each of those persons, and

    (c)   the year of birth of each of those persons.

(4) Subject to subsections (5) to (7), the appropriate person shall notify the donor whether the appropriate person holds the information mentioned in subsection (3) and, if the appropriate person does so, shall comply with the request.

(5) The appropriate person need not comply with a request under subsection (3) if the appropriate person considers that special circumstances exist which increase the likelihood that compliance with the request would enable the donor to identify any of the persons falling within paragraphs (a) to (c) of subsection (3).

(6) In the case of a donor who consented as described in subsection (1)(a), the Authority need not comply with a request made to it under subsection (3) where the person who held the licence referred to in subsection (1)(a) continues to hold a licence under paragraph 1 of Schedule 2, unless the donor has previously made a request under subsection (3) to the person responsible and the person responsible—

    (a)   has notified the donor that the information concerned is not held, or
    (b)   has failed to comply with the request within a reasonable period.

(7) In the case of a donor who consented as described in subsection (1)(b), the Authority need not comply with a request made to it under subsection (3) where the person who held the licence referred to in subsection (1)(b) continues to hold a licence under paragraph 1A of Schedule 2, unless the donor has previously made a request under subsection (3) to the person responsible and the person responsible—

    (a)   has notified the donor that the information concerned is not held, or
    (b)   has failed to comply with the request within a reasonable period.

(8) In this section "the appropriate person" means—

    (a)   in the case of a donor who consented as described in paragraph
    (a)   of subsection (1)—
        (i)   where the person who held the licence referred to in that paragraph continues to hold a licence under paragraph 1 of Schedule 2, the person responsible, or
        (ii)   the Authority, and
    (b)   in the case of a donor who consented as described in paragraph
    (b)   of subsection (1)—
        (i)   where the person who held the licence referred to in that paragraph continues to hold a licence under paragraph 1A of Schedule 2, the person responsible, or
        (ii)   the Authority.

(9) In this section "the relevant statutory provisions" has the same meaning as in section 31ZA.]

Prospective Amendment: Section prospectively substituted, together with ss 31ZA–31ZG, for this section as originally enacted, by the Human Fertilisation and Embryology Act 2008, s 24 with effect from a date to be appointed.

[31ZE Provision of information about donor-conceived genetic siblings

(1) For the purposes of this section two relevant individuals are donor conceived genetic siblings of each other if a person ("the donor") who is not the parent of either of them would or might, but for the relevant statutory provisions, be the parent of both of them.

(2) Where—

    (a) the information on the register shows that a relevant individual ("A") is the donor-conceived genetic sibling of another relevant individual ("B"),

    (b) A has provided information to the Authority ("the agreed information") which consists of or includes information which enables A to be identified with the request that it should be disclosed to—
        (i) any donor-conceived genetic sibling of A, or
        (ii) such siblings of A of a specified description which includes B, and

    (c) the conditions in subsection (3) are satisfied,

then, subject to subsection (4), the Authority shall disclose the agreed information to B.

(3) The conditions referred to in subsection (2)(c) are—

    (a) that each of A and B has attained the age of 18,
    (b) that B has requested the disclosure to B of information about any donor-conceived genetic sibling of B, and
    (c) that each of A and B has been given a suitable opportunity to receive proper counselling about the implications of disclosure under subsection (2).

(4) The Authority need not disclose any information under subsection (2) if it considers that the disclosure of information will lead to A or B identifying the donor unless—

    (a) the donor has consented to the donor's identity being disclosed to A or B, or
    (b) were A or B to make a request under section 31ZA(2)(a), the Authority would be required by regulations under that provision to give A or B information which would identify the donor.

(5) In this section—

    "relevant individual" has the same meaning as in section 31;
    "the relevant statutory provisions" has the same meaning as in section 31ZA.]

Prospective Amendment: Section prospectively substituted, together with ss 31ZA–31ZG, for this section as originally enacted, by the Human Fertilisation and Embryology Act 2008, s 24 with effect from a date to be appointed.

[31ZF Power of Authority to keep voluntary contact register

(1) In this section and section 31ZG, a "voluntary contact register" means a register of persons who have expressed their wish to receive information about any person to whom they are genetically related as a consequence of the provision to any person of treatment services in the United Kingdom before 1 August 1991.

(2) The Authority may—

(a) set up a voluntary contact register in such manner as it thinks fit,

(b) keep a voluntary contact register in such manner as it thinks fit,

(c) determine criteria for eligibility for inclusion on the register and the particulars that may be included,

(d) charge a fee to persons who wish their particulars to be entered on the register,

(e) arrange for samples of the DNA of such persons to be analysed at their request,

(f) make such arrangements as it thinks fit for the disclosure of Information on the register between persons who appear to the Authority to be genetically related, and

(g) impose such conditions as it thinks fit to prevent a person ("A") from disclosing information to a person to whom A is genetically related ("B") where that information would identify any person who is genetically related to both A and B.

(3) The Authority may make arrangements with any person by whom a voluntary contact register is kept before the commencement of this section for the supply by that person to the Authority of the information contained in the register maintained by that person.]

Prospective Amendment: Section prospectively substituted, together with ss 31ZA–31ZG, for this section as originally enacted, by the Human Fertilisation and Embryology Act 2008, s 24 with effect from a date to be appointed.

[31ZG Financial assistance for person setting up or keeping voluntary contact register

(1) The Authority may, instead of keeping a voluntary contact register, give financial assistance to any person who sets up or keeps a voluntary contact register.

(2) Financial assistance under subsection (1) may be given in any form, and in particular, may be given by way of—

(a) grants,

(b) loans,

(c) guarantees, or

(d) incurring expenditure for the person assisted.

(3) Financial assistance under subsection (1) may be given on such terms and conditions as the Authority considers appropriate.

(4) A person receiving assistance under subsection (1) must comply with the terms and conditions on which it is given, and compliance may be enforced by the Authority.]

Prospective Amendment: Section Prospectively substituted, together with ss 31, 31ZA–31ZF, for s 31 as originally enacted, by the Human Fertilisation and Embryology Act 2008, s 24 with effect from a date to be appointed.

31A The Authority's register of licences

(1) The Authority shall keep a register recording the grant, suspension or revocation of –

(a) every licence under paragraph 1 or 2 of Schedule 2 authorising activities in relation to gametes or embryos intended for use for human application, *and*

(b) every licence under paragraph 1A of Schedule 2 [, and

(c) every licence under paragraph 3 of Schedule 2 authorising activities in connection with the derivation from embryos of stem cells that are intended for human application.]

(2) The register shall specify, in relation to each such licence –

(a) the activities authorised,

(b) the address of the premises to which the licence relates,

(c) the name of the person responsible and, *if applicable, the nominal licensee,* [the name of the holder of the licence (if different)] and

(d) any variations made.

(3) The Authority shall make such of the information included in the register as it considers appropriate available to the public in such manner as it considers appropriate.

Amendment: SI 2007/1522.

Prospective Amendment: Words in italics prospectively repealed and subsequent words in square brackets substituted by Human Fertilisation and Embryology Act 2008 with effect from a date to be appointed.

31B The Authority's register of serious adverse events and serious adverse reactions

(1) The Authority shall keep a register containing information provided to it under this Act about any serious adverse event or serious adverse reaction.

(2) The Authority shall make such of the information included in the register as it considers appropriate available to the public in such manner as it considers appropriate.

Amendment: SI 2007/1522.

32 Information to be provided to Registrar General

(1) This section applies where a claim is made before the Registrar General that a *man* [person] is or is not the *father* [parent] of a child and it is necessary

or desirable for the purpose of any function of the Registrar General to determine whether the claim is or may be well-founded.

(2) The Authority shall comply with any request made by the Registrar General by notice to the Authority to disclose whether any information on the register kept in pursuance of section 31 of this Act tends to show *that the man may be the father of the child by virtue of section 28 of this Act* [that the person may be a parent of the child by virtue of any of the relevant provisions] and, if it does, disclose that information.

[(2A) In subsection (2) "the relevant statutory provisions" means –

    (a)   sections 28 of this Act, and
    (b)   sections 35 to 47 of the Human Fertilisation and Embryology Act 2008.]

(3) In this section and section 33 [33A] of this Act, 'the Registrar General' means the Registrar General for England and Wales, the Registrar General of Births, Deaths and Marriages for Scotland or the Registrar General for Northern Ireland, as the case may be.

Prospective Amendment: Words in italics prospectively repealed and subsequent words in square brackets substituted by Human Fertilisation and Embryology Act 1990, Schedule 6; para 33 with effect from a date to be appointed.

33 Restrictions on disclosure of information

(1) No person who is or has been a member or employee of the Authority shall disclose any information mentioned in subsection (2) below which he holds or has held as such a member or employee.

(2) The information referred to in subsection (1) above is –

    (a)   any information contained or required to be contained in the register kept in pursuance of section 31 of this Act, and
    (b)   any other information obtained by any member or employee of the Authority on terms or in circumstances requiring it to be held in confidence.

(3) Subsection (1) above does not apply to any disclosure of information mentioned in subsection (2)(a) above made –

    (a)   to a person as a member or employee of the Authority,
    (b)   to a person to whom a licence applies for the purposes of his functions as such,
    (c)   so that no individual to whom the information relates can be identified,
    (d)   in pursuance of an order of a court under section 34 or 35 of this Act,
    (e)   to the Registrar General in pursuance of a request under section 32 of this Act, or
    (f)   in accordance with section 31 of this Act.

(4) Subsection (1) above does not apply to any disclosure of information mentioned in subsection (2)(b) above –

(*a*) made to a person as a member or employee of the Authority,

(*b*) made with the consent of the person or persons whose confidence would otherwise be protected, or

(*c*) which has been lawfully made available to the public before the disclosure is made.

(*5*) No person who is or has been a person to whom a licence applies, no person who is or has been a person to whom a third party agreement applies, and no person to whom directions have been given shall disclose any information falling within section 31(2) of this Act which he holds or has held as such a person.

(*6*) Subsection (5) above does not apply to any disclosure of information made –

(*a*) to a person as a member or employee of the Authority,

(*b*) to a person to whom a licence applies for the purposes of his functions as such,

[(*ba*) to a person to whom a third party agreement applies for the purposes of his functions under the third party agreement,]⁴

(*c*) so far as it identifies a person who, but for sections 27 to 29 of this Act, would or might be a parent of a person who instituted proceedings under section 1A of the Congenital Disabilities (Civil Liability) Act 1976, but only for the purpose of defending such proceedings, or instituting connected proceedings for compensation against that parent,

(*d*) so that no individual to whom the information relates can be identified,

(*e*) in pursuance of directions given by virtue of section 24(5) or (6) of this Act,

[(*f*) necessarily –

(*i*) for any purpose preliminary to proceedings, or

(*ii*) for the purposes of, or in connection with, any proceedings,

(*g*) for the purpose of establishing, in any proceedings relating to an application for an order under subsection (1) of section 30 of this Act, whether the condition specified in paragraph (a) or (b) of that subsection is met,

(*h*) under section 3 of the Access to Health Records Act 1990 (right of access to health records)[or]³]¹

(*i*) under Article 5 of the Access to Health Records (Northern Ireland) Order 1993 (right of access to health records)

(*6A*) Paragraph (f) of subsection (6) above, so far as relating to disclosure for the purposes of, or in connection with, any proceedings, does not apply –

(*a*) to disclosure of information enabling a person to be identified as a person whose gametes were used, in accordance with consent given under paragraph 5 of Schedule 3 to this Act, for the purposes of treatment services in consequence of which an identifiable individual was, or may have been, born, or

(*b*) to disclosure, in circumstances in which subsection (1) of section 34 of this Act applies, of information relevant to the determination of the question mentioned in that subsection.

(6B) In the case of information relating to the provision of treatment services for any identifiable individual –

    (a)   *where one individual is identifiable, subsection (5) above does not apply to disclosure with the consent of that individual;*

    (b)   *where both a woman and a man treated together with her are identifiable, subsection (5) above does not apply –*

        (i)   *to disclosure with the consent of them both, or*

        (ii) *if disclosure is made for the purpose of disclosing information about the provision of treatment services for one of them, to disclosure with the consent of that individual.*

(6C) For the purposes of subsection (6B) above, consent must be to disclosure to a specific person, except where disclosure is to a person who needs to know –

    (a)   *in connection with the provision of treatment services, or any other description of medical, surgical or obstetric services, for the individual giving the consent,*

    (b)   *in connection with the carrying out of an audit of clinical practice, or*

    (c)   *in connection with the auditing of accounts.*

(6D) For the purposes of subsection (6B) above, consent to disclosure given at the request of another shall be disregarded unless, before it is given, the person requesting it takes reasonable steps to explain to the individual from whom it is requested the implications of compliance with the request.

(6E) In the case of information which relates to the provision of treatment services for any identifiable individual, subsection (5) above does not apply to disclosure in an emergency, that is to say, to disclosure made –

    (a)   *by a person who is satisfied that it is necessary to make the disclosure to avert an imminent danger to the health of an individual with whose consent the information could be disclosed under subsection (6B) above, and*

    (b)   *in circumstances where it is not reasonably practicable to obtain that individual's consent.*

(6F) In the case of information which shows that any identifiable individual was, or may have been, born in consequence of treatment services, subsection (5) above does not apply to any disclosure which is necessarily incidental to disclosure under subsection (6B) or (6E) above.

(6G) Regulations may provide for additional exceptions from subsection (5) above, but no exception may be made under this subsection –

    (a)   *for disclosure of a kind mentioned in paragraph (a) or (b) of subsection (6A) above, or*

    (b)   *for disclosure, in circumstances in which section 32 of this Act applies, of information having the tendency mentioned in subsection (2) of that section.]¹*

(7) This section does not apply to the disclosure to any individual of information which –

(a) falls within section 31(2) of this Act by virtue of paragraphs (a) to (bb) of that subsection, and
(b) relates only to that individual or, in the case of an individual treated together with another, only to that individual and that other.

(8) ...

(9) In subsection (6)(f) above, references to proceedings include any formal procedure for dealing with a complaint.

Prospective Amendment: Substituted, by subsequent s 33A, together with ss 33B–33D, for this section as originally enacted, by the Human Fertilisation and Embryology Act 2008, s 25 with effect from a date to be appointed.

[33A Disclosure of information

(1) No person shall disclose any information falling within section 31(2) which the person obtained (whether before or after the coming into force of section 24 of the Human Fertilisation and Embryology Act 2008) in the person's capacity as—

(a) a member or employee of the Authority,
(b) any person exercising functions of the Authority by virtue of section 8B or 8C of this Act (including a person exercising such functions by virtue of either of those sections as a member of staff or as an employee),
(c) any person engaged by the Authority to provide services to the Authority,
(d) any person employed by, or engaged to provide services to, a person mentioned in paragraph (c),
(e) a person to whom a licence applies,
(f) a person to whom a third party agreement applies, or
(g) a person to whom directions have been given.

(2) Subsection (1) does not apply where—

(a) the disclosure is made to a person as a member or employee of the Authority or as a person exercising functions of the Authority as mentioned in subsection (1)(b),
(b) the disclosure is made to or by a person falling within subsection (1)(c) for the purpose of the provision of services which that person is engaged to provide to the Authority,
(c) the disclosure is made by a person mentioned in subsection (1)(d) for the purpose of enabling a person falling within subsection (1)(c) to provide services which that person is engaged to provide to the Authority,
(d) the disclosure is made to a person to whom a licence applies for the purpose of that person's functions as such,
(e) the disclosure is made to a person to whom a third party agreement applies for the purpose of that person's functions under that agreement,

(f)   the disclosure is made in pursuance of directions given by virtue of section 24,

(g)   the disclosure is made so that no individual can be identified from the information,

(h)   the disclosure is of information other than identifying donor information and is made with the consent required by section 33B,

(i)   the disclosure—

    (i)   is made by a person who is satisfied that it is necessary to make the disclosure to avert an imminent danger to the health of an individual ("P"),

    (ii)   is of information falling within section 31(2)(a) which could be disclosed by virtue of paragraph (h) with P's consent or could be disclosed to P by virtue of subsection (5), and

    (iii) is made in circumstances where it is not reasonably practicable to obtain P's consent,

(j)   the disclosure is of information which has been lawfully made available to the public before the disclosure is made,

(k)   the disclosure is made in accordance with sections 31ZA to 31ZE,

(l)   the disclosure is required or authorised to be made—

    (i)   under regulations made under section 33D, or

    (ii)   in relation to any time before the coming into force of the first regulations under that section, under regulations made under section 251 of the National Health Service Act 2006,

(m)   the disclosure is made by a person acting in the capacity mentioned in subsection (1)(a) or (b) for the purpose of carrying out the Authority's duties under section 8A,

(n)   the disclosure is made by a person acting in the capacity mentioned in subsection (1)(a) or (b) in pursuance of an order of a court under section 34 or 35,

(o)   the disclosure is made by a person acting in the capacity mentioned in subsection (1)(a) or (b) to the Registrar General in pursuance of a request under section 32,

(p)   the disclosure is made by a person acting in the capacity mentioned in subsection (1)(a) or (b) to any body or person discharging a regulatory function for the purpose of assisting that body or person to carry out that function,

(q)   the disclosure is made for the purpose of establishing in any proceedings relating to an application for an order under subsection (1) of section 54 of the Human Fertilisation and Embryology Act 2008 whether the condition specified in paragraph (a) or (b) of that subsection is met,

(r)   the disclosure is made under section 3 of the Access to Health Records Act 1990,

(s)   the disclosure is made under Article 5 of the Access to Health Records (Northern Ireland) Order 1993, or

(t)   the disclosure is made necessarily for—

    (i)   the purpose of the investigation of any offence (or suspected offence), or

(ii)   any purpose preliminary to proceedings, or for the purposes of, or in connection with, any proceedings.

(3) Subsection (1) does not apply to the disclosure of information in so far as—

(a)   the information identifies a person who, but for sections 27 to 29 of this Act or sections 33 to 47 of the Human Fertilisation and Embryology Act 2008, would or might be a parent of a person who instituted proceedings under section 1A of the Congenital Disabilities (Civil Liability) Act 1976, and

(b)   the disclosure is made for the purpose of defending such proceedings, or instituting connected proceedings for compensation against that parent.

(4) Paragraph (t) of subsection (2), so far as relating to disclosure for the purpose of the investigation of an offence or suspected offence, or for any purpose preliminary to, or in connection with proceedings, does not apply—

(a)   to disclosure of identifying donor information, or

(b)   to disclosure, in circumstances in which subsection (1) of section 34 of this Act applies, of information relevant to the determination of the question mentioned in that subsection, made by any person acting in a capacity mentioned in any of paragraphs (c) to (g) of subsection (1).

(5) Subsection (1) does not apply to the disclosure to any individual of information which—

(a)   falls within subsection (2) of section 31 of this Act by virtue of any of paragraphs (a) to (e) of that subsection, and

(b)   relates only to that individual or, in the case of an individual who is treated together with, or gives a notice under section 37 or 44 of the Human Fertilisation and Embryology Act 2008 in respect of, another, only to that individual and that other.

(6) In subsection (2)—

(a)   in paragraph (p) "regulatory function" has the same meaning as in section 32 of the Legislative and Regulatory Reform Act 2006, and

(b)   in paragraph (t) references to "proceedings" include any formal procedure for dealing with a complaint.

(7) In this section "identifying donor information" means information enabling a person to be identified as a person whose gametes were used in accordance with consent given under paragraph 5 of Schedule 3 for the purposes of treatment services or non-medical fertility services in consequence of which an identifiable individual was, or may have been, born.]

Prospective Amendment: Prospectively substituted, by subsequent s 33A, together with ss 33B–33D, for this section as originally enacted, by the Human Fertilisation and Embryology Act 2008, s 25 with effect from a date to be appointed.

33B Consent required to authorise certain disclosures

(1) This section has effect for the purposes of section 33A(2)(h).

(2) Subject to subsection (5), the consent required by this section is the consent of each individual who can be identified from the information.

(3) Consent in respect of a person who has not attained the age of 18 years ("C") may be given—

  (a) by C, in a case where C is competent to deal with the issue of consent, or

  (b) by a person having parental responsibility for C, in any other case.

(4) Consent to disclosure given at the request of another shall be disregarded unless, before it is given, the person requesting it takes reasonable steps to explain to the individual from whom it is requested the implications of compliance with the request.

(5) In the case of information which shows that any identifiable individual ("A") was, or may have been, born in consequence of treatment services, the consent required by this section does not include A's consent if the disclosure is necessarily incidental to the disclosure of information falling within section 31(2)(a).

(6) The reference in subsection (3) to parental responsibility is—

  (a) in relation to England and Wales, to be read in accordance with the Children Act 1989;

  (b) in relation to Northern Ireland, to be read in accordance with the Children (Northern Ireland) Order 1995;

  (c) in relation to Scotland, to be read as a reference to parental responsibilities and parental rights within the meaning of the Children (Scotland) Act 1995.

Prospective Amendment: Prospectively substituted, by subsequent s 33A, together with ss 33B–33D, for this section as originally enacted, by the Human Fertilisation and Embryology Act 2008, s 25 with effect from a date to be appointed.

33C Power to provide for additional exceptions from section 33A(1)

(1) Regulations may provide for additional exceptions from section 33A(1).

(2) No exception may be made under this section for—

  (a) disclosure of a kind mentioned in paragraph (a) or (b) of subsection (4) of section 33A, or

  (b) disclosure in circumstances in which section 32 of this Act applies of information having the tendency mentioned in subsection (2) of that section, made by any person acting in a capacity mentioned in any of paragraphs (c) to (g) of subsection (1) of section 33A.

Prospective Amendment: Prospectively substituted, by subsequent s 33A, together with ss 33B–33D, for this section as originally enacted, by the Human Fertilisation and Embryology Act 2008, s 25 with effect from a date to be appointed.

33D Disclosure for the purposes of medical or other research

(1) Regulations may—

(a) make such provision for and in connection with requiring or regulating the processing of protected information for the purposes of medical research as the Secretary of State considers is necessary or expedient in the public interest or in the interests of improving patient care, and

(b) make such provision for and in connection with requiring or regulating the processing of protected information for the purposes of any other research as the Secretary of State considers is necessary or expedient in the public interest.

(2) Regulations under subsection (1) may, in particular, make provision—

(a) for requiring or authorising the disclosure or other processing of protected information to or by persons of any prescribed description subject to compliance with any prescribed conditions (including conditions requiring prescribed undertakings to be obtained from such persons as to the processing of such information),

(b) for securing that, where prescribed protected information is processed by a person in accordance with the regulations, anything done by that person in so processing the information must be taken to be lawfully done despite any obligation of confidence owed by the person in respect of it,

(c) for requiring fees of a prescribed amount to be paid to the Authority in prescribed circumstances by persons in relation to the disclosure to those persons of protected information under those regulations,

(d) for the establishment of one or more bodies to exercise prescribed functions in relation to the processing of protected information under those regulations,

(e) as to the membership and proceedings of any such body, and

(f) as to the payment of remuneration and allowances to any member of any such body and the reimbursement of expenses.

(3) Where regulations under subsection (1) require or regulate the processing of protected information for the purposes of medical research, such regulations may enable any approval given under regulations made under section 251 of the National Health Service Act 2006 (control of patient information) to have effect for the purposes of the regulations under subsection (1) in their application to England and Wales.

(4) Subsections (1) to (3) are subject to subsections (5) to (8).

(5) Regulations under subsection (1) may not make any provision requiring or authorising the disclosure or other processing, for any purpose, of protected information, where that information is information from which an individual may be identified, if it would be reasonably practicable to achieve that purpose otherwise than pursuant to such regulations, having regard to the cost of and technology available for achieving that purpose.

(6) Regulations under this section may not make provision for or in connection with the processing of protected information in a manner inconsistent with any provision made by or under the Data Protection Act 1998.

(7) Subsection (6) does not affect the operation of provisions made under subsection (2)(b).

(8) Before making any regulations under this section the Secretary of State shall consult such bodies appearing to the Secretary of State to represent the interests of those likely to be affected by the regulations as the Secretary of State considers appropriate.

(9) In this section—

"prescribed" means prescribed by regulations made by virtue of this section,
"processing", in relation to information, means the use, disclosure, or obtaining of the information or the doing of such other things in relation to it as may be prescribed for the purposes of this definition, and
"protected information" means information falling within section 31(2).]

Amendments: Words inserted: Human Fertilisation and Embryology (Disclosure of Information) Act 1992, s 1(2)–(4). Subsection repealed: Data Protection Act 1998, s 74(2), Sch 16, Pt I. Words repealed, inserted, and sub-section inserted: Access to Health Records (Northern Ireland) Order 1993, SI 1993/1250. Words inserted and substituted and paragraph inserted: SI 2007/1522.

Prospective Amendment: Prospectively substituted, together with ss 33A–33C, for s 33 as originally enacted, by the Human Fertilisation and Embryology Act 2008, s 25 with effect from a date to be appointed.

34 Disclosure in interests of justice

(1) Where in any proceedings before a court the question whether a person is or is not the parent of a child by virtue of sections 27 to 29 of this Act [or section 33 to 47 of the Human Fertilization and Embryology Act 2008] falls to be determined, the court may on the application of any party to the proceedings make an order requiring the Authority –

  (a)   to disclose whether or not any information relevant to that question is contained in the register kept in pursuance of section 31 of this Act, and
  (b)   if it is, to disclose so much of it as is specified in the order,

but such an order may not require the Authority to disclose any information falling within *section 31(2)(b)* [section 31 (2) (c) to (e)] of this Act.

(2) The court must not make an order under subsection (1) above unless it is satisfied that the interests of justice require it to do so, taking into account –

  (a)   any representations made by any individual who may be affected by the disclosure, and
  (b)   the welfare of the child, if under 18 years old, and of any other person under that age who may be affected by the disclosure.

(3) If the proceedings before the court are civil proceedings, it –

(a)   may direct that the whole or any part of the proceedings on the application for an order under subsection (2) above shall be heard in camera, and

(b)   if it makes such an order, may then or later direct that the whole or any part of any later stage of the proceedings shall be heard in camera.

(4) An application for a direction under subsection (3) above shall be heard in camera unless the court otherwise directs.

Prospective Amendment: Words in italics prospectively repealed and subsequent words in square brackets inserted by Human Fertilisation and Embryology Act 2008, s 56, Sch 6, Pt 1, para 34 with effect from a date to be appointed.

35 Disclosure in interests of justice: congenital disabilities, etc

(1) Where for the purpose of instituting proceedings under section 1 of the Congenital Disabilities (Civil Liability) Act 1976 (civil liability to child born disabled) it is necessary to identify a person who would or might be the parent of a child but for *sections 27 to 29 of this Act*, [the relevant statutory provision] the court may, on the application of the child, make an order requiring the Authority to disclose any information contained in the register kept in pursuance of section 31 of this Act identifying that person.

(2) Where, for the purposes of any action for damages in Scotland (including any such action which is likely to be brought) in which the damages claimed consist of or include damages or solatium in respect of personal injury (including any disease and any impairment of physical or mental condition), it is necessary to identify a person who would or might be the parent of a child but for *sections 27 to 29 of this Act*,[the relevant statutory provision] the court may, on the application of any party to the action or, if the proceedings have not been commenced, the prospective pursuer, make an order requiring the Authority to disclose any information contained in the register kept in pursuance of section 31 of this Act identifying that person.

[(2A) In subsections (1) and (2) "the relevant statutory provisions" means –

(a)   sections 27 to 29 of this Act, and

(b)   sections 33 to 47 of the Human Fertilisation and Embryology Act 2008.]

(3) Subsections (2) to (4) of section 34 of this Act apply for the purposes of this section as they apply for the purposes of that.

(4) ...

Prospective Amendment: Subsection prospectively inserted; words in italics prospectively repealed and subsequent words in square brackets substituted by Human Fertilisation and Embryology Act 1990, Schedule 6, para 35 with effect from a date to be appointed.

["Mitochondrial donation

35A Mitochondrial donation

(1) Regulations may provide for any of the relevant provisions to have effect subject to specified modifications in relation to cases where—

(a) an egg which is a permitted egg for the purposes of section 3(2) by virtue of regulations made under section 3ZA(5), or

(b) an embryo which is a permitted embryo for those purposes by virtue of such regulations, has been created from material provided by two women.

(2) In this section "the relevant provisions" means—

(a) the following provisions of this Act—

(i)   section 13(6C) (information whose provision to prospective parents is required by licence condition),

(ii)   section 31 (register of information),

(iii) sections 31ZA to 31ZE (provision of information), and

(iv)   Schedule 3 (consents to use or storage of gametes, embryos or human admixed embryos etc), and

(b) section 54 of the Human Fertilisation and Embryology Act 2008 (parental orders).]

Prospective Amendment: Prospectively inserted by the Human Fertilisation and Embryology Act 2008, s 26 with effect from a date to be appointed.

"Fees

35B Fees

(1) The Authority may charge a fee in respect of any of the following—

(a) an application for a licence,

(b) the grant or renewal of a licence,

(c) an application for the revocation or variation of a licence, or

(d) the exercise by the Authority of any other function conferred on it by or under this Act or by or under any other enactment—

(i)   in relation to a licence,

(ii)   in relation to premises which are or have been premises to which a licence relates,

(iii) in relation to premises which are or have been relevant third party premises in relation to a licence, or

(iv)   in relation to premises which, if an application is granted, will be premises to which a licence relates or relevant third party premises.

(2) The amount of any fee charged by virtue of subsection (1) is to be fixed in accordance with a scheme made by the Authority with the approval of the Secretary of State and the Treasury.

(3) In fixing the amount of any fee to be charged by virtue of that subsection, the Authority may have regard to the costs incurred by it—

(a) in exercising the functions conferred on it by or under this Act (apart from sections 31ZA to 31ZG and 33D), and

(b) in exercising any other function conferred on it by or under any other enactment.

(4) The Authority may also charge such fee as it thinks fit in respect of any of the following—

(a) the giving of notice under section 31ZA(1) or 31ZB(1), or

(b) the provision of information under section 31ZA, 31ZB or 31ZE.

(5) In fixing the amount of any fee to be charged by virtue of subsection (4) the Authority may have regard to the costs incurred by it in exercising the function to which the fee relates.

(6) When exercising its power to charge fees under section 8(2), 31ZF(2)(d) or this section, the Authority may fix different fees for different circumstances.]

Prospective Amendment: Prospectively inserted by Human Fertilisation and Embryology Act 2008, s 27, with effect from a date to be appointed.

****

Conscientious objection

38 Conscientious objection

(1) No person who has a conscientious objection to participating in any activity governed by this Act shall be under any duty, however arising, to do so.

(2) In any legal proceedings the burden of proof of conscientious objection shall rest on the person claiming to rely on it.

(3) In any proceedings before a court in Scotland, a statement on oath by any person to the effect that he has a conscientious objection to participating in a particular activity governed by this Act shall be sufficient evidence of that fact for the purpose of discharging the burden of proof imposed by subsection (2) above.

[Enforcement

38A Inspection, entry, search and seizure

(1) Schedule 3B (which makes provisions about inspection, entry, search and seizure) has effect.

(2) Nothing in this Act makes it unlawful for a member or employee of the Authority to keep any embryo, human admixed embryo or gametes in pursuance of that person's functions as such.]

Prospective Amendment: Prospectively inserted by Human Fertilisation and Embryology Act 2008, s 28(1) with effect from a date to be appointed.

39 Powers of members and employees of Authority

(1) Any member or employee of the Authority entering and inspecting premises to which a licence relates, or relevant third party premises, may –

  (a) take possession of anything which he has reasonable grounds to believe may be required –

  (i) for the purpose of the functions of the Authority relating to the grant, variation, suspension and revocation of licences,

  (ia) for the purpose of taking appropriate control measures in the event of a serious adverse event or serious adverse reaction, or

  (ii) for the purpose of being used in evidence in any proceedings for an offence under this Act,

  and retain it for so long as it may be required for the purpose in question, and

  (b) for the purpose in question, take such steps as appear to be necessary for preserving any such thing or preventing interference with it, including requiring any person having the power to do so to give such assistance as may reasonably be required.

(2) In subsection (1) above –

  (a) the references to things include information recorded in any form, and

  (b) the reference to taking possession of anything includes, in the case of information recorded otherwise than in legible form, requiring any person having the power to do so to produce a copy of the information in legible form and taking possession of the copy.

(3) Nothing in this Act makes it unlawful for a member or employee of the Authority to keep any embryo or gametes in pursuance of that person's functions as such.

Amendments: Words inserted and repealed, and paragraph inserted: SI 2007/1522.

Prospective Amendments: Prospectively repealed by Human Fertilisation and Embryology Act 2008, ss 28(3), 66, Sch 8, Pt 1 with effect from a date to be appointed.

40 Power to enter premises

(1) A justice of the peace (including, in Scotland, a sheriff) may issue a warrant under this section if satisfied by the evidence on oath of a member or employee of the Authority that there are reasonable grounds for suspecting that an offence under this Act is being, or has been committed on any premises.

(2) A warrant under this section shall authorise any named member or employee of the Authority (who must, if so required, produce a document identifying himself), together with any constables –

  (a) to enter the premises specified in the warrant, using such force as is reasonably necessary for the purpose, and

  (b) to search the premises and –

(i)   take possession of anything which he has reasonable grounds to believe may be required to be used in evidence in any proceedings for an offence under this Act, or

(ii) take such steps as appear to be necessary for preserving any such thing or preventing interference with it, including requiring any person having the power to do so to give such assistance as may reasonably be required.

(3) A warrant under this section shall continue in force until the end of the period of one month beginning with the day on which it is issued.

(4) Anything of which possession is taken under this section may be retained –

(a) for a period of six months, or

(b) if within that period proceedings to which the thing is relevant are commenced against any person for an offence under this Act, until the conclusion of those proceedings.

(5) In this section –

(a) the reference to things include information recorded in any form, and

(b) the reference in subsection *(2)(b)(i)* above to taking possession of anything includes, in the case of information recorded otherwise than in legible form, requiring any person having the power to do so to produce a copy of the information in legible form, or in a form from which it can readily be produced in visible and legible form and taking possession of the copy.

Prospective Amendment: Prospectively repealed by the Human Fertilisation and Embryology Act 2008, ss 28(3), 66, Sch 8, Pt 1 with effect from a date to be appointed.

Offences

41 Offences

(1) A person who –

(a) contravenes section 3(2) , 3A or *4(1)(c)*[4A(1) or (2)] of this Act, or

(b) does anything which, by virtue of section 3(3) of this Act, cannot be authorised by a licence,

is guilty of an offence and liable on conviction on indictment to imprisonment for a term not exceeding ten years or a fine or both.

(2) A person who –

(a) contravenes section 3(1) or (1A) of this Act, otherwise than by doing something which, by virtue of section 3(3) of this Act, cannot be authorised by a licence,

["(aa) contravenes section 3(1B) of this Act,",]

(b) keeps any gametes in contravention of section 4(1)(a) of this Act,

(ba) uses any gametes in contravention of section 4(1)(b),

[(bb) contravenes section 4(1A) of this Act,]

(c) contravenes section 4(3) of this Act, or

(d)　fails to comply with any directions given by virtue of *section 24(7)(a)* [section 24(5D)]of this Act, is guilty of an offence.

(2A)　A person who contravenes section 3(1B) or 4(1A) is guilty of an offence.

(3)　If a person –

(a)　provides any information for the purposes of the grant of a licence, being information which is false or misleading in a material particular, and

(b)　either he knows the information to be false or misleading in a material particular or he provides the information recklessly,

he is guilty of an offence.

(4)　A person guilty of an offence under subsection (2) or (3) above, *other than an offence to which subsection (4B) applies,* is liable –

(a)　on conviction on indictment, to imprisonment for a term not exceeding two years or a fine or both, and

(b)　on summary conviction, to imprisonment for a term not exceeding six months or a fine not exceeding the statutory maximum or both.

(4A)　Subsection (4B) applies to –

(a)　an offence under subsection (2)(ba) or (d) or (3) committed in the course of providing basic partner treatment services or non-medical fertility services, or

(b)　an offence under subsection (2A).

(4B)　A person guilty of an offence to which this subsection applies is liable –

(a)　on conviction on indictment, to imprisonment for a term not exceeding two years or a fine or both, and

(b)　on summary conviction, to imprisonment for a term not exceeding three months or a fine not exceeding the statutory maximum or both.

(5)　A person who discloses any information in contravention of *section 33* [section 33A] of this Act is guilty of an offence and liable –

(a)　on conviction on indictment, to imprisonment for a term not exceeding two years or a fine or both, and

(b)　on summary conviction, to imprisonment for a term not exceeding six months or a fine not exceeding the statutory maximum or both.

(6)　A person who –

(a)　fails to comply with a requirement made by virtue of section 39(1)(b) or (2)(b) or 40(2)(b)(ii) or (5)(b) of this Act, or

(b)　intentionally obstructs the exercise of any rights conferred by a warrant issued under section 40 of this Act,

is guilty of an offence.

(7) A person who without reasonable excuse fails to comply with a requirement imposed by regulations made by virtue of *section 10(2)(a)* [section 19B(3)(a) or 20B(3)(e)] of this Act is guilty of an offence.

(8) Where a person to whom a licence applies *or the nominal licensee* [or the holder of the licence] gives or receives any money or other benefit, not authorised by directions, in respect of any supply of gametes *or embryos,* [embryos or human admixed embryos] he is guilty of an offence.

(9) A person guilty of an offence under subsection *(6)*, (7) or (8) above is liable on summary conviction to imprisonment for a term not exceeding six months or a fine not exceeding level five on the standard scale or both.

(10) It is a defence for a person ('the defendant') charged with an offence of doing anything which, under section 3(1) or 4(1) of this Act, cannot be done except in pursuance of a licence to prove –

> *(a)   that the defendant was acting under the direction of another, and*
> *(b)   that the defendant believed on reasonable grounds –*
> > *(i)   that the other person was at the material time the person responsible under a licence, a person designated by virtue of section 17(2)(b) of this Act as a person to whom a licence applied, or a person to whom directions had been given by virtue of section 24(9) of this Act, and*
> > *(ii)   that the defendant was authorised by virtue of the licence or directions to do the thing in question.*

[(10) It is a defence for a person ("the defendant") charged with an offence of doing anything which, under section 3(1) or (1A), 4(1) or 4A(2), cannot be done except in pursuance of a licence to prove—

> (a)   that the defendant was acting under the direction of another, and
> (b)   that the defendant believed on reasonable grounds—
> > (i)   that the other person was at the material time the person responsible under a licence, a person designated by virtue of section 17(2)(b) of this Act as a person to whom a licence applied, or a person to whom directions had been given under section 24(5A) to (5D), and
> > (ii)   that the defendant was authorised by virtue of the licence or directions to do the thing in question.

(10A) It is a defence for a person ("the defendant") charged with an offence of doing anything which, under section 3(1A) or (1B) or 4(1A), cannot be done except in pursuance of a licence or a third party agreement to prove—

> (a)   that the defendant was acting under the direction of another, and
> (b)   that the defendant believed on reasonable grounds—
> > (i)   that the other person was at the material time the person responsible under a licence, a person designated by virtue of section 17(2)(b) of this Act as a person to whom a licence

applied, a person to whom a third party agreement applied, or a person to whom directions had been given under section 24(5A) to (5D), and

(ii)   that the defendant was authorised by virtue of the licence, third party agreement or directions to do the thing in question.]

(11) It is a defence for a person charged with an offence under this Act to prove –

(a)   that at the material time he was a person to whom a licence or third party agreement applied or to whom directions had been given, and

(b)   that he took all such steps as were reasonable and exercised all due diligence to avoid committing the offence.

Amendment: Section number inserted: Criminal Justice and Public Order Act 1994, s 156(2). Words, paragraph and subsections inserted, and words repealed: SI 2007/1522.

Prospective Amendment: Words in italics repealed and subsequent words in square brackets substituted, Sub-s (2), para (aa) inserted by the Human Fertilisation and Embryology Act 2008, s 29(1), (3)(a); for effect in relation to the Criminal Justice Act 2008, s 282, subsections repealed, substituted and inserted by Human Fertilisation and Embryology Act 2008, ss 29(1), (10), 66, Sch 8, Pt 1.

42 Consent to prosecution

No proceedings for an offence under this Act shall be instituted –

(a)   in England and Wales, except by or with the consent of the Director of Public Prosecutions, and

(b)   in Northern Ireland, except by or with the consent of the Director of Public Prosecutions for Northern Ireland.

Miscellaneous and General

43 Keeping and examining gametes and embryos in connection with crime, etc

(1) Regulations may provide –

(a)   for the keeping and examining of gametes or embryos, in such manner and on such conditions (if any) as may be specified in regulations, in connection with the investigation of, or proceedings for, an offence (wherever committed), or

(b)   for the storage of gametes, in such manner and on such conditions (if any) as may be specified in regulations, where they are to be used only for such purposes, other than treatment services, as may be specified in regulations.

(2) Nothing in this Act makes unlawful the keeping or examination of any gametes or embryos in pursuance of regulations made by virtue of this section.

(3) In this section 'examination' includes use for the purposes of any test.

****

45 Regulations

(1) The Secretary of State may make regulations for any purpose for which regulations may be made under this Act.

[(1A) Subsection(1) does not enable the Secretary of state to make regulations by virtue of section 19(6)(which confers regulation-making powers on the Authority).]

(2) The power to make regulations [under this Act] shall be exercisable by statutory instrument.

(3) Regulations may make different provision for different cases.

[(3) The power to make regulations under this Act may be exercised—

    (a)   either in relation to all cases to which the power extends, or in relation to those cases subject to specified exceptions, or in relation to any specified cases or classes of case, and

    (b)   so as to make, as respects the cases in relation to which it is exercised—

        (i)   the full provision to which the power extends or any less provision (whether by way of exception or otherwise);

        (ii)   the same provision for all cases in relation to which the power is exercised, or different provision as respects the same case or class of case for different purposes;

        (iii)   any such provision either unconditionally, or subject to any specified condition.

(3A) Any power of the Secretary of State or the Authority to make regulations under this Act includes power to make such transitional, incidental or supplemental provision as the Secretary of State or the Authority considers appropriate.]

(4) The Secretary of State shall not make regulations by virtue of section 3(3)(c), 4(2) or (3), 30, 31(4)(a), 33(6G), or 43 of this Act or paragraph 1(1)(g) or 3 of Schedule 2 to this Act unless a draft has been laid before and approved by resolution of each House of Parliament.

[(4) The Secretary of State shall not make regulations by virtue of any of the provisions specified in subsection (4A) unless a draft has been laid before and approved by a resolution of each House of Parliament.

(4A) Those provisions are—

section 1(6);

section 3(3)(c);

section 3ZA(5);

section 4(2) or (3);

section 4A(5) or (11);

section 20A(3);

section 20B(2);

section 24(4B);

section 31ZA(2)(a);

section 33C;

section 33D;

section 35A;

section 43;

paragraph 1(1)(g), 1ZC or 3A(1)(c) of Schedule 2.]

(5) A statutory instrument containing regulations [made by the Secretary of State] shall, if made without a draft having been approved by resolution of each House of Parliament, be subject to annulment in pursuance of a resolution of either House of Parliament.

(6) In this Act 'regulations' means regulations under this section.

Amendment: Words inserted, Human Fertilisation and Embryology (Disclosure of Information) Act 1992, s 2(2).

Prospective amendment: Sub-s (1A) and words in square brackets prospectively inserted; Sub-s (3), substituted, by subsequent sub-ss (3), (3A); Sub-s (4), substituted, by subsequent sub-ss (4), (4A), by the Human Fertilisation and Embryology Act 2008, s 30(1), (2), (3), (4), (5) with effect from a date to be appointed.

[45A Power to make consequential provision

(1) The Secretary of State may by order make such provision modifying any provision made by or under any enactment as the Secretary of State considers necessary or expedient in consequence of any provision made by regulations under any of the relevant provisions of this Act.

(2) For the purposes of subsection (1), "the relevant provisions of this Act" are—

   (a)   section 1(6) (power to include things within the meaning of "embryo" and "gametes" etc);
   (b)   section 4A(11) (power to amend definition of "human admixed embryo" and other terms).

(3) Before making an order under this section containing provision which would, if included in an Act of the Scottish Parliament, be within the legislative competence of that Parliament, the Secretary of State must consult the Scottish Ministers.

(4) Before making an order under this section containing provision which would be within the legislative competence of the National Assembly for Wales if it were included in a Measure of the Assembly (or, if the order is made after the Assembly Act provisions come into force, an Act of the Assembly), the Secretary of State must consult the Welsh Ministers.

(5) Before making an order under this section containing provision which would if included in an Act of the Northern Ireland Assembly, be within the legislative competence of that Assembly, the Secretary of State must consult the Department of Health, Social Services and Public Safety.

(6) In this section—

"enactment" means—

(a)   an Act of Parliament (other than this Act),
(b)   an Act of the Scottish Parliament,
(c)   a Measure or Act of the National Assembly for Wales, or
(d)   Northern Ireland legislation,
whenever passed or made;

"modify" includes amend, add to, revoke or repeal;
"the Assembly Act provisions" has the meaning given by section 103(8) of the Government of Wales Act 2006.]

Prospective Amendment: Prospectively inserted by the Human Fertilisation and Embryology Act 2008, s 31 with effect from a date to be appointed.

[45B Orders

(1) The power to make an order under section 8C(1)(c) or 45A of this Act shall be exercisable by statutory instrument.

(2) The power to make an order under section 8C(1)(c) or 45A of this Act includes power to make such transitional, incidental or supplemental provision as the Secretary of State considers appropriate.

(3) A statutory instrument containing an order made by the Secretary of State by virtue of section 8C(1)(c) shall be subject to annulment in pursuance of a resolution of either House of Parliament.

(4) The Secretary of State shall not make an order by virtue of section 45A unless a draft has been laid before and approved by a resolution of each House of Parliament.]

Prospective Amendment: Prospectively inserted by the Human Fertilisation and Embryology Act 2008, s 32 with effect from a date to be appointed.

46 Notices

(1) This section has effect in relation to any notice required or authorised by this Act to be given to or served on any person.

(2) The notice may be given to or served on the person –

(a)   by delivering it to the person,
(b)   by leaving it at the person's proper address, or
(c)   by sending it by post to the person at that address.

(3) The notice may –

(a)   in the case of a body corporate, be given to or served on the secretary or clerk of the body,

(b)   in the case of a partnership, be given to or served on any partner, and

(c)   in the case of an unincorporated association other than a partnership, be given to or served on any member of the governing body of the association.

(4) For the purposes of this section and section 7 of the Interpretation Act 1978 (service of documents by post) in its application to this section, the proper address of any person is the person's last known address and also –

(a)   in the case of a body corporate, its secretary or its clerk, the address of its registered or principal office, and

(b)   in the case of an unincorporated association or a member of its governing body, its principal office.

(5) Where a person has notified the Authority of an address or a new address at which notices may be given to or served on him under this Act, that address shall also be his proper address for the purposes mentioned in subsection (4) above or, as the case may be, his proper address for those purposes in substitution for that previously notified.

47 Index

The expressions listed in the left-hand column below are respectively defined or (as the case may be) are to be interpreted in accordance with the provisions of this Act listed in the right-hand column in relation to those expressions.

Expression	*Relevant provision*
Activities governed by this Act	Section 4(5)
[Appeals Committee	Section 20A(2)]
Authority	Section 2(1)
Basic partner treatment services	Section 2(1)
Carry, in relation to a child	Section 2(3)
Competent authority	Section 2(1)]¹
Directions	Section 2(1)
[Distribution, in relation to gametes or embryos intended for human application	Section 2(1)
Embryo [(except in section 4A or in the term "human admixed embryos")]	Section 1
[First Directive	Section 1A]¹
Gametes, eggs or sperm [(except in section 4A)]	Section 1
[Human admixed embryo	Section 4A(6)

Human application	Section 2(1)]
Keeping, in relation to embryos or gametes	Section 2(2)
Licence	Section 2(1)
Licence committee	*Section 9(1)*
Nominal licensee	*Section 17(3)*
Non-medical fertility services	Section 2(1)
[Nuclear DNA (in relation to an embryo)	Section 2 (1)]
Partner-donated sperm	Section 1(5)
Person responsible	Section 17(1)
Person to whom a licence applies	Section 17(2)
Person to whom a third party agreement applies	Section 2A(3)
Processing, in relation to gametes or embryos intended for human application	Section 2(1)
Procurement, in relation to gametes or embryos intended for human application	Section 2(1)
Relevant third party premises, in relation to a licence	Section 2A(2)
Second Directive	Section 1A
Serious adverse event	Section 2(1)
Serious adverse reaction	Section 2(1)
Statutory storage period	Section 14(3) to (5)
Store, and similar expressions, in relation to embryos [human admixed embryos] or gametes	Section 2(1)
Third Directive	Section 1A
Third party	Section 2A(2)
Third party agreement	Section 2A(1)
Traceability	Section 2(1)
Treatment services	Section 2(1)

Amendments: Entries inserted and words substituted: SI 2007/1522.

Prospective Amendment: Entries prospectively inserted, substituted and repealed by the Human Fertilisation and Embryology Act 2008; s 65, Sch 7, para 13(d); s 68(2) with effect from a date to be appointed.

48 Northern Ireland

(1) This Act (except *sections 33(6)(h) and* [sections 33A(2)(r) and]37) extends to Northern Ireland.

(2) ...

Amendments: Human Fertilisation and Embryology (Disclosure of Information) Act 1992, s 2(4): Northern Ireland Act 1998, s 100(2), Sch 15.

Prospective Amendment: Words in italics prospectively repealed and subsequent words in square brackets inserted by Human Fertilisation and Embryology Act 2008, s 65, Sch 7, para 14 with effect from a date to be appointed.

49 Short title, commencement, etc

(1) This Act may be cited as the Human Fertilisation and Embryology Act 1990.

(2) This Act shall come into force on such day as the Secretary of State may by order made by statutory instrument appoint and different days may be appointed for different provisions and for different purposes.

(3) Sections 27 to 29 of this Act shall have effect only in relation to children carried by women as a result of the placing in them of embryos or of sperm and eggs, or of their artificial insemination (as the case may be), after the commencement of those sections.

(4) Section 27 of the Family Law Reform Act 1987 (artificial insemination) does not have effect in relation to children carried by women as the result of their artificial insemination after the commencement of sections 27 to 29 of this Act.

(5) Schedule 4 to this Act (which makes minor and consequential amendments) shall have effect.

(6) An order under this section may make such transitional provision as the Secretary of State considers necessary or desirable and, in particular, may provide that where activities are carried on under the supervision of a particular individual, being activities which are carried on under the supervision of that individual at the commencement of sections 3 and 4 of this Act, those activities are to be treated, during such period as may be specified in or determined in accordance with the order, as authorised by a licence (having, in addition to the conditions required by this Act, such conditions as may be so specified or determined) under which that individual is the person responsible.

(7) Her Majesty may by Order in Council direct that any of the provisions of this Act shall extend, with such exceptions, adaptations and modifications (if any) as may be specified in the Order, to any of the Channel Islands.

Schedule 1
The Authority: Supplementary Provisions

Section 5

Status and capacity

1

The Authority shall not be regarded as the servant or agent of the Crown, or as enjoying any status, privilege of immunity of the Crown; and its property shall not be regarded as property of, or property held on behalf of, the Crown.

2

The Authority shall have power to do anything which is calculated to facilitate the discharge of its functions, or is incidental or conducive to their discharge, except the power to borrow money.

Expenses

3

The Secretary of State may, with the consent of the Treasury, pay the Authority out of money provided by Parliament such sums as he thinks fit towards its expenses.

Appointment of members

4

(1) All the members of the Authority (including the chairman and deputy chairman who shall be appointed as such) shall be appointed by the Secretary of State.

(2) In making appointments the Secretary of State shall have regard to the desirability of ensuring that the proceedings of the Authority, and the discharge of its functions, are informed by the views of both men and women.

(3) The following persons are disqualified from being appointed as chairman or deputy chairman of the Authority –

(a)   any person who is, or has been, a medical practitioner registered under the Medical Act 1983 (whether fully, provisionally or with limited registration), or under any repealed enactment from which a provision of that Act is derived,

(b)   any person who is, or has been, concerned with keeping or using gametes or embryos outside the body, and

(c)   any person who is, or has been, directly concerned with commissioning or funding any research involving such keeping or use, or who has actively participated in any decision to do so.

(4) The Secretary of State shall secure that at least one-third but fewer than half of the other members of the Authority fall within sub-paragraph (3)(a), (b) or (c) above, and that at least one member falls within each of paragraphs (a) and (b).

[4A

(1) A person ("P") is disqualified for being appointed as chairman, deputy chairman, or as any other member of the Authority if—

(a)   P is the subject of a bankruptcy restrictions order or interim order,

(b)   a bankruptcy order has been made against P by a court in Northern Ireland, P's estate has been sequestered by a court in Scotland, or under the law of Northern Ireland or Scotland, P has made a composition or arrangement with, or granted a trust deed for, P's creditors, or

(c)   in the last five years P has been convicted in the United Kingdom, the Channel Islands or the Isle of Man of an offence and has had a qualifying sentence passed on P.

(2) Where P is disqualified under sub-paragraph (1)(b) because a bankruptcy order has been made against P or P's estate has been sequestered, the disqualification ceases—

(a)   on P obtaining a discharge, or

(b)   if the bankruptcy order is annulled or the sequestration of P's estate is recalled or reduced, on the date of that event.

(3) Where P is disqualified under sub-paragraph (1)(b) because of P having made a composition or arrangement with, or granted a trust deed for, P's creditors, the disqualification ceases—

(a)   at the end of the period of five years beginning with the date on which the terms of the deed of composition or arrangement or trust deed are fulfilled, or

(b)   if, before then, P pays P's debts in full, on the date on which the payment is completed.

(4) For the purposes of sub-paragraph (1)(c), the date of conviction is to be taken to be the ordinary date on which the period allowed for making an appeal or application expires or, if an appeal or application is made, the date on which the appeal or application is finally disposed of or abandoned or fails by reason of its non prosecution.

(5) In sub-paragraph (1)(c), the reference to a qualifying sentence is to a sentence of imprisonment for a period of not less than three months (whether suspended or not) without the option of a fine.]

Prospective Amendment: Prospectively inserted by Human Fertilisation and Embryology Act 2008, s 5, Sch 1, paras 1, 2 with effect from a date to be appointed.

Tenure of office

5

(1) Subject to the following provisions of this paragraph, a person shall hold and vacate office as a member of the Authority in accordance with the terms of his appointment.

(2) A person shall not be appointed as a member of the Authority for more than three years at a time.

(3) A member may at any time resign his office by giving notice to the Secretary of State.

(4) A person who ceases to be a member of the Authority shall be eligible for re-appointment (whether or not in the same capacity).

[(4A) A person holding office as chairman, deputy chairman or other member of the Authority is to cease to hold that office if the person becomes disqualified for appointment to it.]

(5) If the Secretary of State is satisfied that a member of the Authority –

    (a)   has been absent from meetings of the Authority for six consecutive months or longer without the permission of the Authority, or

    (b)   *has become bankrupt or made an arrangement with his creditors, or, in Scotland, has had his estate sequestrated or has granted a trust deed for or entered into an arrangement with his creditors, or*

    (c)   is unable or unfit to discharge the *functions of a member* [person's functions as chairman, deputy chairman or other member],

the Secretary of State may *declare his office as a member of the Authority vacant, and notify the declaration in such manner as he thinks fit; and thereupon the office shall become vacant* [remove the member from office as chairman, deputy chairman or other member].

Prospective Amendment: Subparagraph (4A) prospectively inserted, sub-para (5)(b) prospectively repealed; words in italics repealed and subsequent words in square brackets prospectively substituted Human Fertilisation and Embryology Act 2008, s 5, Sch 1, paras 1, 3(b)(iii) with effect from a date to be appointed.

Disqualification of members of Authority for House of Commons and Northern Ireland Assembly

6...

Remuneration and pensions of members

7

(1) The Authority may –

    (a)   pay to the chairman such remuneration, and

    (b)   pay or make provision for paying to or in respect of the chairman or any other member such pensions, allowances, fees, expenses or gratuities, as the Secretary of State may, with the approval of the Treasury, determine.

(2) Where a person ceases to be a member of the Authority otherwise than on the expiry of his term of office and it appears to the Secretary of State that there are special circumstances which make it right for him to receive compensation, the Authority may make to him a payment of such amount as the Secretary of State may, with the consent of the Treasury, determine.

Staff

8

(1) The Authority may appoint such employees as it thinks fit, upon such terms and conditions as the Authority, with the approval of the Secretary of State and the consent of the Treasury, may determine.

(2) The Authority shall secure that any employee whose function is, or whose functions include, the inspection of premises is of such character, and is so qualified by training and experience, as to be a suitable person to perform that function.

(3) The Authority shall, as regards such of its employees as with the approval of the Secretary of State it may determine, pay to or in respect of them such pensions, allowances or gratuities (including pensions, allowances or gratuities by way of compensation for loss of employment), or provide and maintain for them such pension schemes (whether contributory or not), as may be so determined.

(4) If an employee of the Authority –

    (a)   is a participant in any pension scheme applicable to that employment, and

    (b)   becomes a member of the Authority,

he may, if the Secretary of State so determines, be treated for the purposes of the pension schemes as if his service as a member of the Authority were service as employee of the Authority, whether or not any benefits are to be payable to or in respect of him by virtue of paragraph 7 above.

Proceedings

9

(1) *The* [Subject to any provision of this Act, the] Authority may regulate its own proceedings, and make such arrangements as it thinks appropriate for the discharge of its functions.

(2) The Authority may pay to the members of any committee or subcommittee such fees and allowances as the Secretary of State may, with the consent of the Treasury, determine.

Prospective Amendment: Words in italics repealed and subsequent words in square brackets prospectively substituted by Human Fertilisation and Embryology Act 2008, s 65, Sch 7, para 15(a).

10

(1) A member of the Authority who is in any way directly or indirectly interested in a licence granted or proposed to be granted by the Authority shall, as soon as possible after the relevant circumstances have come to his knowledge, disclose the nature of his interest to the Authority.

(2) Any disclosure under sub-paragraph (1) above shall be recorded by the Authority.

(3) Except in such circumstances (if any) as may be determined by the Authority under paragraph 9(1) above, the member shall not participate after the disclosure in any deliberation or decision of the Authority *or any licence committee* with respect to the licence, and if he does so the deliberation or decision shall be of no effect.

Prospective Amendment: Words in italics prospectively repealed by Human Fertilisation and Embryology Act 2008, s 65, 66, Sch 7, para 15(b), Sch 8, Pt 1 with effect from a date to be appointed.

11

The validity of any proceedings of the Authority, or of any committee or sub-committee, shall not be affected by any vacancy among the members or by any defect in the appointment of a member.

Instruments

12

The fixing of the seal of the Authority shall be authenticated by the signature of the chairman or deputy chairman of the Authority or some other member of the Authority authorised by the Authority to act for that purpose.

13

A document purporting to be duly executed under the seal of the Authority, or to be signed on the Authority's behalf, shall be received in evidence and shall be deemed to be so executed or signed unless the contrary is proved.

Investigation by Parliamentary Commissioner

14

The Authority shall be subject to investigation by the Parliamentary Commissioner.

[Application of Statutory Instruments Act 1946

15

The Statutory Instruments Act 1946 applies to any power to make orders or regulations conferred by an Act on the Authority as if the Authority were a Minister of the Crown.]

Prospective Amendment: Prospectively inserted by Human Fertilisation and Embryology Act 2008, s 65, Sch 7, para 15(c) with effect from a date to be appointed.

Schedule 2
Activities for which Licences may be Granted

Section 11 etc

Licences for treatment

1

(1) A licence under this paragraph may authorise any of the following in the course of providing treatment services –

(a) bringing about the creation of embryos *in vitro,*

(b) procuring, keeping, testing, processing or distributing embryos,

(c) procuring, testing, processing, distributing or using gametes

[(ca) using embryos for the purpose of training persons in embryo biopsy, embryo storage or other embryological techniques,]

(d) other practices designed to secure that embryos are in a suitable condition to be placed in a woman *or to determine whether embryos are suitable for that purpose,*

(e) placing any *embryo* [permitted embryo] in a woman,

(f) mixing sperm with the egg of a hamster, or other animal specified in directions, for the purpose of testing the fertility or normality of the sperm, but only where anything which forms is destroyed when the test is complete and, in any event, not later than the two cell stage, and

(g) such other practices [, apart from practices falling within section 4A(2)] as may be specified in, or determined in accordance with, regulations.

(2) Subject to the provisions of this Act, a licence under this paragraph may be granted subject to such conditions as may be specified in the licence and may authorise the performance of any of the activities referred to in sub-paragraph (1) above in such manner as may be so specified.

(3) A licence under this paragraph cannot authorise any activity unless it appears to the Authority to be necessary or desirable for the purpose of providing treatment services.

(4) A licence under this paragraph cannot authorise altering the genetic structure of any cell while it forms part of an embryo.

[(4) A licence under this paragraph cannot authorise altering the nuclear or mitochondrial DNA of a cell while it forms part of an embryo, except for the purpose of creating something that will by virtue of regulations under section 3ZA(5) be a permitted embryo.]

[(4A) A licence under this paragraph cannot authorise the use of embryos for the purpose mentioned in sub-paragraph (1)(ca) unless the Authority is satisfied that the proposed use of embryos is necessary for that purpose.]

(5) A licence under this paragraph shall be granted for such period not exceeding five years as may be specified in the licence.[(6) In this paragraph, references to a permitted embryo are to be read in accordance with section 3ZA.]

Prospective Amendment: Subparagraph and words inserted; words in italics repealed and subsequent words in square brackets prospectively inserted; sub-para (4) prospectively repealed and substituted; Para (4A), inserted by Human Fertilisation and Embryology Act 2008, s 11(2), Sch 2, paras 1, 2(a) with effect from a date to be appointed.

[Embryo testing

1ZA

(1) A licence under paragraph 1 cannot authorise the testing of an embryo, except for one or more of the following purposes—

    (a)   establishing whether the embryo has a gene, chromosome or mitochondrion abnormality that may affect its capacity to result in a live birth,

    (b)   in a case where there is a particular risk that the embryo may have any gene, chromosome or mitochondrion abnormality, establishing whether it has that abnormality or any other gene, chromosome or mitochondrion abnormality,

    (c)   in a case where there is a particular risk that any resulting child will have or develop—

        (i)   a gender-related serious physical or mental disability,

        (ii)   a gender-related serious illness, or

        (iii)   any other gender-related serious medical condition,

establishing the sex of the embryo,

    (d)   in a case where a person ("the sibling") who is the child of the persons whose gametes are used to bring about the creation of the embryo (or of either of those persons) suffers from a serious medical condition which could be treated by umbilical cord blood stem cells, bone marrow or other tissue of any resulting child, establishing whether the tissue of any resulting child would be compatible with that of the sibling, and

    (e)   in a case where uncertainty has arisen as to whether the embryo is one of those whose creation was brought about by using the gametes of particular persons, establishing whether it is.

(2) A licence under paragraph 1 cannot authorise the testing of embryos for the purpose mentioned in sub-paragraph (1)(b) unless the Authority is satisfied—

    (a)   in relation to the abnormality of which there is a particular risk, and

    (b)   in relation to any other abnormality for which testing is to be authorised under sub-paragraph (1)(b), that there is a significant risk that a person with the abnormality will have or develop a serious physical or mental disability, a serious illness or any other serious medical condition.

(3) For the purposes of sub-paragraph (1)(c), a physical or mental disability, illness or other medical condition is gender-related if the Authority is satisfied that—

    (a)   it affects only one sex, or
    (b)   it affects one sex significantly more than the other.

(4) In sub-paragraph (1)(d) the reference to "other tissue" of the resulting child does not include a reference to any whole organ of the child.

Sex selection

1ZB

(1) A licence under paragraph 1 cannot authorise any practice designed to secure that any resulting child will be of one sex rather than the other.

(2) Sub-paragraph (1) does not prevent the authorisation of any testing of embryos that is capable of being authorised under paragraph 1ZA.

(3) Sub-paragraph (1) does not prevent the authorisation of any other practices designed to secure that any resulting child will be of one sex rather than the other in a case where there is a particular risk that a woman will give birth to a child who will have or develop—

    (a)   a gender-related serious physical or mental disability,
    (b)   a gender-related serious illness, or
    (c)   any other gender-related serious medical condition.

(4) For the purposes of sub-paragraph (3), a physical or mental disability, illness or other medical condition is gender-related if the Authority is satisfied that—

    (a)   it affects only one sex, or
    (b)   it affects one sex significantly more than the other.

Power to amend paragraphs 1ZA and 1ZB

1ZC

(1) Regulations may make any amendment of paragraph 1ZA (embryo testing).

(2) Regulations under this paragraph which amend paragraph 1ZA may make any amendment of sub-paragraphs (2) to (4) of paragraph 1ZB (sex selection) which appears to the Secretary of State to be necessary or expedient in consequence of the amendment of paragraph 1ZA.

(3) Regulations under this paragraph may not enable the authorisation of—

    (a)   the testing of embryos for the purpose of establishing their sex, or
    (b)   other practices falling within paragraph 1ZB(1),

except on grounds relating to the health of any resulting child.

(4) For the purposes of this paragraph, "amend" includes add to and repeal, and references to "amendment" are to be read accordingly.]

Prospective Amendment: Paras 1ZA–1ZC prospectively inserted by the Human Fertilisation and Embryology Act 2008, s 11(2), Sch 2, paras 1, 3 with effect from a date to be appointed.

Licences for non-medical fertility services

1A

(1) A licence under this paragraph may authorise any of the following in the course of providing non-medical fertility services –

    (a)   procuring sperm, and
    (b)   distributing sperm.

[(1A) A licence under this paragraph cannot authorise the procurement or distribution of sperm to which there has been applied any process designed to secure that any resulting child will be of one sex rather than the other.]

(2) Subject to the provisions of this Act, a licence under this paragraph may be granted subject to such conditions as may be specified in the licence and may authorise the performance of any of the activities referred to in sub-paragraph (1) above in such manner as may be so specified.

(3) A licence under this paragraph shall be granted for such period not exceeding five years as may be specified in the licence.

Prospective Amendment: Subparagraph (1A) prospectively inserted by Human Fertilisation and Embryology Act 2008, s 11(2), Sch 2, paras 1, 4.

Licences for storage

2

(1) A licence under this paragraph or paragraph 1 or 3 of this Schedule may authorise the storage of gametes or embryos or both.

[(1A) A licence under this paragraph or paragraph 3 may authorise the storage of human admixed embryos (whether or not the licence also authorises the storage of gametes or embryos or both).]

(2) Subject to the provisions of this Act, a licence authorising such storage [as is mentioned in sub-paragraph (1) or (1A)] may be granted to such conditions as may be specified in the licence and may authorise storage in such manner as may be so specified.

(3) A licence under this paragraph shall be granted for such period not exceeding five years as may be specified in the licence.

Prospective Amendment: Subparagraph (1A) and words in square brackets prospectively inserted by Human Fertilisation and Embryology Act 2008, s 11(2), Sch 2, paras 1, 5(b) with effect from a date to be appointed.

Licences for research

3

(1) A licence under this paragraph may authorise any of the following –

    (a)   *bringing about the creation of embryos in vitro, and*

    (b)   *keeping or using embryos,*

for the purposes of a project of research specified in the licence.

(2) A licence under this paragraph cannot authorise any activity unless it appears to the Authority to be necessary or desirable for the purpose of –

    (a)   *promoting advances in the treatment of infertility,*

    (b)   *increasing knowledge about the causes of congenital disease,*

    (c)   *increasing knowledge about the causes of miscarriages,*

    (d)   *developing more effective techniques of contraception, or*

    (e)   *developing methods for detecting the presence of gene or chromosome abnormalities in embryos before implantation,*

or for such other purposes as may be specified in regulations.

(3) Purposes may only be so specified with a view to the authorisation of projects of research which increase knowledge about the creation and development of embryos, or about disease, or enable such knowledge to be applied.

(4) A licence under this paragraph cannot authorise altering the genetic structure of any cell while it forms part of an embryo, except in such circumstances (if any) as may be specified in or determined in pursuance of regulations.

(5) A licence under this paragraph may authorise mixing sperm with the egg of a hamster, or other animal specified in directions, for the purpose of developing more effective techniques for determining the fertility or normality of sperm, but only where anything which forms is destroyed when the research is complete and, in any event, not later than the two cell stage.

(6) No licence under this paragraph shall be granted unless the Authority is satisfied that any proposed use of embryos is necessary for the purposes of the research.

(7) Subject to the provisions of this Act, a licence under this paragraph may be granted subject to such conditions as may be specified in the licence.

(8) A licence under this paragraph may authorise the performance of any of the activities referred to in sub-paragraph (1) or (5) above in such manner as may be so specified.

(9) A licence under this paragraph shall be granted for such period not exceeding three years as may be specified in the licence.

Prospective Amendment: Para 3 prospectively repealed and substituted, by subsequent paras 3, 3A, by the Human Fertilisation and Embryology Act 2008, s 11(2), Sch 2, paras 1, 6 with effect from a date to be appointed.

[Licences for research

3

(1) A licence under this paragraph may authorise any of the following—

    (a)   bringing about the creation of embryos *in vitro*, and

    (b)   keeping or using embryos,

for the purposes of a project of research specified in the licence.

(2) A licence under this paragraph may authorise mixing sperm with the egg of a hamster, or other animal specified in directions, for the purpose of developing more effective techniques for determining the fertility or normality of sperm, but only where anything which forms is destroyed when the research is complete and, in any event, no later than the two cell stage.

(3) A licence under this paragraph may authorise any of the following—

    (a)   bringing about the creation of human admixed embryos *in vitro*, and

    (b)   keeping or using human admixed embryos,

for the purposes of a project of research specified in the licence.

(4) A licence under sub-paragraph (3) may not authorise the activity which may be authorised by a licence under sub-paragraph (2).

(5) No licence under this paragraph is to be granted unless the Authority is satisfied that any proposed use of embryos or human admixed embryos is necessary for the purposes of the research.

(6) Subject to the provisions of this Act, a licence under this paragraph may be granted subject to such conditions as may be specified in the licence.

(7) A licence under this paragraph may authorise the performance of any of the activities referred to in sub-paragraph (1), (2) or (3) in such manner as may be so specified.

(8) A licence under this paragraph may be granted for such period not exceeding three years as may be specified in the licence.

(9) This paragraph has effect subject to paragraph 3A.

Purposes for which activities may be licensed under paragraph 3

3A

(1) A licence under paragraph 3 cannot authorise any activity unless the activity appears to the Authority—

    (a)   to be necessary or desirable for any of the purposes specified in sub-paragraph (2) ("the principal purposes"),

    (b)   to be necessary or desirable for the purpose of providing knowledge that, in the view of the Authority, may be capable of being applied for the purposes specified in sub-paragraph (2)(a) or (b), or

    (c)   to be necessary or desirable for such other purposes as may be specified in regulations.

(2) The principal purposes are—

   (a)   increasing knowledge about serious disease or other serious medical conditions,
   (b)   developing treatments for serious disease or other serious medical conditions,
   (c)   increasing knowledge about the causes of any congenital disease or congenital medical condition that does not fall within paragraph (a),
   (d)   promoting advances in the treatment of infertility,
   (e)   increasing knowledge about the causes of miscarriage,
   (f)   developing more effective techniques of contraception,
   (g)   developing methods for detecting the presence of gene, chromosome or mitochondrion abnormalities in embryos before implantation, or
   (h)   increasing knowledge about the development of embryos.]

General

4

(1) A licence under this Schedule can only authorise activities to be carried on –

   (a)   on premises specified in the licence or, in the case of activities to which section 3(1A)(b) or (1B) or 4(1A) applies, on relevant third party premises, and
   (b)   under the supervision of an individual designated in the licence.

(1A) A licence which authorises activities falling within paragraph 1 or 1A above may not also authorise activities falling within paragraph 3 above.

(2) A licence cannot –

   (a)   ...
   (b)   apply to more than one project of research,
   (c)   authorise activities to be carried on under the supervision of more than one individual, or
   (d)   apply to premises of the person who holds the licence in different places.

Amendments: Subparagraphs substituted and repealed, and word and paragraph inserted: SI 2007/1522.

Schedule 3
Consents to Use *of Gametes or Embryos* [or Storage of Gametes, Embryos or Human Admixed Embryos etc]

Section 12 etc

Consent

1

A consent under this Schedule must be given in writing and, in this Schedule, "effective consent" means a consent under this Schedule which has not been withdrawn

[1

(1) A consent under this Schedule, and any notice under paragraph 4 varying or withdrawing a consent under this Schedule, must be in writing and, subject to sub-paragraph (2), must be signed by the person giving it.

(2) A consent under this Schedule by a person who is unable to sign because of illness, injury or physical disability (a "person unable to sign"), and any notice under paragraph 4 by a person unable to sign varying or withdrawing a consent under this Schedule, is to be taken to comply with the requirement of sub-paragraph (1) as to signature if it is signed at the direction of the person unable to sign, in the presence of the person unable to sign and in the presence of at least one witness who attests the signature.

(3) In this Schedule "effective consent" means a consent under this Schedule which has not been withdrawn.]

Prospective Amendment: Para 1 prospectively inserted by Human Fertilisation and Embryology Act 2008, s 13, Sch 3, paras 1, 3 with effect from a date to be appointed.

2

(1) A consent to the use of any embryo must specify one or more of the following purposes –

    (a)   use in providing treatment services to the person giving consent, or that person and another specified person together,

    (b)   use in providing treatment services to persons not including the person giving consent, *or*

    [(ba) use for the purpose of training persons in embryo biopsy, embryo storage or other embryological techniques, or]

    (c)   use for the purposes of any project of research,

and may specify conditions subject to which the embryo may be so used.

[(1A) A consent to the use of any human admixed embryo must specify use for the purposes of any project of research and may specify conditions subject to which the human admixed embryo may be so used.]

(2) A consent to the storage of any gametes or any embryo must –

(a)   specify the maximum period of storage (if less than the statutory storage period), and

(b)   state what is to be done with the gametes or embryo if the person who gave the consent dies or is unable because of incapacity to vary the terms of the consent or to revoke it,

and may specify conditions subject to which the gametes or embryo may remain in storage.

[(2) A consent to the storage of any gametes, any embryo or any human admixed embryo must—

(a)   specify the maximum period of storage (if less than the statutory storage period),

(b)   except in a case falling within paragraph (c), state what is to be done with the gametes, embryo or human admixed embryo if the person who gave the consent dies or is unable, because the person lacks capacity to do so, to vary the terms of the consent or to withdraw it, and

(c)   where the consent is given by virtue of paragraph 8(2A) or 13(2), state what is to be done with the embryo or human admixed embryo if the person to whom the consent relates dies,

and may (in any case) specify conditions subject to which the gametes, embryo or human admixed embryo may remain in storage.

(2A) A consent to the use of a person's human cells to bring about the creation *in vitro* of an embryo or human admixed embryo is to be taken unless otherwise stated to include consent to the use of the cells after the person's death.

(2B) In relation to Scotland, the reference in sub-paragraph (2)(b) to the person lacking capacity is to be read as a reference to the person—

(a)   lacking capacity within the meaning of the Age of Legal Capacity (Scotland) Act 1991, or

(b)   being incapable within the meaning of section 1(6) of the Adults with Incapacity (Scotland) Act 2000.]

(3) A consent under this Schedule must provide for such other matters as the Authority may specify in directions.

(4)   A consent under this Schedule may apply –

(a)   to the use or storage of a particular embryo, or

(b)   in the case of a person providing gametes, to the use of storage of any embryo whose creation may be brought about using those gametes,

and in the paragraph (b) case the terms of the consent may be varied, or the consent may be withdrawn, in accordance with this Schedule either generally or in relation to a particular embryo or particular embryos

[(4) A consent under this Schedule may apply—

(a)   to the use or storage of a particular embryo or human admixed embryo, or

(b)   in the case of a person providing gametes or human cells, to the use or storage of—

    (i)   any embryo or human admixed embryo whose creation may be brought about using those gametes or those cells, and

    (ii) any embryo or human admixed embryo whose creation may be brought about using such an embryo or human admixed embryo.

(5) In the case of a consent falling within sub-paragraph (4)(b), the terms of the consent may be varied, or the consent may be withdrawn, in accordance with this Schedule either generally or in relation to—

(a)   a particular embryo or particular embryos, or

(b)   a particular human admixed embryo or particular human admixed embryos.]

Prospective Amendment: Words in italics prospectively repealed and subsequent sub-para (ba) substituted; sub-para (1A) prospectively inserted; sub-para (2) prospectively substituted, by subsequent sub-paras (2), (2A), (2B); sub-para (4) prospectively substituted, by subsequent sub-paras (4), (5) by Human Fertilisation and Embryology Act 2008, s 13, Sch 3 with effect from a date to be appointed.

Procedure for giving consent

3

(1) Before a person gives consent under this Schedule –

(a)   he must be given a suitable opportunity to receive proper counselling about the implications of taking the proposed steps, and

(b)   he must be provided with such relevant information as is proper.

(2) Before a person gives consent under this Schedule he must be informed of the effect of paragraph 4 [and, if relevant, paragraph 4A] below.

Prospective Amendment: Words prospectively inserted by Human Fertilisation and Embryology Act 2008, s 13, Sch 3, paras 1, 5 with effect from a date to be appointed.

Variation and withdrawal of consent

4

(1) The terms of any consent under this Schedule may from time to time be varied, and the consent may be withdrawn, by notice given by the person who gave the consent to the person keeping the gametes *or embryo* [, human cells, embryo or human admixed embryo] to which the consent is relevant.

(2) *The* [Subject to sub-paragraph (3), the] terms of any consent to the use of any embryo cannot be varied, and such consent cannot be withdrawn, once the embryo has been used –

(a)   in providing treatment services, or

[(aa) in training persons in embryo biopsy, embryo storage or other embryological techniques, or]

(b)   for the purposes of any project of research.

[(3) Where the terms of any consent to the use of an embryo ("embryo A") include consent to the use of an embryo or human admixed embryo whose creation may be brought about in vitro using embryo A, that consent to the use of that subsequent embryo or human admixed embryo cannot be varied or withdrawn once embryo A has been used for one or more of the purposes mentioned in sub-paragraph (2)(a) or (b).

(4) Subject to sub-paragraph (5), the terms of any consent to the use of any human admixed embryo cannot be varied, and such consent cannot be withdrawn, once the human admixed embryo has been used for the purposes of any project of research.

(5) Where the terms of any consent to the use of a human admixed embryo ("human admixed embryo A") include consent to the use of a human admixed embryo or embryo whose creation may be brought about in vitro using human admixed embryo A, that consent to the use of that subsequent human admixed embryo or embryo cannot be varied or withdrawn once human admixed embryo A has been used for the purposes of any project of research.]

Prospective Amendment: Words in italics repealed and subsequent words in square brackets prospectively substituted; sub-paras (3)–(5) prospectively inserted; Human Fertilisation and Embryology Act 2008, s 13, Sch 3, paras 1, 6(1), (2), (3)(a), (3)(b) with effect from a date to be appointed.

[4A

(1) This paragraph applies where—

    (a)   a permitted embryo, the creation of which was brought about *in vitro*, is in storage,

    (b)   it was created for use in providing treatment services,

    (c)   before it is used in providing treatment services, one of the persons whose gametes were used to bring about its creation ("P") gives the person keeping the embryo notice withdrawing P's consent to the storage of the embryo, and

    (d)   the embryo was not to be used in providing treatment services to P alone.

(2) The person keeping the embryo must as soon as possible take all reasonable steps to notify each interested person in relation to the embryo of P's withdrawal of consent.

(3) For the purposes of sub-paragraph (2), a person is an interested person in relation to an embryo if the embryo was to be used in providing treatment services to that person.

(4) Storage of the embryo remains lawful until

    (a)   the end of the period of 12 months beginning with the day on which the notice mentioned in sub-paragraph (1) was received from P, or

    (b)   if, before the end of that period, the person keeping the embryo receives a notice from each person notified of P's withdrawal under sub-paragraph (2) stating that the person consents to the destruction of the embryo, the time at which the last of those notices is received.

(5) The reference in sub-paragraph (1)(a) to a permitted embryo is to be read in accordance with section 3ZA.]

Prospective Amendment: Prospectively inserted by Human Fertilisation and Embryology Act 2008, s 13, Sch 3, paras 1, 7 with effect from a date to be appointed.

Use of gametes for treatment of others

5

(1) A person's gametes must not be used for the purposes of treatment services [or non-medical fertility services] unless there is an effective consent by that person to their being so used and they are used in accordance with the terms of the consent.

(2) A person's gametes must not be received for use for those purposes unless there is an effective consent by that person to their being so used.

(3) This paragraph does not apply to the use of a person's gametes for the purpose of that person, or that person and another together, receiving treatment services.

Prospective Amendment: Words in square brackets prospectively inserted by Human Fertilisation and Embryology Act 2008, s 13, Sch 3, paras 1, 8 with effect from a date to be appointed.

In vitro fertilisation and subsequent use of embryo

6

(1) A person's gametes [or human cells] must not be used to bring about the creation of any embryo *in vitro* unless there is an effective consent by that person to any embryo[,] the creation of which may be brought about with the use of those gametes [or human cells] being used for one or more of the purposes mentioned in *paragraph 2(1)* [paragraph 2(1)(a),(b),(ba) and (c)] above.

(2) An embryo the creation of which was brought about *in vitro* must not be received by any person unless there is an effective consent by *each person whose gametes were used to bring about the creation of* [each relevant person in relation to] the embryo to the use for one or more of the purposes mentioned in paragraph *2(1)* [paragraph 2(1)(a),(b),(ba) and (c)] above of the embryo.

(3) An embryo the creation of which was brought about *in vitro* must not be used for any purpose unless there is an effective consent by *each person whose gametes were used to bring about the creation of* [each relevant person in relation to] the embryo to the use for that purpose of the embryo and the embryo is used in accordance with those consents.

[(3A) If the Authority is satisfied that the parental consent conditions in paragraph 15 are met in relation to the proposed use under a licence of the human cells of a person who has not attained the age of 18 years ("C"), the Authority may in the licence authorise the application of sub-paragraph (3B) in relation to C.

(3B) Where the licence authorises the application of this subparagraph, the effective consent of a person having parental responsibility for C—

(a)   to the use of C's human cells to bring about the creation of an embryo *in vitro* for use for the purposes of a project of research, or

(b)   to the use for those purposes of an embryo in relation to which C is a relevant person by reason only of the use of C's human cells,

is to be treated for the purposes of sub-paragraphs (1) to (3) as the effective consent of C.

(3C) If C attains the age of 18 years or the condition in paragraph 15(3) ceases to be met in relation to C, paragraph 4 has effect in relation to C as if any effective consent previously given under subparagraphs (1) to (3) by a person having parental responsibility for C had been given by C but, subject to that, sub-paragraph (3B) ceases to apply in relation to C.

(3D) Sub-paragraphs (1) to (3) have effect subject to paragraphs 16 and 20.

(3E) For the purposes of sub-paragraphs (2), (3) and (3B), each of the following is a relevant person in relation to an embryo the creation of which was brought about in vitro ("embryo A")—

(a)   each person whose gametes or human cells were used to bring about the creation of embryo A,

(b)   each person whose gametes or human cells were used to bring about the creation of any other embryo, the creation of which was brought about in vitro, which was used to bring about the creation of embryo A, and

(c)   each person whose gametes or human cells were used to bring about the creation of any human admixed embryo, the creation of which was brought about in vitro, which was used to bring about the creation of embryo A.]

(4) Any consent required by this paragraph is in addition to any consent that may be required by paragraph 5 above.

Prospective Amendment: Words in square brackets inserted; words in italics prospectively repealed and subsequent words in square brackets prospectively inserted; sub-paras (3A)–(3E) inserted by the Human Fertilisation and Embryology Act 2008, s 13, Sch 3, paras 1, 9(1), (5) with effect from a date to be appointed.

Embryos obtained by lavage, etc

7

(1) An embryo taken from a woman must not be used for any purpose unless there is an effective consent by her to the use of the embryo for that purpose and it is used in accordance with the consent.

(2) An embryo taken from a woman must not be received by any person for use for any purpose unless there is an effective consent by her to the use of the embryo for that purpose.

(3) *This paragraph does* [Sub paragraphs (1) and (2) do] not apply to the use, for the purpose of providing a woman with treatment services, of an embryo taken from her.

[(4) An embryo taken from a woman must not be used to bring about the creation of any embryo in *vitro* or any human admixed embryo in *vitro.*]

Prospective Amendment: Para 7, in sub-para (3) words in italics prospectively repealed and subsequent words inserted; sub-para (4) prospectively inserted by the Human Fertilisation and Embryology Act 2008, s 13, Sch 3, paras 1, 10(1), (3) with effect from a date to be appointed.

Storage of gametes and embryos

8

(1) A person's gametes must not be kept in storage unless there is an effective consent by that person to their storage and they are stored in accordance with the consent.

(2) An embryo the creation of which was brought about *in vitro* must not be kept in storage unless there is an effective consent, by each *person whose gametes were used to bring about the creation of* [relevant person in relation to]the embryo, to the storage of the embryo and the embryo is stored in accordance with those consents.

[(2A) Where a licence authorises the application of paragraph 6(3B) in relation to a person who has not attained the age of 18 years ("C"), the effective consent of a person having parental responsibility for C to the storage of an embryo in relation to which C is a relevant person by reason only of the use of C's human cells is to be treated for the purposes of sub-paragraph (2) as the effective consent of C.

(2B) If C attains the age of 18 years or the condition in paragraph 15(3) ceases to be met in relation to C, paragraph 4 has effect in relation to C as if any effective consent previously given under subparagraph (2) by a person having parental responsibility for C had been given by C but, subject to that, sub-paragraph (2A) ceases to apply in relation to C.

(2C) For the purposes of sub-paragraphs (2) and (2A), each of the following is a relevant person in relation to an embryo the creation of which was brought about in vitro ("embryo A")—

    (a)   each person whose gametes or human cells were used to bring about the creation of embryo A,

    (b)   each person whose gametes or human cells were used to bring about the creation of any other embryo, the creation of which was brought about in vitro, which was used to bring about the creation of embryo A, and

    (c)   each person whose gametes or human cells were used to bring about the creation of any human admixed embryo, the creation of which was brought about in vitro, which was used to bring about the creation of embryo A.]

(3) An embryo taken from a woman must not be kept in storage unless there is an effective consent by her to its storage and it is stored in accordance with the consent.

[(4) Sub-paragraph (1) has effect subject to paragraphs 9 and 10; and sub-paragraph (2) has effect subject to paragraphs 4A(4), 16 and 20.]

Prospective Amendment: Para 8, in sub-para (2) words in italics prospectively repealed and subsequent words in square brackets inserted; sub-paras (2A)–(2C), (4) prospectively inserted by the Human Fertilisation and Embryology Act 2008, s 13, Sch 3, paras 1, 11(1), (3) with effect from a date to be appointed.

[Cases where consent not required for storage

9

(1) The gametes of a person ("C") may be kept in storage without C's consent if the following conditions are met.

(2) Condition A is that the gametes are lawfully taken from or provided by C before C attains the age of 18 years.

(3) Condition B is that, before the gametes are first stored, a registered medical practitioner certifies in writing that C is expected to undergo medical treatment and that in the opinion of the registered medical practitioner—

    (a)   the treatment is likely to cause a significant impairment of C's fertility, and
    (b)   the storage of the gametes is in C's best interests.

(4) Condition C is that, at the time when the gametes are first stored, either—

    (a)   C has not attained the age of 16 years and is not competent to deal with the issue of consent to the storage of the gametes, or
    (b)   C has attained that age but, although not lacking capacity to consent to the storage of the gametes, is not competent to deal with the issue of consent to their storage.

(5) Condition D is that C has not, since becoming competent to deal with the issue of consent to the storage of the gametes—

    (a)   given consent under this Schedule to the storage of the gametes, or
    (b)   given written notice to the person keeping the gametes that C does not wish them to continue to be stored.

(6) In relation to Scotland, sub-paragraphs (1) to (5) are to be read with the following modifications—

    (a)   for sub-paragraph (4), substitute—

(4) Condition C is that, at the time when the gametes are first stored, C does not have capacity (within the meaning of section 2(4) of the Age of Legal Capacity (Scotland) Act 1991) to consent to the storage of the gametes.", and

(b)　in sub-paragraph (5), for "becoming competent to deal with the issue of consent to the storage of the gametes" substitute "acquiring such capacity.

10

(1)　The gametes of a person ("P") may be kept in storage without P's consent if the following conditions are met.

(2)　Condition A is that the gametes are lawfully taken from or provided by P after P has attained the age of 16 years.

(3)　Condition B is that, before the gametes are first stored, a registered medical practitioner certifies in writing that P is expected to undergo medical treatment and that in the opinion of the registered medical practitioner—

(a)　the treatment is likely to cause a significant impairment of P's fertility,
(b)　P lacks capacity to consent to the storage of the gametes,
(c)　P is likely at some time to have that capacity, and
(d)　the storage of the gametes is in P's best interests.

(4)　Condition C is that, at the time when the gametes are first stored, P lacks capacity to consent to their storage.

(5)　Condition D is that P has not subsequently, at a time when P has capacity to give a consent under this Schedule—

(a)　given consent to the storage of the gametes, or
(b)　given written notice to the person keeping the gametes that P does not wish them to continue to be stored.

(6)　In relation to Scotland—

(a)　references in sub-paragraphs (3) and (4) to P lacking capacity to consent are to be read as references to P being incapable, within the meaning of section 1(6) of the Adults with Incapacity (Scotland) Act 2000, of giving such consent,
(b)　the references in sub-paragraphs (3) and (5) to P having capacity are to be read as references to P not being so incapable, and
(c)　that Act applies to the storage of gametes under this paragraph to the extent specified in section 84A of that Act.

11

A person's gametes must not be kept in storage by virtue of paragraph 9 or 10 after the person's death.[Creation, use and storage of human admixed embryos

12

(1)　A person's gametes or human cells must not be used to bring about the creation of any human admixed embryo in vitro unless there is an effective consent by that person to any human admixed embryo, the creation of which may be brought about with the use of those gametes or human cells, being used for the purposes of any project of research.

(2) A human admixed embryo the creation of which was brought about in vitro must not be received by any person unless there is an effective consent by each relevant person in relation to the human admixed embryo to the use of the human admixed embryo for the purposes of any project of research.

(3) A human admixed embryo the creation of which was brought about in vitro must not be used for the purposes of a project of research unless—

(a) there is an effective consent by each relevant person in relation to the human admixed embryo to the use of the human admixed embryo for that purpose, and

(b) the human admixed embryo is used in accordance with those consents.

(4) If the Authority is satisfied that the parental consent conditions in paragraph 15 are met in relation to the proposed use under a licence of the human cells of a person who has not attained the age of 18 years ("C"), the Authority may in the licence authorise the application of sub-paragraph (5) in relation to C.

(5) Where the licence authorises the application of this subparagraph, the effective consent of a person having parental responsibility for C—

(a) to the use of C's human cells to bring about the creation of a human admixed embryo in vitro for use for the purposes of a project of research, or

(b) to the use for those purposes of a human admixed embryo in relation to which C is a relevant person by reason only of the use of C's human cells,

is to be treated for the purposes of sub-paragraphs (1) to (3) as the effective consent of C.

(6) If C attains the age of 18 years or the condition in paragraph 15(3) ceases to be met in relation to C, paragraph 4 has effect in relation to C as if any effective consent previously given under subparagraphs (1) to (3) by a person having parental responsibility for C had been given by C but, subject to that, sub-paragraph (5) ceases to apply in relation to C.

(7) Sub-paragraphs (1) to (3) have effect subject to paragraphs 16 and 20.

13

(1) A human admixed embryo the creation of which was brought about in vitro must not be kept in storage unless—

(a) there is an effective consent by each relevant person in relation to the human admixed embryo to the storage of the human admixed embryo, and

(b) the human admixed embryo is stored in accordance with those consents.

(2) Where a licence authorises the application of paragraph 12(5) in relation to a person who has not attained the age of 18 years ("C"), the effective consent of a person having parental responsibility for C to the storage of a human admixed embryo in relation to which C is a relevant person by reason only of the use of C's human cells is to be treated for the purposes of sub-paragraph (1) as the effective consent of C.

(3) If C attains the age of 18 years or the condition in paragraph 15(3) ceases to be met in relation to C, paragraph 4 has effect in relation to C as if any effective consent previously given under subparagraph (1) by a person having parental responsibility for C had been given by C but, subject to that, sub-paragraph (2) ceases to apply in relation to C.

(4) Sub-paragraph (1) has effect subject to paragraphs 16 and 20.

14

For the purposes of paragraphs 12 and 13, each of the following is a relevant person in relation to a human admixed embryo the creation of which was brought about in vitro ("human admixed embryo A")—

(a)   each person whose gametes or human cells were used to bring about the creation of human admixed embryo A,

(b)   each person whose gametes or human cells were used to bring about the creation of any embryo, the creation of which was brought about in vitro, which was used to bring about the creation of human admixed embryo A, and

(c)   each person whose gametes or human cells were used to bring about the creation of any other human admixed embryo, the creation of which was brought about in vitro, which was used to bring about the creation of human admixed embryo A.]

[Parental consent conditions

15

(1) In relation to a person who has not attained the age of 18 years ("C"), the parental consent conditions referred to in paragraphs 6(3A) and 12(4) are as follows.

(2) Condition A is that C suffers from, or is likely to develop, a serious disease, a serious physical or mental disability or any other serious medical condition.

(3) Condition B is that either—

(a)   C is not competent to deal with the issue of consent to the use of C's human cells to bring about the creation in vitro of an embryo or human admixed embryo for use for the purposes of a project of research, or

(b)   C has attained the age of 16 years but lacks capacity to consent to such use of C's human cells.

(4) Condition C is that any embryo or human admixed embryo to be created in vitro is to be used for the purposes of a project of research which is intended to increase knowledge about—

(a)   the disease, disability or medical condition mentioned in sub-paragraph (2) or any similar disease, disability or medical condition, or

(b)   the treatment of, or care of persons affected by, that disease, disability or medical condition or any similar disease, disability or medical condition.

(5) Condition D is that there are reasonable grounds for believing that research of comparable effectiveness cannot be carried out if the only human cells that can be used to bring about the creation *in vitro* of embryos or human admixed embryos for use for the purposes of the project are the human cells of persons who—

(a)   have attained the age of 18 years and have capacity to consent to the use of their human cells to bring about the creation in vitro of an embryo or human admixed embryo for use for the purposes of the project, or

(b)   have not attained that age but are competent to deal with the issue of consent to such use of their human cells.

(6) In relation to Scotland, sub-paragraphs (1) to (5) are to be read with the following modifications—

(a)   for sub-paragraph (3) substitute—

(3) Condition B is that C does not have capacity (within the meaning of section 2(4ZB) of the Age of Legal Capacity (Scotland) Act 1991) to consent to the use of C's human cells to bring about the creation in vitro of an embryo or human admixed embryo for use for the purposes of a project of research,

(b)   in sub-paragraph (5)(a), for "have capacity to consent" substitute "are not incapable (within the meaning of section 1(6) of the Adults with Incapacity (Scotland) Act 2000) of giving consent", and

(c)   in sub-paragraph (5)(b), for "are competent to deal with the issue of" substitute "have capacity (within the meaning of section 2(4ZB) of the Age of Legal Capacity (Scotland) Act 1991) to.]

Parental consent conditions

16

(1) If, in relation to the proposed use under a licence of the human cells of a person who has attained the age of 18 years ("P"), the Authority is satisfied—

(a)   that the conditions in paragraph 17 are met,

(b)   that paragraphs (1) to (4) of paragraph 18 have been complied with, and

(c)   that the condition in paragraph 18(5) is met,

the Authority may in the licence authorise the application of this paragraph in relation to P.

(2) Where a licence authorises the application of this paragraph, this Schedule does not require the consent of P—

  (a)   to the use (whether during P's life or after P's death) of P's human cells to bring about the creation in vitro of an embryo or human admixed embryo for use for the purposes of a project of research,
  (b)   to the storage or the use for those purposes (whether during P's life or after P's death) of an embryo or human admixed embryo in relation to which P is a relevant person by reason only of the use of P's human cells.

(3) This paragraph has effect subject to paragraph 19.

Consent to use of human cells etc not required: adult lacking capacity

17

(1) The conditions referred to in paragraph 16(1)(a) are as follows.

(2) Condition A is that P suffers from, or is likely to develop, a serious disease, a serious physical or mental disability or any other serious medical condition.

(3) Condition B is that P lacks capacity to consent to the use of P's human cells to bring about the creation in vitro of an embryo or human admixed embryo for use for the purposes of a project of research.

(4) Condition C is that the person responsible under the licence has no reason to believe that P had refused such consent at a time when P had that capacity.

(5) Condition D is that it appears unlikely that P will at some time have that capacity.

(6) Condition E is that any embryo or human admixed embryo to be created in vitro is to be used for the purposes of a project of research which is intended to increase knowledge about—

  (a)   the disease, disability or medical condition mentioned in sub-paragraph (2) or any similar disease, disability or medical condition, or
  (b)   the treatment of, or care of persons affected by, that disease, disability or medical condition or any similar disease, disability or medical condition.

(7) Condition F is that there are reasonable grounds for believing that research of comparable effectiveness cannot be carried out if the only human cells that can be used to bring about the creation in vitro of embryos or human admixed embryos for use for the purposes of the project are the human cells of persons who—

  (a)   have attained the age of 18 years and have capacity to consent to the use of their human cells to bring about the creation in vitro of an embryo or human admixed embryo for use for the purposes of the project, or
  (b)   have not attained that age but are competent to deal with the issue of consent to such use of their human cells.

(8) In this paragraph and paragraph 18 references to the person responsible under the licence are to be read, in a case where an application for a licence is being made, as references to the person who is to be the person responsible.

(9) In relation to Scotland—

    (a)   references in sub-paragraphs (3) to (5) to P lacking, or having, capacity to consent are to be read respectively as references to P being, or not being, incapable (within the meaning of section 1(6) of the Adults with Incapacity (Scotland) Act 2000) of giving such consent, and

    (b)   sub-paragraph (7) is to be read with the following modifications—

        (i)   in paragraph (a), for "have capacity to consent" substitute "are not incapable (within the meaning of section 1(6) of the Adults with Incapacity (Scotland) Act 2000) of giving consent", and

        (ii)   in paragraph (b), for "are competent to deal with the issue of" substitute "have capacity (within the meaning of section 2(4ZB) of the Age of Legal Capacity (Scotland) Act 1991) to.

Consulting carers etc in case of adult lacking capacity

18

(1) This paragraph applies in relation to a person who has attained the age of 18 years ("P") where the person responsible under the licence ("R") wishes to use P's human cells to bring about the creation in vitro of an embryo or human admixed embryo for use for the purposes of a project of research, in a case where P lacks capacity to consent to their use.

(2) R must take reasonable steps to identify a person who—

    (a)   otherwise than in a professional capacity or for remuneration, is engaged in caring for P or is interested in P's welfare, and

    (b)   is prepared to be consulted by R under this paragraph of this Schedule.

(3) If R is unable to identify such a person R must nominate a person who—

    (a)   is prepared to be consulted by R under this paragraph of this Schedule, but

    (b)   has no connection with the project.

(4) R must provide the person identified under sub-paragraph (2) or nominated under sub-paragraph (3) ("F") with information about the proposed use of human cells to bring about the creation in vitro of embryos or human admixed embryos for use for the purposes of the project and ask F what, in F's opinion, P's wishes and feelings about the use of P's human cells for that purpose would be likely to be if P had capacity in relation to the matter.

(5) The condition referred to in paragraph 16(1)(c) is that, on being consulted, F has not advised R that in F's opinion P's wishes and feelings would be likely to lead P to decline to consent to the use of P's human cells for that purpose.

(6) In relation to Scotland, the references in sub-paragraphs (1) and (4) to P lacking, or having, capacity to consent are to be read respectively as references

to P being, or not being, incapable (within the meaning of section 1(6) of the Adults with Incapacity (Scotland) Act 2000) of giving such consent.

Effect of acquiring capacity

19

(1) Paragraph 16 does not apply to the use of P's human cells to bring about the creation in vitro of an embryo or human admixed embryo if, at a time before the human cells are used for that purpose, P—

    (a)   has capacity to consent to their use, and

    (b)   gives written notice to the person keeping the human cells that P does not wish them to be used for that purpose.

(2) Paragraph 16 does not apply to the storage or use of an embryo or human admixed embryo whose creation in vitro was brought about with the use of P's human cells if, at a time before the embryo or human admixed embryo is used for the purposes of the project of research, P—

    (a)   has capacity to consent to the storage or use, and

    (b)   gives written notice to the person keeping the human cells that P does not wish them to be used for that purpose.

(3) In relation to Scotland, the references in sub-paragraphs (1)(a) and (2)(a) to P having capacity to consent are to be read as references to P not being incapable (within the meaning of section 1(6) of the Adults with Incapacity (Scotland) Act 2000) of giving such consent.

Use of cells or cell lines in existence before relevant commencement date

20

(1) Where a licence authorises the application of this paragraph in relation to qualifying cells, this Schedule does not require the consent of a person ("P")—

    (a)   to the use of qualifying cells of P to bring about the creation in vitro of an embryo or human admixed embryo for use for the purposes of a project of research, or

    (b)   to the storage or the use for those purposes of an embryo or human admixed embryo in relation to which P is a relevant person by reason only of the use of qualifying cells of P.

(2) "Qualifying cells" are human cells which—

    (a)   were lawfully stored for research purposes immediately before the commencement date, or

    (b)   are derived from human cells which were lawfully stored for those purposes at that time.

(3) The "commencement date" is the date on which paragraph 9(2)(a) of Schedule 3 to the Human Fertilisation and Embryology Act 2008 (requirement for consent to use of human cells to create an embryo) comes into force.

Conditions for grant of exemption in paragraph 20

21

(1) A licence may not authorise the application of paragraph 20 unless the Authority is satisfied—

    (a)   that there are reasonable grounds for believing that scientific research will be adversely affected to a significant extent if the only human cells that can be used to bring about the creation in vitro of embryos or human admixed embryos for use for the purposes of the project of research are—

        (i)   human cells in respect of which there is an effective consent to their use to bring about the creation in vitro of embryos or human admixed embryos for use for those purposes, or

        (ii)   human cells which by virtue of paragraph 16 can be used without such consent, and

    (b)   that any of the following conditions is met in relation to each of the persons whose human cells are qualifying cells which are to be used for the purposes of the project of research.

(2) Condition A is that—

    (a)   it is not reasonably possible for the person responsible under the licence ("R") to identify the person falling within sub-paragraph (1)(b) ("P"), and

    (b)   where any information that relates to P (without identifying P or enabling P to be identified) is available to R, that information does not suggest that P would have objected to the use of P's human cells to bring about the creation in vitro of an embryo or human admixed embryo for use for the purposes of the project.

(3) Condition B is that—

    (a)   the person falling within sub-paragraph (1)(b) ("P") is dead or the person responsible under the licence ("R") believes on reasonable grounds that P is dead,

    (b)   the information relating to P that is available to R does not suggest that P would have objected to the use of P's human cells to bring about the creation in vitro of an embryo or human admixed embryo for use for the purposes of the project, and

    (c)   a person who stood in a qualifying relationship to P immediately before P died (or is believed to have died) has given consent in writing to the use of P's human cells to bring about the creation in vitro of an embryo or human admixed embryo for use for the purposes of the project.

(4) Condition C is that—

    (a)   the person responsible under the licence ("R") has taken all reasonable steps to contact—

        (i)   the person falling within sub-paragraph (1)(b) ("P"), or

(ii)   in a case where P is dead or R believes on reasonable grounds that P is dead, persons who could give consent for the purposes of sub-paragraph (3)(c),

but has been unable to do so, and

(b)   the information relating to P that is available to R does not suggest that P would have objected to the use of P's human cells to bring about the creation in vitro of an embryo or human admixed embryo for use for the purposes of the project.

(5) The HTA consent provisions apply in relation to consent for the purposes of sub-paragraph (3)(c) as they apply in relation to consent for the purposes of section 3(6)(c) of the Human Tissue Act 2004; and for the purposes of this sub-paragraph the HTA consent provisions are to be treated as if they extended to Scotland.

(6) In sub-paragraph (5) "the HTA consent provisions" means subsections (4), (5), (6), (7) and (8)(a) and (b) of section 27 of the Human Tissue Act 2004.

(7) In this paragraph references to the person responsible under the licence are to be read, in a case where an application for a licence is being made, as references to the person who is to be the person responsible.

(8) Paragraphs 1 to 4 of this Schedule do not apply in relation to a consent given for the purposes of sub-paragraph (3)(c).]

Prospective Amendment: Schedule prospectively inserted by Human Embryology and Fertilisation Act 2008 s 14(5), Sch 4 with effect from a date to be appointed.

[Interpretation

22

(1) In this Schedule references to human cells are to human cells

which are not—

(a)   cells of the female or male germ line, or
(b)   cells of an embryo.

(2) References in this Schedule to an embryo or a human admixed embryo which was used to bring about the creation of an embryo ("embryo A") or a human admixed embryo ("human admixed embryo A") include an embryo or, as the case may be, a human admixed embryo which was used to bring about the creation of—

(a)   an embryo or human admixed embryo which was used to bring about the creation of embryo A or human admixed embryo A, and
(b)   the predecessor of that embryo or human admixed embryo mentioned in paragraph (a), and
(c)   the predecessor of that predecessor, and so on.

(3) References in this Schedule to an embryo or a human admixed embryo whose creation may be brought about using an embryo or a human admixed embryo are to be read in accordance with subparagraph (2).

(4) References in this Schedule (however expressed) to the use of human cells to bring about the creation of an embryo or a human admixed embryo include the use of human cells to alter the embryo or, as the case may be, the human admixed embryo.

(5) References in this Schedule to parental responsibility are—

  (a)   in relation to England and Wales, to be read in accordance with the Children Act 1989,
  (b)   in relation to Northern Ireland, to be read in accordance with the Children (Northern Ireland) Order 1995, and
  (c)   in relation to Scotland, to be read as references to parental responsibilities and parental rights within the meaning of the Children (Scotland) Act 1995.

(6) References in this Schedule to capacity are, in relation to England and Wales, to be read in accordance with the Mental Capacity Act 2005.

(7) References in this Schedule to the age of 18 years are, in relation to Scotland, to be read as references to the age of 16 years.]

Prospective Amendment: Schedule prospectively inserted by Human Embryology and Fertilisation Act 2008s 14(5), Sch 4 with effect from a date to be appointed.

[Schedule 3ZA
Circumstances in which Offer of Counselling Required as Condition of Licence for Treatment

[PART 1
KINDS OF TREATMENT IN RELATION TO WHICH COUNSELLING MUST BE OFFERED]

Prospective Amendment: Prospectively inserted by Human Fertilisation and Embryology Act 2008, s 14(5), Sch 4 with effect from a date to be appointed.

1

The treatment services involve the use of the gametes of any person and that person's consent is required under paragraph 5 of Schedule 3 for the use in question.

2

The treatment services involve the use of any embryo the creation of which was brought about in vitro.

3

The treatment services involve the use of an embryo taken from a woman and the consent of the woman from whom the embryo was taken was required under paragraph 7 of Schedule 3 for the use in question.]

Prospective Amendment: Prospectively inserted by Human Fertilisation and Embryology Act 2008, s 14(5), Sch 4 with effect from a date to be appointed.

[PART 2
EVENTS IN CONNECTION WITH WHICH COUNSELLING MUST BE OFFERED

4

A man gives the person responsible a notice under paragraph (a) of subsection (1) of section 37 of the Human Fertilisation and Embryology Act 2008 (agreed fatherhood conditions) in a case where the woman for whom the treatment services are provided has previously given a notice under paragraph (b) of that subsection referring to the man.

5

The woman for whom the treatment services are provided gives the person responsible a notice under paragraph (b) of that subsection in a case where the man to whom the notice relates has previously given a notice under paragraph (a) of that subsection.

6

A woman gives the person responsible notice under paragraph (a) of subsection (1) of section 44 of that Act (agreed female parenthood conditions) in a case where the woman for whom the treatment services are provided has previously given a notice under paragraph (b) of that subsection referring to her.

7

The woman for whom the treatment services are provided gives the person responsible a notice under paragraph (b) of that subsection in a case where the other woman to whom the notice relates has previously given a notice under paragraph (a) of that subsection.]

Prospective Amendment: Schedule prospectively inserted by Human Embryology and Fertilisation Act 2008 s 14(5), Sch 4 with effect from a date to be appointed.

Schedule 3A
Supplementary Licence Conditions: Human Application

Section 14A

Traceability and coding system

1

Licence conditions shall require that all persons to whom a licence applies adopt such systems as the Authority considers appropriate to secure –

    (a)   in relation to traceability, compliance with the requirements of Article 8 (traceability) of the first Directive and Article 9 (traceability) of the third Directive, and

    (b)   in relation to the coding of information, compliance with the requirements of Article 25 (coding of information) of the first Directive and Article 10 (European coding system) of the third Directive.

2

Licence conditions imposed in accordance with paragraph 1 may specify the coding system which must be applied in relation to gametes and embryos intended for human application.

Serious adverse events and serious adverse reactions

3

Licence conditions shall require such –

    (a)   systems to report, investigate, register and transmit information about serious adverse events and serious adverse reactions, and

    (b)   accurate, rapid and verifiable procedures for recalling from distribution any product which may be related to a serious adverse event or serious adverse reaction,

to be in place as are necessary to secure compliance with the requirements of Article 11 (notification of serious adverse events and reactions) of the first Directive and Article 5 (notification of serious adverse reactions) and Article 6 (notification of serious adverse events) of the third Directive.

Third party agreements and termination of licensed activities

4

For the purpose of securing compliance with the requirements of Articles 21(5) (tissue and cell storage conditions) and 24 (relations between tissue establishments and third parties) of the first Directive, licence conditions shall specify the requirements that must be met in relation to the termination of storage activities authorised by the licence and in relation to third party agreements.

Requirements for procurement of gametes and embryos

5

Licence conditions shall require all persons to whom a licence applies who are authorised to procure gametes or embryos, or both, to comply with the requirements (including as to staff training, written agreements with staff, standard operating procedures, and appropriate facilities and equipment) laid down in Article 2 (requirements for the procurement of human tissues and cells) of the second Directive.

Selection criteria and laboratory tests required for donors of reproductive cells

6

In relation to partner-donated sperm which is not intended to be used without processing or storage, licence conditions shall require compliance with the selection criteria for donors and the requirements for laboratory tests laid down in section 2 (partner donation (not direct use)) of Annex III (selection criteria and laboratory tests required for donors of reproductive cells) to the second Directive.

7

In relation to donations of gametes or embryos other than partner-donated sperm or partner-created embryos, licence conditions shall require compliance with the selection criteria for donors and the requirements for laboratory tests laid down in section 3 (donations other than by partners) of Annex III to the second Directive.

8

Licence conditions shall require that the laboratory tests required by sections 2 and 3 of Annex III to the second Directive to be carried out for the purpose of selecting gametes or embryos for donation, meet the requirements of section 4 (general requirements to be met for determining biological markers) of Annex III to the second Directive.

Donation and procurement procedures and reception at the tissue establishment

9

In relation to –

(a)   donation and procurement procedures, and
(b)   the reception of gametes and embryos at the premises to which a licence relates or at relevant third party premises,

licence conditions shall require compliance with the requirements of Article 15(3) (selection, evaluation and procurement) and Article 19(4) to (6) (tissue and cell reception) of the first Directive and with the requirements laid down in the provisions of the second Directive listed in the right-hand column, the subject-matter of which are described in the left-hand column in respect of those provisions.

	Relevant provisions of the second Directive
1 Donation and procurement procedures	
Consent and donor identification (record of consent, method of identification, donor interview)	Annex IV, point 1.1
Donor evaluation: other than partner-donated sperm and partner-created embryos and autologous donors (assessment of donor's medical and behavioural information)	Annex IV, point 1.2
Procurement procedures for gametes and embryos (requirements relating to procurement procedures and instruments)	Annex IV, point 1.3
Donor documentation (record of donor and the procurement)	Annex IV, point 1.4
Packaging (requirements as to packaging and shipping containers)	Annex IV, point 1.5
Labelling of the procured gametes and embryos (minimum labelling requirements)	Annex IV, point 1.6
Labelling of the shipping container (minimum labeling requirements)	Annex IV, point 1.7
2 Reception of tissues and cells at the tissue establishment	
Verification upon arrival (procedures for verification and requirement for quarantine until verification)	Annex IV, points 2.1 to 2.3
Registration of data (other than in respect of partner-donated sperm and partner-created embryos)	Annex IV, point 2.4
Registration of data (partner-donated sperm and partner-created embryos)	Annex IV, point 2.5

Requirements for holding a licence under paragraph 1, 1A or 2 of Schedule 2

10

Licence conditions shall require compliance with the requirements laid down in the provisions of the third Directive listed in the right-hand column, the subject-matter of which are described in the left-hand column in respect of those provisions.

	Relevant provisions of the third Directive
Organisation and management (requirements as to organisational structure, management systems, and third party agreements)	Annex I, Part A
Personnel (number, competence, responsibilities and training)	Annex I, Part B
Equipment and materials (appropriate for use, validation, maintenance, and specifications)	Annex I, Part C
Facilities and premises (suitability, environment, storage, and maintenance)	Annex I, Part D
Documentation and records (standard operating procedures, document control, record reliability)	Annex I, Part E
Quality review (quality management system, investigations, corrective action, and reviews)	Annex I, Part F

Requirements for holding a licence for gametes and embryo preparation processes

11

In respect of gametes and embryos preparation processes, licence conditions shall require compliance with –

(a) the requirements of Article 20(2) and (3) (tissue and cell processing) and Article 21(2) to (4) of the first Directive, and

(b) the requirements laid down in the provisions of the third Directive listed in the right-hand column, the subject-matter of which are described in the left-hand column in respect of those provisions.

	Relevant provisions of the third Directive
Reception of gametes and embryos at the tissue establishment	Annex II, Part A

Processing of gametes and embryos (validation, documentation and evaluation of critical procedures)	Annex II, Part B
Storage and release of gametes and embryos (criteria to be complied with, including standard operating procedure)	Annex II, Part C
Distribution and recall of gametes and embryos (criteria to be complied with, including procedures to be adopted)	Annex II, Part D
Final labelling of gametes and embryo containers for distribution (information to be shown on container label or in accompanying documentation)	Annex II, Part E
External labelling of the shipping container (information to be shown on label on shipping container)	Annex II, Part F

Interpretation of this Schedule

12

In this Schedule, 'partner-created embryos' means embryos created using the gametes of a man and a woman who declare that they have an intimate physical relationship.

Amendment: Schedule inserted: SI 2007/1522.

Section 28

[Schedule 3B
Inspection, Entry, Search And Seizure

Inspection of statutory records

1

(1) A duly authorised person may require a person to produce for inspection any records which the person is required to keep by, or by virtue of, this Act.

(2) Where records which a person is so required to keep are stored in any electronic form, the power under sub-paragraph (1) includes power to require the records to be made available for inspection—

    (a)   in a visible and legible form, or
    (b)   in a form from which they can be readily produced in a visible and legible form.

(3) A duly authorised person may inspect and take copies of any records produced for inspection in pursuance of a requirement under this paragraph.

Arranging inspections

2

(1) Where a person—

    (a)   makes an enquiry to the Authority which concerns the making of a relevant application by that person, or

    (b)   has made a relevant application to the Authority which the Authority has not yet considered, the Authority may arrange for a duly authorised person to inspect any of the premises mentioned in sub-paragraph (3).

(2) For the purposes of sub-paragraph (1) a "relevant application" means—

    (a)   an application for authorisation for a person to carry on an activity governed by this Act which the person is not then authorised to carry on, or

    (b)   an application for authorisation for a person to carry on any such activity on premises where the person is not then authorised to carry it on.

(3) The premises referred to in sub-paragraph (1) are—

    (a)   the premises where any activity referred to in subparagraph (2) is to be carried on;

    (b)   any premises that will be relevant third party premises for the purposes of any application.

(4) The power in sub-paragraph (1) is exercisable for purposes of the Authority's functions in relation to licences and third party agreements.

Entry and inspection of premises

3

(1) A duly authorised person may at any reasonable time enter and inspect any premises to which a licence relates or relevant third party premises.

(2) The power in sub-paragraph (1) is exercisable for purposes of the Authority's functions in relation to licences and third party agreements.

4

(1) Subject to sub-paragraph (2), the Authority shall arrange for any

premises to which a licence relates to be inspected under paragraph 3 by a duly authorised person at intervals not exceeding two years.

(2) The Authority need not comply with sub-paragraph (1) where the premises in question have been inspected in pursuance of paragraph 2 or 3 at any point within the previous two years.

Entry and search in connection with suspected offence

5

(1) If a justice of the peace is satisfied on sworn information or, in Northern Ireland, on a complaint on oath that there are reasonable grounds for believing—

    (a)   that an offence under this Act is being, or has been committed on any premises, and

    (b)   that any of the conditions in sub-paragraph (2) is met in relation to the premises, the justice of the peace may by signed warrant authorise a duly authorised person, together with any constables, to enter the premises, if need be by force, and search them.

(2) The conditions referred to are—

    (a)   that entry to the premises has been, or is likely to be, refused and notice of the intention to apply for a warrant under this paragraph has been given to the occupier;

    (b)   that the premises are unoccupied;

    (c)   that the occupier is temporarily absent;

    (d)   that an application for admission to the premises or the giving of notice of the intention to apply for a warrant under this paragraph would defeat the object of entry.

(3) A warrant under this paragraph shall continue in force until the end of the period of 31 days beginning with the day on which it is issued.

(4) In relation to Scotland—

    (a)   any reference in sub-paragraph (1) to a justice of the peace includes a reference to a sheriff, and

    (b)   the reference in that sub-paragraph to "on sworn information" is to be read as a reference to "by evidence on oath".

Execution of warrants

6

(1) Entry and search under a warrant under paragraph 5 is unlawful if any of sub-paragraphs (2) to (4) and (6) is not complied with.

(2) Entry and search shall be at a reasonable time unless the person executing the warrant thinks that the purpose of the search may be frustrated on an entry at a reasonable time.

(3) If the occupier of the premises to which the warrant relates is present when the person executing the warrant seeks to enter them, the person executing the warrant shall—

    (a)   produce the warrant to the occupier, and

    (b)   give the occupier—

        (i)   a copy of the warrant, and

        (ii)   an appropriate statement.

(4) If the occupier of the premises to which the warrant relates is not present when the person executing the warrant seeks to enter them, but some other person is present who appears to the person executing the warrant to be in charge of the premises, the person executing the warrant shall—

    (a)   produce the warrant to that other person,

    (b)   give that other person—

        (i)   a copy of the warrant, and

        (ii)   an appropriate statement, and

    (c)   leave a copy of the warrant in a prominent place on the premises.

(5) In sub-paragraphs (3)(b)(ii) and (4)(b)(ii), the references to an appropriate statement are to a statement in writing containing such information relating to the powers of the person executing the warrant and the rights and obligations of the person to whom the statement is given as may be prescribed by regulations made by the Secretary of State.

(6) If the premises to which the warrant relates are unoccupied, the person executing the warrant shall leave a copy of it in a prominent place on the premises.

(7) Where the premises in relation to which a warrant under paragraph 5 is executed are unoccupied or the occupier is temporarily absent, the person executing the warrant shall when leaving the premises, leave them as effectively secured as the person found them.

Seizure in the course of inspection or search

7

(1) A duly authorised person entering and inspecting premises under paragraph 3 may seize anything on the premises which the duly authorised person has reasonable grounds to believe may be required for—

    (a)   the purposes of the Authority's functions relating to the grant, revocation, variation or suspension of licences, or

    (b)   the purpose of taking appropriate control measures in the event of a serious adverse event or serious adverse reaction.

(2) A duly authorised person entering or searching premises under a warrant under paragraph 5 may seize anything on the premises which the duly authorised person has reasonable grounds to believe may be required for the purpose of being used in evidence in any proceedings for an offence under this Act.

(3) Where a person has power under sub-paragraph (1) or (2) to seize anything, that person may take such steps as appear to be necessary for preserving that thing or preventing interference with it.

(4) The power under sub-paragraph (1) or (2) includes power to retain anything seized in exercise of the power for so long as it may be required for the purpose for which it was seized.

(5) Where by virtue of sub-paragraph (1) or (2) a person ("P") seizes anything, P shall leave on the premises from which the thing was seized a statement giving particulars of what P has seized and stating that P has seized it.

Supplementary provision

8

(1) Power under this Schedule to enter and inspect or search any premises includes power to take such other persons and equipment as the person exercising the power reasonably considers necessary.

(2) Power under this Schedule to inspect or search any premises includes, in particular—

    (a)   power to inspect any equipment found on the premises,

    (b)   power to inspect and take copies of any records found on the premises, and

    (c)   in the case of premises to which a licence relates or premises which are relevant third party premises in relation to a licence, power to observe the carrying-on of the licensed activity on the premises.

(3) Any power under this Schedule to enter, inspect or search premises includes power to require any person to afford such facilities and assistance with respect to matters under that person's control as are necessary to enable the power of entry, inspection or search to be exercised.

9

(1) A person's right to exercise a power under this Schedule is subject to production of evidence of the person's entitlement to exercise it, if required.

(2) As soon as reasonably practicable after having inspected premises in pursuance of arrangements made under paragraph 2 or after having exercised a power under this Schedule to inspect or search premises, the duly authorised person shall—

    (a)   prepare a written report of the inspection, or as the case may be, the inspection and search, and

    (b)   if requested to do so by the appropriate person, give the appropriate person a copy of the report.

(3) In sub-paragraph (2), the "appropriate person" means—

    (a)   in relation to premises to which a licence relates, the person responsible, or

    (b)   in relation to any other premises, the occupier.

Enforcement

10

A person who—

(a)   fails without reasonable excuse to comply with a requirement under paragraph 1(1) or 8(3), or

(b)   intentionally obstructs the exercise of any right under this Schedule,

is guilty of an offence and liable on summary conviction to a fine not exceeding level 5 on the standard scale.

Interpretation

11

In this Schedule—

(a)   "duly authorised person", in the context of any provision, means a person authorised by the Authority to act for the purposes of that provision, and

(b)   "licensed activity", in relation to a licence, means the activity which the licence authorises to be carried on.]

Prospective Amendment: Schedule prospectively inserted by Human Fertilisation and Embryology Act 2008, s 28(2), Sch 5 with effect from a date to be appointed.

INDEX